THE
POTTER'S
HANDS

WHAT OTHERS ARE SAYING . . .

"I'm convinced many of the church's woes result from too little Bible and too much everything else. In *The Potter's Hands* Jason Lawson invites the believer to be molded and shaped daily by God through His Word. It's God's Word that will accomplish what God wants (Is. 55:11). We just need to be molded by its truth. Read this book. Better yet, be molded by it."

DR. ROBERT HEFNER
Sr. Pastor, Pleasant Garden Baptist Church, NC

"*The Potter's Hands* is 366 daily devotions that will lead, guide, and teach us the ways of God for the rest of our lives and generations to come. Over the past several years I have found Jason to be a credible deliverer of The Word of God. I can assure you his devotions are straight from the Potter's hands."

SARAH MARTIN BYRD
Author of: *Guardian Spirit, The Color of My Heart, The River Keeper, In the Coal Mine Shadows,* and *The Manger Mouse*

"It is no secret that God often does His best work through us as His people when we are broken, dependent, and surrendered before Him. *The Potter's Hands* is a perfect example of this truth. This devotional flows out of Jason's journey with Jesus during a challenging season in his life. It is God-centered, Bible-based, and simple, yet challenging to all who desire to set their heart in a fresh way on God's perspective and hope during those difficult and perplexing seasons of life."

DR. J. CHRIS SCHOFIELD
Wake Forest, NC

A 366-DAY JOURNEY TO

KNOWING GOD

THE

POTTER'S

HANDS

JASON LAWSON

AMBASSADOR INTERNATIONAL
GREENVILLE, SOUTH CAROLINA & BELFAST, NORTHERN IRELAND
www.ambassador-international.com

The Potter's Hands
A 366-Day Journey to Knowing God

©2021 by Jason Lawson
All rights reserved

ISBN: 978-1-64960-118-6, hardcover
ISBN: 978-1-64960-257-2, paperback
eISBN: 978-1-64960-168-1

Cover Design by Hannah Linder Designs
Interior Typesetting by Dentelle Design

Scripture taken from the New American Standard Bible 1995 (NASB1995) New American Standard Bible®, Copyright © 1960, 1971, 1977, 1995 by The Lockman Foundation. All rights reserved.

AMBASSADOR INTERNATIONAL
Emerald House
411 University Ridge, Suite B14
Greenville, SC 29601
United States
www.ambassador-international.com

AMBASSADOR BOOKS
The Mount
2 Woodstock Link
Belfast, BT6 8DD
Northern Ireland, United Kingdom
www.ambassadormedia.co.uk

The colophon is a trademark of Ambassador, a Christian publishing company.

But now, O LORD, You are our Father, We are the clay, and You our potter;
And all of us are the work of Your hand.

Isaiah 64:8

WHAT OTHERS ARE SAYING, CONTINUED . . .

"*The Potter's Hands* will help you deepen your prayer life; It will teach you Biblical names of God that you may have never known! Jason's careful research and artful presentation will truly help you grow in your walk with the Lord."

ALEX MCFARLAND
Author, apologist *Truth For A New Generation*
www.alexmcfarland.com

"Jason loves Jesus, his family, and his church. In this book he speaks from his heart and invites the reader to journey with him to become clay in the Potter's hands. Jason's writing reveals the love of God in his life, encourages us, and seeks to grow us day by day."

RICK TREXLER
College Ministry Coordinator, Salem, VA

"I've had the privilege to co-labor with Jason among the strangers (refugees) in our land. The substance for his ministry to tough places is reflected in this work. These devotions ministered to me and reminded me that my story and my ministry is simply about God's ministry to me."

BILL JOHNSON
Pastor of Reach the Nations Community Church, Clarkston, GA

TABLE OF CONTENTS

DEDICATED TO

The two little boys and a little girl—
May many more adventures await you!

&

My beautiful wife—
I love you, Boo!

Special thanks to
Dr. Richard Pace—
Thanks for the idea!
1953 - 2020

PREFACE

Has God ever flipped your world upside down for His glory? That happened to me in 2018. I was stressed to the max with ministry and family things, not to mention our third child was on the way. I found myself at an emotional breaking point on a Saturday morning when I woke up overwhelmed and anxious beyond words. I quickly spiraled down into what I thought was a mental breakdown. I was trying to prepare breakfast for my family, but I couldn't even pour orange juice into their smoothies because my hand was shaking so badly. I called my pastor and asked if we could talk, though I mostly just cried. That was the most scared I have ever been! Now, I understand I was having a panic attack, but at the time, I thought I was falling apart. Honestly, I thought my wife was going to leave me because she needed a husband who could at least make smoothies for the family. I thought the church I worked for was going to ask me to step down because they needed a youth pastor who could do the job. I thought I was on the verge of being broken beyond repair and left all alone. That was a dark day in my life, but then God intervened and began a process of shinning His light into my darkness.

- My wife assured me she wasn't leaving and that she and the kids would walk through anything with me.
- Pastor Steve Corts of Center Grove Baptist Church in Winston-Salem, NC, told me something that would alter my mindset forever. He said, *"There are two ways to read the Bible. We can read it as a book about us or a book about God. How we begin reading the Bible will ultimately determine what we take from it. If we begin treating it as a*

book about us, we will always miss the truth God intended for us." I had been reading the Bible wrong!

- The counselor I started going to challenged me to find something fun to do, like working out or taking up a hobby. This would be challenging with three children under four years old. Alone time was at a premium, and nap times were sacred silent times for fear of waking up the kids. Writing a book was on my bucket list, so I decided to write 366 devotions over a one-year span and compile them into a book.

So there it was; God had placed my family and me on a journey to write a year's worth of daily devotionals that did not focus on me but on Him. There were three rules I followed for each devotional: First, I was not writing to impress people; I was writing to teach. Second, I was to pray and listen over every devotional. And third, the devotionals were not to be about me but about God. That is what I have tried to do.

Now to prepare you for this journey, let me focus you in the right direction. In the phrase *"Clay in the Potter's hands,"* what is the subject? The clay or the Potter's hands? It is so easy to put ourselves as the center of everything but we are merely clay in the Potter's hands. It is the Potter Who knows what will be useful to Him. He molds us, puts us through the fire, and then uses us as He desires. He is the beginning and the end; we are simply His vessels. My prayer for you as you embark on this year-long journey is that you will encounter the loving Potter that I did. There are still days I struggle, but I know beyond a shadow of a doubt that God is with me, and He is shaping me into a vessel of honor, useful to the Master (2 Timothy 2:21). I'm praying for you!

JASON LAWSON

JANUARY

The Potter's Hands Are Strong and Wise

THE POTTER'S HANDS

"Can I not, O house of Israel, deal with you as this potter does?"
declares the LORD. "Behold, like the clay in the potter's hand,
so are you in My hand, O house of Israel."

Jeremiah 18:6

God's heartbeat echoes as He speaks to Jeremiah, directing him to go down to the local potter's house and to watch him fashion clay on the wheel. God had fashioned Jeremiah, so He knew how difficult it was for Jeremiah to step out and be His messenger. God had heard Jeremiah cry out *"Alas, Lord GOD!"* when the call to be a prophet was given. Now the Heavenly Potter was using a visual image to declare to His children, His masterful design, His sovereign plan and His superior wisdom.

The Father had created a covenant with Israel, but Israel had turned its back on Him. Now the King of Kings was once again revealing His heart to His Chosen, saying, *"Will you surrender to Me? I am the wise Potter Who formed you and purposed you. You may think you know what's best for your life, and most of that is based on your feelings and desires, but you were not formed to fulfill your plans; no more than a screwdriver was formed to hammer in a nail. It can be done, but it will destroy the screwdriver. You may live your life trying to fulfill your plans but in the end, it will destroy you. Please, My children, hear My voice and turn back to Me! You may be marred, but in My hands I will remake you into another vessel as it pleases Me."*

God's call to surrender to His forming still stands today. The Potter's hands are strong and wise! They do not slip nor make mistakes. You may not like your personality, your size, or your skillset, but the Potter did not make a mistake. Cancer, depression, being very short, these are not mistakes when in the Potter's hands. There is no greater calling than to be used by the Potter, but there also may be no greater challenge than to surrender yourself to Him. Will you trust the Potter's hands?

———

VESSEL FOR HONOR

Therefore, if anyone cleanses himself from these things, he will be a vessel for honor, sanctified, useful to the Master, prepared for every good work.

2 Timothy 2:21

There are two main points that need to be spotlighted in this verse: First, this vessel will be *"Useful to the Master,"* and second, we will be *"A vessel for honor."* So when you look at these two points you can see that our lives are not about us, they are about the Potter! As John the Baptist says, *"Jesus must increase and I must decrease"* (John 3:30). I am a vessel formed by the hands of the Potter, not for my own doings but so that I may be useful to the Potter. When He uses me, I become a vessel for honor. Prior to this, I actually dishonor my Creator. In the Western part of the world, we may not totally understand this honor. We tend to have a mindset of "innocence and guilt." This is why we question whether it's okay to go five miles per hour over the speed limit? Much of the Eastern part of the world focuses on "honor and shame." Honor, in this sense, is worth living and dying for. It is what makes a person who they are. Honor is what separates you from anyone or anything else. Yet at the same time, when I bring honor, I am intricately connected to all of creation. Many people would lay down their lives to protect their honor. Scripture teaches us that the honor of a vessel, when used by the Master, is the greatest of all honor. First Timothy 6:1 says, *"All who are under the yoke as slaves are to regard their own masters as worthy of all honor so that the name of God and our doctrine will not be spoken against."* Any honor we receive is the Master's! But we only receive true honor when we are being used by the Potter. When we try to make a name for ourselves, we are as helpless as a bowl trying to beckon someone to pick it up. It is helpless apart from the one who uses it. We live and die for the honor of the Potter. So then let this be your prayer today: *"Now to the King eternal, immortal, invisible, the only God, be honor and glory forever and ever. Amen"* (1 Timothy 1:17).

WHO ARE YOU O MAN

On the contrary, who are you O man, who answers back to God?
The thing molded will not say to the molder, "Why did you make me like this," will it?

Romans 9:20

A hand consists of fingers, a palm, the back of the hand, fingernails, knuckles, skin, nerves, muscles, ligaments, nerves, blood, cells, atoms, neurons, etc. It's insane how many working parts there are in the hand, not to mention the other thousands of parts that make up your body. Now consider what the practical purpose of the shape and size of your hand is? Are you a doctor or a teacher? Do you use your hands to tighten bolts on a car or wipe tears from the eyes of a crying child? It would be so easy to say to the Heavenly Potter, "You missed the mark! Things would have been so much easier if You had only made my hand a different shape!" We do this every day. So many treatments have been developed to correct the "mistakes" made by the Potter. We can change our hair color, our body shape, our metabolism, our eyesight, and even our personality. Why do we need to change or alter these parts? Did the Potter slip and make a mistake? How impertinent we are. *"You turn things around! Shall the potter be considered as equal with the clay, That what is made would say to its maker, 'He did not make me'; Or what is formed say to him who formed it, 'He has no understanding?'"* (Isaiah 29:16).

Could you even imagine if God responded to our complaints in the same manner He did to Job? *"Now gird up your loins like a man, And I will ask you, and you instruct Me!"* How quickly we would realize our place. We are the clay, and the Potter does not have to answer our questioning of His intent. No, He made us as vessels to serve Him. Yet, on the flip side, why would we need the information we are asking for? If the Potter knows all, makes no mistakes, and formed us completely, then how would it be to stop trying to fix the Creator's perfection and start trusting in His love for the creation?

———

THE BREATH OF LIFE

Your hands fashioned and made me altogether, And would You destroy me?
Remember now, that You have made me as clay;
And would You turn me into dust again?

Job 10:8–9

Have you ever heard someone say, "I'm just a modern-day Job"? What do you think that means? This person is probably crying out in despair, *"Why is all this happening to me? If the Potter is a good God and He loves me, then why is He allowing this to take place? Why doesn't He stop this?"* While these questions make sense, I believe Job hit on something that may give a new perspective. Job said, *"And would You turn me into dust again?"* How important it is to remember that we were once dust. Genesis 2:7 says, *"Then the LORD God formed man of dust from the ground, and breathed into his nostrils the breath of life; and man became a living being."* It was the Potter Who took the dust and molded us into a vessel. He, being the Creator, could have filled His vessel with anything He desired—good, bad, pleasure, or pain. Instead, He chose to fill His vessel with a part of Himself—His very breath. That breath transformed us from dust into a living *"nephesh,"* which is the Hebrew word for 'soul.' Our soul is the seat of our emotions, thoughts, and desires. The Potter took His creation and blew into it His breath of life. That life became in us passion, dreams, hope, love, joy, and hurt. But remember, that breath He breathed was life to us, His life *in* us! So the soul that is active in us, those desires, emotions, and thoughts, were birthed out of the very lungs of the Potter. Job's question is a valid question. *"And would You turn me into dust again?"* The very thing that separates us from dust is the breath of God in us. No, the Potter does not desire to destroy us by separating us from His breath of life. He is fashioning us back to that vessel where the only thing in us is His breath. *O Lord, please wash this vessel, so that the only thing in me is Your breath of Life!*

THE POTTER BECAME THE FATHER

But now, O LORD, You are our Father, We are the clay, and You our potter;
And all of us are the work of Your hand.

Isaiah 64:8

This verse is a beautiful line of poetry but do not miss the absolute absurdity that is stated in it! Isaiah speaks here of two things: (1) the Father, Creator, Potter, and (2) the creation, clay, work of His hand. So in essence, Isaiah is telling us of the relationship between these two entities. But the mental image that Isaiah lays before us is that of a potter creating something at his wheel. When he finishes his vessel, the potter sits it on the table in front of himself and declares, "This is my beloved child! I love them, and I am its father!" How can the creation be adopted into the family of the Creator? You do not make a mudpie and then adopt it as your child! What has to take place for the 'work of Your hand' to become the 'love of Your life'?

Actually, the process is not all that complex, though we may never understand the depths of it. Basically we, the creation, were created by the Potter but then disobeyed our Creator by following Satan. Satan then became our master. The Potter would then have to purchase us back from our new master at a very high price, the life of His only Son. Remember that we are merely clay formed into the image of God. The Potter would deliver His only Son to death, which purchased us and made us slaves to Him. He could have ruled over us with an iron fist, and we would have deserved every ounce of it. But our Heavenly Master did not strike fear into our hearts with His position but rather showed His love for us by declaring that we were no longer slaves but His sons and daughters. The Potter became the Father of His creation!

"For you have not received a spirit of slavery leading to fear again, but you have received a spirit of adoption as sons by which we cry out, 'Abba! Father'" (Romans 8:15).

"For the anxious longing of the creation waits eagerly for the revealing of the sons of God" (Romans 8:19).

CREATED IN THE IMAGE OF GOD

God created man in His own image, in the image of God He created him;
male and female He created them.

Genesis 1:27

We were created in the image of the Potter. What does that mean? Does God have two hands, a nose, and two eyes? Maybe, but possibly the image we were created in was not physical but spiritual since God is Spirit (John 4:24). But what does this image look like? The Bible gives us a pretty clear view of it in Colossians 3:9–15. Let's look at how this comes together. *"Do not lie to one another, since you laid aside the old self with its evil practices, and have put on the new self who is being renewed to a true knowledge according to the image of the One who created him"* (vs. 9–10).

If you take a step back and look at the whole grand panoramic from Genesis 1 to Colossians 3, you will see that when God created us, we were fashioned in His likeness. Through the mutilation of sin, we have undergone spiritual plastic surgery so that we look like Satan and his 'evil practices.' This is much like the mirrors in a carnival funhouse that distorts our appearance; we are distortions of God's image. When we come to Christ, we take off this old self and put on a new self. This new self is being renewed to the image of the Potter. What does this image of God look like? Well, we get a list of attributes in Colossians 3:12–14; *"a heart of compassion, kindness, humility, gentleness, and patience; bearing with one another, and forgiving each other, love, peace, and thankfulness."*

Another word for 'renewed' is 'grown.' Much like the fruit of the Spirit is grown in us by the Spirit. The image of God is renewed in us through His power, not our determination. When we become renewed to the image of our Creator, our physical appearance may not change, but our spiritual appearance will become unrecognizable. We will no longer look like ourselves but like the Potter.

THE GLORIOUS WORKS OF GOD

For we are His workmanship created in Christ Jesus for good works,
which God prepared beforehand so that we would walk in them.

Ephesians 2:10

I can just see the Potter going to His workshop, pulling out some clay, and shaping it into a person. He then carves out a mouth, forms a nose, and creates two eye sockets. Finally, He paints with every color on His palette. Once He finishes, He leans in and breathes the breath of life into its nostrils, and as the Potter's creation comes to life, He lovingly calls it by name for the first time. How great are the works of the Potter's hands.

What are these good works that we are to walk in? Usually, we see these works as 'tasks' God has assigned for us to do, and while He does have tasks for us to do during this life, it is interesting to note that when you look at the works of God's hands—Creation, Salvation and even the Restoration to come—these works have all been completed. The Potter rested on the seventh day because creation was completed (Genesis 2:1–2), Jesus said from the cross, *"It is finished"* (John 19:30), and even our eternal reign in Heaven with Christ has been completed because Jesus has spoken it in the Revelation. So if the works God prepared for us to walk in are completed, then what does this mean?

Isaiah 6:3 says, *"And one called out to another and said, 'Holy, Holy, Holy, is the LORD of hosts, The whole earth is full of His glory.'"* Another interpretation of this is *"The fullness of the whole earth is His glory."* Possibly what God is pointing us to is not what we are to accomplish but to simply walk in the glory of His works. When we walk down the streets, plant a garden, talk to a friend, or eat a meal with family, we are walking in the glory of the Potter. When we walk in the glory of what God has already done, we are drawn into worship!

"All Your works shall give thanks to You, O LORD, And Your godly ones shall bless You" (Psalm 145:10).

———

THE SPIRIT'S UNCOVERING

But to each one is given the manifestation of the Spirit for the common good.

1 Corinthians 12:7

The Potter's presence among humanity has been key since the beginning of time. Without His presence, we are void of power, direction, hope, and fellowship. During the Old Testament, the Father's presence was seen as the pillar of cloud by day and of fire by night. His presence rested on the Ark of the Covenant in the Holy of Holies and went before Israel into battle. Then, Jesus' presence was seen in human form during the thirty-three years of the Gospels. Finally, the Holy Spirit's presence is inside those who believe in Christ. The Spirit is what teaches us and testifies with our spirit that we are children of God.

First Corinthians 12:7 tells us that those who are saved through Jesus Christ have been given a manifestation of the Spirit. The word 'manifestation' literally means '*uncovering,*' so we have had the Spirit of God uncovered in us for the common good. Acts 1:8 reminds us that the Holy Spirit comes on us with power! This uncovering of the Spirit is a revealing of superhuman power. So when Paul says each of us is given an uncovering of the Spirit for the common good, he is saying this is no mere event, it is THE event of our lifetime! And that event comes with powerful responsibility.

"*For the body is not one member, but many*" (1 Corinthians 12:14). The "common good" of those many parts can be understood in the image of a symphony. If every instrument were a trumpet, then the music would lack that depth that can be felt by a bass drum. If every instrument were a tuba, then we would lack the gentleness of a flute. For a symphony to create music, each instrument must play for the common good of the music. Likewise, we have received a powerful uncovering of the Spirit, not so we can be superhuman but so that together we can work as the body of Christ. We know what this is by abiding with the Potter.

WHO IS THE POTTER?

Seeing that His divine power has granted to us everything pertaining to life and godliness, through the true knowledge of Him who called us by His own glory and excellence.

2 Peter 1:3

Who is the Potter? Isn't this the most important question we could ask? As a vessel created in the image of God, shouldn't we know the Potter. Peter tells us in 2 Peter 1:3 that *God has granted us everything pertaining to life and godliness through the true knowledge of Him.* The Potter equipped us with everything we need to live a godly life when He created us to be in relationship with Him. But the clause in this is, the 'granting' comes 'through the true knowledge' of God. It is impossible to live a godly life apart from knowing Who He is. In fact, John 17:3 says, *"This is eternal life, that they may know You, the only true God, and Jesus Christ whom You have sent."* Therefore, eternity is bound up in knowing the Lord, so again the most important question is, "Who is the Potter?"

God is love (1 John 4:16), *God is our refuge and strength* (Psalm 46:1), *Jesus is the way, the truth and the life* (John 14:6), *God is Light* (1 John 1:5), *God is Spirit* (John 4:24), *Jesus is the bread of life* (John 6:35), *Jesus is the door of the sheep* (John 10:7), *The LORD is our Shepherd* (Psalm 23:1), *Jesus is the resurrection and the life* (John 11:25), *The LORD is our strength and shield* (Psalm 28:7), *God is a consuming fire* (Hebrews 12:29), *The LORD is gracious, righteous and full of compassion* (Psalm 116:5), *The LORD of hosts is, holy, holy, holy* (Isaiah 6:3), *God our Savior is the bearer of our burdens* (Psalm 68:19), *The Father of lights is the giver of every good gift* (James 1:17), *God is with us* (Matthew 1:23).

It is through knowing the Potter, Who formed us in His image, designed us to walk in His works, and gifted us through His Spirit, that we are granted everything pertaining to life and godliness. Do you know the Potter?

THE POTTER'S PLAN

"For I know the plans that I have for you," declares the LORD,
"plans for welfare and not for calamity to give you a future and a hope."

Jeremiah 29:11

Every decision we make boils down to, are we going to surrender to God or reclaim the throne of our life. Jeremiah points out the Potter has a plan for our life, which we were designed for. Is it possible to conduct our lives based on our plans and still be successful? Depending on your definition of 'success,' yes. Worldly speaking, we can make a lot of money, reach a high level of fame, and even make a great impact doing things our way. But will we be able to make an eternal difference? No!

If the designer of a new coffee pot says that in order to make the best cup of coffee, you need to follow these steps with this amount of coffee, but you use a different process with more grounds, most likely the coffee will be bad. But there is a chance it might taste good or even better to your palette. Yet to the designer of the coffee pot, it is subpar. The best cup of coffee is determined by who the judge is. If everything revolves around you, then you are the judge; make the coffee your way. But if the maker of the coffee pot is the judge, then no matter what your preference is, his way is best.

The Potter has a plan for your life, and He formed you to accomplish that plan. It's a plan for welfare, not for calamity, and to give you a future and a hope. We want the welfare, future, and hope, but we don't necessarily want the Potter's plan. Acts 26:14 says, *"And when we had all fallen to the ground, I heard a voice saying to me in the Hebrew dialect, 'Saul, Saul, why are you persecuting Me? It is hard for you to kick against the goads.'"* Just like Saul, we find ourselves kicking against the goads of God. He is Creator, and we are His; therefore, it is not our preferences that determine success but rather if we are accomplishing the plans of the Potter.

———————

FEARFULLY AND WONDERFULLY

I will give thanks to You, for I am fearfully and wonderfully made;
Wonderful are Your works, And my soul knows it very well.

Psalm 139:14

David speaks in this psalm of giving thanks to the Potter for the way he was formed. That sounds very wholesome, but in reality, we are not always so thankful for our height, weight, body shape, personality, or genetic predisposition to certain illnesses. Sometimes it's hard being who we are. But maybe the reason David could be so thankful was because he understood something about why God formed him the way He did.

Two Hebrew words from this verse that we need to define are: *"fearfully"* or *yare*, which means "to inspire reverence or godly fear," and *"wonderfully"* or *palah*, which means "to be distinguished, be separated."

In short, when David says he is fearfully and wonderfully made, he is saying, "I was made to inspire others to fear God. I'm distinguished as one who has the fingerprint of the Potter!" When the world, who is so busy trying to change who they are so they can be someone they were never meant to be, sees someone relishing in their Creator's genius, they have to stop and wonder what David knows that they do not?

Do we always like our "flaws" and "challenges"? No, but those "flaws" and "challenges" are the very gifts the Potter formed into us so that we can use them for His glory. You may be short, so was Zacchaeus and Jesus went to his house. You may have a chronic illness, so did the man with leprosy, and yet He was touched by Jesus. You may suffer from depression, but so did Elijah, and yet he heard God's still small voice. You may struggle with temptation, but so did the woman caught in adultery, and she found forgiveness. We were fearfully and wonderfully made not for our benefit and enjoyment but because the Potter knew what we needed to inspire others to reverence Him.

———

BODY SOUL AND SPIRIT

Now may the God of peace Himself sanctify you entirely; and may your spirit and soul and body be preserved complete, without blame at the coming of our Lord Jesus Christ. Faithful is He who calls you, and He also will bring it to pass.

1 Thessalonians 5:23–24

We have a self-absorbed tendency to study the clay as if we may find some grand understanding about our being, but I want us to take a second and look at the clay to see if we find some grand understanding about the Potter's being. We are all made up of a body, soul, and spirit, and these three entities are in the hand of the Potter. He is the One Who sanctifies us entirely, preserves us completely, calls us with faithfulness, and brings His plan to pass. What does this look like?

Our body is much like the structure of a sculpture, the size, shape, texture, and color. All of these attributes help the vessel to accomplish the purpose of the Potter. Our soul is our mind, the seat of our desires, emotions, and thoughts. This is the command center for our body, deciding whether to obey the Lord or to become our own master. Our spirit is the communication center of our body and soul. God is Spirit and therefore communicates with our spirit. It is important to also note that Satan is a spirit and therefore can communicate with our spirit, too (1 John 4:1). How do we know what our intended purpose is unless the Creator tells us?

Our soul may tell us a lot of logical things, and our body may have a seemingly perfect lean toward a certain skill, but if we are not hearing from the Potter Himself, then we are in grave danger of missing His hand. When Christ formed us, He gave us a body to work within our finite realm. He gave us a soul so we could understand, feel, and effectively serve. He also gave us a spirit so we could communicate with Him. When all three of these unique gifts work together with the Potter, we abide in His hand and work in His power.

THE POTTER'S HOME

Or do you not know that your body is a temple of the Holy Spirit who is in you, whom you have from God, and that you are not your own? For you have been bought with a price: Therefore glorify God in your body.

1 Corinthians 7:19–20

For most of the Bible, the image of a temple was a physical structure that provided the means to have your sins covered, to be ceremonially washed from your sins, to worship God through obedience, and a location where you could come to the presence of God. We can't fathom what it must have been like to be a priest standing in the Holy Place, with the menorah on his left, the table of showbread on his right, the altar of incense in front of him and beyond that, the very presence of God, separated from him only by a veil. The voice that spoke creation into existence, the hands that wove our DNA together, and the heart that would do anything to redeem humanity would be mere feet away. The presence of God Almighty!

But all of that changed with Jesus' death on the cross. The veil was torn, and access was granted. The Holy Spirit was given to Christians, and it was then that the temple of God was no longer a structure made by human hands but rather within the very bodies the Potter Himself had formed. God designed His own sanctuary with such holy precision that science has spent thousands of years trying to understand our bodies, but they have just scratched the surface because our bodies are the fingerprint of the Potter!

How does this change our worship? Are we more drawn to the awe of standing mere feet from God's presence than we are to His Spirit residing inside us? To stand at the veil knowing that El Shaddai is on the other side is enough to drop us to our knees, yet how many days begin without us so much as thanking the Spirit for waking us up? Is it possible to not know the Potter, Whose home we are?

THE TESTING OF THE POTTER

The refining pot is for silver and the furnace for gold, But the LORD tests hearts.

Proverbs 17:3

When a potter begins to work with clay, they start by slamming the clay down on a table to make sure that all of the air pockets have been removed. The reason for this is that when the clay goes into the kiln, it is heated to very high temperatures. The heat causes the air in the pockets to expand and can cause the clay to explode, destroying the work of the potter. Therefore it is so important to slam the clay down when you start.

Proverbs 17:3 tells us that the Potter tests our hearts. He is searching for those air pockets of sin that will destroy us when we go through the fires of temptation. During this testing it can feel like God is slamming us down repeatedly. It can feel like God is abusing us. When these moments of testing come, it is easy to lash out at God in anger. Our prayers become consumed with self-preservation and cynical accusations against the Almighty. We question His kindness, His love, and His wisdom. We can go to church and complain about life in the name of a "prayer request" and even chastise others who speak of the goodness of God. Have you found yourself secretly joking about the person who says they are *"Too blessed to be stressed"* or *"God is good all the time"*? We joke about them because we do not feel blessed, and God does not feel good during these seasons. When our heart bubbles up and overflows with the dross of the filth within, it's because God is exposing our sin and pulling out the air pockets.

Do we trust the Potter enough to endure His testing so that, in the end, we will be solid and useful to the Maker? One way to know if you trust Him is to listen to the words of your mouth. Are your words those of praise or anger? Are they words of edification or doubt? Are they filled with love or are they hollow? Trust the Potter to remove what is deadly within you.

A CLAY PITCHER IN THE POTTER'S HANDS

Behold, I have made your face as hard as their faces and your forehead as hard as their foreheads. Like emery harder than flint I have made your forehead. Do not be afraid of them or be dismayed before them, though they are a rebellious house.

Ezekiel 3:8–9

A clay pitcher in the hands of the Potter is at the mercy of the Potter. If He dropped it, it would shatter and be useless. Also, a pitcher is filled with whatever the Potter desires. If it is filled with something rancid and full of decay, then the pitcher will be marked as a vessel of dishonor and not be used for things of honor. Finally, a pitcher is placed where the Potter desires. If he places the pitcher so that it teeters on the edge of a shelf, then the pitcher has no say in it. Likewise, we are at the mercy of our Maker. We are in His hands, filled with what He desires, and placed where He wants us to be. We cannot control our lives, but we can choose to be obedient to the Potter.

Ezekiel was called to be a Prophet. He did not ask for this job, but he was created for it! Ezekiel 2:6 says, *"And you, son of man, neither fear them nor fear their words, though thistles and thorns are with you and you sit on scorpions; neither fear their words nor be dismayed at their presence, for they are a rebellious house."* God tells Ezekiel that where He is placing him is dangerous, and it will appear that he is teetering on the edge of death. Yet, he is not to fear because Ezekiel was formed by the Potter to have a face as hard as their face. He was made for this. He is in the hands of the Potter; nothing will reach him apart from the Potter's will. Ezekiel has also been filled with the words of the Potter, the same words that have the power to create, give life, and destroy. Finally, it may look like the Potter has placed Ezekiel in a dangerous place, but in reality, he is exactly where he was created to be. A clay pitcher may seem fragile but in the hands of the Potter, it is stronger than it could ever imagine.

———————

BREAKING POINTS

For You have tried us, O God; You have refined us as silver is refined.

Psalm 66:10

Do you know where your breaking point is? Do you know just how much you can take before you snap under the pressure? How many times have you approached that point and cried out to God, *"Why are You allowing this?"* The truth of the matter is, the Potter knows your breaking point better than you do because He formed you. He knows exactly how much you can take. The interesting thing is, even though God knows our breaking point, He will often lead us past it. This can seem heartless and cruel. How could the Good Father do that to His children?

The word "tried" in Psalm 66:10 means "to test, prove or examine." God has tested us so that we will be refined. Why does God test us? First Peter 1:6–7 tells us, *"In this you greatly rejoice, even though now for a little while, if necessary, you have been distressed by various trials, so that the proof of your faith, being more precious than gold which is perishable, even though tested by fire, may be found to result in praise and glory and honor at the revelation of Jesus Christ."* According to this, there are various trials, and they can be distressing, but the purpose of these trials is so that our faith may produce praise, glory, and honor to Jesus. So in essence, the Potter Who knows us even better than we know ourselves allows us to go beyond our breaking point to refine our faith in Him. In those moments, nothing matters except our faith because it is not our strength that gets us through the trials; it is the power of the Spirit in us. And it is through God, bringing us through these trials, that our faith produces praise to the Father, glory to His Son, and honor to the Spirit of the Potter. Once again we see, life is not about us; we are merely clay. Life has everything to do with the glory of God! That is why He takes us past our breaking point, because He can, and then He brings us back with a more refined faith in Him.

DIAMOND IN THE ROUGH

Now in the first year of Cyrus king of Persia, in order to fulfill the word of the LORD by the mouth of Jeremiah, the LORD stirred up the spirit of Cyrus king of Persia, so that he sent a proclamation throughout all his kingdom, and also put it in writing, saying: "Thus says Cyrus king of Persia, 'The LORD, the God of heaven, has given me all the kingdoms of the earth and He has appointed me to build Him a house in Jerusalem, which is in Judah.'"

Ezra 1:1–2

Have you ever found a "diamond in the rough"? A diamond so precious found among the unnoticeable common. A diamond passed by daily by so many, and yet found by you. A "diamond in the rough" is very special indeed because it is yours!

Since the beginning of time, there have been billions of people. Every single one of them were handcrafted by the Potter for a very specific purpose. Of those billions of people, never has there been a duplicate. Every person formed by the Potter is unique, and that makes them special.

King Cyrus was a perfect example of a "diamond in the rough." He sent out this proclamation to everyone saying that the Lord had appointed him to a task. That means of the billions of people to walk on planet earth, he was the man the Potter designed to build Him a house in Jerusalem. He was precious in the eyes of God because God had formed him for just such a task. But how did Cyrus know that out of the billions of people and billions of options, he was the one appointed for this task? He knew it because *'the LORD had stirred up the spirit of the king.'* The Holy Spirit of God was communicating with the spirit of a man to reveal His custom-made plan for him. The Spirit of the Potter is still doing that today with His creation. Are you searching for His stirring, that leading, that passionate drawing to serve the Almighty? You are the Potter's diamond in the rough.

———

THREE LUMPS OF CLAY

*Before I formed you in the womb I knew you, And before you were born
I consecrated you; I have appointed you a prophet to the nations.*

Jeremiah 1:5

The Hebrew word for consecrated is *qadash*, which means "to be set apart." Think of it this way: A potter had three lumps of clay; with one he formed a coffee cup, with another, he formed a water pitcher, and with the third, he formed a bedpan. All three of these vessels are unique and set apart for different tasks.

The coffee cup is designed to hold a small amount of hot liquid, which will bring warmth and comfort on cold mornings. A coffee cup does not have any responsibility other than to be drunk out of.

The water pitcher is designed not to be drunk out of but to be poured from. It is a vessel of service in that it will give a refreshing drink on a hot day or can be used to pour over dirty hands or feet. A water pitcher's responsibility is to be poured out for the purpose of refreshing.

The bedpan is designed to hold the refuse of a person who is unable to get out of bed. While this seems like a vessel of great dishonor, for the person who is unable to get up, it is a vessel of greatest service. It does not bring comfort on a cold day nor refreshing on a hot day; it simply allows for relief to a person in need.

All three of these lumps of clay have very different purposes, that is because they are consecrated. They have been set apart to serve. Likewise, the Potter consecrated us before we were ever born. You may think, "I sure would rather be a water pitcher than a bedpan," but that choice is not up to the clay but to the Potter. We can run from His plan, but in the end, there will be no peace. Take comfort in the fact that God knew you before He formed you, He consecrated you before you were born, and He has appointed you to the task He desires. *"Dear Lord, please help me submit to Your design, not stand contrary to You as if I know better."*

CHRIST JESUS THE LORD

Therefore as you have received Christ Jesus the Lord, so walk in Him,
having been firmly rooted and now being built up in Him and established in your faith,
just as you were instructed, and overflowing with gratitude.

Colossians 2:6–7

Over the next six days, we are going to be breaking these two verses into smaller bites so we can understand the Potter better. Today we will just be looking at, *"Therefore as you have received Christ Jesus the Lord."*

"Christ Jesus Lord." Those three words carry with them so much weight. "Christ" is Greek for the Hebrew word *Messiah*. The Christ was the long-awaited Seed of the woman who would crush the head of the serpent (Genesis 3:15). For Paul to say, *"receive Christ Jesus as Lord,"* was to make a claim of monumental proportions because the Jews had waited for over 4,000 years for the Christ to come.

Whereas "Christ" carries with it such dignity and grander, "Jesus," on the other hand, carried obscurity and humility. Jesus did not come from wealth, importance, or notoriety. On the contrary, He came from meager means as the son of a carpenter. Jesus was known as a teacher and miracle worker but saying He was the Son of God is what led Him to the cross.

"Lord" is another word that carries a punch. The Greek word *kyrios* means "he to whom a person or thing belongs, about which he has power of deciding." In English we would use the word "master." Your master is whomever you obey, not with your words but with your actions.

Paul is spurring these Christians to receive Jesus the Son of a carpenter, as the long-awaited Messiah, and to make Him the Master and decision maker of their life. This is by the Potter's design. These are big words and ones we should not so quickly read over.

———

THE FOG OF HIS PRESENCE

Therefore as you have received Christ Jesus the Lord, so walk in Him,
having been firmly rooted and now being built up in Him and established in your faith,
just as you were instructed, and overflowing with gratitude.

Colossians 2:6–7

As we continue to journey through Paul's words of encouragement to the Church in Colossae, we hear him say, *"so walk in Him."* Remember that Paul has just told them to receive Jesus the Son of a carpenter as the long-awaited Messiah and to make Him the Master and decision maker of their life. Now that they have done that, they are to walk in Him. What does this mean?

There have been several times when I have ended up hiking in a fog bank. The fog imposes on you, not letting you see more than a few feet. Your hair and clothing drip with the moisture in the air. Your eyes adjust to the glare even though the sunlight is blocked. The presence of fog can even be felt in the core of your being.

Walking in Jesus is much like walking in a fog bank. Just as walking in the fog can be dangerous, so can walking in Jesus, to the careless. God's ways are not our ways (Isaiah 55:8). He conceals the path in front of us, causing us to either depend on His leading or to try to figure it out for ourselves. Often, the Potter's plan doesn't make sense, which produces uncertainty that leads to anxiety, fear, and then doubt. Doubt is what leads us to self-reliance, which is how we walk right off a cliff. No, walking in Jesus is being in His presence every second of every day. Just like walking in fog, it encompasses you and drips off of you, but it also restricts your view. The Potter is continuing to refine us for His use, and that is why He wants your total trust. Trusting Him is the only way to walk in the fog of His presence but remember trusting the Potter is the death of self. May God open our eyes to see His glorious presence, may He open our ears to hear His voice, and may He open our hearts to trust His leading.

———

THE POTTER'S LOVE

Therefore as you have received Christ Jesus the Lord, so walk in Him,
having been firmly rooted and now being built up in Him and established in your faith,
just as you were instructed, and overflowing with gratitude.

Colossians 2:6–7

Reality is defined as what is 'real.' Whether or not you believe in reality has no bearing on what is real. Real is real, no matter what. So let's look at what is 'real.' The Potter, Who holds all power, including the power to create from nothing and then give it life, formed you from the dust of the earth; He holds you, fills you, and uses you as He wills. All of this is in accordance with the plan He had for you before you were ever born. Now, you may not like this arrangement, you may not even believe in the Potter, but whether you believe or like it holds no bearing on the reality of the Potter's hand. His hands are wise and strong! You can rebel against Him or you can submit to His ability to create and sustain for His glory. But at the end of the day, your life is all about His glory, not yours.

This is why Paul tells the church in Colossae to be *"firmly rooted."* Jeremiah tells us that a tree planted by the water with its roots extended by the stream does not fear the heat or drought but has green leaves and bears fruit (Jeremiah 17:8). Your roots are so vitally important, but even more important is what your roots are planted in. A plant that has roots yet has been pulled out of the dirt will wither and die from lack of nutrients. Likewise, we will wither if we are not rooted in Christ.

Ephesians 3:17–18 says, *"So that Christ may dwell in your hearts through faith; and that you, being rooted and grounded in love, may be able to comprehend with all the saints what is the breadth and length and height and depth."* How can we trust the Potter's hand if we are not rooted in His love? Things won't always feel good but we must know that He is good. Your roots must run deep into the Potter's love!

THE PERFECT FOUNDATION

Therefore as you have received Christ Jesus the Lord, so walk in Him,
having been firmly rooted and now being built up in Him and established in your faith,
just as you were instructed, and overflowing with gratitude.

Colossians 2:6–7

Paul continues to exhort the church in his letter to the Colossians by saying, "You have received Jesus, you are walking in Him, you are firmly rooted, now be built up in Him." The Greek word for 'being built up' is *epoikodomeō* and it means "being built upon, or to finish, the structure of which the foundation has already been laid." So the foundation has been laid, and we are to build upon it. But what is the foundation? We find the answer in 1 Corinthians 3:11–13: *"For no man can lay a foundation other than the one which is laid, which is Jesus Christ. Now if any man builds on the foundation with gold, silver, precious stones, wood, hay, straw, each man's work will become evident; for the day will show it because it is to be revealed with fire, and the fire itself will test the quality of each man's work."* Jesus Christ is the foundation; your life must be built upon Him. But there is something else that I want you to notice in this passage. We are to build upon the foundation of Jesus, and then on the day of judgment, the quality of what we have built will be tested with fire. Understand that if you built with anything subpar, it will be burned up. If everything you build is burned up, it is important to note that your foundation will not burn up because Jesus is fireproof in that He is holy. Therefore, anything you use to build yourself up that is not of the same likeness as Jesus will be consumed. We are to build ourselves up in holiness and Christlikeness.

O Father, so much of my life is reflective of me. My speech is about me, my desires are about me, my prayers are about me. Captivate me with Your holiness, otherwise on that day, I will have nothing to give to You other than a perfect foundation.

LIFE, IN EVERY WAY, IS ABOUT THE POTTER

Therefore as you have received Christ Jesus the Lord, so walk in Him,
having been firmly rooted and now being built up in Him and established in your faith,
just as you were instructed, and overflowing with gratitude.

Colossians 2:6–7

Let's continue to put the pieces together. Envision a cross with arrows pointing left, right, up, and down. The left side of the cross points back toward our past; Paul said, *"as you have received Christ Jesus the Lord."* The right side of the cross points to our future, *"so walk in Him."* Then the bottom of the cross points to the ground, *"having been firmly rooted."* Finally, the top of the cross points to the sky, *"now being built up in Him."* So we see that Paul reminds us that we are surrounded by the Potter's work, past and present, grounding and growing. Finally, Paul connects the four points when he says, *"established in your faith, just as you were instructed."* To be established means "to make firm your conviction of the truth." We are to become firm in the conviction of our faith. Don't be misled into believing faith means being certain of your religion. Religion says, "I am a denomination, preference, or style." Faith says, "the Potter is loving, trustworthy, and holy." Being established in our faith and firm in our convictions means we've received Jesus the Christ as Lord and Master, now we are walking in His surrounding presence day by day, which is causing us to grow roots deeper into His love. It is on this foundation of Jesus that we are growing up in Christlike holiness. To be established is to be unshakable, not in who you are but in Who the Potter is. Nothing comes to you except what passes through His hands, and the Potter's hands are strong and wise. Does this mean nothing bad will ever happen? 'Bad' is a word we have devised to describe things that do not go the way we want, yet here we are reminded that life, in every way, is about the Potter, not me.

———————

THE EUCHARIST OF GRATITUDE

Therefore as you have received Christ Jesus the Lord, so walk in Him,
having been firmly rooted and now being built up in Him and established in your faith,
just as you were instructed, and overflowing with gratitude.

Colossians 2:6–7

Just within these two short verses, Paul has delivered a whole semester of seminary, yet he has broken it down into bitesize nuggets that anyone can grasp.

"Receive Christ Jesus as Lord." This is Salvation.

"Walk in Him." This is Sanctification.

Sanctification begins as we become *"firmly rooted"* in His love.

It is developed as we are *"built up"* in His holiness.

Next, we become *"established in your faith"* as we trust Him.

Finally, we are to *"overflow with gratitude."* To live a life of gratitude is a double-sided sword. Sure anyone can say thank you when they get what they want but to say thank you for having what you want stripped away requires death of self. The Potter has the ability and the freedom to give and to take away (Job 1:21). Gratitude applies to the giving and the taking away. To learn this gratitude is to truly trust the Potter.

To better understand this, look at the Greek word for gratitude, *eucharistia*, which is made up of two words—*eu* means "well," and *charizomai* means "to give freely." You probably recognize the word *eucharistia* as being where we get the English word *eucharist*. The Eucharist is the bread and wine of communion. The symbols that Christ gave us to help us remember His broken body and blood poured out. Not just broken and poured out but *freely given, well!* Jesus freely gave His life so that we could have that salvation and sanctification; without it, we would have no hope. Jesus' gift of His life is the source of gratitude. If you are not overflowing with gratitude, then maybe you need to return to the Eucharist. See the Potter's nail-pierced hand as it sculpts and forms you into a vessel of great gratitude to Him.

TO WHOM WILL YOU COMPARE?

Even to your old age I will be the same, And even to your graying years I will bear you!
I have done it, and I will carry you; And I will bear you and I will deliver you.

Isaiah 46:4

In this verse, God is delivering a message of His unchanging presence, through Isaiah, to the remnant of Israel who are in captivity (vs. 3). But in verse five, God asks a question, *"To whom would you liken Me And make Me equal and compare Me, That we would be alike?"* The Potter is speaking of idols, man-made gods. What could stand equal to the Creator of all things? A cow? A goat? A creation of your own mind? No, anything we devise will crumble because we are the creation, not the Creator. The Potter formed us and breathed life into us; we form idols yet have no power to give life. Therefore to whom could we compare the Almighty? God declares several things in verse four:

- *"I have done it."* This literally means "I have made." The Potter is staking His claim on you saying, "I made you, you did not make Me."
- *"I will carry you."* The Greek word is *nasa*, and it means "to lift up, to take away." This brings understanding when we look at the space agency NASA. It is responsible for *lifting up* rockets into space *to take away* astronauts and bring them back. God lifts us up and carries us; we do not lift Him up.
- *"I will bear you."* Again God is comparing Himself with the idols of Israel. He is saying, "you bear or drag your handmade idols because they cannot walk. I bear or drag you because apart from Me, you can do nothing."
- *"I will deliver you."* The Lord declares His might when He compares His power to save with our idol's inability to do anything.

To whom would you liken Me? What is My equal? Certainly not us nor the work of our hands! Nothing can create, carry, bear, or deliver. None but the Potter; that is why we can trust Him with our very lives.

SURRENDERING THE LITTLE THINGS

Indeed, the very hairs of your head are all numbered. Do not fear;
you are more valuable than many sparrows.

Luke 12:7

Is it possible to control our lives? Only to a certain extent. Circumstances come at us from all directions. In most of these, we cannot control their onset, just our reaction to them. But our lack of control doesn't stop us from trying to sway things as much as possible. Two physical traits we have all tried to control would be our weight and our hairstyle. All of us have gone through either weight loss diets or protein muscle-building diets. Not that either of these are wrong, but they are our attempt to control our body size. The second area we seek to control is our hairstyles. One year we have long hair, the next year short. One month our hair is natural, and the next, it's dyed a different color. Some days our hair is straight, and others it's curly. Some of us lost part of our hair years ago, so we just shaved it all off. We can change our hairstyle pretty much whenever we want, and usually the reason we change it is because we want to. Simply put, we control the situation to fit what we like.

Does God care if we go on a diet or change our hair color? I don't know, but what I believe He cares more about is who gets the authority and control? Who gets the final say in our decision making? Do you consult the Potter as to if you should cut the hair He gave you? Many people would say God is not concerned about something as trivial as the length of your hair. But according to Luke 12:7, God cares enough about your hair to know the exact number you have on your head. God is not some dictator Who says, *"Do it because I said so."* He loves you so much that even the number of hairs you have were considered when He formed you. He wants control of your life, and seeing as you cannot control your circumstances, maybe we should hand control over to the One Who can control all things and cares even for the little things.

FINITE VS. INFINITE

But now faith, hope, love, abide these three; but the greatest of these is love.

1 Corinthians 13:13

One of the most beautiful expressions of the Potter's love for us is the interweaving of the infinite with the finite. When we look around at creation, everything is finite: the trees, the animals, the lakes, and the clouds. But in the midst of this temporal world, there are glimpses of eternity. These glimpses are of the presence and character of God. First Corinthians 13 is a chapter that describes some of this weaving of the finite and the infinite. Verses eight through twelve speak of the revelations of God through prophecy, tongues, and knowledge, which help us understand an infinite God in a finite world. Basically, these gifts of the Spirit are words of understanding given by the Spirit to one of His followers. That servant is then to speak, proclaim, or teach those words to others so they will have an understanding of God also. Yet Paul tells us that these gifts will be done away with at the proper time. Verse thirteen tells of three things that likewise reveal the character of God but will not be done away with. These three are eternal. We will be looking at these three over the next few days. The first of these is faith.

Second Corinthians 5:7 says, *"For we walk by faith, not by sight."* Hebrews 11:6 tells us, *"And without faith it is impossible to please Him, for he who comes to God must believe that He is a rewarder of those who seek Him."* If we as humans, eternal beings living in a finite world, are to please our eternal Father, then we are to not trust the temporary things around us that we can see. We are to cling to the eternal things of the Potter which we cannot see. The Potter is eternal, His plan is eternal, we His creation are eternal, yet our actions are finite when we trust the power and logic of man (Psalm 118:8). But when we walk by faith, we please the Potter. He smiles on His creation because our actions are dependent on Him, and that is worship, which is eternal.

HOPE IN THE UNSEEN

But now faith, hope, love, abide these three; but the greatest of these is love.

1 Corinthians 13:13

The word hope is defined as "an expectation of something." In Scripture the word hope is used 132 times; sixty-four of those are in the Old Testament, sixty-eight of those are in the New Testament. What is interesting is, of those sixty-eight New Testament instances, only two of them are found in the Gospels, and of those two only one is spoken by Jesus. That one is in reference to a hope that is misplaced (John 5:45). Why might it be that Jesus, our Hope, did not use this word in describing His salvation? Possibly, Paul sheds a little light on this: *"And not only this, but also we ourselves, having the first fruits of the Spirit, even we ourselves groan within ourselves, waiting eagerly for our adoption as sons, the redemption of our body. For in hope we have been saved, but hope that is seen is not hope; for who hopes for what he already sees? But if we hope for what we do not see, with perseverance we wait eagerly for it"* (Romans 8:23–25).

Maybe the Old Testament writers wrote about hope because they hoped for the Messiah to come. Likewise, the New Testament writers wrote about hope because they hoped for the Messiah to return. But Jesus did not speak of hope because in the Gospels, the Messiah could be seen, and as Paul said, *"Who hopes for what he already sees?"*

Today, we hope for the Messiah's return. First Corinthians 13:13 tells us that hope abides, therefore *"with perseverance we wait eagerly for it."* The creation waits for the Potter to return and take up His vessel. We hope in Him, and our hope is eternal.

———

THE POTTER'S LOVE

But now faith, hope, love, abide these three; but the greatest of these is love.

1 Corinthians 13:13

Love is arguably the most impacting word in the world, and that is why I firmly believe that everyone does what they do because of love. It is a word that both life and death hang on. Paul tells us in this verse that while some things are finite and will end, others are infinite and will remain eternally. Of those eternal gifts from God, the greatest of them is love. How well do you understand love?

- **Love is a noun in that it is a person**: God—1 John 4:16: "*We have come to know and have believed the love which God has for us. God is love, and the one who abides in love abides in God, and God abides in him.*"

- **Love is a noun in that it is a place**: The Body of Christ—Ephesians 4:16: "*From whom the whole body, being fitted and held together by what every joint supplies, according to the proper working of each individual part, causes the growth of the body for the building up of itself in love.*"

- **Love is a noun in that it is a thing**: Fruit of the Spirit—Galatians 5:22–23: "*But the fruit of the Spirit is love, joy, peace, patience, kindness, goodness, faithfulness, gentleness, self-control; against such things there is no law.*"

- **Love is a verb in that it is an action**: Labor—1 Thessalonians 1:3: "*Constantly bearing in mind your work of faith and labor of love and steadfastness of hope in our Lord Jesus Christ in the presence of our God and Father.*"

Usually, we see love as a wonderful feeling toward someone close, but from these verses, we can see the Potter's plan for us to love others is laid out. God is love, and His Spirit fleshes that out in us, the body of Christ. We are to toil, labor, and even travail in our love for others. Loving is often difficult and even dangerous, but we must endure because we are God's lighthouse of eternal love.

———

UNALTERABLE BLUEPRINT

You also, as living stones, are being built up as a spiritual house for a holy priesthood
to offer up spiritual sacrifices acceptable to God through Jesus Christ.

1 Peter 2:5

In Lilburn, Georgia, there is a Hindu temple that is an architectural work of art. It is comprised of more than 34,000 pieces of stone, which were hand carved in India. Even greater still is that there is no steel holding up the structure; the stones were carved to fit together like puzzle pieces and then held together by a giant keystone at the top of the temple.

Very much like this Hindu temple, Peter writes in his first letter that we are being built up as a spiritual house. When the Potter formed us, He not only handcrafted us for His purposes but He also designed us to interlock with other living stones. This structure is a spiritual house for God, just like the tabernacle in the Old Testament. When you study the blueprint of the Tabernacle as laid out in Scripture, you will see that everything about it had a purpose; nothing was arbitrary. Even the rings that held up the curtains were described in great detail. So if God took this much care to have His earthly dwelling place constructed, how much more will He meticulously form the stones that will make up His spiritual house? The Potter's purpose in making you was not so you could play games, make money, or even do good things. His hands mashed you, formed you, and smoothed you out with such precision that when the Potter places you next to another living stone, you will unite with them in a way that could only be described as worship. The solidarity of believers is not for a lost world's sake but for He Who lives in us. How dare we destroy what the Potter formed with our self-centered acts and quarreling between brothers and sisters. We were formed by the Potter's hand; any attempt to strengthen what He has made will weaken His temple (Psalm 133).

WILL YOU TRUST THE POTTER?

Know that the LORD Himself is God; It is He who has made us,
and not we ourselves; We are His people and the sheep of His pasture.

Psalm 100:3

If you ever visit the home of a Jewish family, when you enter you would see a little box hanging on the doorpost called a *mezuzah*. Inside this box would be a piece of paper with the *shema* written on it. The *shema* is found in Deuteronomy 6, *"Hear, O Israel! The LORD is our God, the LORD is one! You shall love the LORD your God with all your heart and with all your soul and with all your might"* (verses 4–5). Whenever a Jew would walk in or out of their house, they would reach up and touch the *mezuzah*, remembering that the Lord is God. How powerful would it be for us to practice this tradition? To be reminded daily that we are not God.

Psalm 100:3 reminds us that it is the Potter Who made us, not we ourselves. The Potter formed us in His image. He designed us for His plan. He gifted us and equipped us so that we could walk in Him. He crafted us, leaving His fingerprint on us. He put us through the fire of affliction so that we would be hardened and tempered for His great work. He then fills us with what He desires, and He places us, a vessel of honor, where we need to be to accomplish His task. Everything about our lives has been orchestrated by the Potter for us to walk in.

Now, we must choose, are we going to trust the Potter? Are we willing to trust Him when we hurt? When we are wronged? When it costs us everything? Will you trust Him, even when you ask Him to intervene and He does not? We cannot alter or try to strengthen what God has prepared, even when all logic says otherwise. The Potter's vessel was created to love Him, with all its heart, soul, and might. Our heart, soul, and might are not our own; they belong to the Potter, for His use. The Potter's hands are strong and wise, and we can trust Him!

FEBRUARY

The Savior's Wounds Are Death and Life

THE LAMB OF GOD

The next day he saw Jesus coming to him and said,
"Behold, the Lamb of God who takes away the sin of the world!"

John 1:29

When God had finished creating Adam and Eve, He looked back at all He had created, and He saw that it was *"very good"* (Genesis 1:31). The Potter had formed it perfectly according to His pleasure, but it was short-lived because Adam and Eve would disobey God's one command; they would eat from the tree of the knowledge of good and evil. The consequence that God had already laid before them was death. God knew they would disobey, and He already knew that He would act as the Savior of His creation. But that did not negate the consequence He gave them; someone would have to die. Their blood poured out, their soul separated from God's presence, destined to Hell. The Savior had already begun His journey to the cross. For four thousand years, the Savior would draw closer to the cross, closer to the nails, closer to death.

Four thousand years after Adam and Eve tasted the forbidden fruit, a little baby was born, the seed of the woman (Genesis 3:15). This baby would grow up into a man thirty years old. One day as He was walking through the town of Bethany beyond the Jordan, John the Baptist would make an exclamation, *"Behold the Lamb of God who takes away the sin of the world!"* The word John used for *"takes away"* was *airō,* which means "to bear away what has been raised." John was prophesying that Jesus would bear away, or carry off, all the sins of the world—every bit of our disobedience—and they would be raised up. God was revealing what was to come. My sin and your disobedience would be laid on Jesus, and He would be raised up on the cross. He would die so we could live. The Savior, the spotless Lamb of God, would become the sacrifice for the world. The Savior's death would become our life! The Savior's wounds are death and life.

———

THE SAVIOR'S FACE

For He grew up before Him like a tender shoot, And like a root out of parched ground;
He has no stately form or majesty That we should look upon Him,
Nor appearance that we should be attracted to Him.

Isaiah 53:2

For four thousand years, the Jews had been waiting and watching for the Messiah, yet most of them missed Him. When you stop to think about it, what would a Savior look like? If you were tasked to go to the airport to pick up someone you had never met nor knew anything about, you didn't even know what day or hour their flight would arrive, how would you even begin? You could make a sign with their name on it, but then anyone could come up and say that was their name. Truth be told, if we were still waiting and watching for the Son of God to make His entrance on this earth, I believe we would miss Him, too. We would be looking for the same appearance those in the Gospels were looking for.

But the people of the Gospels were not totally without help. Isaiah had already told them not to look in the palaces. He prophesied that the Messiah would have no stately form or majesty. How does the King of Kings not have majesty? Oh, the Savior has majesty. *"And He is the radiance of His glory and the exact representation of His nature, and upholds all things by the word of His power. When He had made purification of sins, He sat down at the right hand of the Majesty on high"* (Hebrews 1:3). Jesus was the very radiance of glory and majesty, but Philippians 2:6 tells us, *"who, although He existed in the form of God, did not regard equality with God a thing to be grasped."* The Greek word for "grasped" means "utilized." The Savior had glory, radiance, and majesty but He did not utilize it. He was willing to leave all of that behind and come to earth as a little baby, a tender shoot. There was nothing about His earthly appearance that would draw us to Him because it wasn't His face that would save us; it was His heart.

THE WAY IN WHICH WE SHOULD GO

He was despised and forsaken of men, A man of sorrows and acquainted with grief;
And like one from whom men hide their face He was despised,
and we did not esteem Him.

Isaiah 53:3

Take a second to imagine a city of peace, beauty, and love. This city is like Heaven on earth; there is no pain, no sadness, and no sickness. It is a city set majestically on a mountain and emanates glory and honor. Rumor has it that its gates are wide open, and all can live there. Your heart longs to go to this city, so you go to the mountain; you can see the city perched high above the clouds, but no matter where you go, you cannot find the road that leads to this wonderful place. Though this city is perfect, it is inaccessible and therefore not a source of hope or joy.

We, as Christians, have just such a city that awaits us. New Jerusalem will one day be a city of peace and wholeness for all who believe, but what good is that if there were no way to get there? *"Jesus said to him, [Thomas] 'I am the way, and the truth, and the life; no one comes to the Father but through Me'"* (John 14:6). Jesus is the road to that city, but the question is how did He become that road? Isaiah tells us that Jesus would be a man of sorrow and acquainted with grief. Jesus, Who had never sinned, thereby not knowing sorrow, pain, grief, or sickness, would not save mankind from a distance but would step out of Heaven and come to earth, becoming acquainted with the effects of death so that He could be the road to the Father. But when He came into our world, He was not received with a royal welcome. No, He was despised and forsaken. The city was prepared, the road was made for us, but we wanted to kill the Creator, not follow the Savior. *"He was in the world, and the world was made through Him and the world did not know Him. He came to His own, and those who were His own did not receive Him"* (John 1:10–11).

———

PERSONAL SAVIOR

Surely our griefs He Himself bore, And our sorrows He carried;
Yet we ourselves esteemed Him stricken, Smitten of God, and afflicted.

Isaiah 53:4

Today, God's grace becomes personal. Isaiah reminds us that the sorrows and grief Jesus was acquainted with in verse three are our sorrows and grief. Jesus bore all of humanity's grief but Isaiah makes it personal; He bore my grief.

This verse introduces what we could call the "God's Perspective Paradox." This is when we say something, but from God's perspective, the opposite is true. For example, when Pilate questioned Jesus he said, "I am innocent of this Man's blood." And the people responded, "His blood shall be on us" (Matthew 27:24–25). What Pilate was saying was, "I want no part of killing Jesus." But in God's perspective, to have none of Jesus' blood on you is to be lost. The people were saying, "We take responsibility for killing Him." But God's perspective is, the blood of Jesus must be on you if you are to be saved. What Pilate meant as good was actually bad, and what the people meant as bad was actually their only hope.

Isaiah points to another "God's Perspective Paradox:" *"Yet we ourselves esteemed Him stricken, Smitten of God and afflicted."* The people's perspective was that God was punishing this Man because He was a blasphemer, but from God's perspective, Jesus was spotless. To understand this paradox, ask yourself, was Jesus smitten of God? The Savior was perfect, but He carried my sorrow and was acquainted with my grief; He bore my sins and imperfections. The wages of my sin is death (Romans 6:23). Therefore, Jesus also took on my death. This death is not just to stop breathing but to be separated from God. Was Jesus smitten of God? Was the Savior struck down by God? Yes, but not because of His sin like the people before Pilate thought. It was because of my sin and your sin. Oh, what a Savior!

HE WAS PIERCED THROUGH

But He was pierced through for our transgressions, He was crushed for our iniquities;
The chastening for our well-being fell upon Him, And by His scourging we are healed.

Isaiah 53:5

Let's take a journey. When Jesus was on trial before the religious leaders, He told them that now they would see the Son of Man seated at the right hand of Power. They then spit in His face, they struck Him, and some slapped Him (Matthew 26:67). While these are not mortal blows, they are insults. They are the chastising which brought us well-being.

We continue with Pilate, who in John 19:1 orders Jesus scourged. The Romans were so skilled in the art of flogging that they could take a man to the brink of death yet keep him alive. Jesus lost massive amounts of blood and was disfigured beyond the image of a man (Isaiah 52:14). But it was by His scourging that we are healed.

Next, we visit the cross. Our Savior was forced to carry His cross to Golgotha, where He was made to lay on it with arms stretched out. Then long metal spikes were hammered into His hands and feet. The cross would be raised up so that Jesus was totally exposed, mutilated, drained of life, and a symbol of disobedience. But Jesus was innocent. It was for our transgressions that He was pierced through.

Finally, we come to the end of our journey. Physical pain is temporary because the body is finite, but a crushed spirit who can stand? (Proverbs 18:14). Jesus would cry out to His Father, *"My God, My God, why have You forsaken Me?"* (Matthew 27:46). But there would be no reply. Jesus would have the weight of our iniquities placed on Him, and the Father would crush Him with the wrath that was meant for me.

Jesus was chastened, scourged, pierced, and crushed so that we could have peace, healing, and life. The Savior's wounds are death and life! Praise the Savior!

OPPOSITE OPPOSITION

All of us like sheep have gone astray, Each of us has turned to his own way;
But the LORD has caused the iniquity of us all To fall on Him.

Isaiah 53:6

Opposite opposition—these two words describe objects that lie on different extremes of a spectrum that, when brought together, respond with a reaction. Light and dark, at rest and in motion, alive and dead—these are examples of opposites that are in opposition with one another. When light encounters dark, only one can win. When an object at rest is acted upon by an equal or greater force, then the object ceases to be at rest. When something that is alive encounters death, life is no more—opposite opposition.

Isaiah writes about the greatest opposite opposition in verse six: *"But the LORD has caused the iniquity of us all to fall on Him."* He was writing about holy and perverse or, to state it more simply, clean and dirty. All of us have turned from God, disobeying Him and perverting His love. This perversion or sin is what Isaiah calls iniquity. The Lord caused my iniquity to fall on Jesus. You cannot say that Jesus is the most holy being because that is to imply that someone could one day become more holy than Him. No, Jesus is holy, completely, fully, cannot be added to. Therefore when the Lord caused our iniquity to fall on the Holy, there was an opposite opposition. Only one could remain, the other did not lessen or diminish but it ceased to be. The Savior's wounds are death and life! Jesus' life is greater than your death, so when this opposite opposition happened, your death transferred to Him, and His life transferred to you. His death is now your life. Perversion was no match for the holiness of the Savior; that is why He is the Risen Savior! If He loves you enough to take your death, do not fear death, He has already overcome the grave. Trust Him enough to walk the path He asks of you, and do not turn away when things get hard; press into the Savior.

TOTAL SURRENDER

He was oppressed and He was afflicted, Yet He did not open His mouth;
Like a lamb that is led to slaughter, And like a sheep that is silent before its shearers,
So He did not open His mouth.

Isaiah 53:7

Over the past several weeks, we have been talking about trusting God with total surrender. No matter what God pours in you, where He places you, or what fire of affliction He asks you to walk through. But what does this total trust, total submission, and total obedience to the Father look like? In chapter fifty-three, Isaiah wrote what we know as the *"Suffering Servant"* passage, and he depicted Jesus leaving His glory in Heaven, coming in poverty as One Who would never be looked upon as the Messiah. Basically, Isaiah had laid out a job description of the Savior: Poverty, Pain, and Penalty.

Jesus came to the earth as a baby, born to a poor family. He grew up knowing sickness, pain, and rejection. He obeyed everything the Father had for Him to do, then the night before His death, He would pour out His heart to God saying, *"If it is possible, let this cup pass from Me; yet not as I will, but as You will"* (Matthew 26:39). Jesus was honest before the Lord, He did not want the pain, but He was surrendered to what the Father wanted.

The next day as Jesus stood before Pilate and Herod, the very people who had the power to set Him free, He did not open His mouth. He did not make a defense nor plead for His life because He was totally surrendered to the Father's will. It did not matter if He liked it, wanted it, was uncomfortable with it, or thought it was unfair. No, Jesus knew the Father had heard His prayer but was unwilling to let the cup pass. So Jesus drank the cup to the bitter end.

You will know if you are totally surrendered to the Father's will when He does not let the cup of pain pass, and you simply grasp the cup with a closed mouth. What is there to say? *"Not as I will, but as You will."*

TO WHOM THE STROKE WAS DUE

By oppression and judgment He was taken away; And as for His generation, who considered That He was cut off out of the land of the living For the transgression of my people, to whom the stroke was due?

Isaiah 53:8

All through Scripture, we see God's ultimatum—obedience is life, but disobedience is death. This was laid down in the Garden of Eden and was carried all the way to the cross. *"For the wages of sin is death, but the free gift of God is eternal life in Christ Jesus our Lord"* (Romans 6:23). So the line was drawn in the sand, but all of humanity has disobeyed God (Romans 3:23). Every one of us deserves death and far more.

> *So all these curses shall come on you and pursue you and overtake you until you are destroyed, because you would not obey the LORD your God by keeping His commandments and His statutes which He commanded you. They shall become a sign and a wonder on you and your descendants forever. Because you did not serve the LORD your God with joy and a glad heart, for the abundance of all things* (Deuteronomy 28:45–47).

God's wrath is severe, lethal, and final, but He made known His consequences from the beginning. He also made known His love! *"When you were dead in your transgressions and the uncircumcision of your flesh, He made you alive together with Him, having forgiven us all our transgressions, having canceled out the certificate of debt consisting of decrees against us, which was hostile to us; and He has taken it out of the way, having nailed it to the cross"* (Colossians 2:13–14). As Isaiah reminds us, the stoke of punishment, the fierceness of God's wrath, the finality of death, *was* ours but it was laid on the Savior. We have been given the love of the Father and a new assignment. *"And walk in love, just as Christ also loved you and gave Himself up for us, an offering and a sacrifice to God as a fragrant aroma"* (Ephesians 5:2). Go walk in love!

A PERSPECTIVE FROM ON THE CROSS

His grave was assigned with wicked men, Yet He was with a rich man in His death,
Because He had done no violence, Nor was there any deceit in His mouth.

Isaiah 53:9

Isaiah makes a prophecy in verse nine that is unique. He says that the Savior's grave would be assigned with wicked men. Of course, Isaiah's prophecy was fulfilled in the Gospels when Jesus is crucified between two thieves (Luke 23:32–33). But why is this prophecy so unique? Hebrews 7:26 says, *"For it was fitting for us to have such a high priest, holy, innocent, undefiled, separated from sinners and exalted above the heavens."* When you look at this list of attributes for Jesus, of course He was holy, innocent, undefiled, and exalted above the heavens, but separated from sinners? How was Jesus separated from sinners? He was always surrounded by sinners. The Pharisees were constantly pointing their finger at Jesus' company. Mary anointing His feet, Jesus eating at Zacchaeus' house, the woman caught in adultery thrown at His feet, and even the unorthodox disciples. If the Savior was separated from sinners, then this has to mean something other than His proximity to them. Jesus was not separated from sinners in that He was distanced from them but rather distinct from them. The sin that condemned the two criminals was the same that condemned Jesus, but as one of the criminals said on the cross, the condemnation of Jesus was unjust. *"Do you not even fear God, since you are under the same sentence of condemnation? And we indeed are suffering justly, for we are receiving what we deserve for our deeds; but this man has done nothing wrong"* (Luke 23:40–41). Jesus is our High Priest because He was *"separated from sinners,"* but He is the cleansing sacrifice because *"His grave was assigned with wicked men."* I am that wicked man, yet through the Savior's wounds, His death is my life. O Lord, help us to have a perspective from on the cross not just from the empty tomb.

A PLEASING SACRIFICE

But the LORD was pleased To crush Him, putting Him to grief; If He would render Himself as a guilt offering, He will see His offspring, He will prolong His days, And the good pleasure of the LORD will prosper in His hand.

Isaiah 53:10

The Savior's wounds are death and life; what does this mean? When Jesus' blood was shed, the forgiveness of sins was made available to those who believe. Life was given to them, but to Jesus there had to come death, a crushing of Himself by the Father—much like grapes are crushed to get their juice, much like seeds are crushed in a mortar to get their oils, Jesus was likewise crushed and made contrite to get His purifying blood. This was pleasing to the Father. Why? Psalms 51:17 says, *"The sacrifices of God are a broken spirit; A broken and a contrite heart, O God, You will not despise."* Why does God delight in a contrite spirit? Because a contrite spirit is an obedient spirit. *"For My hand made all these things, Thus all these things came into being,"* declares the LORD. *"But to this one I will look, To him who is humble and contrite of spirit, and who trembles at My word"* (Isaiah 66:2). Total obedience requires total trust, and total trust requires total surrender. The Father loves a crushed, contrite spirit because that is a spirit that can only depend on Him. But God does not crush our spirits just so we will be doormats; to those who bow with a contrite heart, He gives the kingdom of Heaven (Matthew 5:3). The Savior's wounds brought His death but gave us life. His life in us likewise produces a death in us, a death to sin (Romans 8:11–17). We are to suffer with Him so that we may also be glorified with Him (vs. 17). Crushed, bruised, broken, contrite, lowly, poor, humble, these are the sacrifices of God that are pleasing to Him, not because He is sadistic but because He gives resurrected, whole, eternal, restored, beautiful life to all those who die to sin, starting with His own Son.

LIGHT IN THE DARKNESS

As a result of the anguish of His soul, He will see it and be satisfied; By His knowledge the Righteous One, My Servant, will justify the many, As He will bear their iniquities.

Isaiah 53:11

The night before Jesus was crucified, He was in the garden of Gethsemane praying with His disciples and He told them, *"My soul is deeply grieved, to the point of death; remain here and keep watch with Me"* (Matthew 26:38). The Savior would begin to pray, pouring out His soul to the Father, and as Luke tell us, His sweat would become like drops of blood (Luke 22:44). Anguish, literally meaning "heavy, wearisome labor," would churn like the waves of the ocean within the soul of the Prince of Peace. Jesus' soul was so troubled that He began sweating blood, yet something happened because right after He was praying to the Father to allow the cup to pass, He turned around and told the disciples to get up and get going (Matthew 26:46). Jesus went from 'anguish' to 'it's go time' within just a couple of verses; what happened? According to Isaiah 53:11, something "satisfied Him." The Dead Sea Scrolls records this verse as saying, *"He shall see light and be satisfied."*

The cross was not easy for the Savior—the wounds, the anguish, the betrayal, the weight, and the silence of the Father—but Jesus went from sweating blood to "Let's go" because He saw the light. He communed with the Father in prayer, and even though Jesus' request was to let the cup pass, the Father said "No." Jesus was the Servant, and His task was to bear our iniquities. He was able to be obedient to the Father because He was reminded of God's glorious and mighty hand. There is great light in communing with the Father. This light shines on the truth that we are forgiven!

———

FATHER FORGIVE THEM

Therefore, I will allot Him a portion with the great,
And He will divide the booty with the strong; Because He poured out Himself to death,
And was numbered with the transgressors; Yet He Himself bore the sin of many,
And interceded for the transgressors.

Isaiah 53:12

"*Father, forgive them; for they do not know what they are doing*" (Luke 23:34). "*And forgive us our debts, as we also have forgiven our debtors*" (Matthew 6:12). "*Whenever you stand praying, forgive, if you have anything against anyone, so that your Father who is in heaven will also forgive you your transgressions*" (Mark 11:25). "*And if he sins against you seven times a day, and returns to you seven times, saying, 'I repent,' forgive him*" (Luke 17:4).

The cry from the cross was to forgive the very people who plotted against Him, sold Him out for thirty pieces of silver, hit Him in the face, told lies trying to condemn Him, mashed the crown of thorns down on His head, spit in His face, laid the purple robe over His ripped open flesh, denied ever knowing Him, doubted Him, whipped Him draining His life, forced Him to carry the cross up Calvary, cast lots for His clothes, and hammered the nails into His hands and feet. Yes, the Savior cried out, "*Father forgive them; for they do not know what they are doing.*" Jesus interceded for the transgressors, and then He poured Himself out to death.

But He didn't just intercede for the Jewish accusers or the Roman executioners or His fearful followers; He interceded for *me*. Jesus asked God to forgive *me* for my selfishness, hate, lust, pride, gossip, greed, lack of compassion, doubt, jealousy, vanity, disrespect, lies, and deceitful ways. Yes, Jesus interceded for me, then He poured Himself out to death. The Savior's wounds are death and life!

DRINKING THE SOUR CUP

After this, Jesus, knowing that all things had already been accomplished,
to fulfill the Scripture, said, "I am thirsty." A jar full of sour wine was standing there;
so they put a sponge full of the sour wine upon a branch of hyssop and brought it
up to His mouth. Therefore when Jesus had received the sour wine, He said,
"It is finished!" And He bowed His head and gave up His spirit.

John 19:28–30

John records what we could call the mystery of the cross. If everything had already been accomplished to fulfill the Scripture, then why did Jesus say, *"I am thirsty"*? Why would the Savior spend one moment more on that excruciating cross than He had to? Verse thirty even says, *"He bowed His head and gave up His spirit."* Jesus had the power to lay down His life, so why did He say, *"I am thirsty"* and drink the sour wine? Possibly, the reason Jesus took this extra step points back to when He was praying in the Garden. He asked God to let this cup pass (Matthew 26:39), but the Father had said no. Therefore, Jesus was going to have to drink the cup of suffering. The Savior went to the cross, endured the mocking and the torture, even experienced the silence of the Father, and then in the last few seconds, He said, *"I am thirsty,"* so that He could physically drink the mouth-twisting, nonsatisfying, sour cup that the Father had set aside just for His Son. Sour to the last drop!

Digging a step further into the injustice of this cup, John 1:3 says, *"All things came into being through Him, and apart from Him nothing came into being that has come into being."* This means that the grapes that were used to make the sour wine were created by Jesus. He could have made them sweet but He designed them to be sour, to complete His task on earth. Just like Jesus created human beings, He could have designed them not to sin, but He gave them the freedom to love or hate Him. And that is why He was on the cross drinking the sour wine; He loved them to the end!

BROUGHT TO TEARS

Jesus wept.

John 11:35

What could possibly make the Savior of the world weep? Jesus knew that Lazarus had died, but He also knew that He was going to raise him from the dead, so why would Jesus weep?

When Lazarus got sick, his sisters sent word to Jesus saying, *"Lord, behold, he whom You love is sick"* (John 11:3). Again, after Lazarus died, Jesus would weep, and the people watching would say, *"See how He loved him!"* (John 11:36). In each of these verses, the Greek word for love is *phileō,* which means "brotherly love or to be friendly to someone." So Mary and Martha and those watching Him weep saw the love of a friend that ran deep but do not miss how Jesus would describe His love for Lazarus and his family. *"Now Jesus loved Martha and her sister and Lazarus"* (John 11:5). This word for love is *agapaō,* which means "to love dearly." This is the same word for love that was used in John 3:16 to describe the love the Father has for the world. The love Jesus felt for Lazarus was not that of a brother but that of a Savior! I believe Jesus wept at Lazarus' tomb not because of his death but because of His love. Jesus' love was pure, complete, and incomprehensible; those around Him did not understand His great love, and my fear is that today we still do not grasp His all-encompassing love. First John 3:1 says, *"See how great a love the Father has bestowed on us, that we would be called children of God; and such we are. For this reason the world does not know us, because it did not know Him."* The love that the Father bestowed on us was Jesus Himself! The world does not know Him; It does not know of His love, and this wounds the Savior. His love is Who He is, and that draws Him to weep for mankind.

Lord, please teach us of Your great love. May we know the patient, kind, selfless, and complete love which You have for us! We love because You first loved us.

THE LOSS OF A FRIEND

And he threw the pieces of silver into the temple sanctuary and departed;
and he went away and hanged himself.

Matthew 27:5

Can you imagine what the relationships must have been like for Jesus and the disciples? For three years they had spent so much time together, experienced so many things, and probably stayed up late talking about everything on earth and Heaven above. During this three-year period, the Savior was able to watch these men grow from fishermen and tax collectors into disciples and apostles. He saw them on days they laughed, and He comforted them on days they hurt. When politics and the state of the world seemed to fall in on them, Jesus was there to point them to the Father. They grew from a teacher-pupil relationship to friends.

Often we forget that the disciples didn't know what was coming (e.g., that Judas was going to betray Jesus). They just knew they were a band of brothers, learning from Jesus and seeing Him do amazing things. Judas himself did not even understand what he was doing (Matthew 27:3). But when Judas came to the pentacle of his plan, Jesus exposed Himself to a painful wound. *"Immediately Judas went to Jesus and said, "Hail, Rabbi!" and kissed Him. And Jesus said to him, "Friend, do what you have come for." Then they came and laid hands on Jesus and seized Him"* (Matthew 26:49–50). Jesus came to earth to die so that humanity could be saved, but I'm sure it still hurt to have that plan enacted by His friend. Yet the pain Jesus felt from being betrayed by His friend was not the wound that hurt the most; the heart-wrenching wound came when Judas took his guilt and, instead of running to his Friend, he hung himself. Jesus didn't have the opportunity to tell Judas, "I still love you" or "I forgive you." Jesus was betrayed by His friend, but even worse His friend lost sight of the Hope, Who loved him so much!

———————————

NEW LIFE

Having canceled out the certificate of debt consisting of decrees against us,
which was hostile to us; and He has taken it out of the way, having nailed it to the cross.

Colossians 2:14

"Therefore if anyone is in Christ, he is a new creature; the old things passed away; behold, new things have come" (2 Corinthians 5:17). Old and new, just like the two sides of a coin, only one can face up. Either the Savior has made you new through His death on the cross or you are still old, clinging to your sins. Why do we insist on clinging to the death and decay that plagues us like a cancer? Why don't we let go of ourselves and allow God to make us new? As Paul says in Colossians 2:14, it is our sins that are *"hostile to us."* Sin is much like a hot, boiling pot of water on a stove; when we pick it up barehanded, it burns our skin and instantly begins to destroy the cells in our fingers. Our refusing to surrender to the Savior is much like continuing to hold the boiling pot of water, feeling its pain yet denying its reality. Paul points out that Jesus took away that hostility by nailing it to the cross but understand that before Jesus nailed it into the wooden beam, He nailed it to Himself!

For you have been called for this purpose, since Christ also suffered for you, leaving you an example for you to follow in His steps, who committed no sin, nor was any deceit found in His mouth; and while being reviled, He did not revile in return; while suffering, He uttered no threats, but kept entrusting Himself to Him who judges righteously; and He Himself bore our sins in His body on the cross, so that we might die to sin and live to righteousness; for by His wounds you were healed. For you were continually straying like sheep, but now you have returned to the Shepherd and Guardian of your souls (1 Peter 2:21–25).

Turning to the Savior does mean total surrender, but it also means total life. Let go of the sin that continues to harm you, receive the healing that Jesus is dying to give.

———

MY PAIN AND HIS COMFORT

Blessed be the God and Father of our Lord Jesus Christ, the Father of mercies and God of all comfort, who comforts us in all our affliction so that we will be able to comfort those who are in any affliction with the comfort with which we ourselves are comforted by God. For just as the sufferings of Christ are ours in abundance, so also our comfort is abundant through Christ.

2 Corinthians 1:3–5

Prior to Jesus' coming to this earth, He reigned in Heaven. The Prince of Peace had no needs, no wants, nor any problems, but that all changed as He stepped into this world. Jesus would experience sickness, He would know the pain of scrapes and cuts, and He would know the hurt of a broken heart. The Savior understands pain, so it is through His afflictions that He is able to comfort us in ours. Pain can be relentless but in the hands of the Master, it can be a most powerful tool. James 1:2–4 says, *"Consider it all joy, my brethren, when you encounter various trials, knowing that the testing of your faith produces endurance. And let endurance have its perfect result, so that you may be perfect and complete, lacking in nothing."* How can anyone count trials as joy? I can only think of one possible reason. You have faith that God is greater than the trial, and He will deliver you and even make you stronger. The Savior was able to find joy in His wounds because His faith in His Father was greater than His fears; therefore, He knew that though His wounds were death, they would also be life. Now, when I walk through trials, I experience hurts and fears, but I can find the joy of the Holy Spirit because Jesus knows how to comfort me; he has already walked through it. We can rest in His hands even in our darkest hour but only if we truly trust Him. You will know you trust the Savior when you stop running, stop protecting, and stop talking. Life will not be painless but comfort and joy can be found in Jesus' wounds.

———

THE PRICE OF PEACE

Saying, "Behold, we are going up to Jerusalem, and the Son of Man will be delivered to the chief priests and the scribes; and they will condemn Him to death and will hand Him over to the Gentiles. They will mock Him and spit on Him, and scourge Him and kill Him, and three days later He will rise again.

Mark 10:33–34

The Savior's wounds are death and life. According to these two verses, Jesus points out ten wounds that He would receive, each one separated by the word *"and."* Over the next ten days, we will look into each wound that would bring death to His life yet Life to our death.

First, Jesus told the disciples that they would be going up to Jerusalem. On the surface there are no wounds here, but when you meditate on what Jerusalem was, then you see the scar of rebellion. The name Jerusalem means "peace." Jesus was not going to Jerusalem to experience peace, but death. The Holy City was the site of the Temple and in those walls was the Holy of Holies where the 'Shekhinah Glory' of God rested over the mercy seat. The Father, Who had led Israel through the wilderness, gone before His children into battle, and had given them the Promise Land, had dwelt in Jerusalem; now His holy presence was seen in the flesh of His Son Who was going to the City of Peace to bring forgiveness for our rebellion by the breaking of His body. Peace for Jesus was not the absence of pain but rather the absence of accusation brought on those who would believe in Him. The first wound of the Savior did not draw blood; it was a broken heart. Jesus' heart broke because humanity was separated from the Father, pain and sickness were destroying His creation, and the enemy was celebrating. The only provision for this was for the Savior to go to Jerusalem. Peace for us would come at a very high price, one that Jesus was willing to pay.

MISGUIDED SERVICE

Saying, "Behold, we are going up to Jerusalem, and the Son of Man will be delivered to the chief priests and the scribes; and they will condemn Him to death and will hand Him over to the Gentiles. They will mock Him and spit on Him, and scourge Him and kill Him, and three days later He will rise again."

Mark 10:33–34

Today as we continue to look at Jesus' prophecy of what was about to happen to Him, we see another great emotional wound. The Son of Man told His disciples that He would be delivered to the chief priests. The word delivered also means "betrayed." Oftentimes, for us who live on this side of the cross, we have a bird's-eye view of the whole story, but we must remember that those who were walking through it did not have this luxury. They could only see what was right in front of them. What I mean by this is, often we make the chief priests and the religious leaders out to be villains because of how they handled Jesus' trial, but we have to remember who these men were and what their role was in relation to the Father. The chief priests were God's liaison to the people and the people's liaison to God. They offered the sacrifices so that the sins of God's children would be covered. They followed the law of God so that they could once a year go into the very presence of God. The chief priest was one chosen by God to potentially know Him more than any other human because of sheer proximity to Him. These men, though sinners, were men who were looking for the Messiah and employed to serve the Father in the house of the Lord. If there was ever a friend of the Savior or a safe house for the Christ, it would be in the fellowship of the chief priest, but instead, Jesus would be betrayed into their hands, and they would be the leading voice in the cry to crucify Him. Those who serve the Lord with misguided hearts, as sincere as they may be, are the very ones who carry out the works of the dark. Oh, that they would have known the God they served.

———

LIGHT AND DARKNESS

*Saying, "Behold, we are going up to Jerusalem, and the Son of Man will be
delivered to the chief priests and the scribes; and they will condemn Him to death
and will hand Him over to the Gentiles. They will mock Him and spit on Him,
and scourge Him and kill Him, and three days later He will rise again."*

Mark 10:33–34

Isaiah 9:2 says, *"The people who walk in darkness will see a great light; Those who
live in a dark land, The light will shine on them."* For those who live in darkness, can
you imagine the liberation they must experience when they see this great light!
Not only to see the light but to be loved by the Light, protected by the Light, and
led by the Light (Exodus 13:21). But how sad it is for those who are in the light
to walk in darkness. *"But if your eye is bad, your whole body will be full of darkness.
If then the light that is in you is darkness, how great is the darkness"* (Matthew 6:23).

Jesus told His disciples that they would be delivered to the scribes. The
scribes were lawyers charged to know the Law of Moses and to help the children
of Israel walk in it. They knew the Law of God forward and backward, yet in
their opportunity they had embraced their folly. The Law which was given to
a people who walked in darkness was to be a lighthouse. God knew when He
gave the Law that no human would ever be able to follow it completely; it was
a light that shone on our sins. But it also was a light that shone on the Savior.
The scribes, above all, should have recognized the Savior's fulfilling of the Law
but they had become so blinded by themselves that they would miss the light of
Messiah and would try to extinguish that Light on the cross. But just like water
to a grease fire, it only made the Light shine brighter! The Savior was wounded
by those who should have known Him best, but they betrayed Him to death. Of
these, I am one. How great is the grace found in the Savior's wounds!

———————

CHILDISH CONDEMNATION

Saying, "Behold, we are going up to Jerusalem, and the Son of Man will be delivered to the chief priests and the scribes; and they will condemn Him to death and will hand Him over to the Gentiles. They will mock Him and spit on Him, and scourge Him and kill Him, and three days later He will rise again."

Mark 10:33–34

When a child comes in the room mimicking his or her parents and announces, "You have been naughty, go to bed without supper," we smile because, cute as they are, they do not have the authority to send us to bed. He or she is the child and not the parent. Likewise, there is an amount of silliness in today's wound inflicted on the Savior. Jesus told the disciples that the religious leaders would condemn Him to death. This is laughable because John 14:6 says that Jesus is ". . . the way, the truth and the life." He is life and the giver of life (John 1:4). What are humans but the creation of the Savior? (John 1:3). What man has the authority to say to Life, "You have been judged, and You are condemned to no longer be Life?" Jesus has all authority to look at those men and say, "How dare you presume to demand such a thing, I am Life and the giver of Life, and if you could even take My Life from Me then you would cease to have life because I gave you part of Myself when I gave life to you." No one can take the Savior's Life, but because of His great love for us, the Savior laid His life down. *"For this reason the Father loves Me, because I lay down My life so that I may take it again. No one has taken it away from Me, but I lay it down on My own initiative. I have authority to lay it down, and I have authority to take it up again. This commandment I received from My Father"* (John 10:17–18). These men did not have the authority to take Jesus' life, yet they had the audacity to condemn Him to death. This was the perfect picture of a temper tantrum, but Jesus accepted the condemnation and willingly laid down His life so as to save those who would kill Him. The Savior's wounds are death and life.

ETHNIC SALVATION

Saying, "Behold, we are going up to Jerusalem, and the Son of Man will be delivered to the chief priests and the scribes; and they will condemn Him to death and will hand Him over to the Gentiles. They will mock Him and spit on Him, and scourge Him and kill Him, and three days later He will rise again."

Mark 10:33–34

The chief priests and the scribes would hand Jesus over to the Gentiles. To understand this racial wound, I want to preface it by stating that Jesus was not racist. He understood the sovereignty of God, and He understood the fullness of time for the Gentiles to receive the Gospel, which had not yet come. So please read to the end.

The word gentile in Greek is *ethnos*, which means "foreign nations not worshipping the true God." *Ethnos* is where we get the word ethnicity; therefore, another way to understand gentiles is the English word, foreigner. Basically, in the Old Testament, it meant someone of a different ethnicity or race. It is not a derogatory word, just a differentiating word. But because of the persecution, violence, and violations of the Jews during the exile and the intertestamental period, at the hands of some of the Gentile ethnicities, the word gentile became a more negative word. They were seen as unclean and pagan.

Jesus knew Malachi 1:11 said, *"My name will be great among the nations."* This included the Gentile nations, but Jesus also understood the Father's task, which was for Him to go to the lost sheep of the house of Israel (Matthew 15:24). Jesus knew that the day of salvation for the Gentiles was coming, but at the time He was handed over to them, they did not know the Father. They knew their own power, their own idols, their own laws. The hands of the Gentiles would be the instrument that would break the Savior's body, shed His blood, and end His life. No nation would be innocent of the blood of Jesus—Jew or Gentile; we are all guilty, we are all condemned, we are all loved by the Savior.

———

HE KNEW WHO HIT HIM

Saying, "Behold, we are going up to Jerusalem, and the Son of Man will be
delivered to the chief priests and the scribes; and they will condemn Him to death
and will hand Him over to the Gentiles. They will mock Him and spit on Him,
and scourge Him and kill Him, and three days later He will rise again."

Mark 10:33–34

Words have the power to give life or to kill (Proverbs 18:21). Jesus spoke words of Life, but He would receive words of death. When He had been arrested and waited to be questioned by the Sanhedrin, they mocked Him, blindfolded Him, beat Him, and then said, *"Prophesy, who hit You?"* (Luke 22:64–65). Later, He was taken to Pilate's official residence, where an entire Roman battalion would gather around Him to mock Him. They would start by stripping the Savior of His clothes. They would then put a scarlet robe on Him and shove a crown of thorns on His head. They would put a reed in His hand and kneel in front of Him saying, *"Hail, King of the Jews!"* Eventually, the soldiers took the reed back and began hitting Jesus in the head (Matthew 27:27–30). Finally, while Jesus was hanging on the cross, it would seem the entire world would turn their back on Him. The religious leaders, scribes, the rulers, the people passing by, and the criminals hanging next to Him would mock Him saying, *"If you are the Son of God, come down from the cross"* (Matthew 27:39–44). Every word was another blow to the Savior.

"Prophesy, who hit You?" Don't you know, He knew! With every blow they gave, Jesus could recall the day He wove them together in their mother's womb. He knew how many hairs were on their heads. He not only knew them but He also loved them! Their mocking voices were not alone; no, there was another voice that was heard that day, it was the voice of the Savior saying, *"Father, forgive them; for they do not know what they are doing"* (Luke 23:34).

SPIT IN HIS EYES

Saying, "Behold, we are going up to Jerusalem, and the Son of Man will be
delivered to the chief priests and the scribes; and they will condemn Him to death
and will hand Him over to the Gentiles. They will mock Him and spit on Him,
and scourge Him and kill Him, and three days later He will rise again."

Mark 10:33–34

As Jesus was standing before His accusers, they were filled with such hate. They would look at the Savior, and with the venom of a serpent, they would spit in His face. This wound was not designed to break the body but rather to break the spirit of a man. This was an insult reserved for someone who was below life. Even as a child, we learn we are not to spit on people, but these religious leaders were saying, "this creature in front of us is not even worthy of being called a person." Jesus would stand there with their spit running down His forehead, stinging as it ran into His eyes. I can only imagine Jesus' thoughts went back to the blind man He had encountered not that long ago. The Lord had spit in the dirt and mixed it up, making mud which He smeared into this blind man's eyes (John 9:6). Was this an insult? No, but was this blind man humbled as he walked to the pool to wash? Probably, but did his humility lead to worship when his eyes were opened? Yes! This once-blind man who could now see told everyone of his encounter with the Savior. Now, Jesus would stand before His accusers, and with their spit running down His face, He would humble Himself. His humility would lead to the worship of *"a great multitude that no one could number, from every nation, from all tribes and peoples and languages, standing before the throne and before the Lamb, clothed in white robes with palm branches in their hands, and crying out with a loud voice, "Salvation belongs to our God who sits on the throne, and to the Lamb!"* (Revelation 7:9–10). Their spit was meant to break, but in reality it restored! The Savior's wounds are death and life.

SCOURGED BEYOND ABILITY

*Saying, "Behold, we are going up to Jerusalem, and the Son of Man will be
delivered to the chief priests and the scribes; and they will condemn Him to death
and will hand Him over to the Gentiles. They will mock Him and spit on Him,
and scourge Him and kill Him, and three days later He will rise again."*

Mark 10:33–34

The Romans would scourge Jesus, inflicting excruciating pain on Him and causing the loss of massive amounts of blood. The soldiers would lay open His flesh from head to foot, causing His body to tremble and collapse. Weakened from His already-grueling torture, the weight of the cross He was forced to carry would crush Him. It would seem that the sadistic game the soldiers were playing had passed the point of realistic expectation. Jesus had been betrayed, beaten, spit on, mocked, deprived of sleep, whipped, and then forced to carry a wooden cross large enough to hold the weight of a man and long enough to keep his feet from touching the ground. Finally, Jesus would collapse because the torture was more than a human could take. If the soldiers were to finish this execution, they would have to grab someone and force them to carry the cross. They would grab a man named Simon from Cyrene, who was the father of Rufus and Alexander, who had come in from the country (Mark 15:21; Luke 23:26). Simon would carry the cross to the top of Golgotha, where he would relinquish it back to the Savior.

Why did Jesus hand His cross over to Simon? What purpose did this serve? Evil men beat Him, condemned men mocked Him, religious men hated Him, loyal men forsook Him, and an innocent man helped Him, but all men needed Him! Simon may not have known the pain of the nails, but he knew the weight of the cross. *O Lord, may we know the crushing weight of Your cross. It was rightly mine, but You took it back when You reached Calvary!*

———————

THE SERPENT'S VENOM

Saying, "Behold, we are going up to Jerusalem, and the Son of Man will be delivered to the chief priests and the scribes; and they will condemn Him to death and will hand Him over to the Gentiles. They will mock Him and spit on Him, and scourge Him and kill Him, and three days later He will rise again."

Mark 10:33–34

The wounds of the Savior leading up to the cross have been physical, emotional, and social, but on the cross, the wound the Savior received was spiritual. This wound was prophesied long ago, all the way back in the Garden of Eden when God cursed the serpent saying, *"And I will put enmity Between you and the woman, And between your seed and her seed; He shall bruise you on the head, And you shall bruise him on the heel"* (Genesis 3:15). Jesus would receive a wound on His heel, a wound inflicted by a serpent, a venomous, poisonous, death-filled wound that would stop His heart. The sun would refuse to shine, the earth would tremble, the rocks would crack and, literally, all hell would break loose as the Savior cried out with all He had left, *"My God, My God, why have You forsaken Me?"* (Mark 15:34). The Savior would hang His head and life would fade out of His body, His heart would stop beating, blood would cease to run through His veins, His lungs would stop expanding and contracting, His body would begin to grow cold as death consumed Him. Blood would flow from the nail holes in His hands and feet, but unseen to our eyes, there was another trail of blood trickling from His heel. The wound of Satan, delivered with such hate, received with such love.

In my mind's eye, I can see the Savior's lifeless body hanging on the cross. His body broken, His blood poured out, Satan rejoicing, the Father satisfied, but I stand at the cross looking at the Savior's wounds. Am I the executioner, the betrayer, the condemning judge, the brutal soldier, the mocking crowd? Was it my sin that was the venom of the serpent?

THE WOUNDS OF HEALING

Saying, "Behold, we are going up to Jerusalem, and the Son of Man will be delivered to the chief priests and the scribes; and they will condemn Him to death and will hand Him over to the Gentiles. They will mock Him and spit on Him, and scourge Him and kill Him, and three days later He will rise again."

Mark 10:33–34

What wounds does the Savior have in the resurrection? After all that Jesus had been through, He was now restored, made new, reborn. But there is still a wound found in His resurrection. After Jesus rose from the dead, He appeared to the disciples. They thought He might be a ghost, but Jesus responded to their disbelief in Luke 24:39, *"See My hands and My feet, that it is I Myself; touch Me and see, for a spirit does not have flesh and bones as you see that I have."* The Savior did not look the same as He did three days ago. Where His head bore the marks of a crown of thorns, there was now fresh skin. Where His flesh was laid open by the whip, now there was no carnage. His body had been made new with the exception that His hands and feet still bore the scars of the nails. These scars gave witness to the reality of the cross. But the beauty of the Savior's scars is that they are wounds of healing. Malachi 4:2 says, *"But for you who fear My name, the sun of righteousness will rise with healing in its wings; and you will go forth and skip about like calves from the stall."* His wounds of death were healed into scars of life.

Paul says he bears on his body the brand marks of Jesus (Galatians 6:17). Those who follow the Savior will bear His wounds, but these wounds will not end in death; no, they will begin in death, the death of self, but they end in life! (2 Corinthians 5:17). The Savior's wounds are death and life! The Savior's wounds are our death and our life! *O Father, help me to receive Your wounds of death on this earth, so I may walk in Your Life in Heaven.*

———————

THE BLOOD OF THE SAVIOR

Little children, make sure no one deceives you; the one who practices righteousness is righteous, just as He is righteous; the one who practices sin is of the devil; for the devil has sinned from the beginning. The Son of God appeared for this purpose, to destroy the works of the devil.

1 John 3:7–8

For this reason, the Savior came to the earth—to destroy the works of the devil. Jesus came as a tiny baby to lead a rebellion against the prince of darkness and to overthrow the powers of death and the grave. The paintings we grew up seeing of Jesus hanging on the cross may seem mild and painless but understand that the battle the Son of God waged on Satan was far from bloodless. Hebrews 12:4 says, *"You have not yet resisted to the point of shedding blood in your striving against sin."* Understand that Jesus came to earth knowing it was going to be bloody. He said in John 12:31–32, *"Now judgment is upon this world; now the ruler of this world will be cast out. And I, if I am lifted up from the earth, will draw all men to Myself."* The Savior was not playing games then, and He is not playing games now. He came to destroy the works of the devil, and the devil will not go quietly. Satan will kick and scream and deceive whomever he can by whatever means he can. He will destroy homes with business, he will destroy churches with apathy, he will destroy relationships with greed, and he will destroy lives with lust, but the Son of Man will destroy Satan with love! Jesus came to take sin away (1 John 3:5). Satan desires to destroy, but the Savior desires to restore (John 10:10). Satan wants to steal our joy, but the joy of the Lord is our strength! (Nehemiah 8:10). Satan will lash out at the Savior and will mortally wound Him, but Jesus will, in death, do what man could never do—destroy the works of the devil! Satan made Him bleed, but it was His blood that brought life! *Praise God we serve a living Savior!*

THE BANNER OF SALVATION

And I saw between the throne (with the four living creatures) and the elders a Lamb standing, as if slain, having seven horns and seven eyes, which are the seven Spirits of God, sent out into all the earth.

Revelation 5:6

The Savior's wounds are death and life, but they are also eternal. John writes in Revelation of a vision of Heaven, and while he is having this vision, he sees Jesus as a Lamb that has been slain. Now understand that this Lamb is not a defeated Lamb but an exalted King, the only One worthy to open the seven seals on the scroll (Revelation 5:5). So what does this mean? To understand this imagery, we need to go all the way back to the Old Testament. Leviticus 16 tells of two goats that, on the Day of Atonement, would be brought to the high priest who would take one of them and slaughter it as a sacrifice before God to cover the sins of the people. The second goat would then be brought to the high priest, who would lay hands on the head of the goat and confess the sins of the people of Israel. Then the goat would be led away and released into the wilderness, being considered unclean and therefore forsaken.

The Savior atoned for our sins in both of these ways. He would have all our sins laid on Him and become forsaken as unclean, even though He had never sinned. He was slaughtered on the cross so that His blood would cover our sins. Jesus, the Lamb of God, would be the sacrifice that would forgive and wash away our sins. Much like a child who falls into a mud puddle, the parent may forgive them for their action but then the parent still has to wash away the mud.

John looks and sees Jesus, the Lamb Who was slain but is not defeated. He overcame death and the grave, thereby forgiving and cleansing us of all our disobedience. Even in Heaven, the Savior bears the wounds of redemption, which are not the marks of death but the banner of Salvation!

MARCH

The Counselor's Insights Are Freeing and Trustworthy

WONDERFUL COUNSELOR

For a child will be born to us, a son will be given to us; And the government will rest on His shoulders; And His name will be called Wonderful Counselor, Mighty God, Eternal Father, Prince of Peace.

Isaiah 9:6

What do you do when life seems too big and the world is moving too fast for you to keep up? Stress is a very real thing, and distress soon follows. Angry, worried, helpless, sad, restless, afraid, and overwhelmed—these are all emotions that we feel from time to time or even a lot of the time, but what do you do with them? Any emotion, positive or negative, can lead us further from God if we focus on it instead of Him. That's why God is not as concerned about our emotions as He is the fruit of His Spirit grows in us. Emotions come and go, but the Fruit of the Spirit is a lifestyle grown in us by abiding with Him.

But don't think that God is indifferent to how we feel; on the contrary, Isaiah tells us that one of the names of God is *"Wonderful Counselor,"* and while counselor doesn't solely mean a psychologist, He does counsel us on our emotions. God is the creator of emotions, and there are many references in the Bible as to how God feels. The question is, do we take the time to listen to the Counselor's insights? Who better to counsel us about our emotions than the very One Who designed them? We often turn to the insights of pop culture, celebrities, doctors, self-help books, or friends, but at best they are speaking out of their experience, at worse they are speaking out of Satan's influence. They cannot speak directly to your soul because they do not know it. Job's friends, for example, spoke to him out of their own wisdom, which was feeble and unhelpful, but then God points to His sustaining hand at work all around the world. Job listened and was changed. Our emotions are not God, so be careful not to worship how you feel. The Counselor's insights are freeing and trustworthy; we must simply listen and surrender to Him.

SLEEP IN PEACE

*In peace I will both lie down and sleep, For You alone,
O LORD make me to dwell in safety.*

Psalm 4:8

It would be easy to focus on the words *peace, sleep,* or *safety* in this verse, but I believe the word that makes all of those words stand out is *"alone."* We all want the peace to lie down and sleep safely, but there is just something about the night that steals it from us. The night has a way of exaggerating and shrouding things. Without light, you can't tell what makes the noises, and if you have a little light, then the shadows play with your eyes. Not to mention your mind can start working in overdrive. So many nights are spent thinking about something that happened the day before or all the things that might happen the next day. Yes, we want peace, but often the night is full of stress and distress. Why? It's because of that one little word, *"alone."*

We fear the noises, and we stress over everything we have going on because we are working so hard to do things in our own power. Can I protect my family from an intruder? Can we make it if I get fired? What if the house catches on fire? Can I get to safety? If our children get abducted, what will we do? Everything is suffocating us, and that is destroying our rest.

David reminds us that the Lord *"alone"* brings peace, sleep, and safety. We can try all we want, but it will never work. The Counselor tells us to come to Him, and He will give us rest! (Matthew 11:28). But the thing we fear most is the very thing God asks of us, to lose control. We cannot handle everything that life throws at us, and we certainly can't get all our ducks lined up perfectly. We can't stop sickness, nor can we change the past, but the Counselor *"alone"* makes us dwell in safety. Run to Him and let go; it's the only way to find peace. *O Father, I have tried for so long to perfect my life. I'm holding so much, but nothing is working, and I'm just tired. I give up! Into Your hands I commit my life, my family, my past, and my future. Please help me sleep in peace. Amen.*

DEEPLY GRIEVED

But I have a baptism to undergo, and how distressed I am until it is accomplished!

Luke 12:50

What comfort there is to know that we are not alone when it comes to feeling distressed. Jesus felt distressed on more than one occasion. Matthew 26:37–38 says, *"And He took with Him Peter and the two sons of Zebedee, and began to be grieved and distressed. Then He said to them, 'My soul is deeply grieved, to the point of death; remain here and keep watch with Me.'"* Jesus, the One Who Isaiah said would be named *"Wonderful Counselor"* was distressed and grieved to the point of death. That is because stress is a normal part of our lives. When Jesus came to earth, He walked through the same muck and mire we do (Hebrews 4:15).

For many of us, we choose to turn to things that we can control like stress eating, pornography, or maxing out our charge card. Others will run from the stressors, so they will leave their family, quit their job, or change churches. And still others will choose to mask their distress with other emotions like laughing when really you want to cry. Often it is easier to hide by pointing at others, so no one sees what's really going on—we gossip, blame others, and post messages on social media. But none of these things takes our stress away; on the contrary, it makes us even more distressed.

So what did Jesus do when He was distressed? What was His pressure valve? Matthew 26:39 says, *"And He went a little beyond them, and fell on His face and prayed, saying, 'My Father, if it is possible, let this cup pass from Me; yet not as I will, but as You will.'"* The Counselor went before the Father and fell on His face in humility. He poured out His heart, and then He left it in the Father's hands. He prayed a surrendered prayer, and then He accepted whatever the Father desired. Things will happen that will take you to the end of your rope, but the Counselor's insights are freeing and trustworthy; follow His advice, humbly take it to the Father, surrender it, and leave it.

———

THE PATH WE ARE TO WALK

He humbled you and let you be hungry, and fed you with manna which you did not know, nor did your fathers know, that He might make you understand that man does not live by bread alone, but man lives by everything that proceeds out of the mouth of the LORD.

Deuteronomy 8:3

God spoke through Isaiah the prophet and said, *"For My thoughts are not your thoughts, Nor are your ways My ways"* (Isaiah 55:8). It is no secret that God operates very differently from how we do. The ways of God are higher than ours, and this baffles our minds. How do we trust a God Who leads us so out of the realm of logic? To us, we feel like the world is spinning out of control and going to hell in a handbasket, but the Counselor is whispering to us, "Come with Me and let's smell the roses." For us, it seems we are coming unglued, but God is more concerned about those roses than He is about helping us. How do we make sense of this?

In Deuteronomy 8:3, God is giving the people of Israel some very important insights about His character. He said that He allowed them to go hungry so that they would be humbled. The path God had for them was one of humility. Then He goes on to say that He provided them with food; it wasn't steak and baked potatoes, but rather the food of uncertainty. They did not know what kind of bread it was that God was providing. Sometimes God has us walk a path of humility while surrounded by uncertainty. Why? To teach us that even on our best day, we cannot do enough or be enough to sustain life. No, we live by the Word of the Lord. That Word is the insights of the Counselor; without it we shrivel up and die of starvation. The path of life we are walking is one of humility and uncertainty and dependence on God; that is why it is paramount that we listen to the words of the Counselor. *Please open my ears Lord to hear Your voice as I walk this path of humility, uncertainty, and dependence on You. I love You!*

HOPE FOR LIFE

For whatever was written in earlier times was written for our instruction, so that through perseverance and the encouragement of the Scriptures we might have hope. Now may the God who gives perseverance and encouragement grant you to be of the same mind with one another according to Christ Jesus.

Romans 15:4–5

Where does your hope lie? Now before you answer "Jesus," ask yourself if you worry when problems arise? Or do you get stressed out when things take an unexpected turn? Or even whether you struggle with thinking about how things might turn out? These are all signs that your hope may not be in Jesus. If your hope is in a Sovereign God, then He can handle all these things. If your hope is in a non-sovereign you, then your hope will crumble.

Paul is telling the Christians in Rome that they can have hope through the perseverance and encouragement of the Scripture. You are not strong enough to persevere on your own, nor can you pull yourself up by your bootstraps to rise above the waves of life. That is why when we look at the waves, just like Peter, we begin to sink (Matthew 14:28–30). But when we look to the Sovereign Counselor, we are able to rise above the storm.

So, where does your hope lie? In your inability or God's Sovereignty? Hope, when founded in Christ, can carry us through the darkest night. Open the Scripture and seek for the instructions of the Counselor. Fall in love with the book of Psalms. Hear the words of David as he cries out for forgiveness, rejoices in the Majesty of God, and writhes in distress as he feels the world crashing in on him. Learn from King Solomon in the book of Proverbs as he shares insights on how to live your life. And experience the footsteps of the Counselor as you read the Gospels. Your hope lies not in your ability but God's Sovereignty, so get to know the One Who gives perseverance, encouragement, and hope in the living pages of Scripture.

MARCH 6

THE FATHER'S HUG

You have enclosed me behind and before, And laid Your hand upon me.

Psalm 139:5

In the morning hours, as I sat reading Psalm 139:5 and contemplating its meaning, my son got out of bed and came to where I was sitting. He stood next to me, and I reached over and hugged him, asked him how he slept, and told him I loved him. He smiled at me and told me he loved me, too. This was a sweet moment that I love to remember, but when I told him to go on back to bed, he quietly said, "But I wanted you to hold me." It wasn't time for him to get up, and I knew this was a ploy to stay up longer, but I closed my Bible and sat it on the table. My son climbed over the arm of my chair and got into my lap. I spread my blanket over him, he snuggled into my chest, and I wrapped my arms around him. We sat there for a while just being together, listening to each other breathe. The sunlight began to break, and together we started a new day. Finally, I told him to run on back to bed; I picked my Bible up again and re-read Psalm 139:5, *"You have enclosed me behind and before, And laid Your hand upon me."* Possibly, the Fatherly way of saying this verse is, "I, Your Heavenly Father, have embraced you in a hug. I wrap you in My arms, and we sit together."

The first six verses of Psalm 139 are all about how much the Counselor knows us. He intimately knows us and watches our every move (vs. 2–3). He knows what we will say before we ever form the word on our tongue (vs. 4). The Counselor's love for us is so ardent, so complete, so all-encompassing, that we cannot grasp it (vs. 6). We sit in His arms, and He wraps us up! We are never alone! Nothing can ever separate His arms from being around us! Nothing can possibly make it through His embrace! The Counselor loves us, and we can rest in Him.

———————

OVERCOMING ANXIETY

Search me, O God, and know my heart; Try me and know my anxious thoughts;
And see if there be any hurtful way in me, And lead me in the everlasting way.

Psalm 139:23–24

The Wonderful Counselor has great insights in these two verses—please, do not miss them. David was a man who had the courage to fight a giant yet knew the fears of hiding in the wilderness. As he wrote this Psalm, he prayed and asked God to search him and to know his heart and thoughts; that's because our hearts and thoughts are linked. The heart is not the muscle that pumps blood but rather our soul, the seat of emotions and thoughts. David asked the Counselor to search his soul to see if there was any anxiety or anything hurtful.

The Counselor puts both *"anxious thoughts"* and *"any hurtful way"* into the same category because anxiety in our soul is hurtful. It can damage our lives, physically, emotionally, socially, and mentally. The words *"any hurtful way"* literally means "way of pain." We need to be very careful not to allow any anxious thoughts to put us on the way of pain, but how do we stop this?

The Counselor continues to direct us through David's prayer by saying, *"and lead me in the everlasting way."* To avoid the hurt and pain of an anxious soul, we need to be led in the eternal path, not the temporal. Anxiety draws its power from getting you to focus on temporary circumstances. It says, look at that giant! How are you going to survive this? This is impossible! But David knew that to overcome anxiety, he needed God to lead him in the everlasting way, that which is eternal. Anxiety says, "This situation is too big." God says, "I am bigger!" Eternity always trumps the temporary, but we must focus our faith there. Finally, the Counselor reminds us that you cannot just wander through this life; you must be led in the everlasting way. We are led by the Counselor's insights, which free us from anxiety, and are trustworthy, leading to life! Today ask the Counselor to search your soul and to lead you in His ways.

HEALING JOY

A joyful heart is good medicine, But a broken spirit dries up the bones.

Proverbs 17:22

It is so easy to confuse joy and happiness. We can lump them both together using them synonymously, or we can polarize them by saying, "happiness is of this world" and "joy is eternal." Joy and happiness are not the same, but they are not opposites either. Christians, if not careful, can drain every ounce of fun out of the life God has given us. The Potter did not form us, nor did the Savior die for us, so that we could be sour-faced grumps with miserable souls and bad health due to a judgmental outlook filled with pessimism and skepticism. No, Jesus came to give us life more abundant! (John 10:10).

What we need for our sick soul, according to Solomon, is some good medicine. The prescription for a sick soul is "joy." A different translation of this verse says, *"A joyful heart causes good healing."* Often we are miserable because we lack joy; the lack of joy zaps our happiness, and the lack of happiness makes us miserable. This is a cycle that we will see tomorrow, *"dries up the bones."* If your life feels dried up, then perhaps you need to heed the Counselor's prescription and ask Him for a joyful heart. It is true that joy is not based on our circumstances, so if you are miserable with a sick soul, then joy can come in, and in spite of the darkness, it will start *"causing good healing."* Once that healing begins, you may even find yourself enjoying some happiness.

Often our miserable disposition comes from our lack of faith in God. We cannot see how God could love us or use us or protect us, so we see the world through dismal glasses. We point a finger at everything and everyone, saying the world is going to hell in a handbasket when really we simply lack joy. Joy is a fruit of the Spirit, a result of spending time with the Counselor. You can keep trying to find happiness from things, people, or opportunities, or you can run to the Father and experience His healing joy.

CAN DRY BONES LIVE AGAIN?

A joyful heart is good medicine, But a broken spirit dries up the bones.

Proverbs 17:22

The hand of the LORD was upon me, and He brought me out by the Spirit of the LORD and set me down in the middle of the valley; and it was full of bones. He caused me to pass among them round about, and behold, there were very many on the surface of the valley; and lo, they were very dry. He said to me, "Son of man, can these bones live?" And I answered, "O Lord GOD, You know" (Ezekiel 37:1–3).

What a truth the Counselor has in these verses. Can our dried up bones live? Solomon tells us that a broken spirit dries up the bones (Proverbs 17:22), and then we see Ezekiel in a valley of dry bones.

It seems like we are living in a world of dry bones because so many people have broken spirits and no hope. Can't you just hear the voice of the Counselor, *"Can your dry bones live again? Don't you believe that you can be revived?"* The sad thing is that many of us do not believe we can be revived; our spirits just seems too dry. But take note, like we saw yesterday, a joyful heart brings good healing, not just to us but to the whole valley of dry bones. How beautiful it is to be revived by the joy of the Lord, only to realize the dried up, sour-faced prunes next to you are watching you, wondering why you are different. We become a beacon of life.

Then He said to me, "Prophesy to the breath, prophesy, son of man, and say to the breath, 'Thus says the Lord GOD, 'Come from the four winds, O breath, and breathe on these slain, that they come to life.'"' So I prophesied as He commanded me, and the breath came into them, and they came to life and stood on their feet, an exceedingly great army (Ezekiel 37:9–10).

O Lord, please breathe on us that we can live again! Bring Your healing to these dry bones, and through Your joy, we may become an exceedingly great army! Can these dry bones live? O Lord God, You know!

WAITING ON HOPE

Hope deferred makes the heart sick But desire fulfilled is a tree of life.

Proverbs 13:12

Another way of saying this is, "Hope that is drawn out makes the heart weak." In Hebrew, the root word for "to hope" means "to wait." Anytime we have to wait a long time for something that we are hoping for, we begin to feel discouraged. When you look through the lens of a life or death situation, you can see how losing hope could mean losing life itself.

In 1 Samuel 13, we see the story of King Saul as he prepares the people of Israel to go to battle with the Philistines. Israel is in a bad place, and without the help of God, they will not win this fight. People were hiding in caves, pits, and cellars (vs. 6), some were running away (vs. 8), and the ones still following Saul were trembling (vs. 7). Saul was waiting for the prophet Samuel to offer the sacrifice to God and ask for His help in battle, but Samuel was late. Saul looked around at the situation, and because the wait was wearing on everyone, hope was beginning to be lost. Saul's heart was growing weak and sick, so instead of holding on to hope, he took matters into his own hands. He asked for the sacrifice so he could offer it instead of Samuel (vs. 9). As soon as he finished, Samuel came walking up and asked, *"What have you done?"* (vs. 11). Saul's response was basically, "I lost hope."

Waiting on God for relief or healing is very difficult. When that waiting is drawn out, our hope becomes weaker and weaker because we know we do not have the power to do it on our own. We lash out, grasping for anything that could restore hope even if it's not from the God Who seems late. But the Counselor Who is outside of time, Who can raise the dead and heal the sick, is never late. Those who wait on the Lord will renew their strength; they will sore on eagle's wings (Isaiah 40:31). Don't lose heart, hope in Christ!

———

TWO TREES

Hope deferred makes the heart sick But desire fulfilled is a tree of life.

Proverbs 13:12

In the Garden of Eden, there were two trees called "The Tree of Life" and "The Tree of the Knowledge of Good and Evil" (Genesis 2:9). Both of these trees bore fruit, and the outcome of eating these fruits was very different. If you ate from "The Tree of Life," you would live forever (Genesis 3:22). But if you ate from "The Tree of the Knowledge of Good and Evil," you would die (Genesis 2:17). Adam and Eve would spend their time in the Garden in the presence of Life and Death.

"The desire of the righteous is only good, But the expectation of the wicked is wrath" (Proverbs 11:23). We all are full of desires which we long for. These desires are much like a fire that burns within us; they may be as small as a match or as huge as a forest fire. These desires may be for righteous things, or they may be for evil. What we run after is the difference between Life and Death. *"When the woman saw that the tree was good for food, and that it was a delight to the eyes, and that the tree was desirable to make one wise, she took from its fruit and ate; and she gave also to her husband with her, and he ate"* (Genesis 3:6). Eve saw the fruit, and she desired it; that desire burned in her until she ate it, and because of that, she was separated from "The Tree of Life." An evil desire brings wrath, but a righteous desire is good. Solomon even says that the fulfillment of that good desire is a tree of life.

Just like Adam and Eve, we spend our lives in the presence of two trees. One is the tree of righteous desires, which is a tree of life, and the other is the tree of evil desires, which is a tree of wrath. Our desires for the fruits of these trees burn within us. Without the insights of the Counselor, we would reach out and take the fruit of wrath. His insights free us from these evil desires, and they are trustworthy, leading to life. But are we listening?

———

GUARDING OUR HEART AT ALL COST

Watch over your heart with all diligence, For from it flow the springs of life.

Proverbs 4:23

Can you imagine what it must have been like to be a night watchman on the wall of Jerusalem during the Old Testament? They watched the shadows for a scout who could tell an enemy army where the weak points were. The watchmen would have to be on their guard every second of the night, not allowing themselves to get sleepy or distracted. It wouldn't matter if they felt healthy or sick; they would have to be prepared to sound the alarm. The enemy was watching and wanted to exploit a distracted watchman.

Solomon warns us to watch over our hearts with the same diligence that a watchman watched over the wall. One weak moment and Satan would have an inroad into our heart. And why would that be so bad? What damage could he do? Solomon continues to tell us that our heart is the source, or spring, of life. John 14:6 says, *"Jesus said to him, 'I am the way, and the truth, and the life; no one comes to the Father but through Me.'"* So if from our heart flows life, and Jesus is life, then we are to guard our hearts because it is overflowing with Jesus. If Satan could get past our guard and start to pollute the spring of Jesus flowing out of our lives, then we would fall prey to any lie Satan threw at us, not to mention the lost world around us. Matthew 12:34 tells us the mouth speaks out of what fills the heart, so if Satan's lies fill our hearts, then that is what we talk about. Jesus was talking to the religious leaders when He told them this; He was saying, you think you are good and clean but listen to what you are saying, you are filled with Satan's lies, not the Counselor's truths. Far be it for the very watchman who protects the city to be the gateway through which the death of the city comes. The Counselor speaks love, forgiveness, and grace not perversion, hatred, and condemnation. What flows out of your mouth?

THINK, BELIEVE, ACT

Finally, brethren, whatever is true, whatever is honorable, whatever is right,
whatever is pure, whatever is lovely, whatever is of good repute,
if there is any excellence and if anything worthy of praise, dwell on these things.

Philippians 4:8

The Apostle Paul gives the Christians in Philippi eight things to *"dwell"* on. The word *"dwell"* means "to meditate," focusing our mind and soul on the words of the Counselor. So over the next eight days, we are going to look at these eight categories of meditation.

The first category Paul points us to is *"whatever is true."* Sometimes the easiest way to understand what a word means is to look at its opposite word. The opposite of true is a lie or a distortion. The Counselor tells us to meditate, focusing our thoughts on things that are true, not things that are lies or distortions of the truth. What is so bad about thinking on things that are distortions? Ultimately to distort the truth is to distort God and His Word because God is truth (John 14:6). What does this look like? When we put a situation, like terrorism, sickness, failure, or death, in the foreground of our focus and God in the background, He becomes distorted, tipping the scales in the opposite direction. All of a sudden, God is no longer all powerful, or if He is, He is not loving. How could God be loving and allow such atrocities? We begin to see God as unstable, much like an abusive father; one minute He hugs you and the next He hits you. You lose trust in Him and with that, you no longer try to find out what He wants; you create a new god in your likeness instead of God creating you in His likeness.

But when we meditate on what is true, we see God in the right light. We hear the voice of the Counselor as He leads us through the challenges of life such as terrorism, sickness, failure, and death. The Counselor is not weak; He is wise. What we think on is what we will believe to be true, and what we believe is what will determine our actions.

———

SONGS OF ASCENTS

Finally, brethren, whatever is true, whatever is honorable, whatever is right,
whatever is pure, whatever is lovely, whatever is of good repute,
if there is any excellence and if anything worthy of praise, dwell on these things.

Philippians 4:8

Paul tells us to dwell on whatever is honorable. The Greek word for honorable is *semnos* which means "inspires reverence or admiration and supreme dignity." What do you have in your life that inspires you to fear the Lord? When life seems to be the most hectic and everything is coming unraveled, what do you look to—from where do you draw inspiration?

In the book of Psalms, you have several types of psalms, written by a number of different people over the course of hundreds of years. Some of the psalms deal with praise, some with vengeance, and some with sorrow, but the focus of all of them is the Counselor's insights being freeing and trustworthy. Even when David was running for his life, He still looked to God for strength and wisdom.

Psalms 120–134 are a set of fifteen psalms which are called *"Songs of Ascents."* What this actually meant is unsure, but there are several theories. One of the more traditional views is that the city of Jerusalem sat on a mountain, so no matter where people traveled from during the three times of the year when God commanded everyone to go to Jerusalem for the feasts, they would be ascending a hill. Families would sing these Psalms of Ascents as they traveled to Jerusalem. This helped them dwell on the fear of the Lord as they drew closer to God's presence in the Temple. I challenge you to read these psalms daily, at least some of them, just to help you dwell on things that are honorable. When life gets you down, these can help point you toward worship. Meditate on the Counselor's insights and ascend into His presence with praise.

JESUS APPROVED

Finally, brethren, whatever is true, whatever is honorable, whatever is right, whatever is pure, whatever is lovely, whatever is of good repute, if there is any excellence and if anything worthy of praise, dwell on these things.

Philippians 4:8

Can you imagine what was going through Zacchaeus' mind when Jesus told him He was going to come to his house? What would you do if Jesus said He was coming to your house to take part in whatever you usually do? Would you have to think of an excuse why you couldn't watch a TV show or listen to a song? This is because most of the time, we do what we want with no thought for whether Jesus would approve of it.

Paul tells us that we should dwell on things that are *"right."* This means that our thoughts should center on things Jesus approves of. Our mind is the house of our soul, and our thoughts are what we decorate our mind with. If you paint a room white then leave it for a few years, it would still look white, but against the original white swatch, you could see just how dirty the walls had become. You do not see it because you are used to it. It's the same with our thoughts. If Jesus spent the day with us, we would quickly see just how dirty our minds have become. We focus on the movies we watch and think they are *"right"* because it's just entertainment, but if Jesus was sitting next to us on the couch, we would probably feel uncomfortable with almost every movie we watch. The same goes for the songs we listen to, the conversations we have with others, and the games we play. We don't mean to be mesmerized by sinful things; we just grow accustomed to them.

Zacchaeus didn't allow the state of his house to stop Jesus from coming by; he opened the door and allowed the Counselor in. And what happened was, Zacchaeus saw a lot of things that weren't *"right,"* and it changed his life! Are you willing to allow Jesus into your home and mind so He can show you what *"right"* really is?

———

DWELLING VERSUS SOJOURNING

Finally, brethren, whatever is true, whatever is honorable, whatever is right,
whatever is pure, whatever is lovely, whatever is of good repute,
if there is any excellence and if anything worthy of praise, dwell on these things.

Philippians 4:8

Today, there are two things we need to look at. First, Paul tells us to dwell on whatever is pure. The word pure means "exciting reverence or immaculate." It is like a yard that has been perfectly manicured so that the grass is lush and green with no signs of weeds anywhere. Then one morning when the owner walks out, they discover a dandelion in the middle of the grass. The yard is no longer immaculate because there is a mixture of grass and weeds, and if the dandelion were to be left to grow long enough, it would spread its seeds and the grass would be ruined. The Counselor teaches us it's the same with our thoughts. If we allow negative or sinful thoughts into our minds, then we are at odds with God's desire for us. These thoughts, if not taken captive, will spread and consume our minds (2 Corinthians 10:5). The secret to dwelling on what is pure is that it cannot be mixed with anything because purity is based on its singularity. We are to constantly be on guard for anything impure.

The second thing we need to look at is what does it mean to dwell on something. The Bible talks about two words that are vital for us—*dwell* and *sojourn*. The word sojourn means "to temporarily visit," while the word dwell means "to settle down or establish." So when the Counselor tells us to dwell on whatever is pure, this means it's not just something we do during our quiet time or while we are temporarily at church; no, we are to continuously meditate on what is pure, which we already know can't be mixed with negative or sinful thoughts. If this sounds time consuming, it is! We can never quit, and we must always be watchful, like a night watchman watching for the morning. Our soul waits on the Lord (Psalm 130:6).

SING A NEW SONG

*Finally, brethren, whatever is true, whatever is honorable, whatever is right,
whatever is pure, whatever is lovely, whatever is of good repute,
if there is any excellence and if anything worthy of praise, dwell on these things.*

Philippians 4:8

How easy it is to allow our soul to stray to things not edifying to Christ, others, or ourselves. Today we look at what Paul says about dwelling on whatever is lovely. This is a most difficult facet to focus on. In our fallenness, we so quickly look to the ugly instead of the lovely.

When David found out that Saul and Jonathan were killed in battle, he chanted a song in their honor (2 Samuel 1:17–27). One of the lines says, *"Saul and Jonathan, beloved (lovely) and pleasant in their life, And in their death they were not parted; They were swifter than eagles, They were stronger than lions."* Saul had been a threat to David's life for years, and now he would never be a threat again. On the other hand, David's friend and confidant, Jonathan, had also been killed. These two people had played opposite roles in David's life, but when David remembered them in this song, he said that both of them were beloved or lovely. He saw the lovely where we are so quick to become critical. Instead of looking at others with love, we merely see their faults in comparison to ourselves. David had every right to rejoice in Saul's demise, but instead of criticizing him or tearing him down, David simply said he was lovely. Not just lovely but equally as lovely as Jonathan! Could you imagine equating your enemy to your beloved friend? This can be done only when we are dwelling on whatever is lovely. The Counselor's insights are freeing and trustworthy; that is why David was able to show love to Saul. He had trusted God's protection, and that had freed him to sing. For many of us, we are not able to sing such a song of forgiveness because we are blinded by our own critical spirit. *O LORD, help us to sing a new song!* (Psalm 96:1).

HOW ARE YOU KNOWN

Finally, brethren, whatever is true, whatever is honorable, whatever is right,
whatever is pure, whatever is lovely, whatever is of good repute,
if there is any excellence and if anything worthy of praise, dwell on these things.

Philippians 4:8

How are you known? All of us are a 'son' or a 'daughter.' Most are known as 'brother' or 'sister.' Many are called 'husband' or 'wife.' Scores of us are known as 'father' or 'mother.' Beyond these we can be known as friend, coworker, athlete, collector, big mouth, or that bald guy, but often what we are known by is in line with our reputation. That reputation is likely a sign of what we believe to be most important. For example, the person who is known as a servant is often the person volunteering and doing what others do not want to do.

In the English language, a word that ends in '-ian' carries the meaning "of." The word Christian ends in '-ian,' therefore giving the meaning "of Christ." So when we say, "I am a Christian," we are saying, "I am of Christ." With our mouth, this is easy to say, but do we live up to that reputation? First Thessalonians 5:21–22 says, *"But examine everything carefully; hold fast to that which is good; abstain from every form of evil."* If we are *'of Christ,'* then we represent Him, but if we are surrounding ourselves with lifestyles that are ungodly, then we become known as ungodly. We must be very careful of this, not just in action but, as the Counselor points out, in thought as well. Today we learn that we are to dwell on whatever is of good repute or of good reputation. Just like a train car that follows the car in front of it, our body will follow our mind. Therefore, it is vital that we dwell on things that are of good repute because what we think about is what we will do, and that is how we will be known. As an ambassador of Christ, we need to be pointing the lost to Christ through the way we live, not chasing them away because of our hypocrisy (2 Corinthians 5:20).

SATAN'S LORDSHIP

Finally, brethren, whatever is true, whatever is honorable, whatever is right,
whatever is pure, whatever is lovely, whatever is of good repute,
if there is any excellence and if anything worthy of praise, dwell on these things.

Philippians 4:8

Paul tells us to dwell on things that have excellence. This same Greek word used for *"excellence"* is also used in 2 Peter 1:5–7, which says, *"Now for this very reason also, applying all diligence, in your faith supply moral 'excellence,' and in your moral excellence, knowledge, and in your knowledge, self-control, and in your self-control, perseverance, and in your perseverance, godliness, and in your godliness, brotherly kindness, and in your brotherly kindness, love."* In these verses, Peter lists several attributes of a Christlike life. The first of these attributes is moral excellence, which is one of the same things Paul tells us to dwell on. Moral excellence is virtue or goodness. Does your mind think on the things of God or the things of you? As long as we are the focus of our thoughts, then we will never move beyond 'Point A.'

Peter tells us to 'add' to our moral excellence, knowledge, self-control, perseverance, godliness, brotherly kindness, and love; this means there is a progression. We cannot get to 'knowledge' until we go through 'excellence.' Ask yourself the question, what do I think about virtue? If you want to test yourself in this, set an alarm to go off every hour. When you hear the alarm, immediately write down what you are thinking about. Don't sugarcoat it or alter it in any way. Then take that thought and hold it up to the attributes listed in Philippians 4:8 and 2 Peter 1:5–7 and see if it is considered morally excellent. Odds are our thoughts are often not on the things of God. The Counselor's insights are freeing and trustworthy, but we must listen to Him. Are you tired of having Satan wreak havoc in your life? Stop giving him ownership of your mind. If you are not dwelling on whatever is excellent, then you are surrendering to his lordship.

HALLELUJAH!

Finally, brethren, whatever is true, whatever is honorable, whatever is right,
whatever is pure, whatever is lovely, whatever is of good repute,
if there is any excellence and if anything worthy of praise, dwell on these things.

Philippians 4:8

"*GOD INHABITS THE PRAISES OF HIS CHILDREN.*" What is praise? It is to tell the attributes of God. He is worthy of all praise and honor, and we praise Him when we dwell on how great He is. When we praise the world for how powerful it is, or when we praise people for how wise they are, or even when we praise ourselves for our ability, we begin to become distressed, depressed, and dissatisfied. We, the creation, can do nothing without the Creator; that is why the Counselor asks us to dwell on things worthy of praise. "*Let the words of my mouth and the meditation of my heart Be acceptable in Your sight, O LORD, my rock and my Redeemer*" (Psalm 19:14). May I be filled with praise of the Almighty! Let's end by looking at what this praise looks like.

> *After these things I heard something like a loud voice of a great multitude in heaven, saying, "Hallelujah! Salvation and glory and power belong to our God; because His judgments are true and righteous; for He has judged the great harlot who was corrupting the earth with her immorality, and He has avenged the blood of His bond-servants on her." And a second time they said, "Hallelujah! Her smoke rises up forever and ever." And the twenty-four elders and the four living creatures fell down and worshiped God who sits on the throne saying, "Amen. Hallelujah!" And a voice came from the throne, saying, "Give praise to our God, all you His bond-servants, you who fear Him, the small and the great." Then I heard something like the voice of a great multitude and like the sound of many waters and like the sound of mighty peals of thunder, saying, "Hallelujah! For the Lord our God, the Almighty, reigns* (Revelation 19:1–6).

LOOK AT US!

When he saw Peter and John about to go into the temple, he began asking to receive alms. But Peter, along with John, fixed his gaze on him and said "Look at us!"

Acts 3:3–4

Acts 3 is the story of a lame man who would beg for alms at the temple gate called *"Beautiful."* Peter had been so timid just a short time before but now filled with the Holy Spirit, he was bold and running after what Jesus had called him to. Peter and John were going to the temple to pray, and this man, born lame, saw them coming. The Bible makes no reference to whether this man knew Peter or John, but it does make a point to say that the man saw them coming and began asking them for money. This is important to take note of. The next verse tells us that Peter and John fixed their eyes on the lame man. So if we put two and two together, then we note that the lame man sees Peter and John, then they fix their eyes on the man, this means they should be looking at each other. But Peter's next words to the lame man were, *"Look at us!"* Why? What happened? The man looked at them, started asking for money, but before he even received their response, he had already looked away. In psychology there is a theory called Learned Hopelessness, where someone has been conditioned to a negative circumstance time and time again, to the point that even if you changed the circumstance, they continue doing what they have always done because they have learned they cannot change their life. They feel hopeless. This man had looked at people for so long, hoping for a little money, that when Peter and John come up with the power of the Spirit, this man had already looked away. But Peter tells him, it's not money I have, but in the name of Jesus, get up and walk! The lame man then got up, leaping and praising God. The Counselor teaches us that hope is not bound up in our circumstances but in Who He is!

———————

A DREAM OF HEAVEN

Come to Me, all who are weary and heavy-laden, and I will give you rest.

Matthew 11:28

I had a dream once that the rapture happened, and I was standing outside the heavenly city along with my wife, my kids, and my parents. We waited with millions of others to go before God. No one was impatient or rude; everyone was joyful and excited. Finally, my time came. I entered a large tent, and there in front of me was the Son, the Father, and the Spirit. Jesus reached out His arms to me, and I collapsed into His embrace! Then I fell on my face before the Father and praised Him! Finally, I went before the Spirit and worshipped Him! As I walked out of the tent, I was rejoined by my family, and together we walked into Heaven.

There was a highway that ran through the city, and it reflected a golden light. I looked up at the top of a high mountain, which was where the light came from. The mountain had a winding path that led to the top, and people were coming and going on it. I remember thinking to myself, *"This is not exactly how I thought Heaven would be. I thought God would be here with us, not us having to climb a mountain to get to His presence."* Then I heard the voice of God say, *"This is not a journey to Me but a journey with Me."* I often lay in bed at night and relive that dream. I see the mountain, and I think about what God said, *"It's a journey with Me."*

In Matthew 11:28, Jesus tells us to come to Him if we are weary and He will give us rest. Usually I focus on the rest that I am desiring, but after having this dream, I think about the part where Jesus says, *"Come to Me."* What does this mean? Do I have to rise to a certain level to receive rest? No, on the contrary, I could never rise to Jesus; instead, He lowered Himself to earth as a little baby. Now I do not journey to Him; I journey with Him. It is true, we are so busy that we start to unravel and wear-out, but the Counselor stands with us saying, *"Find rest in My presence."*

EVERYTHING FOR EVERYBODY

Take My yoke upon you and learn from Me, for I am gentle and humble in heart, and You will find rest for your souls. For My yoke is easy and My burden is light.

Matthew 11:29–30

Once again, we find ourselves looking at what the Counselor says about rest. It must be pretty important since God felt the need to tell us that on the seventh day of creation He rested. So if we are to rest, why is it we feel worn out and thread bear? Maybe because we take verses like 1 Corinthians 9:22 out of context. *"To the weak I became weak, that I might win the weak; I have become all things to all men, so that I may by all means save some."* If we are not careful, we will read this as, "I have become everything for everybody so that I may by all means save some." This is not what Paul was saying. We think busyness is next to Godliness, but this is dangerous. When we focus on what we are doing, then our eyes are off the Master, the true source of our strength. Also, when we are constantly on the go, we can easily forget to ask God what His desire is. Without instructions we just do what logically seems like a good idea, but God's ways are not our ways (Isaiah 55:8–9). In church we feel pressured into being everything for everybody. We think to ourselves, *If I don't do this, then no one else will, these people will go to hell, and it will be on my head!* No wonder people walk away from churches every day. With this mindset, we equate obedience with busyness, and we end up worn out and disillusioned with the church, with Scripture, and with God. The Counselor is saying, "STOP!" He desires us to come to Him, take off the burden of being everything for everybody, and allow Him to put His yoke upon us. His yoke is easy, and His burden is light. This is where we find rest for our souls, not in filling every hole in our schedule with stuff. The Counselor is gentle and humble in heart; He's not a cruel taskmaster, so stop being one to yourself. Learn from Him and find rest.

———

WAIT

Yet those who wait for the LORD Will gain new strength;
They will mount up with wings like eagles,
They will run and not get tired, They will walk and not become weary.

Isaiah 40:31

Imagine that you are standing in a room having a conversation with God. He tells you to face forward and not to turn to the right or left (Proverbs 4:25–27). Then He tells you, "If you believe I am all powerful, take two steps forward." So you do. Then He says, "If you believe I have a plan for you, take two more steps forward." Again you do. This pattern continues until you are one step from the wall. God says, "If you believe I love everyone, take two steps forward." After one step, your nose is touching the wall. What should you do? You can't move to the right or left, but you can't go forward either. It is easy to try to make something happen. We begin to look around and realize no one else is standing with their nose against the wall. Before long we have slid down until we are at a door, and we take that last step and say, "Okay, what's next?"

But the Counselor is not interested in "what's next," He's still working on "what's now." We get so hung up on completing the task right now that we forget He is never going to ask us to do something that, with Him, is impossible. So, yes, there are times when what God asks of us seems impossible, and for us, it is impossible, but nothing is impossible for Him. Often we think we have to finish this task now or else bad things will happen, they could die and go to hell, this great opportunity will go to someone else, it will cost me money, or life will pass me by. But God is outside of time. He knows exactly when that person will die, if this opportunity is for you, how to give you more money, and what real Life is. With faith, we can wait with our nose at a wall as long as it takes because God is still in control. If we wait on the Lord, we will mount up on wings like eagles and fly over the wall, but only if we wait on Him.

CONDEMNING GOD

So do not worry about tomorrow; for tomorrow will care for itself.
Each day has enough trouble of its own.

Matthew 6:34

"Each day has enough trouble of its own." That is for sure! Every day we can be consumed with the anxiety of cancer, school shootings, terrorist attacks, car trouble, getting fired, divorce, and brain-eating amoebas. The weight of possibility is so heavy it can crush us in an instant. But the Counselor tells us not to worry about tomorrow or today (Philippians 4:6). How is this possible? Matthew 6:25–26 says, *"For this reason I say to you do not be worried about your life, as to what you will eat or what you will drink; nor for your body as to what you will put on. Is not life more than food and the body more than clothing? "Look at the birds of the air, that they do not sow, nor reap nor gather into barns, and yet your heavenly Father feeds them. Are you not worth much more than they?"*

God is Jehovah-Jireh, which means, "God Our Provider." But Satan comes in and sows seeds of doubt saying, "Will God really provide for your needs? He provides food and covering for the animals, but the world is full of hungry and cold people? God obviously cares more for the animals than He does for you." If we are not careful, we will believe this lie, and we will doubt God's provision. We end up in a paralyzing mess of confusion saying, "The question is not can God provide but will He?" This is dangerous because it puts us in the place of judging God's goodness, and we condemn Him when we don't get our way.

Our doubt makes us anxious. Psalm 127:1–2 says, *"Unless the LORD builds the house, They labor in vain who build it; Unless the LORD guards the city The watchman keeps awake in vain. It is vain for you to rise up early, To retire late, To eat the bread of painful labors; For He gives to His beloved even in his sleep."* Will you trust the Provider, or will you labor in vain, anxiously worrying if you are enough to keep up?

BARBARIC GOD?

Jesus answered, "It was neither that this man sinned, nor his parents;
but it was so that the works of God might be displayed in him."

John 9:3

"Why do bad things happen to good people?" This is an age-old question that has led many weak Christians to become bitter atheists. How could a God of love (1 John 4:7–8) allow good people to be treated with such evil? Many people have said, if this is how God treats His creation, then I don't want any part of Him. Sadly, the church seems to crumble at this question. Either they have no idea how to answer, or they have a very scholarly answer, which produces more confusion. We can't deny that sickness, famine, violence, rape, molestation, murder, genocide, and torture happen every day. Even babies who are still in the womb are killed with inhuman methods that would rival the Roman persecution of the early church. Why would God allow this? We must look at this from different angles.

The Bible tells us that no one is good except for God alone (Psalm 53:3; Luke 18:19). We all deserve death (Romans 6:23).

God told us that bad things were going to happen because of sin (John 15:20; Genesis 2:17; Matthew 24:12).

If God removed the most heinous sin, then the next most heinous sin would be most heinous. If God kept removing the worst sin, then eventually there would be no sin. If God removed all sin, there would be no free choice, and with no free choice, God would be forcing us to love Him. That is not His heart.

No, we hurt and go through sickness for a few different reasons. Sometimes it is discipline for our sins (Hebrews 12:11). And, there is such a thing as a generational curse (Exodus 20:5). Finally, the Counselor teaches us sometimes bad things happen to people who are seeking Him so they can find Him (John 9:3; 1 Peter 5:10).

SIN SECRETS

When I kept silent about my sin, my body wasted away Through my groaning all day long. For day and night Your hand was heavy upon me; My vitality was drained away as with the fever heat of summer. Selah.

Psalm 32:3–4

In Psalm 32, David writes very openly about the consequences of sin and the help that comes through the Lord. Churches preach a message of "Grace Covers All," which is true, but that's not a license to keep on sinning. We must also listen to the Father when He says, *"If we confess our sins, He is faithful and righteous to forgive us our sins and to cleanse us from all unrighteousness"* (1 John 1:9). Sin that is hidden is detrimental, but sin that is confessed is forgiven. In Psalm 32, the Counselor gives us a clear view of the effects of sin on the body, as well as the healing that comes from confessing.

The Effects of Sin: *"When I kept silent about my sin, my body wasted away Through my groaning all day long. For day and night Your hand was heavy upon me; My vitality was drained away as with the fever heat of summer. Selah"* (Psalm 32:3–4).

The Confessing of Sin: *"I acknowledged my sin to You And my iniquity I did not hide; I said, "I will confess my transgressions to the LORD"; And You forgave the guilt of my sin. Selah"* (Psalm 32:5).

The Effects of Repentance: *"Many are the sorrows of the wicked, But he who trusts in the LORD, lovingkindness shall surround him. Be glad in the LORD and rejoice, you righteous ones; And shout for joy, all you who are upright in heart"* (Psalm 32:10–11).

When we hide a sin secret from God, we live in misery. We waste away, with no life by day or rest by night; nothing provides relief. The pleasures of earth cannot revive our shriveled soul. Listen to the Counselor's insights, confess your sins, and be forgiven so that you can rejoice and shout for joy!

THE NEARNESS OF GOD

The LORD is near to the broken hearted and saves those who are crushed in spirit.

Psalm 34:18

David knew the ups and downs of life. He was the youngest of his brothers and a lowly shepherd of sheep, yet at a young age, he would be called out of the fields to be anointed as the next king of Israel. He would hear the people's songs as he returned from battle, praising him over king Saul, yet he also knew the fear of hiding in caves while running for his life. The fear of the Lord and the fear of man are not opposite ends of a spectrum but rather two sides of the same coin. The direction we face determines whom we fear.

David would write Psalm 34 after an experience that threatened his life (1 Samuel 21:10–15). He could sing of the Lord's goodness because he focused on the nearness of the Lord to the brokenhearted and the crushed in spirit. God knows the heart of those He created. He sees those who are broken by sickness, disease, and pain. The Counselor is near to those who are crushed by depression, anxiety, and guilt. Isaiah 57:15 says, *"For thus says the high and exalted One Who lives forever, whose name is Holy, 'I dwell on a high and holy place, And also with the contrite and lowly of spirit In order to revive the spirit of the lowly And to revive the heart of the contrite.'"*

What insights does the Counselor have for those who are brokenhearted and crushed? Freedom lies in His presence. We will not know a trial free life until we are in Heaven, so broken hearts and crushed spirits will happen to us, but God is near to us and saves us. As Isaiah said, He revives the spirit of the lowly and the heart of the contrite. We can sing of His salvation even while we are walking in the valley of the shadow of death, not because He takes us out of the valley and sits us in Glory but because He left Glory and walks with us in the valley. The fear of the Lord and the fear of man are not two separate locations but rather our perspective from the valley. Are you looking at God or your trials?

TURN SEEK FIND

I sought the LORD, and He answered me, And delivered me from all my fears.

Psalm 34:4

In 2 Chronicles 15, we learn about what happened when King Asa received a prophecy from the Counselor. *"Now the Spirit of God came on Azariah the son of Oded, and he went out to meet Asa and said to him, 'Listen to me, Asa, and all Judah and Benjamin: the LORD is with you when you are with Him. And if you seek Him, He will let you find Him; but if you forsake Him, He will forsake you'"* (verses 1–2). So God spoke to Asa and basically told him, I'm right here; stand with me, and I'll stand with you but walk away, and you will stand alone.

The story continues in verse three: *"For many days Israel was without the true God and without a teaching priest and without law."* Can you even imagine? They were without God for many days, alone, vulnerable, and weak. But in verse four, everything changed: *"But in their distress they turned to the LORD God of Israel, and they sought Him, and He let them find Him."* This is a very important verse so let's break it down.

While Israel was in this low point of distress, they turned to the Lord; then they sought God, and finally God revealed Himself to them. Notice the pattern here; distress led to a turning, which led to a seeking, which led to a finding. This pattern is still applicable today. If we try to do things on our own, God will allow us to go many days without Him; this is the foundation for distress. Our distress will either point us to God or to fear. But if we will turn to the Counselor, and seek His insights, then He will let you find Him. How can we be distressed if we know the Father? *"And those who know Your name will put their trust in You, For You, O LORD, have not forsaken those who seek You"* (Psalm 9:10).

MARCH 30

HIDDEN TOXIC

For the mind set on the flesh is death, but the mind set on the Spirit is life and peace.

Romans 8:6

What do you think about? Could you imagine having a cartoon thought bubble pop up over your head so everyone could see what you were thinking? Would you find yourself staying away from certain people because you would be ashamed for them to see your thoughts? Life would be very different!

The Apostle Paul asked the Christians in Rome an interesting question about their sin lives. It's found in Romans 6:21. *"Therefore what benefit were you then deriving from the things of which you are now ashamed? For the outcome of those things is death."* What benefit do we glean from the thoughts we would be ashamed for others to know? Consider it logically; what is the long-term effect of thinking about lust, jealousy, bitterness, pride, or anger? Those thoughts may bring instant gratification, but the long-term effects of living the double life of outwardly looking good while inwardly thinking sinful thoughts is depression, anxiety, low self-esteem, and ultimately death. But if we are thinking thoughts that are like Christ—things like love, compassion, gratitude, forgiveness, and encouragement—then we are happy to express those thoughts to others, and we live in freedom.

Satan desires for us to believe that our daydreams are harmless and safe places to think about the things we would never act on, but truth be told, even if we never act on our bad thoughts, they act on us and affect others. The poison that is seeping into our souls through our carnal thoughts is lethal to us and toxic to those around us. Yet when our mind is set on the Spirit, then our soul begins to heal, and we become a spring of reviving water to those around us. The result of shameful thoughts is death, but the result of Christ-like thoughts is *"life and peace."* You choose what pours into you, and you choose what you show to others.

GREATER THAN EVIL

Peace I leave with you; My peace I give to you; not as the world gives do I give to you. Do not let your heart be troubled, nor let it be fearful.

John 14:27

Jesus said He gives us peace but not as the world gives peace. What does that mean? While the world is looking for a life that is free of war, Christians should understand that we will never know a war-free life until we are in Heaven. Therefore the peace which Jesus leaves us is not the promise of no pain, strain, or death but rather the promise of His presence through His Holy Spirit. Peace is not the absence of war but knowing Who the Counselor is in the midst of the war. This is how Jesus can say, *"Do not let your heart be troubled, nor let it be fearful."* Peace is not the absence of war; it is not allowing the things of this world to agitate or distress us. *"For God has not given us a spirit of timidity, but of power and love and discipline"* (2 Timothy 1:7). The Spirit that is inside us is powerful and greater than anything this world or Satan himself has to throw at us (1 John 4:4). So if we have this Spirit of peace and power, why do we struggle with fearing the struggles of this world?

First John 4:18 says, *"There is no fear in love; but perfect love casts out fear, because fear involves punishment, and the one who fears is not perfected in love."* Basically, we fear this world because we do not know the Father's love, the power of the Son's death, or the presence of the Spirit. Let's look at these briefly. The Father's love is entirely freely given and not earned; therefore, nothing you do will make Him take it back. The Son's death is all inclusive. No sin can elude the grace of Jesus' blood. The Spirit's presence is all encompassing. There is nowhere we can go that we will be truly alone.

We do not need to look at evil as if it no longer exists because of what Jesus did. Evil does exist, but we need to see the love of the Father, the blood of the Son, and the presence of the Spirit as greater than the evil.

APRIL

The Servant's Towel Is Worn and Waiting

LIVING BACKWARDS

For even the Son of Man did not come to be served, but to serve,
and to give His life a ransom for many.

Mark 10:45

The Son of Man came to serve, but who would ever recognize Him as the Messiah while He was wearing the towel of a servant? One of the greatest lessons Jesus taught was that of *'Position.'* What is our position before God? What is our position before man? Our position before both of those is one of a humble servant. The Father has called us to a life of humility which is diabolically opposed to our fallen nature. Our sinful self tells us to rise to a position of power so that others would serve us, yet Christ, the King of kings, came not to be served but to serve. This is why so few recognized Him as the Messiah; He didn't fit their idea of an all-powerful Deliverer.

To better understand this idea of a Servant King, think of the word evil. When you read this word, your mind will automatically go to images of hatred, violence, greed, abuse, and manipulation. But maybe you are not reading this word correctly. You read this word based on your past experience because you were taught to read from left to right, but what if I told you this word was different. This word was to be read from right to left. Now when you see the word evil, you would read it as live. Jesus, the Son of God, came not in stately attire or dripping with wealth but came as a humble child, teaching a message of servitude, not dominance. This was backward to what people expected, so they rejected it. Still today, we struggle to embrace this message of backward living because past experience says authority is at the top. We want the power, the honor, and the security that comes from being the best but the Servant's towel is worn and waiting. We are to be servants ever ready to bow and serve; that is what it means to live backward. To truly live! (Luke 22:26–27).

———————

THE LOVE GIVING SERVANT

And walk in love, just as Christ also loved you and gave Himself up for us,
an offering and a sacrifice to God as a fragrant aroma.

Ephesians 5:2

Paul instructs us to imitate God because of our great love for Him as our Heavenly Father (Ephesians 5:1). This is tricky to understand because how do we imitate someone that we cannot see, nor is finite? We are bound by the laws of this world, such as gravity, space, and time; therefore, how can we imitate the One Who created those laws? The answer to this is we have to look to God's human representation, which is Jesus (Hebrews 1:3).

Though Jesus was fully God, He became fully human also, meaning He played by the same laws that we live by. So when we imitate God, we are to look to Jesus and do what He did during those thirty-three years. But what did Jesus do? Jesus did the works that the Father had for Him (John 5:36). Luke 10:27 tells us the work we are to do is *"love."* Paul reminded those in Ephesus that they are to walk in the same love as Jesus, a love that is sacrificial. Jesus gave up Himself as an offering to God, and we are to likewise love those around us as a servant. *"Greater love has no one than this, that one lay down his life for his friends"* (John 15:13). This is not an easy discipline to live by because the world around us tells us to look out for ourselves, but Jesus says to give up self; this is what is pleasing to God. We can think of it like going to a great ball, those who are attending the party will walk in the room and instantly look for their friends and the best seat in the house, but when the servants at the ball walk into the room, they instantly look for where the need is. They look for those whose cup is empty and who needs food on their plate. Jesus was the One Who hosted the party and could have sat down to be served, but instead, He put on the towel of a Servant and began seeking those who were in need. Like Christ, we are to walk the path of a love giving servant.

A JOURNEY OF LIGHT

For you were formerly darkness, but now you are Light in the Lord;
walk as children of Light.

Ephesians 5:8

The Servant's towel is worn and waiting. It is worn because it is used often; it is waiting because the Servant stands ready to help those in need. One of the jobs of the Servant is to shine the Light so that those in darkness can see the way— much like a lighthouse shines in the fog, alerting ships to the dangers ahead.

Isaiah 9:2 says, *"The people who walk in darkness will see a great light; Those who live in a dark land, The light will shine on them."* There is hope for all people living in darkness because there will come a Light that will eradicate the darkness. Light and dark cannot coexist; by definition, one must overpower the other.

Isaiah's prophecy was stated again many years later by Zacharias at the birth of John the Baptist. *"To shine upon those who sit in darkness and the shadow of death, To guide our feet into the way of peace"* (Luke 1:79). Death will overshadow humanity, and they will dwell in a place separated from peace. This is true for us today; we desire peace, yet we feel overshadowed by evil and death.

Isaiah's prophecy would also be stated by Paul. *"For God, who said, "Light shall shine out of darkness," is the One who has shone in our hearts to give the Light of the knowledge of the glory of God in the face of Christ"* (2 Corinthians 4:6). This Light is the knowledge of God's glory, and it is seen in Christ. Jesus is the Light Who came to the darkness shining and pointing to the Father's glory.

Finally, we learn from Ephesians 5:8 that we are to walk as children of the Light. So from all of these verses, we see that humanity lacks peace because they live in the darkness of death's shadow, but the Light of the glory of God through Jesus is coming, not just eradicating the darkness but adopting us as children of the Light! This Light illuminates all things, but the Father's desire is for us to see His love (Isaiah 60:1–3).

———

SEEING THE BEAUTY

Therefore be careful how you walk, not as unwise men but as wise.

Ephesians 5:15

If you have ever had the opportunity to do any kind of hiking, then you know that no matter where you go, there is beauty to be seen. There is beauty in a mountainous horizon, a stream that runs through a valley, the dunes of sand in the desert, the fields of crops in the country, the skyline of buildings near a city, or the changing color of leaves in the forest. Everywhere has beauty, but there can be danger in beauty as well. When you are hiking, if you are not careful, you will look at the beauty and forget to keep an eye on the path. Next thing you know, you will be tripping over a root and flying headlong down the trail. To enjoy the beauty, we have to be wise with an eye out for stumbling blocks.

In Ephesians 5:15, Paul tells us to be careful to walk wisely. The Greek word for *"be careful"* is *blepō*, which literally means "to see." He is saying, when you walk in life, be wise and look where you are going, or else you will get tripped up.

It is important to know that Paul is not speaking literally when he says you need to look at the ground in front of you; he is metaphorically saying, be wise and use your mind's eye to see the stumbling blocks. Our mind is the battlefield of so many skirmishes. Eve did not eat the fruit in the garden until she had processed it in her mind (Genesis 3:6). We must be ever careful to utilize Godly wisdom when seeing the world around us. If we are not taking every thought captive (2 Corinthians 10:5), testing the spirits (1 John 4:1), and walking in the light of Scripture (Psalm 119:105), then we are hiking on rocky terrain with our eyes closed. The outcome will be brokenness and pain.

Lord Jesus, You see the road before me, please help me to walk wisely with my eyes open to follow wherever You lead.

A WONDROUSLY CONFUSING EVENING

[Jesus] got up from supper, and laid aside His garments; and taking a towel, He girded Himself. Then He poured water into the basin and began to wash the disciples' feet and to wipe them with the towel with which He was girded.

John 13:4-5

The meal is wrapping up, and the smell of food is still in the air. The sounds of men talking are bouncing off the walls along with the shadows cast by candlelight. Suddenly, Jesus gets up, leaning on John's shoulder to help Him. He has a twinkle in His eye, which the disciples knew meant they were about to learn something new, something backward, something incredible.

They each waited for Jesus to begin speaking but instead of standing to teach, Jesus walked over to the edge of the room and picked up a towel and a bowl of water. Just when they thought nothing Jesus did would surprise them, He begins to take off His robe. Thinking this was odd even for Jesus, they watched with uncertainty. Jesus would take the towel and wrap it around His waist and then gently carry the bowl of water back to the table where the disciples sat with eyes and mouths open. Finally, without a word spoken, Jesus kneels down, takes Thomas' foot, and begins washing it in the water. Everyone could hear the splashing of the water in the bowl. Thomas was too caught off guard to ask any questions, so he just sat there while the dirt turned into mud, causing the clear water in the bowl to cloud to brown. This continues until the Servant has washed all the disciples' feet and dried them on the towel around His waist. After Jesus finishes, He places the bowl of water back against the wall along with the towel. He puts His robe back on, and with a smirk on His face, He walks back over to the very confused disciples and sits down. What an incredibly wondrous and confusing evening this was for the disciples. The Servant's towel is worn and waiting!

UNWORTHY SLAVES

If I then, the Lord and the Teacher, washed your feet,
you also ought to wash one another's feet.

John 13:14

After Jesus washed the feet of the disciples, He gave them a command. On the one hand, this command was authoritative; Jesus said, *"If I then, the Lord,"* the word Lord means "Master." He is saying, "If I am your master, then obey Me." On the other hand, this command was a teaching lesson; Jesus said, *"If I then . . . the Teacher."* He was also saying, "I'm trying to teach you a truth." But what was that truth? Love others, or help your brothers? Jesus told Peter the reason He only washed his feet was because he was already clean, thereby only needing his feet washed (John 13:10). If being clean is symbolic of salvation, then what is the washing of feet. Confessing your daily sins? If so, is that something we can do for others? What is the lesson? Jesus reveals Himself in three ways in this passage: (1) Lord/Master (2) Teacher (3) Servant. The command is given by the Lord and Teacher, but it is understood in the Servant.

"Which of you, having a slave plowing or tending sheep, will say to him when he has come in from the field, 'Come immediately and sit down to eat'? But will he not say to him, 'Prepare something for me to eat, and properly clothe yourself and serve me while I eat and drink; and afterward you may eat and drink'? He does not thank the slave because he did the things which were commanded, does he? So you too, when you do all the things which are commanded you, say, 'We are unworthy slaves; we have done only that which we ought to have done'" (Luke 17:7–10). The lesson of the Servant is, we cannot serve others as Jesus did unless we totally, willingly, and joyfully empty ourselves of self. Is it possible for us to walk in salvation if we still cling to self? Can we be saved if we are the master of our lives? *"We are unworthy slaves; we have done only that which we ought to have done."*

———————

TWELVE LEGIONS OF ANGELS

Or do you think that I cannot appeal to My Father, and He will at once put at My disposal more than twelve legions of angels? "How then will the Scriptures be fulfilled, which say that it must happen this way?

Matthew 26:53–54

While Jesus was on earth, there were a few times that He really revealed His humanity. He knew the Father's plan, but He also didn't necessarily want to go through the pain. Satan tempted Jesus with shortcuts to being Savior (Matthew 4:8–10) also Jesus would sweat blood as He cried for this cup to pass (Luke 22:41–44). Jesus even knew He could bypass the pain by asking the Father to send twelve legions of angels to wipe out those who opposed Him, but He also knew the Father's heart was that not one soul would perish (Matthew 18:14), so Jesus continued on the path that led to Calvary.

Ephesians 6:10 says, *"Finally, be strong in the Lord and in the strength of His might."* The Greek word for might is *ischys,* and it means "ability." This is a very challenging verse when you really think about it. Be strong, take courage, find hope in the Lord and in the strength of His ability. God has all power, all ability, and all strength; nothing can stand against Him, nothing can outsmart Him nor overpower Him, but that doesn't mean that He always uses that ability. God could heal every cancer, release every sex slave, protect every persecuted person, but He doesn't. He has the ability, but His plan sometimes requires Him to hold back the twelve legions of angels and allow His Son to go to the cross. Yes, we are to be strong in the Lord and in the strength of His mighty ability, but we are also to trust His heart. Jesus, the Servant, went through the pain and agony of the cross but now sits at the right hand of the Father, exalted and honored. Likewise, we are to trust the Father even when it cost us everything because there is coming a day when we will be restored, and there will be no more tears (Revelation 21:4). Jesus served because He trusted the Father.

———

A CHRISTLIKE PATIENCE

Love is patient, love is kind and is not jealous;
love does not brag and is not arrogant.

1 Corinthians 13:4

Over the next several days, we will be working our way through the fifteen attributes of love mentioned in 1 Corinthians 13:4-7. We will look at them through the lens of the Servant. The first thing we need to understand is what love is. As a noun, the book of 1 John tells us that God is love (1 John 4:8). As a verb, we understand that love is how God responds and acts toward us. I am a firm believer that everyone does what they do because of love. What I mean is that a person will do many things searching for love, and they will end up in many different places—lust, acceptance, dependence, etc. But we know that God is love, so they may not know it, but they are seeking the fulfillment that only God can give. That is what we as the body of Christ are called to do, point people to real Love.

Paul starts out his list of love attributes with, *"Love is patient"* (1 Corinthians 13:4), and he ends it with *"Love never fails"* (1 Corinthians 13:8). Now anyone can show some patience, but only the Servant can show patience that never fails. He is slow to anger and full of compassion, even to those who cried out for Him to be crucified. Our patience has boundaries, but His patience is limitless. This is not to say that God will overlook the sins of humanity; no, He will bring about justice to its fullest extent, but He waits patiently for us to turn if we will. A servant is not given the luxury of getting impatient; he waits for as long as it takes. A person becomes impatient when someone else's affairs interfere with his or her own, but a servant has surrendered all desires and plans to that of their Master. Once we have totally surrendered, totally trusted, and totally obeyed, then we can love with Christlike patience (Nahum 1:3; James 1:19).

───────────

I AM NOT KIND

Love is patient, love is kind and is not jealous;
love does not brag and is not arrogant.

1 Corinthians 13:4

O Lord, please give us open hearts to understand Your lesson for us today, so that we may walk in it.

"*Love is kind.*" This seems to be rather point blank and simple; when we show kindness to others, we show love to them, but these three words are not quite as simple as we may think. To understand these three words, we need to know the basics of grammar. Usually, we think of love as a verb or an action. We love others, or someone loves us. But Paul wrote the word love in 1 Corinthians 13:4 not as a verb but as a noun. A noun is "a person, place, or thing," so when we read "*love is kind,*" we must read it as if love has substance; it is something, an entity. Most of the time, when we read this verse we take ownership of it, saying, "I am kind when I love." But that is thinking of love as a verb instead of a noun. If love is an entity, then I am not kind, but rather love is. This is monumentally important because it takes the ownership out of my hands and puts it in love's hands.

First John 4:16 says, "*We have come to know and have believed the love which God has for us. God is love, and the one who abides in love abides in God, and God abides in him.*" Again this word for love is a noun, it is a Person (God), and it is a place (God's presence). When we put all this together, we realize that kindness is not something I do because I am not love. Rather it is something that comes out of me when I abide in God Who is Love. Kindness is a fruit of being in God's presence (Galatians 5:22). I am not love; God is love (noun). Therefore I can only love (verb) when I am connected to God, just as the branch of an apple tree is not an apple, it only bears apples when connected to the apple tree. It should humble us to understand that we are not kind, but God produces kindness in us when we are in His love. It is all Him, not me! "*He [Jesus] must increase, but I must decrease*" (John 3:30).

AN AFFAIR WITH THE WORLD

Love is patient, love is kind and is not jealous;
love does not brag and is not arrogant.

1 Corinthians 13:4

Jealousy is defined as "to burn with zeal or boil with envy." The root of jealousy is discontentment. If God is love, then we can find nothing lacking in Him; there is nothing to be discontent about. God is full and complete, and in Him, there is no void.

But there is a flip side to jealousy: *"For you shall not worship any other god, for the LORD, whose name is Jealous, is a jealous God"* (Exodus 34:14). This verse might cause the wheels in your head to start turning; how can God be love, and love is not jealous, yet God is jealous? What does this mean? Well, in God, there is nothing to be discontent about because His love is complete. But God is jealous because there is something that He wants: He is discontent because He desires our love. When we divide our love between Him and the things of this world, He is jealous because He is the rightful recipient of our love (Ezekiel 16).

So what does this tell us about the Servant? The Creator formed this world and then created us to abide in His complete love, but we neglected and squandered His love. So the Servant came to this earth to put His love on display for all to see (John 3:16). The Servant's love was displayed in a manger, among the disciples, on the cross, and leaving the tomb. The Savior did all this, but He is not interested in a divided heart. He gave us everything so that there would be nothing to be discontent about. Yet we had an affair with the world and expected God to be okay with it. He is a jealous God! We need to understand, Jesus serves us, but He is not our servant. We are not His Master, telling Him what to do. No, He obeys the Father by washing our feet, but His love for us is to be met with our love. Love is not jealous; it is complete. Do you love Him completely, or are you having an affair with the world?

I AM THAT I AM

Love is patient, love is kind and is not jealous; love does not brag and is not arrogant.

1 Corinthians 13:4

Moses knelt down in front of the burning bush, and with his face pressed into the dirt, he conversed with the Almighty. God revealed His plan for Moses to go to Egypt and to speak out against the Pharaoh, demanding the freedom of the Hebrews. Moses was afraid of this massive call, so he questioned God as to a name he could refer to Him as, and God said, *"I Am who I Am"* (Exodus 3:14). The *"I Am"* would go on to say, *"Thus you shall say to the sons of Israel, 'The LORD, the God of your fathers, the God of Abraham, the God of Isaac, and the God of Jacob, has sent me to you.' This is My name forever, and this is My memorial-name to all generations"* (Exodus 3:15). To this very day, God will be known as the *"I Am."* But *"I Am"* what? Throughout Scripture, God made *"I Am"* statements that revealed a little more of His character. In Matthew 11:29, it says, *"Take My yoke upon you and learn from Me, for I am gentle and humble in heart, and you will find rest for your souls."* Jesus made a point in this verse to say I am humble in heart. What does this mean? In short, the Great I Am is saying, "I am lowly, bowed down to the ground, a mere Servant." How ironic for the Master to claim humility. Most people would see this as a weakness, but to the One Who holds all power, He did not need to proclaim His greatness. We see this again in 1 Corinthians 13:4 when Paul says, *"love does not brag."* Remember that the word *"love"* in this verse is a noun, thereby pointing to a person, place, or thing. God is love, and He has no need to brag because He simply is the *"I Am."* To brag is to embellish yourself or to display yourself excessively. How could Jesus embellish Himself? Something that is the best cannot be made better, and Jesus did not have to excessively display Himself because He simply is the *"I Am."* The Servant did not have to boast of His love because He is love in the flesh and in the Spirit.

HUMBLE LOVE

Love is patient, love is kind and is not jealous; love does not brag and is not arrogant.

1 Corinthians 13:4

"As far as the east is from the west, So far has He removed our transgressions from us" (Psalm 103:12). Have you ever stopped to think about the reality of this verse? The Servant loves us so much that He took our sins and removed them as far as the east is from the west! This phrase, *"as far as the east is from the west,"* is interesting because just how far is that? It depends on which way you are facing. If you have repented from your sins and have turned away from them, then your disobedience is infinitely distanced from you, but we must be careful because the moment we turn back to face a sinful life, we instantly go from facing east to facing west. What I mean is, our sins have been forgiven, but the moment we turn away from God, we are face to face with sin again. So east and west are ever growing apart, but one small about-face brings sin right back to your doorstep.

The same principle is seen in 1 Corinthians 13:4 when Paul says love is not arrogant. Arrogance means "puffed up," like a balloon. You cannot be puffed up and humble at the same time, just like you cannot face east and west at the same time. Arrogance and humility are ever growing apart, but it only takes a small about-face to bring a sense that you are above others, and that makes loving them impossible. Jesus came not puffed up with arrogance but as a humble Servant. He never turned to the right or to the left because that would have been like deviating from true east. Anything off from true east is some sort of west. Any deviation from humility is arrogance.

O Lord, please help us to keep our faces toward You. So many things in this world beg for our attention, and that pulls us from Your path. You never deviated or changed, and in humility, You love us. May we also humbly love others!

———

GRACE TO THE RUDE

Does not act unbecomingly; it does not seek its own, is not provoked, does not take into account a wrong suffered.

1 Corinthians 13:5

Love does not act unbecomingly, which means "rude." As parents, we teach our children not to be rude. "Don't talk when others are talking." These are things that are considered disrespectful. Why is it rude to interrupt someone? Because doing so says, "you are less important than me." Basically, being rude is to degrade someone to a status below you. Could you imagine what it would be to love all people with a love that isn't rude? Jesus tells us to even love our enemies (Luke 6:27).

So how do we show a love that isn't rude to those who hate us and try to destroy us? How can we elevate our enemies to a level of equality and treat them with dignity? They want to see us killed, silenced forever, yet we are to meet them, not just with peace but with kindness? This makes no sense! Not only is it illogical, but it is unjust. They deserve what they have coming because of what they have dished out. As kids we are taught not to be rude, but as adults we learn that rudeness is how we treat people who treat us rudely. We grow up living by the rule, "An eye for an eye." This is justice, and a world without justice is anarchy. But when we look at the world through the lens of the Servant's love, we see that Jesus looked upon the very people who were killing Him, who wanted to see Him silenced, who were rudely spitting on Him and slapping Him. He looked on them not with a vengeance of justice, but He raised them up to a level of brother and sister. The justice they deserved was poured out on Him, and He took it. Love is not rude; it is restoring. When someone does something to us that demands a just response of rudeness, we should remember, not only did the Servant give us mercy but also grace at the cross. How can we receive His grace and not also give it? We can't!

———

DEATH TO THE GIVER

Does not act unbecomingly; it does not seek its own, is not provoked,
does not take into account a wrong suffered.

1 Corinthians 13:5

Love does not seek its own. It is one thing to serve someone out of our surplus, but it is a whole other thing to serve out of our poverty (Mark 12:44). When we give out of our poverty, it takes from us what we need to live. But only when we begin to give out of our poverty do we actually start to Live!

Do nothing from selfishness or empty conceit, but with humility of mind regard one another as more important than yourselves; do not merely look out for your own personal interests, but also for the interests of others. Have this attitude in yourselves which was also in Christ Jesus, who, although He existed in the form of God, did not regard equality with God a thing to be grasped, but emptied Himself, taking the form of a bond-servant, and being made in the likeness of men. Being found in appearance as a man, He humbled Himself by becoming obedient to the point of death, even death on a cross. For this reason also, God highly exalted Him, and bestowed on Him the name which is above every name, so that at the name of Jesus every knee will bow, of those who are in heaven and on earth and under the earth, and that every tongue will confess that Jesus Christ is Lord, to the glory of God the Father (Philippians 2:3–11).

1. Jesus looked out for the interest of others. (vs. 4)
2. Jesus emptied Himself, taking the form of a bond-servant. (vs. 7)
3. Jesus humbled Himself to obedience, even to death. (vs. 8)
4. Jesus was given the name above every name. (vs. 9)
5. We are to have this attitude in us. (vs. 5)
6. This glorifies God our Father! (vs. 11)

SHARPENED FOR WHAT PURPOSE?

Does not act unbecomingly; it does not seek its own, is not provoked,
does not take into account a wrong suffered.

1 Corinthians 13:5

Today we will look at what it means when love is not provoked. The literal meaning of the word provoked is "to make sharp, to irritate, arouse to anger." Love is not easily angered or irritated or even sharpened. Let's dive deeper to see what this could mean for us and the people we love.

Being provoked carries with it a picture of two things rubbing together, creating friction and wearing on each other until they become sharp. This picture is also used in Proverbs 27:17, *"Iron sharpens iron, So one man sharpens another."* Typically we see this proverb as a beneficial thing, very much the picture of accountability. But not all friction and sharpening is edifying. On the one hand, when a seasoned Christian comes alongside a younger Christian and begins to sharpen them, wearing away the burs and rough edges, then this sharpening is good and useful, even something we have been called to do (Hebrews 10:24–25). On the other hand, when we push the buttons of others just to get them agitated, then we are creating friction, which will likewise sharpen them, but their blade will be turned toward us, not toward the enemy. Both of these actions will sharpen our brothers and sisters to a razor-sharp status, but the result of one will be a trusted friend who fights beside us, building us up and protecting us. The other will result in a person who does not trust us, is irritated, and will at a stressful moment, lash out, wounding not just us but the body of Christ. It is so important that we do not provoke others to anger because this will always come back on us.

The love that the Servant has for us is very much the love a father bestows on his children. He does not provoke us or rub us into anger but rather sharpens us, preparing us for battling the real enemy (Ephesians 6:4).

THE MINISTRY OF RECONCILIATION

*Does not act unbecomingly; it does not seek its own, is not provoked,
does not take into account a wrong suffered.*

1 Corinthians 13:5

The one word that defines what it means to not take into account a wrong suffered would be forgiveness. *But not some forgiveness we see when a little child wrongs another and the parent makes them say, "I'm sorry." That is the* kind of forgiveness that gets you off the hook but never changes how you see the other person. Truly when Paul says, *"Love does not take into account a wrong suffered,"* this 'love' is next to impossible for us to understand. That is why it's important to learn that this word 'love' is a noun; it is God Almighty. Rarely have we seen someone wounded so severely that their blood pours out, look to the perpetrator and say, "I forgive you, and I erase the offense." How can we erase the offense? We struggle to forgive our own offenses to ourselves.

Love is an impossibility for you and me. We cannot conjure up inside us an expression of such selflessness as to call it love. We love only because the Servant loved us first (1 John 4:19). How could we look at the person who harmed us and say to them I forgive you and no longer even remember what you did to me? We must come face to face with the God of the universe Who bowed Himself down to our eye level and forgave us first. Peering into His eyes and seeing His complete forgiveness for us is how we can also forgive others. *"Now all these things are from God, who reconciled us to Himself through Christ and gave us the ministry of reconciliation, namely, that God was in Christ reconciling the world to Himself, not counting their trespasses against them, and He has committed to us the word of reconciliation"* (2 Corinthians 5:18–19). It is that reconciliation that we received from Jesus that allows us to walk in the ministry of reconciliation.

THE TRUTH OF YOUR SALVATION

Does not rejoice in unrighteousness, but rejoices with the truth.

1 Corinthians 13:6

What makes God rejoice? What is it that brings joy to the heart of the Father? Remember, we have been learning that the word love as used in 1 Corinthians 13:4–7 is a noun, meaning it is a person, namely God. So in verse six, we see that God does not rejoice in unrighteousness but rejoices with the truth. To understand the impact of this verse, we need to look up a couple of Greek words. The Greek word for rejoice is *chairō*, which means "to be glad or thrive." The Greek word for rejoices is *sygchairō*, which is a combination of two root words—*chairō*, which we have already seen, and *syn*, which means "with." Combined, the word *sygchairō* means "to be glad with." "With" is a small word, but it carries a lot of weight. God is not glad in unrighteousness, but He is glad *"with"* the truth. What is truth? (John 18:38). Jesus gave a very clear answer to this in John 14:6. *"Jesus said to him, 'I am the way, and the truth, and the life; no one comes to the Father but through Me.'"* Jesus is the truth! So now put all of the pieces together. God is love, and He is not glad in unrighteousness or the fallenness of this world, but He is glad in His Son Who is the truth! You can know the truth, and the truth will set you free (John 8:32). The Father rejoices when the Son sets mankind free. Our joy is not completed in our salvation but in Jesus' salvation (Psalm 51:12). If the Father rejoices in the Son's salvation, how can we find our delight in anything less? The things this world has to offer may be fun for a season, but in the end they are death and pain.

May our prayer be the same as King David's, *"Restore to me the joy of Your salvation And sustain me with a willing spirit"* (Psalm 51:12).

Father, please protect us from evil and its unrighteous trappings. And help us to find our joy 'with' the truth of Your salvation. May we know the Truth and be set free by Him.

———

MERCY AND GRACE

Bears all things, believes all things, hopes all things, endures all things.

1 Corinthians 13:7

Psalm 118:24 says, *"This is the day which the LORD has made; Let us rejoice and be glad in it."* We have been given a gift in that we have a new day to love others and to know our Savior more. Do not miss this day!

Paul tells us that Love bears all things, which means to endure or to cover. Basically, nothing gets past love. When I think about a love that bears all things, I think of the traditional American marriage vows. *"To have and to hold, from this day forth, for better or worse, richer or poorer, in sickness or health, forsaking all others until death do us part."* Many people add an unstated escape clause to these vows, which states, *"unless the other person doesn't uphold their end of the bargain."* But God, Who says *"Love bears all things,"* truly means His love endures and covers ALL things; there is no escape clause because there is nothing that can overtake, get past, or overwhelm Him. This is why the "Marriage Vows" or "Covenant" the Lord made with His chosen people was made by Himself. He knew we would mess up. Our love does not bear all because we seek the fulfillment of self. It is so easy for us to confuse love with lust, and that is why God made His covenant with Himself on our behalf (Genesis 15). The Old Covenant was fulfilled in Christ's life and death. The New Covenant was made in His death and resurrection. This covenant is experienced in Christ's mercy and grace toward us. Just like the marriage vows, a bride or groom promises the mercy of forgiveness for the shortcomings of their spouse, and they give the grace of love even if it is undeserved. *"Above all, keep fervent in your love for one another, because love covers a multitude of sins"* (1 Peter 4:8). Love bears all things in the mercy and grace of Christ Jesus. The Servant's towel is worn and waiting, and He stands ready to wash away the dirt of our waywardness and to purify our feet. That is His Mercy and Grace!

BELIEVING THE UNBELIEVABLE

Bears all things, believes all things, hopes all things, endures all things.

1 Corinthians 13:7

This attribute of love is probably the one we most misunderstand because we as fallen humans cannot comprehend *"love never fails"* (1 Corinthians 13:8). We do not believe everything others say because they cannot be trusted to never fail. This has produced in us a spirit of skepticism, even among friends and family. It is easy to believe the word of a trusted source as long as it is logical, but even the illogical words of a friend will be met with skepticism. Why? Because our love does fail. But not God's. His love is true and can be believed even when it doesn't make sense. A prime example of this would be when God spoke to Abraham and called Him to sacrifice his son (Genesis 22:2). If this command had come to me, I can only imagine my thought would have been, *"This is unbelievable."* But according to Hebrews 11:19, Abraham understood something of the love of God. He did not question God in this because he believed in God's word, God's love, and God's power.

God's word was to sacrifice his only son. Abraham recognized God's voice, and He knew God's words were true even if they didn't make sense.

God's love had already been expressed to Abraham in the promise of a son through whom a great nation would come. Abraham believed it because He trusted God's love.

God's power was limitless for Abraham. He had already seen God take a very old man and a very old woman, and through His power, give them a son. He had experienced God's power; therefore, He trusted it.

If God's word said you would have a son and His love promised you a great nation through that son, then His power would raise that dead son. Abraham obeyed because he believed in God's love. Believing the Servant's love is to trust Him even when it makes no sense.

WAIT. HOPE. EXPECT.

Bears all things, believes all things, hopes all things, endures all things.

1 Corinthians 13:7

"*I wait for the LORD, my soul does wait, And in His word do I hope . . . O Israel, hope in the LORD; For with the LORD there is lovingkindness, And with Him is abundant redemption*" (Psalm 130:5,7). The Psalmist cried out saying that his soul waits for the Lord and that he hopes in His word. What does this mean, and what does it have to do with love hoping all things? If you look up the Hebrew word for wait used in this verse, it means, "wait, hope, or expect." They are different words, but they mean the same basic thing—to stay put and look forward with expectation. The Psalmist is saying he is in a season of need, he has cried out for help, and now he waits, watching the horizon with his ears strained to hear the voice of the Lord. But what is he waiting and hoping for? If we are not paying attention, it would be easy to read verse seven and say he waits and expectantly looks for lovingkindness and redemption and to be sure he does long for these things, but that is not what his hope is in. Verse seven says, "*O Israel, hope in the LORD; For with the LORD there is loving kindness, And with Him is abundant redemption.*" His hope is in the Lord, and he waits for the Lord because the lovingkindness and the abundant redemption is with the Lord. The Psalmist's focus was not on the blessings but on the One Who bestowed the blessing. He could hope in all things because he knew the love of the Lord.

How quick we are to run to the Servant and demand His service as if we deserve it, but that is not love, nor is it where hope is grounded. We are to wait, hope, and expect the Lord. He is Love, and He never fails. We do not need to go anywhere else. Wait. Hope. Expect.

ENDURING LOVE

Bears all things, believes all things, hopes all things, endures all things.

1 Corinthians 13:7

The Servant's towel is worn and waiting because a servant is always on duty. A servant watches because his delight is in pleasing his master. This is why Jesus endures all things. Let's dig deeper so we can better understand how to serve through enduring love.

The Greek word for endures is *hypomenō,* which means "to remain or to tarry behind." To endure is to remain unmoved until the task is completed. This word *hypomenō* is also used in Luke 2:43 when Jesus' parents had gone to Jerusalem for a feast when He was twelve years old. They were following what God had prescribed in the Law. Each year Jews were to make the pilgrimage to Jerusalem for the feasts. This was a time of celebrating, remembering, and sacrifices. So Mary and Joseph were focusing on what God had called them to do, but Jesus was also doing what His Father had called Him to do, *"and as they were returning, after spending the full number of days, the boy Jesus stayed behind (hypomenō) in Jerusalem. But His parents were unaware of it."* Jesus endured, or remained, in Jerusalem longer than His earthly parents, why? Verse forty-nine says, *"And He said to them, 'Why is it that you were looking for Me? Did you not know that I had to be in My Father's house?'"* It was Jesus' love for His Father that kept Him enduring in Jerusalem.

We must be careful because we can get so focused on completing our religious tasks that we miss enduring in the Father's house. To tarry in His presence and to remain before His throne, that is what eternal life is all about (John 17:3). Jesus' service is in the interest of the Father; this is why His towel is worn from washing our feet. He came not to be served but to serve (Mark 10:45). But we must remember that we are servants of the King, not the other way around. God owes us nothing yet gives to us at His own expense. The expense of His life!

NEVER ORPHANED

Make sure that your character is free from the love of money, being content with what you have; for He Himself has said, "I will never desert you, nor will I ever forsake you."

Hebrews 13:5

God's interaction with mankind during the Old Testament was different in the Gospel years, and is still different now. In the Old Testament, the Father manifested Himself over the Ark of the Covenant as a pillar of cloud by day and fire by night. But during the Gospels, God manifested Himself as a human being, Jesus, Who lived thirty-three years before ascending to Heaven. Today, God manifests Himself as the Holy Spirit Who dwells in us. God has never left us. He sometimes moves, and we choose not to follow, but He never turns His back on His creation. But with that said, He does not sit by and allow us to habitually profane His presence. God has been known to simply pick up and move when we sin with no thought to His holiness.

In Ezekiel 10:4, the Bible tells us that the glory of the Lord moved to the threshold of the temple. Later in verses eighteen and nineteen, we see that the glory of the Lord followed cherubim from the threshold out to the east gate of the temple. Finally, Ezekiel tells us that the glory of the Lord left the city of Jerusalem all together and stood over a mountain east of the city (Ezekiel 11:23). So because of sin, the glory of the Lord would leave its place enthroned over the ark of the covenant and would move to the threshold, then the east gate, then finally to the top of a mountain outside the city. God will not sit in the midst of sin; He will move but note that God did not leave earth. The Lord Almighty has never deserted His children nor forsaken them. There may be times in our lives when we feel like God has removed Himself from us, and maybe He has moved when we were more focused on the things of this world, but we can rest assured, He will not leave us orphaned. He came to serve not to disown us.

A HEART TO HELP

The LORD is for me among those who help me;
Therefore I will look with satisfaction on those who hate me.

Psalm 118:7

H—hope	H—hurt
E—encourage	A—accuse
L—listen	T—torment
P—partner	E—evil

Does God help us or hate us? We know the churchy answer is that God helps us because He loves us, but in actuality, does God really help us? If we walk through these two acronyms, what do we learn?

The desires of someone who gives help are:

- They desire to give Hope when there seems to be no way out (Lamentations 3:24).
- They desire to Encourage when you are at the end of your rope (Matthew 11:28).
- They desire to Listen to you when you cry out (Psalm 69:33).
- They desire to Partner with you, not leaving you alone (Matthew 28:20).

On the other hand, the desires of someone who harbors hate are:

- They desire to Hurt you by tearing you down (Matthew 5:11).
- They desire to Accuse you of every wrong you do or have ever done (1 Corinthians 13:5).
- They desire to Torment your mind, telling you how worthless you are (2 Corinthians 5:17).
- They desire Evil for you, not good (Matthew 20:28).

Truly we have a God Who desires to help us find His heart. He holds no hate toward us and His heart overflows with love for His children.

———————

THE TABLE HAS BEEN SET

Therefore you too have grief now; but I will see you again,
and your heart will rejoice, and no one will take your joy away from you.

John 16:22

Jesus' love for the disciples ran deep. Over the previous three years, they had experienced many things; they had celebrated, mourned, marveled, and worshipped. Jesus knew they were getting ready to be tested as they had never been before, so He was trying to prepare them to stand strong; He knew His death was going to be life altering for them.

The disciples did not have the luxury of reading the book of John to see the resurrection. They simply had this riddle from Jesus, *"A little while, and you will no longer see Me; and again a little while, and you will see Me"* (John 16:16). Today we worship a risen Savior, but they had a Rabbi Who was saying He was going to disappear for a time and then reappear. Never lose sight of how difficult this was for the disciples to live in real time. Jesus was setting the table for them so they would have what they needed. He knew the main course was going to be His flesh and blood, and they were going to struggle to stomach it. But in the end, He knew they would rejoice! This is like a parent who takes their child to the doctor to get a shot. They know the shot will hurt, but the pain will be short lived, and the pain of the disease would be far worse. Love drives the parent to relinquish their child to momentary pain for greater health; likewise, love drove Jesus to surrender the disciples to momentary pain for an eternal joy!

Much like the disciples, we do not get the whole picture, just a mysterious telling of things to come. They were told He would die and rise again; we are told He will return to take us home. This life is not easy, we are being tested, but once again, the Servant has set the table with everything we need. The main course set before us may be difficult to stomach, but Jesus knows that in the end, the eternal joy far outweighs the momentary struggle.

EYE TO EYE

The LORD supports the afflicted; He brings down the wicked to the ground.

Psalm 147:6

Imagine in your mind a person sitting on a street corner, their clothes ragged, their appearance withered, and the sign in their hand clearly saying they are in need. The thoughts that begin to run through your head may range from, "They are lazy and need to get a job" to "What a poor soul, how can I help?" My intention is not to determine if it is right or wrong to give money to someone on a street corner but to see the Servant's heart. Psalm 147:6 tells us that the Servant supports the afflicted. This means He relieves them in their afflictions. Two ways we generally give support to someone in this situation are, we stand over them with a hand reaching down giving them money, food, or clothing, or we bend our knee so that our eyes are on the same level. When we see them eye to eye, we give dignity. Both of these methods are beneficial to the afflicted, but one gives dignity as well as meets a need.

Jesus supports the afflicted, which means He did not just reach down from Heaven with something in His hand but rather He stepped out of Heaven, bent His knee so we would be eye to eye, and then He reached out His hand so a nail could be hammered into it. He supported the afflicted not with currency but with Himself. Jesus didn't just alleviate a need; He served the broken.

Now revisit your mental image of the homeless person sitting on the street corner. Watch as someone walks up and stoops down eye to eye with them. As they look into each other's eyes, the homeless man reaches out a nail-pierced hand and helps lift up the kneeling person. That is the teaching of the Servant. The Lord raises up those who are bowed down (Psalm 146:8). Jesus came down to meet us eye to eye but are we willing to bow down to see Him eye to eye?

HIDDEN IN PRAYER

O You who hear prayer, To You all men come.

Psalm 65:2

What would be the worst form of torture? While physical torture would be more than I can imagine, I think being ignored every day of your life would be even worse. Loneliness is the closest thing to hell on earth, and it is the definition of Hell itself—separation from God. In prison, one of the worst forms of discipline is solitary confinement, where you are separated so that no one hears your cries nor responds to your words. It is in isolation that we are truly lost and indeed tortured beyond our human ability to cope.

Isolation is what makes the thought of being separated from God unbearable. I cannot fathom even a day without His presence. A life without God's interaction is no life at all. That is one thing that makes being a child of God so amazing; God interacts with us. He listens when we speak! We cry out to Him, and He listens and responds. The Servant's towel is worn, and His ear is waiting. *"The LORD is near to all who call upon Him, To all who call upon Him in truth. He will fulfill the desire of those who fear Him; He will also hear their cry and will save them"* (Psalm 145:18–19). Prayer is the meeting place for God and us, a secret hiding place deep within our souls. He hears us, and all men come to Him. He draws near to all who call on Him. It is in prayer that we abide together, the Servant and His servant. When the waves rise and crash around us, there is solace in prayer because that is where we hide in Him (Psalm 46:1–3). Try to imagine the world in chaos—wars and rumors of wars, natural disasters, and such lawlessness that makes people's love grow cold (Matthew 24:12)—but you sit calmly talking to your Father. That is what peace is, not the absence of war but finding refuge in the open ears of the Servant. Does that mean nothing will ever harm you? No, it means you trust the Father to bring His kingdom on earth as it is in Heaven. He will carry you safely home.

THE GOSPEL OF INCONVENIENCE

And Jesus turned and saw them following, and said to them, "What do you seek?"
They said to Him, "Rabbi (which translated means Teacher), where are You staying?"
He said to them, "Come, and you will see." So they came and saw where He was
staying; and they stayed with Him that day, for it was about the tenth hour.

John 1:38–39

A servant cannot be as concerned about self as he or she is about others; therefore, they must be open to interruptions. For people who are not servant-minded, interruptions and distractions can be irritating, but to a servant, they are opportunities.

One day as Jesus was walking down the street, He sensed that He was being followed. John 1:38 says that Jesus *"turned."* I love this verse because it shows that Jesus was not so task driven that He missed the opportunities around Him. Jesus could have said, "I am the Savior of the world, I don't have time to deviate from My task," but instead, Jesus *"turned"* and saw Andrew and another of John the Baptist's disciples. Jesus asked them what they were seeking, to which they responded, *"where are You staying?"* He could have told them an address, but instead He allowed Himself to be inconvenienced for the rest of the day. Why? Why would Jesus spend a whole day talking to these disciples?

Jesus did not run from distractions but utilized them as opportunities to point people to the Father. Andrew would leave Jesus that day and run to his brother Simon and tell him that they had found the Messiah (John 1:41). This was no small claim! The Jews had been waiting for the Messiah for four thousand years. Simon met Jesus, and his life was never the same. People all over the world, Jew and Gentile, would know Jesus' saving grace through Peter's preaching, and it can all be traced back to the moment when Jesus *"turned."* We needed Jesus to *"turn"* so that we could *"turn"* to Him. The Servant was willing to be inconvenienced.

KING SERVANT FATHER

I am no longer in the world; and yet they themselves are in the world, and I come to You. Holy Father, keep them in Your name, the name which You have given Me, that they may be one even as We are.

John 17:11

There is possibly no more touching passage of Scripture than John 17. We often call it the High Priestly Prayer, and it is here that we not only hear Jesus' heart for His followers but also for us, thousands of years later. In verse twenty Jesus said, *"I do not ask on behalf of these alone, but for those also who believe in Me through their word."* We bear the name Christian today because the disciples shared the Gospel with someone who shared it with someone else and it continued for two thousand years. Jesus prayed for you that night before the cross! How beautiful!

Also in this High Priestly prayer, Jesus prayed that the Holy Father would keep the disciples in the Father's name. Jesus goes on in verse twelve to say, *"While I was with them, I was keeping them in Your name which You have given Me; and I guarded them and not one of them perished but the son of perdition, so that the Scripture would be fulfilled."* Jesus knew that His time on earth was at its end. While He had been here, He guarded the disciples with the Father's name, but now He was leaving to go back to Heaven, so He asked that the Father guard them. If the Father guards you, you are safe.

When Jesus left Heaven, He set aside His equality with God (Philippians 2:6), but now He was going back; He would be returning to His throne at the right hand of the Father (Acts 2:33). While on earth, Jesus served, but in Heaven, He would sit as Prince of Peace, not as servant. Yet even in His righteous royalty, Jesus still served by praying for humanity. Jesus is no slave, but He is a servant. It is Who He is, and it is Who the Father is, so we can rest assured that we are wrapped up in the Name that is above all names! King. Servant. Father.

REMEMBER IT WAS FOR YOU

Jesus came and took the bread and gave it to them, and the fish likewise.

John 21:13

If there was one word that could encapsulate John chapter twenty-one, it would be "remember." When the scene unfolds, we see some of the disciples going fishing. Jesus appeared to them while they were fishing, just like He did three years before (Matthew 4:18–22). Next, Jesus called out to these disciples to throw their nets on the other side of the boat. Even though they had fished all night and caught nothing, they obeyed. When they did, they caught a huge number of fish. This was exactly what happened at the beginning of Jesus' ministry (Luke 5:4–7) .The next reminiscent event of this chapter is that Peter got out of a boat in order to be with Jesus (Matthew 14:28–33). When the disciples got to shore, Jesus had fixed breakfast for them. He reached over, grabbed some bread, and handed it to them just as He had done a few weeks prior during the Lord's supper where He explained that the bread was like His flesh that would be broken for them. Now those nail scarred hands were handing them bread again (Mark 14:22–25). Finally, the last situation that was being relived was when Jesus handed His disciples bread and fish just as He had done at the feeding of the 5,000. This was a memory that was seared into their minds as they watched those five loaves of bread and two fish feed so many. Then to truly ingrain it into their spirits, there were twelve baskets of leftovers that the twelve disciples carried away (Matthew 14:15–21).

Everything Jesus did was to serve mankind. Sometimes He spoke in words of grace and sometimes in words of truth. But either way, His intention was to serve. Jesus ended the book of John with a story of remembrance. Remember what I did. Remember what I am doing. Remember what I am going to do. Remember it is all in obedience to the Father and in service to you!

———

THE VICTORIOUS LION

And one of the elders said to me, "Stop weeping; behold, the Lion that is from the tribe of Judah, the Root of David, has overcome so as to open the book and its seven seals."

Revelation 5:5

While on the island of Patmos, John had a vision of the last days. In this vision, he saw a book that had seven seals. A strong angel came out asking if there was anyone who was worthy to open the seals of the book? They would search all over Heaven and earth and under the earth, but no one was found worthy to open the book. John began to weep, but one of the elders told him to stop because the Lion of Judah had overcome and He could open the book. Jesus is the Lion of Judah, the Root of David, the Lamb standing as if slain. Yes, Jesus had overcome and was worthy to open the seals. What had He overcome? Everything! Jesus had overcome death and the grave, He had overcome the world, He had overcome Satan's tricks and temptations, and now He stood in Heaven ready to open the seven seals of the book that would begin the process of ushering us into the new Heaven and new earth. Jesus had overcome!

But may we never lose sight of what took place for Jesus to overcome and why He went through it. Jesus left Heaven and became a human. He experienced death, which was diabolically contrary to Who He was because Jesus is life. Jesus experienced the Father turning away from Him on the cross because of our sins. All the pain, all the betrayal, all the sins, all the accusations, all the disrespect, all the hatred—He took on all of it for us. He did not have to do any of that. He could have easily destroyed everything and started again with a creation that wouldn't fall short of His glory, but He served mankind with a love that could not be reflected back to Him. The only reason we will stand before the Father as sons and daughters is because the Servant's towel is worn and waiting. He overcame! Praise the Lamb! Praise the Lion of Judah!

MAY

The Commander's Army Is Swift and Fierce

TRUSTING HIS ABILITY

Finally, be strong in the Lord and in the strength of His might.

Ephesians 6:10

Do you trust God? Better yet, is God trustworthy? Will God be moved to your salvation? Will He intervene on your behalf when you fall? The Commander's Army is swift and fierce, but will the Commander dispatch His army when we are attacked? Can we comprehend the mind of the Master? God spoke to Job and said, "*Have you ever in your life commanded the morning, And caused the dawn to know its place, That it might take hold of the ends of the earth, And the wicked be shaken out of it?*" (Job 38:12–13). The Commander has an army, a whole host, and that army even includes the morning. He commands the morning and the dawn, so the wicked are shaken out of it. So great is the power of the Commander of Heaven's army.

We can trust God because He is trustworthy. But what can you trust Him to do? Evil is everywhere; certainly we cannot trust Him to keep evil from us. We will all die, so we cannot trust Him to heal our every sickness. Harm comes to us, therefore we cannot trust God to protect us from pain. So how can we be strong in the strength of the Lord's might?

The Greek word for might is *ischys*, which means "ability." So we are to be strong in the Lord and in the strength of His *ability*. There is no doubt that God's ability is absolute. Will He use that ability how I want and when I want? That is not for me to decide or even know. The Commander of Heaven's army knows the battle plans, and there are times He will be moved to fight for the preserving of my earthly body. There are other times when He will allow my body to decay. Why? Because the battle is not for my body! It is for His glory! It is for our souls! When we look for Him to meet our every whim, we are left wanting, which leads to doubt. However, when we look to Him to save our souls, we will see His ability at work in our lives, and that builds trust, which brings Him glory!

———————

THE PEACE OF GOD

*Be anxious for nothing, but in everything by prayer and supplication with
thanksgiving let your requests be made known to God. And the peace of God,
which surpasses all comprehension, will guard your hearts and your minds in Christ Jesus.*

Philippians 4:6–7

"The peace of God." Isn't that what we long for? Isn't that what we war over
and climb the ladder of success for? Peace. But what is peace? The absence of
war? A state of perpetual bliss? In John 14:27, Jesus says, *"Peace I leave with you;
My peace I give to you; not as the world gives do I give to you. Do not let your heart be
troubled, nor let it be fearful."* Jesus is the giver of peace, but we can be sure that
the peace He gives is not the absence of war because we are surrounded by war.
Likewise, His peace is not perpetual bliss because we go through pain. So what
is this peace that passes all comprehension?

The peace we receive in Christ is His very presence! The peace of God is the
presence of God. Just because God's presence is with you doesn't mean you will
experience smooth sailing. The disciples cried out in fear when the waves were
threatening to overtake their boat, even though Jesus was asleep in the boat.
Jesus' presence does not ensure calm seas but rather a peace that nothing will
come to you unless He ushers it. The very tools Satan uses to steal our joy and
overtake our faith are our heart and our mind. These are the battlefields that
we live in every day. Our heart betrays us. Our mind deceives us into believing
we are in trouble, that we are not enough, or that we cannot control the chaos
around us. But the peace of God, which comes in His presence, reminds us that
life is not about our ability to be enough or to be in control. He is more than
enough, and He is in control. His presence guards our hearts and minds in the
truth that Christ is with us, so we are to cling to Him as a branch clings to the
tree, instead of trying to control the war of chaos around us.

GOD DIDN'T ASK PERMISSION

Now, gird up your loins and arise, and speak to them all which I command you.
Do not be dismayed before them, or I will dismay you before them.

Jeremiah 1:17

God's word came to Jeremiah, *"Before I formed you in the womb I knew you, And before you were born I consecrated you; I have appointed you a prophet to the nations"* (Jeremiah 1:5). This was a high calling and one that made Jeremiah buckle at the knees. Jeremiah cried out, *"Alas, Lord God! Behold, I do not know how to speak, Because I am a youth."* Fear is a powerful emotion that can paralyze us. Jeremiah was afraid of the calling God had just given. God's response to Jeremiah's fear was to remind Him of a few things: (1) You are not God, (2) I am, (3) I have equipped you, and (4) I did not ask your permission. God did not allow Jeremiah to back away because fear tugged at his mind. In fact, God even went a step further. Without skipping a beat, God gave Jeremiah his first assignment. Go proclaim to Judah that judgment is coming. This was a hard task and especially for an already fearful young man, but God sternly told him not to be dismayed before them or God would dismay him before them. God's words were hard, with no loopholes or ways of escape. But God would follow that up with a promise. *"Now behold, I have made you today as a fortified city and as a pillar of iron and as walls of bronze against the whole land, to the kings of Judah, to its princes, to its priests and to the people of the land. "They will fight against you, but they will not overcome you, for I am with you to deliver you," declares the LORD"* (Jeremiah 1:18–19). God did not ask Jeremiah if he wanted the job. He commanded His servant to go, but He also equipped Jeremiah with everything he needed. The Commander gave him the words to speak, and He also gave him His presence for protection; Jeremiah simply came with obedience. The Commander's army is swift and fierce; never forget, we are a part of that army.

TRUTH OVER LIES

I sought the LORD, and He answered me, And delivered me from all my fears.

Psalm 34:4

What is it that produces fear in our lives? Fear is the emotional response to a negative possibility. For example, if you asked people if they were afraid of a small black animal with several legs, many would say yes. Why? Because small black spiders have the possibility to produce poison that can bring sickness or even death. But if I told you the small black animal with many legs is not a spider but an ant, most people would say, I'm not afraid of one ant. Why? Because black ants, while they can pinch, are not poisonous and pose no real threat. We fear the things that produce a negative possibility.

David wrote Psalm 34 in response to an experience he had when he was in a valley of life. He was running for his life from King Saul, and it had led him to Achish, king of Gath. David was seeking deliverance, but when people began talking to the king about how David was known for killing many Philistines, David began to fear. First Samuel 21:12 says, *"David took these words to heart and greatly feared Achish king of Gath."* Why did David fear King Achish? Because the king posed a negative possibility. So David acted like he was a madman, and God helped him escape.

David was in a lose-lose situation. Stay in Israel and be found by King Saul or run to Gath and be captured by King Achish. He feared for his life because of the possibilities. But he cried out to God, and He responded with deliverance from fears. The Commander's army is able to deliver from any fear. Remember, we fear merely the possibilities. Our Commander doesn't operate in possibilities but rather in truth. Jesus is the truth (John 14:6), and the truth will set you free! (John 8:32). Deliverance comes only when we believe the truth over the lies. Possibilities seem so unavoidable, but God is not bound by the limitations of our fearful mind.

THE ARMOR OF COVENANT

Therefore, take up the full armor of God, so that you will be able to resist in the evil day, and having done everything, to stand firm.

Ephesians 6:13

Ephesians, chapter 6, contains a list of armor that Paul tells us to put on. Over the next seven days, we will be taking each piece of armor and learning what it says about God. First, we need to understand why we are putting on this armor that belongs to God? Let's first take a look at 1 Samuel 18:3–4: *"Then Jonathan made a covenant with David because he loved him as himself. Jonathan stripped himself of the robe that was on him and gave it to David, with his armor, including his sword and his bow and his belt."* Jonathan made a covenant with David and then gave him his armor. This act was a sign of trust and submission. This same act is revisited in Romans 13:12, *"The night is almost gone, and the day is near. Therefore let us lay aside the deeds of darkness and put on the armor of light."* Jesus tells us that He is the Light of the world (John 8:12); therefore, the armor of light is His. God gives us His armor because He is in covenant with us. We see this covenant even in the categories of the Bible, the Old and New Testaments, or Old and New covenants. The Old Covenant being one of the Law and the New Covenant is one of grace through Christ. Paul tells us to put on the full armor of God because we are in covenant with Him; we have exchanged clothes. His righteousness we put on, and He takes on our unrighteousness, nailing it to the cross. This covenant is unbreakable and cannot be overturned.

God has given us His armor because of His deep love for us and because He knows we are at war, not against flesh but against evil (Ephesians 6:12). We need to suit up and prepare for the battle ahead. The Commander has given us His armor and sounded the charge, "To battle! To Life!"

THE SHADES OF TRUTH

Stand firm therefore, having girded your loins with truth,
and having put on the breastplate of righteousness.

Ephesians 6:14

On my first day in college art class, my teacher gave me three crayons and a sheet of paper with about fifty squares on it. I was told to color each square a different color using the three crayons. So I would mix colors by pressing harder with one crayon and lighten up on another. The first night wasn't so bad, but each day he would assign the same homework. I was frustrated! Finally, a light bulb started to come on in my head. If you want to paint a masterpiece like the 'Mona Lisa,' you can't just grab a peach crayon and color the face; you have to know how to mix colors. I learned that 'white' mixed with black would give you grey. If you put in one drop of black, you get light grey, but if you pour black in then you get dark grey. There can be millions of shades of grey, but the truth is, white mixed with anything is no longer white.

Jesus came to earth saying that He was the truth (John 14:6). When we put on the belt of truth, we are not putting on a characteristic of Jesus, we are putting on Jesus Himself. It's very easy to mix Jesus with a bit of political correctness and think everything is okay, but the truth is, Jesus mixed with anything is no longer Jesus. If we mix Jesus with a drop of the mindset, *"I'm not as bad as them,"* then we no longer have Jesus because He is the Truth and the truth mixed with anything becomes a partial truth. The color white can only be white if it is not mixed with anything.

We are at war, and our Commander has called us to arms and given us His armor. He didn't give us the ability to tell the truth; He gave us the Truth, Himself! Stop trying to mix Jesus with something that makes Him more palatable. When you do that, your masterpiece stops being a portrait of Christ and looks more and more like a self-portrait.

WATCH OVER YOUR HEART

*Stand firm therefore, having girded your loins with truth,
and having put on the breastplate of righteousness.*

Ephesians 6:14

Imagine that you go on a backpacking trip. It is a hot summer day, and your backpack is heavy. After several hours of strenuous hiking, you reach back to grab your water bottle only to discover that you have left it in the car. Now you are miles from civilization, no one is in sight, and you are extremely thirsty. Finally, as the trail cuts across a cow pasture, you see a hiker walking toward you. You beg for some water. The hiker immediately reaches back and grabs a full bottle of water. He opens the bottle, and you watch as it shines in the sunlight. Then suddenly, the hiker reaches down and picks up a pile of cow manure from the pasture and drops it into the water bottle. He then hands it to you and continues on his way. You feel your throat burning with thirst as you look at the nasty water. What would you do?

Water makes the difference between life and death, but you must consider the source. A well that has been contaminated can bring death faster than no water at all. Proverbs 4:23 says, *"Watch over your heart with all diligence, For from it flow the springs of life."* This means that from our heart flows, not 'a spring,' but 'the spring' of life. Therefore our heart is a spring of Jesus, gushing forth like a geyser. We have been charged to watch over our hearts with all diligence because Satan wants nothing more than to contaminate it like the hiker with the manure. We need the water of life more than oxygen, but if it is contaminated, then it is deadly. This is why God has given us the breastplate of righteousness. It is not our righteousness that protects us but Jesus'. We must daily make sure His breastplate is securely fastened around our heart so that nothing can pollute the spring of living water. We have put on His righteousness, but we must trust Him, not our good works, to deliver us from sin.

VICTORY!

And having shod your feet with the preparation of the gospel of peace.

Ephesians 6:15

The Commander's Army is swift and fierce, but the sooner we understand where their strength comes from, the better off we will be. Their strength is not their numbers, their weapons, or having the high ground, but it comes from the Commander's presence. Isaiah 52:6–12 explains why putting on the boots of peace is so important for us. It's not for the battle but for the victory our Commander has won!

> *Therefore My people shall know My name; therefore in that day I am the one who is speaking, "Here I am." How lovely on the mountains Are the feet of him who brings good news, Who announces peace And brings good news of happiness, Who announces salvation, And says to Zion, "Your God reigns!" Listen! Your watchmen lift up their voices, They shout joyfully together; For they will see with their own eyes When the Lord restores Zion. Break forth, shout joyfully together, You waste places of Jerusalem; For the Lord has comforted His people, He has redeemed Jerusalem. The Lord has bared His holy arm In the sight of all the nations, That all the ends of the earth may see The salvation of our God. Depart, depart, go out from there, Touch nothing unclean; Go out of the midst of her, purify yourselves, You who carry the vessels of the Lord. But you will not go out in haste, Nor will you go as fugitives; For the Lord will go before you, And the God of Israel will be your rear guard.*

I pray that God would help us understand verse six, victory comes in the name of the Commander, victory comes when He says, *"Here I am!"* When the Father steps up to the battle, that is when the captives are set free. That is when we walk out of captivity with our boots on. God goes before us, and God guards behind us! Our job is to bring the good news to the people—we announce peace and we shout, *"God reigns!"*

CLINGING TO FAITH

In addition to all, taking up the shield of faith with which you will be able to extinguish all the flaming arrows of the evil one.

Ephesians 6:16

Where is God when we are surrounded by evil? Satan assaults our souls with accusations of guilt from past mistakes and relentlessly brings down our spirit. There is no rest nor peace when our life falls apart in front of our eyes. Careers, spouses, children, security, sanity, health, and dreams all slip through our fingers like water. We fight for them, but it's like grasping at smoke. We feel totally exposed and vulnerable as Satan shoots his flaming darts at us. If God does not intervene, then we will come to the end we have feared for so long. Satan attacks us mentally, physically, emotionally, spiritually, and socially with things like cancer, unemployment, anxiety, divorce, suicide, and war. It's easy to wonder, "Where is God?" Where is the refuge He promised? We look for the Rider on the white horse, but we do not see Him (Revelation 19:11). Life sometimes hurts, but God never promised us a painless path. In fact, He said we would have trials (John 15:18–21). But God gave us His shield of faith, which extinguishes all the flaming arrows of Satan. The shield of faith is what we cling to when everything else has been stripped from us. It is difficult to fight the battles of a war that has already been won. We ask God why He makes us go through the pain of war if He already has the victory? The shield of faith acknowledges that there will be tears, but it reminds us that one day, God will wipe every tear from our eyes (Revelation 21:4). Faith is what keeps us from running away from the fight. It requires surrendering, submitting, and staying put even when the battle seems hopeless. We do not fight alone, the Commander is with us, but we do fight a very real fight.

Father, please help me to cling to the shield of faith when everything seems to be falling apart. May I trust You even when the war rages.

———————

THE BATTLE WITHIN

And take the helmet of salvation, and the sword of the Spirit,
which is the word of God.

Ephesians 6:17

Of the five senses, all but one takes place solely in our head. Touch can take place anywhere on the body, but it is registered in our brain, which is likewise in our head. So it is easy to see how incredibly important our head is. It is impossible to live without our brain, so whether you are riding a bike, working on a construction site, or waging war on a battlefield, you wear a helmet. Trauma to the head can mean the difference between life and death. Likewise, the trauma inflicted on our minds by Satan can be detrimental to our relationship with God. This is why God gave us His helmet of salvation to protect our mind. The world is a battlefield for Christians, with temptations and persecutions, but the battlefield in our mind can be much worse. The hidden landmines can have lethal consequences. The Bible tells us to take every thought captive because they can be the arrows of the enemy (2 Corinthians 10:5). We are to test every spirit to know whether it is from God or Satan (1 John 4:1). This battle within our minds will overflow into our relationships with others. If we think about the things of this world, then we will act like the world (Proverbs 23:7). We must constantly think on the things that are of God; otherwise, we allow the enemy in, and they will overrun your mind (Philippians 4:8). This may sound excessive but imagine being a soldier in enemy territory. Behind any tree there could be a sniper, and with each step, you risk stepping on a mine. At that moment, would you be willing to divide your thoughts between the dangers at hand and the trivial tasks of everyday life back home? Most certainly not! You would give the danger at hand undivided attention. It's the same way in our daily spiritual battle. We can't think about the things of God and the things of the world because that is where spiritual trauma comes from. God has given us the helmet of salvation to protect our minds.

THE WEAPONS OF OUR WARFARE

And take the helmet of salvation, and the sword of the Spirit,
which is the word of God.

Ephesians 6:17

I remember learning about the Armor of God as a kid and thinking how cool it was to be a knight for God! But whenever the teacher came to the sword of the Spirit, I always felt a little let down because then she would hold up her Bible and say, "The Word of God is the sword of the Spirit." I didn't want a Bible; I wanted a sharp samurai sword or a pirate's cutlass. Running around in the backyard with my Bible was boring. But as I got older, I realized that life was far from playtime in my backyard. I wanted a sword that was actually going to make a difference in the battles I was fighting. This was when I discovered that the Bible was exactly the weapon I wanted. Second Corinthians 10:4 says, *"for the weapons of our warfare are not of the flesh, but divinely powerful for the destruction of fortresses."* Hebrews 4:12 says, *"For the word of God is living and active and sharper than any two-edged sword, and piercing as far as the division of soul and spirit, of both joints and marrow, and able to judge the thoughts and intentions of the heart."* God's word is so powerful that He can fling galaxies across the universe with one word and it is so sharp that He can do major surgery on the cancerous sin within my heart. It was the word of God that Jesus used in His battle against Satan's temptations (Matthew 4:1–11). He knew how to effectively wield His sword. But let's not get too hasty, just as you would never hand a razor-sharp knife to a two-year-old, allowing a baby Christian the freedom to run around waving the sword of the Spirit is very dangerous, too. We can bend the word of God and make it say anything we want, but this will result in hurting those around us and ourselves. Daily we are to practice using the sword of the Spirit with the Spirit as our trainer. This will ensure that we know how to effectively wield the weapons of our warfare!

IS HE YOUR COMMANDER?

O LORD, how my adversaries have increased! Many are rising up against me.
Many are saying of my soul, "There is no deliverance for him in God." Selah.

Psalm 3:1–2

King David would rise from the fields as a shepherd and fall before King Saul. He would rise before the prophet Samuel and fall before his son Absalom. David's life was not an easy ride, but the path laid before him was one planned by God. David's own son would even conspire against him. David would receive a message saying, *"The hearts of the men of Israel are with Absalom"* (2 Samuel 15:13). These were the people who celebrated every time God gave them victory through David's military leadership, yet now they had turned against him, causing David and his family to flee. They would leave their home and pass over the brook Kidron, heading to the wilderness. It was during this time that David would pour out his heart before the Lord saying, *"O LORD, how my adversaries have increased! Many are rising up against me. Many are saying of my soul, "There is no deliverance for him in God." Selah"* (Psalm 3:1–2). David was not just walking through a physical wilderness but also a spiritual wilderness. He was trying to figure out what the Commander of Heaven's army was doing. David's enemies had increased to the point that even his own son was turning the hearts of Israel against him. From a military perspective, David was outnumbered and overpowered. He asked the question, will God still deliver me? The Commander's army is swift and fierce but would He give the signal to move forward or to stay put?

Some days we are on top of the world, and other days the world is on top of us. Our adversaries increase, and we hear the voices of the world saying, "There is no deliverance for them in God." It's in these moments we must ask ourselves, will we follow God, even unto death? He cannot be our Commander unless we can honestly answer that question, "Yes!"

WILDERNESS THANKSGIVING

But You, O LORD, are a shield about me, My glory, and the One who lifts my head.

Psalm 3:3

We continue to follow David as He flees into the wilderness from his son Absalom. David poured his heart out to God, wondering if He would save him, but now we see that David's trust in the Lord is leading the way. David declares that the Commander is a shield surrounding Him and that in the end, the Lord would victoriously lift up his head.

Sometimes even when we are fleeing into the wilderness, we have the assurance that God is still on our side. We can trust in His shield even when there seems to be no hope. The wilderness can be a tricky place. If we look at how low we have fallen, then the wilderness is a demoralizing wasteland, but if we look at how wonderful God is to have created a wilderness for us to retreat to, then we can respond with thanksgiving. Thanksgiving is the difference between being crushed and rising above. David also wrote, *"The LORD is my strength and my shield; My heart trusts in Him, and I am helped; Therefore my heart exults, And with my song I shall thank Him"* (Psalm 28:7). His mantra was, "God is my shield! I trust in Him! I thank Him in song!" Why would anyone thank God for the wilderness seasons of life? Maybe because the wilderness is where God restores the soul, refreshes the spirit and revives the body! While in the wilderness, a man named Shobi brought *"beds, basins, pottery, wheat, barley, flour, parched grain, beans, lentils, parched seeds, honey, curds, sheep, and cheese of the herd, for David and for the people who were with him, to eat; for they said, "The people are hungry and weary and thirsty in the wilderness"* (2 Samuel 17:27–29). Thank God for the wilderness because if we trust Him, it is where we find restoration! When was the last time you were faced with the decision to cry out in fear or to sing a song of thanksgiving?

TOTAL TRUST

I was crying to the LORD with my voice, And He answered me from His holy mountain. Selah. I lay down and slept; I awoke, for the LORD sustains me. I will not be afraid of ten thousands of people Who have set themselves against me round about.

Psalm 3:4-6

Today we finish our journey with David as he runs from Absalom. David writes in Psalm 3:5 that he laid down and slept, for the Lord sustained him. Could you even imagine running for your life and being only one step in front of your enemy, yet you are able to lay down and fall asleep? How was David able to sleep? I believe the answer is found in 2 Samuel 15:26: *"But if He [God] should say thus, 'I have no delight in you,' behold, here I am, let Him do to me as seems good to Him."* This is complete and total surrender. David was running from a human foe, not God. He was not afraid to trust God even though he understood God's desire for him might not be to keep him alive. Someone who fears for their life does not attack a bear or a lion, they do not run out to meet a giant, one on one, and they do not sleep when their enemy is right behind them! But David had completely put his life in the hands of the Commander, and come life or death, David was surrendered to Him. What person, storm, or emotion cripples you? What blocks you and turns you away from what God has called you to do? What would you have to lay down to completely trust God, even to death?

A commander has to make the tough decision to send their soldiers into battle knowing they won't all come home alive. The commander has to believe in the battle plan so implicitly that they will gamble the lives of those who follow their orders on it. God is our Commander, and His battle plan is sure. We can see it in Scripture; He is victorious. But while we are not guaranteed to make it through this battle, for those who trust the Commander completely, we are promised to survive the war!

REMEMBER!

They did not remember His power,
The day when He redeemed them from the adversary.

Psalm 78:42

How much of your early life do you remember? Days, weeks, and years pass by but do we remember the moments that brought change to our lives? How can we teach our children about the goodness of God if we do not remember the times God moved? This is why God told the children of Israel to build altars because He knew they would forget. We see this in Joshua 4:21–24:

> *He said to the sons of Israel, "When your children ask their fathers in time to come, saying, 'What are these stones?' Then you shall inform your children, saying, 'Israel crossed this Jordan on dry ground.' "For the LORD your God dried up the waters of the Jordan before you until you had crossed, just as the LORD your God had done to the Red Sea, which He dried up before us until we had crossed; that all the peoples of the earth may know that the hand of the LORD is mighty, so that you may fear the LORD your God forever.*

We wonder how anyone could ever forget what it was like to walk through the river on dry ground. But the truth is, all of us have had those Jordan River movements, and we forget them all too easily. Doubt is such a corrosive mindset. It can take a memory and quickly deteriorate it to a fairytale. Both those who walked across the Red Sea and those who walked across the Jordan River fell prey to the powers of doubt and forgot the power of God. This is why building an altar is so vital, not just for yourself but for your children's sake. They need to know that pile of rocks came from the bottom of the Jordan River because if they do not learn what God did, then how will they ever trust Him when they are standing on its banks. The Commander has the power to part the waters. He has done it time and time again. How costly doubt can be; it can steal the praises of God from an entire generation. Trusting God can be difficult. Forgetting His power can be easy. We must remember!

———————

IT'S THE GOSPEL

*So he answered, "Do not fear, for those who are with us are more than those who
are with them." Then Elisha prayed and said, "O LORD, I pray, open his eyes that he
may see." And the LORD opened the servant's eyes and he saw; and behold,
the mountain was full of horses and chariots of fire all around Elisha.*

2 Kings 6:16–17

What an incredible story this is! Elisha is a wanted man because God keeps
using him to thwart the plans of the king of Aram. So the king sent his army and
surrounded the city that Elisha and his servant were in. In the morning when
the servant saw that they were surrounded, he became scared for his life and
ran to Elisha. Elisha simply prayed that God would open his servant's eyes. All
of a sudden, the servant was able to see; the army of Heaven was surrounding
Elisha in greater force. God is greater than the armies of this world! But what is
interesting is that even though God's army had greater strength and numbers,
the Commander did not use his army to defeat His foe. Instead, Elisha prayed
that the Arameans would be struck blind, and then he led them to Samaria, right
to the king of Israel. When God opened their eyes, they knew that they had been
defeated. God would not allow Israel to harm the army of Aram, but rather He
had them throw a feast for them and send them on their way.

What a seemingly backward story. God's heavenly army had the upper
hand, yet the Commander never said charge. Israel's army was in position for a
surprise attack, but the Commander never said attack. Instead, the command
that came down from the top was *"Set bread and water before them, that they
may eat and drink and go to their master"* (2 Kings 6:22). There are many times
we cry out for God to unleash His heavenly host on the forces that oppose us
but instead, God doesn't show vengeance; He shows mercy and grace. It's the
Gospel! Praise God for the Commander's wisdom!

TURN BACK

Tell the sons of Israel to turn back and camp before Pi-hahiroth, between Migdol and the sea; you shall camp in front of Baal-zephon, opposite it, by the sea.

Exodus 14:2

If there are ever words that we do not want to hear from the Commander, they are *"turn back."* These two words are so disheartening because they can only mean one thing, you went too far now you are going back toward where you came from. Moses led the children of Israel out of Egypt, the place where they had experienced bondage, crushing workloads, fear, and death. Finally, they were free! God had worked wonders and gloriously freed them without them even lifting a finger in battle. The Egyptians gave them gold and valuables as they walked out of their slavery. They sang, they laughed, they worshipped, and they marveled, then God said, *"turn back."* Why? What happened? Why could God possibly want them to go back toward their bondage?

From our perspective, we cannot fully grasp all that God has in mind but how quickly we are to tell God what needs to take place. For us, *"turn back"* is synonymous with "set back," and when we are finally experiencing freedom from the trials we have been enslaved to, the last thing we want is a set back. Our Commander never gives the signal for retreat, but He does sometimes tell us to *"Turn back"* because His plan is far greater than we can know. We may cringe when God says, *"turn back,"* but had the Israelites not turned back, then Pharaoh never would have pursued them into the Red Sea (Exodus 14:5). Victory was won not because they walked out of Egypt but because they *"turned back."*

Father, we want to walk in Your freedom and Your favor, but it is so hard when we hear things like "Turn back." Please help us to trust You more than our own understanding. Even if You call us to "Turn back" all the way to our Egypt, may we obey Your command with gladness.

———

STAND BY AND SEE

But Moses said to the people, "Do not fear! Stand by and see the salvation of the LORD which He will accomplish for you today; for the Egyptians whom you have seen today, you will never see them again forever."

Exodus 14:13

Yesterday we learned that the Commander gave the orders for Moses and the children of Israel to *"turn back."* Today we are going to look at His next order for them, and it is equally challenging. In verse thirteen, God commands the unarmed, defenseless men, women, and children to *"Do not fear!"* What might they fear? The very armed, very numerous, and very zealous Egyptians that are on their way to recapture the Israelites! All through Scripture, God has a way of telling people not to fear when they are on the cusp of disaster. When a storm is threatening to capsize your boat, and you are a long way from land, that is the perfect time to fear! Fear is the chemical and emotional response God designed your body to produce in a threatening situation; how are you not to fear?

The answer is found in the Commander's next order, "Stand by and see." Fear is the chemical and emotional response to a threat, but God is saying to the Israelites, *"There is no threat. Stand by and see what I'm about to do."* When we come to the point of understanding that God is all powerful, then things change for us. Those things that threaten our lives no longer produce fear in us. The Egyptians in our lives are no more problematic than a butterfly when we stand by and see that God can take those Egyptians and make them disappear. The battle that rages is not our battle; the Commander is fighting for us! *"Do not fear,"* just *"Stand by and see."* God has the power to make fire not burn, lions not kill, giants fall down, storms not capsize, metal float, and the dead to rise. Will God utilize His power against our Egyptians? That is up to the Commander; we must surrender to His battle plan. *"Do not fear!"* *"Stand by and see!"* There is salvation from your Egyptians, but it comes at the hand of the Commander.

GOD IS ENOUGH

The LORD will fight for you while you keep silent.

Exodus 14:14

The commands of God to Moses in Exodus 14 were, *"Turn back," "Do not fear,"* and *"Stand by."* Today we will see another command from our Commanding Officer. *"Keep silent."* It seems God thrives on giving commands that are diabolically contrary to how we are wired. And if the truth be told, God does thrive on that! Why? Because we live in a world that is diabolically opposed to how He wired us. God's commands are not to make us squirm but to put us at peace. You may be thinking, how can commands like *"Turn back"* or *"Keep silent"* bring peace? They contain peace because in the world God created, apart from sin, we would understand that God is enough. What could any opposing force do to us if God is enough? Nothing! But we live in a fallen world that tries to remind us that God is not enough, that we must pull ourselves up and look out for ourselves. When we begin to believe the world, we say things like, "I could never go back to that place!" "I can't wait any longer!" "I'm scared to death!" or "I will not be silent anymore!" Where is God in these comments? We have made him such a weak and insignificant god that he cannot be seen over the waves nor heard over the wind. But we have a Commander Who is not weak nor insignificant and greater still, He fights for us! When we see God for Who He really is, then His commands to turn around, don't worry, stand right here, just rest in silence and watch Me work, actually seem beautiful! This is the God Who is, not the God we wish for. God fights for us, but we must surrender to His Lordship so that we can *"Turn back," "Not fear," "Stand by,"* and *"Keep silent."* His path is the only path to peace, no matter what the world tells us.

Holy Father, we bow before You as a servant bows before their master. Command us and strengthen us to obey. We are not enough, but You, O Lord, are!

———————

GO FORWARD!

Then the LORD said to Moses, "Why are you crying out to Me?
Tell the sons of Israel to go forward."

Exodus 14:15

Today, we will wrap up our series on the commands of God to Moses in Exodus 14. And if the previous commands were tough to swallow, then today's could be all the more. Often we say things like, *"God, I'm tired of waiting." "I'm ready, Lord, put me in."* But then when He says, *"Okay, go,"* we freak out saying, *"I can't do that!"* We don't want inactivity, but we also don't really want to take a step of faith. God told Moses to *"Go forward."* Why is this so hard? Think about it, Moses and the Israelites are bookended by death. One side holds Pharaoh and his army; the other side holds the Red Sea. Moses cries out to God for help, and God basically says, *"If you stay here, you will be overtaken; go forward."* Walking through the Red Sea is so ludicrous that we would never even think that it was an option, so Moses keeps praying. God tells him to *"turn back,"* then Moses has everyone about-face. God tells Moses, *"do not fear,"* so Moses leans into the Commander. God tells Moses to *"stand by,"* So Moses has everyone hold their position. God tells Moses to *"keep silent,"* so Moses shushes everyone. Then Moses waits for the next command, but nothing comes. Everyone looks at each other and then shrugs their shoulders. They wait a little longer, then finally God speaks and says, *"What are you waiting for? Get going through the sea."* The Commander's army is swift and fierce because they know what it means to *"go forward"* into the unknown, into the impossible, into the power of the Commander.

What about you? Do you trust your Commander enough to *"turn back," "do not fear," "stand by," "keep silent,"* and *"go forward"*? This kind of trust is a highly specialized faith, a faith that the average man does not have, a trust that will *"go forward"* into anything. The Bible calls this the *"faith of a child"* (Psalm 116:6). We must trust our Commander as children trust their fathers.

———

EVIL ON EITHER SIDE

The LORD is good, A stronghold in the day of trouble,
And He knows those who take refuge in Him.

Nahum 1:7

The Lord is a stronghold in the day of trouble; what exactly does this mean? I believe God defines it in a word picture found in Nahum 1:6–8. Verse seven says, *"The LORD is good, A stronghold in the day of trouble, And He knows those who take refuge in Him."* Nahum tells us of the protection given by the Lord for those who take refuge in Him. Understand that it does not say that God will provide a stronghold. On the contrary, this verse says that God is the stronghold for those who take refuge in Him. The refuge is found only in Christ.

Now, we look at verse six: *"Who can stand before His indignation? Who can endure the burning of His anger? His wrath is poured out like fire And the rocks are broken up by Him."* Again we see in verse eight, *"But with an overflowing flood He will make a complete end of its site, And will pursue His enemies into darkness."* So basically, what we see in this passage is a "Refuge Sandwich." There is refuge in God, our stronghold, but before us and behind us, there is anger, wrath, overwhelming floods, and darkness. For those who seek refuge in God, they will be surrounded by the goodness of God even though they are engulfed in a war of wrath. Anger before me, darkness behind, but I will rest in peace because the Lord has encircled me with His strong presence. Yes, the presence of our Commander is sure! He keeps us when everything else falls away.

Father, this world is such a backward place. Everything begs us to come find life in it. Everything promises life, protection, and security, but in the end, it is hollow, powerless, and a trap. But You, o Lord, are a fortress that seals us in, behind and before. Today, may we find refuge in You, not in the things of this world which will consume us. May we be consumed in You. You are good! May we trust You as You fight the evil outside the gates.

HE RODE INTO BATTLE

Therefore, since the children share in flesh and blood, He Himself likewise also partook of the same, that through death He might render powerless him who had the power of death, that is, the devil, and might free those who through fear of death were subject to slavery all their lives.

Hebrews 2:14–15

Have you ever questioned God's methods? You have no choice but to go through your days, struggling and broken, longing for a future that you have no guarantee of. All the while, God sits on a throne in Heaven, orchestrating the next set of trials that are supposed to develop you into a vessel of honor. When we see life through this bitter lens, it is easy to question what 'love' really is. But this is a skewed view of life and love. The writer of Hebrews tells us that we are flesh and blood and therefore subject to pain, sickness, and even death. But God showed us His great love by becoming flesh and blood also. He subjected Himself to the same pain, sickness, and even death that we experience. Our Commander is not One Who sits behind the safe line and calls in orders while the ground troops are being picked off one by one. Our Commander crossed the safe line and stepped into battle. He went straight for the enemy and overthrew him, giving us freedom!

On those days when we bitterly question God's love, we need to take a moment to remember that our King didn't just come and fight a good fight and go back home. He came and won victory for us, but that victory came through His death. Our King does not sit on a throne with clean hands. His nail-pierced hands have blood under the fingernails, His blood, the blood that freed us from death and the grave. We have freedom because our Commander rode into battle and laid down His life so we could pick it up! Now Satan is rendered powerless! So on those days when the Devil seems so powerful, stop to remember the truth, Greater is He Who is in us than he that is in the world (1 John 4:4).

———————

NOTHING CAN SEPARATE US

But in all these things we overwhelmingly conquer through Him who loved us.

Romans 8:37

How real is the fight? Is our battle like a game that is played and then walked away from? No, the battle we fight every day is very real, the blood we bleed is reality, and the people who lose their lives in this war do not come back. The fight is real! *"Who will separate us from the love of Christ? Will tribulation, or distress, or persecution, or famine, or nakedness, or peril, or sword"* (Romans 8:35). The Church can sometimes be guilty of handing out weapons that are empty of ammunition. We go to services and hear messages about fighting the enemy and using the sword of the Spirit, then we walk out the doors and are attacked by Satan, only to find we do not know what Scriptures to use. Satan's desire is to bring us to the point of doubting God's love. He does this by utilizing tribulation, distress, persecution, famine, nakedness, peril, and sword. He comes at us with a savage fierceness, and if our spiritual weapons are not loaded, then we are an easy target. Satan wreaks havoc within our churches, and Christians run around in circles complaining, backbiting, and doubting the love of God. The world looks at the church and hears the complaining and backbiting and decides they don't want anything to do with those hypocrites. We have allowed Satan to lure us with finite life to the point we walk away from true eternal life (John 17:3). It's time to stop allowing Satan and his minions to run over the children of God! *"But in all these things we overwhelmingly conquer through Him who loved us"* (Romans 8:37). Overwhelmingly conquer means to gain a surpassing victory. *"In all these things"*—tribulation, distress, persecution, famine, nakedness, peril, and sword—we have gained surpassing victory through Christ! The fight is real, it's difficult, and at times it's scary, but we have victory through Christ; nothing can separate us from that!

NO OTHER NAME

For the LORD your God is the one who goes with you,
to fight for you against your enemies, to save you.

Deuteronomy 20:4

"The LORD your God" is many things in your life. He is Master, Owner, Protector, Savior, Healer, Sustainer, Creator, and so much more. In Deuteronomy 20:4, we see how the Lord our God is specifically three things, and thereby He is enough.

First, Moses tells us that He is the One Who goes with us. The name of God that represents this is Immanuel. *"Therefore the Lord Himself will give you a sign: Behold, a virgin will be with child and bear a son, and she will call His name Immanuel"* (Isaiah 7:14). Immanuel means *"God with us"* therefore, we are never alone! The Lord your God is Immanuel.

Second, this verse tells us that our Commander fights for us against our enemies. The name of God that points to this is Jehovah-Nissi. *"And Moses built an altar, and called the name of it Jehovah Nissi"* (Exodus 17:15). Jehovah Nissi means, "The Lord our banner." This is the name we raise when we are in battle which reminds us that God fights for us, that He is in control, and that He has already won the victory.

Finally, we see that the Lord our God saves us. *"She will bear a Son; and you shall call His name Jesus, for He will save His people from their sins"* (Matthew 1:21) The name Jesus means, "The Lord is Salvation." We call on this precious name because we cannot be saved by any other (Acts 4:12).

The Commander's army is swift and fierce because they know Who their leader is. He is Immanuel, He is Jehovah-Nissi, and He is Jesus! What could possibly stand in our way as we follow our Lord Who is with us, Who is our banner of victory, and Who is our salvation! Walk with your head held high, the Lord your God is righteously victorious!

SLAVES AGAIN

It was for freedom that Christ set us free; therefore keep standing firm and do not be subject again to a yoke of slavery.

Galatians 5:1

Imagine being arrested during World War II and thrown into a concentration camp. Day after day, you live in fear of abuse and death. You smell the stench of the incinerators, and every day you see people that you will not see again. Your body has been bent and made haggard from the work you are forced to do. Hope seems to have drained from your life like water running between your fingers. Then one day, you receive papers that say you have been set free! You walk to the gate and watch it open. In disbelief, you take that first step into freedom; no longer are you captive, but you are free! Once outside the fence, you walk ten feet to the shade of a tree where you sit down. The shade feels nice, and there is plenty of wood from the trees, so you decide to build a house right there. Every morning you wake up free, but you still smell the incinerators and hear the cries of the captives.

How sad it would be for someone to actually build their house ten feet outside the walls of the prison they once were bound in. But that is exactly what we do spiritually. We live our lives bound to sin until Jesus comes and sets us free by grace. Yet often, we never leave the prison of sin; we simply build our house right there in its midst. The sin that once enslaved us slowly creeps back into our lives, and we volunteer to be enslaved again.

Jesus came to set us free; the papers have been signed, our debt paid in full! The gate has been opened, and we are now free to walk out of prison and into a new life. Do not stop ten feet outside the gate but let us continue to run straight, never looking back. The Commander didn't set us free so that we could take up the yoke of slavery again. No, it was for freedom that He set us free.

A+B=C

Submit therefore to God. Resist the devil and he will flee from you.

James 4:7

The Commander's army is swift and fierce. If there was ever a verse that illustrated this it would be James 4:7. Another way of saying this is, "Fall in line as a soldier under the authority of God's command, take your stand against Satan and seeing that he will not be able to defeat you, he will run away." If this is as easy as A+B=C, why don't more Christians live in victory? I believe it is as simple as A+B=C because the Bible promises it, but maybe we misunderstand the equation.

A=submitting to God: This was often used as a military term meaning, "To arrange troops under the command of a leader." Are you truly under His command? Is there something He could ask for that you would hesitate to carry out? Maybe you are holding on to something or someone, refusing to hand them over to God. Without true submission to God, there can be no true retreat of the enemy.

B=resist the devil: This means *to* set one's self against. Oftentimes when we are around other Christians, we talk about sins and vices with such disdain, as if sin was the nastiest thing, but when we are alone, we take out our box of vices and play with them. To truly resist the devil, we must take our stand against his schemes. Not just in word around others but in action, even when we are alone.

C=the enemy retreats as one who sees they cannot overcome. Now, we would like to think the devil runs away, never to be seen nor heard of again, but as in many battles, retreat means to step back and reorganize for a counter-offensive. We must always be on the alert for the devil's attacks.

Constantly we submit to God and resist the devil. Victory is God's, not ours, but if we let our guard down, the enemy will exploit it with savage cruelty.

SHEDDING BLOOD

You have not yet resisted to the point of shedding blood in your striving against sin.

Hebrew 12:4

Our enemy is not like a cartoon antagonist, who has an intimidating build and hollers a lot yet has too much compassion and restraint to actually harm the main character. On the contrary, Satan, our enemy, is void of compassion and is full of deception. Nothing you can imagine would be beneath him. Our enemy is in no hurry; he is willing to lie in wait until we have a weak moment. The snares of Satan are so well hidden that they may lay directly under the noses of Christians for generations, and no one ever sees them. They can even be hidden in our very homes, and we have no idea. In fact, Satan is so crafty that someone could point out his snares in our home, and we will fight to the death for our right to keep them. Television streams into our houses, murder, adultery, and dissatisfaction. The internet puts pornography and lust within our children's bedrooms. And our video games give us guilt-free arenas to carry out sin because it is virtual. But if someone were to suggest to us that television, internet, and video games were gateways for the enemy to ensnare us, we would argue that they are benign. We would even point to the good that these gateways bring. Our enemy is crafty; therefore, Jesus tells us that it would be better to pluck out our eyes or cut off our hands in order to escape these snares (Matthew 18:8–9). This sounds inhuman and barbaric. How could a loving God ask us to take such grotesque actions? It is because of His love for us that He asks us to take these measures. He would rather spend eternity with us lacking a hand than for us to burn in hell for eternity yet having had a lifetime with two hands. The writer of Hebrews is correct in saying we have not resisted our sins to the point of shedding blood. Freeing ourselves from the snares of Satan is going to draw blood, and it very well may mangle us, but we serve a Commander Who can heal and restore.

THE SEWAGE AMONG US

Since the LORD your God walks in the midst of your camp to deliver you and to defeat your enemies before you, therefore your camp must be holy; and He must not see anything indecent among you or He will turn away from you.

Deuteronomy 23:14

This is a powerful verse of Scripture, but it is found in a most unique passage. If you read verses twelve and thirteen, then you actually see that God is giving the children of Israel a law about going to the bathroom. *"You shall also have a place outside the camp and go out there, and you shall have a spade among your tools, and it shall be when you sit down outside, you shall dig with it and shall turn to cover up your excrement* (Deuteronomy 23:12–13). You might wonder why an Almighty God is concerned about the bathroom habits of a nation, but we learn that God was very interested in all the details that kept His children safe. In modern times we understand the dangers of leaving sewage around where we walk and eat. God was laying the groundwork of health that would protect a nation from disease and death. But God was also laying the foundation that would protect against an even greater disease, the disease of sin. In verse fourteen, God shows that deliverance from your enemies was directly related to His presence, and His presence was contingent on the presence of anything indecent. If the Children of God wanted health or protection, then they had to rid themselves of indecent things.

Today this still applies; God's presence is still contingent on the presence of anything indecent in our lives. We cannot expect to abide in His presence if we are allowing the sewage of sin to run rampant within our homes and lives. This is not a way to earn salvation but to walk in holiness. So often we live the sinful way we want, then we turn to God and say, where are You? The Commander fights for us, but we must also rid ourselves of the indecent things around us.

HELD DEEP WITHIN THE ROCK

The steadfast of mind You will keep in perfect peace, Because he trusts in You. Trust in the LORD forever, For in God the LORD, we have an everlasting Rock.

Isaiah 26:3–4

When you are at the top of a mountain, you find that the vegetation has changed compared to that at the bottom of the mountain. At the bottom, you see large trees with broad leaves, but at the top there are mostly bushes and shrubs. At the bottom of the mountain, there is plenty of soil for the trees to root in, but at the top the soil is much more shallow because of the large rock bed. Yet, even at the top of a mountain, you can find a few weathered trees, they are bent and blown, but they still bear leaves, their roots digging deep into the rock of the mountain.

Isaiah tells us that a steadfast mind is kept in perfect peace because it trusts in God. The Hebrew word for mind is *yetser* which means, "form, such as pottery, graven images or man having been formed of the dust of the ground." We are that form which was made by the hand of our Creator, and when we are *"steadfast"* meaning to "rest upon or to lean against," then we are kept at perfect peace; we are like the tree on the mountain. We are not kept from the storms of life; in fact, the tree on the mountain has seen worse storms than the trees in the valley, but it continues to bear its fruit because its roots are held within the rock. Does this mean it can't fall? Of course the tree can fall, mountain tops are littered with fallen trees, but the tree that sinks its roots into the rock depends on the rock to keep it standing. Likewise, we do not have the ability to keep standing through the storms of life, they are too strong and too violent, but when we lean on or rest upon the *"everlasting Rock"* then we are kept at perfect peace, bearing fruit, because we are trusting God to keep us.

DANCING ON THE RUINS

For He has brought low those who dwell on high, the unassailable city; He lays it low, He lays it low to the ground, He casts it to the dust. "The foot will trample it The feet of the afflicted, the steps of the helpless.

Isaiah 26:5–6

Yesterday we saw where Isaiah wrote that we were to trust in the Lord forever because He is our everlasting Rock (Isaiah 26:4). Today we take another step in that passage and see why it is that we can trust our Commander. Isaiah tells us that there is a city that is set against us, that has the high ground. In fact, Isaiah says that it is *"unassailable."* What hope do we have? Impending doom looms over us, and we are overwhelmed with dread. Anxiety engulfs us, despair drains us, and doubt cripples us. What are we to do with unassailable cities? What do we do when our best efforts are not good enough, and our defenses are laid bare?

Satan has a way of exploiting the cracks in the wall around our heart, and it seems that even our best efforts are steamrolled by temptation, and our cries for help are silenced by the static of the world. But Isaiah looks at the unassailable city and remembers the Commander, the everlasting Rock. The Commander's army is swift and fierce, and it is He Who brings the unassailable city down. Yes, *"He lays it low, He lays it low to the ground, He casts it to the dust."* We do not have the strength to fight every battle, and there are days when more is heaped on us than we can handle, but it is the Lord Who destroys the unassailable city in our lives. Maybe not in our time nor in the way we would do it, but that is why our job is to trust in the Lord forever (Isaiah 26:4). The Commander fights on our behalf and brings victory, then we who are the afflicted and the helpless will trample on the dust of the unassailable city. We will dance on the ruins of Satan's stronghold! Take hope! Though the battle seems lost today, we have a Commander Who is working out His plan, and He will win!

EARTHLY ROCKS VERSUS HEAVENLY ROCKS

And they remembered that God was their rock,
And the Most High God their Redeemer.

Psalm 78:35

In Psalm 78, Asaph looked back at the Israelites as they journeyed out of Egypt, and he noted their unfaithfulness. *"He [God] split the rocks in the wilderness And gave them abundant drink like the ocean depths. He brought forth streams also from the rock And caused waters to run down like rivers. Yet they still continued to sin against Him, To rebel against the Most High in the desert"* (Psalm 78:15–17). The Commander freed the Israelites from centuries of bondage in Egypt; then He led them to an earthly rock where they complained about God's provision, so God split the rock and made water flow. This earthly rock met their needs, but they were not satisfied; they still continued to sin and rebel. God used an earthly rock to meet their complaints, but I ask you, what if they had never complained? Would there have been a need for that earthly rock?

Later in the psalm, Asaph tells us, *"And they remembered that God was their rock, And the Most High God their Redeemer"* (Psalm 78:35). The people of Israel would continue to rebel and complain, so God got their attention. Then they remembered that earthly rocks can only meet earthly needs, but our Commander is a Heavenly Rock, and He is the One Who redeems. Again I ask you, would there be a need for an earthly rock if we looked to our Heavenly Rock to meet our needs?

Today, are you looking for your battles to be won by earthly rocks? These rocks can only meet our needs if the Heavenly Rock empowers them. Stop putting your hopes in an earthly rock, turn your eyes to the Heavenly Rock; He is the One Who will redeem you! *"I will lift up my eyes to the mountains [earthly rock]; From where shall my help come? My help comes from the LORD [Heavenly Rock], Who made heaven and earth"* (Psalm 121:1–2).

———

JUNE

The Spirit's Presence Is Near and Active

THE SPIRIT WAS GIVEN

I will ask the Father, and He will give you another Helper, that He may be with you forever; that is the Spirit of truth, whom the world cannot receive, because it does not see Him or know Him, but you know Him because He abides with you and will be in you.

John 14:16–17

Who is this Spirit of truth? The Father led the children of Israel in the wilderness during the Old Testament. In the Gospels, the Son of God ministered in Israel, healing the sick and teaching about the love of God. Now we live in what scholars call the "Church Age," and we do not have a pillar of cloud by day to follow, nor do we have the Son of God walking around in the streets. What are we to do? Jesus taught the disciples that He was going to ask the Father to send another Helper, Someone Who would come to be with us always and to guide us. This Helper is the Holy Spirit, the very One Who has come from the Father, is of the Father, and is the Father is in us. He is near, and He is active. What does this mean? God is and has always been and will always be *Emanuel.* God is with us, dwelling and Abiding with us. He is not going to leave His children orphaned (John 14:18). The invisible Spirit of God is with us to this day, and He helps us. But this is complex to the world because they could see the pillar of cloud in the Old Testament, and they could see Jesus raising the dead, but today they cannot see the Spirit of truth. Today, we are to be the hands and feet of Jesus for the world to see. They are to see in us the God of the universe. This is not done through our power but through the power of the Spirit. This is much like a light bulb. In and of itself, a light bulb is nothing more than glass and wires, but when power is run to it, it brings light to everything around it. We are nothing more than the dust of the earth, but when the Spirit is inside of us, we become a light to the world! God's presence is still on the earth, and He is seen through us as we reflect Him. Apart from Him, we are lost.

———

THE SONG OF THE SPIRIT

But you will receive power when the Holy Spirit has come upon you;
and you shall be My witnesses both in Jerusalem, and in all Judea and Samaria,
and even to the remotest part of the earth.

Acts 1:8

This is a verse that most of us have heard many times before, but I want to look at it from a different perspective. Usually, we focus on the Holy Spirit, and rightly so. That is where we will end today but first, let's look at the word *"My."*

Jesus is speaking in Acts 1:8; therefore, the words *"My witnesses"* belong to Him. We will be Jesus' witnesses; what does that mean? In the Bible we see a system used by the Trinity: the Father stands glorified and Sovereign over all, the Son came to earth to bear witness to the Father, and then the Holy Spirit came to bear witness to the Son. But note that this verse tells us that we will be Jesus' witnesses when and only when the Holy Spirit has come on us. We are the vessel that the Holy Spirit uses to point to the Son Who points to the Father. This is enormous! Each person of the Trinity points to another person of the Trinity, but the Holy Spirit uses us as a spotlight pointed directly on Jesus so all can see Him. He comes upon us and fills us with power so that we can be that witness for Jesus. What do we need the power for? Is it so hard to tell others Who Jesus is? Most certainly yes! How can we put an infinite God into finite words? We would fall so miserably short that the world would look on Him as a mere fairytale at best. We need the power of the Holy Spirit to give us the words so we can sing the Spirit's song. It is a song that awakens a dead heart. What good is it to tell deaf ears of a loving Savior? The power that accompanies the Spirit is just right to raise the dead and heal deaf ears. May the Spirit sing through us a song of redemption, a song of life, and a song of power.

Holy Spirit, may we be available for Your using today so others may know the Son and the Son may know them.

———

THE SPIRIT'S PRESENCE

For the kingdom of God is not eating and drinking,
but righteousness and peace and joy in the Holy Spirit.

Romans 14:17

Paul writes in his letter to the Romans about the freedom we have in Christ, but also the surrendering of our desires so others would not stumble over our freedom. He mainly is dealing with foods and drink, which is why he starts verse seventeen with *"for the kingdom of God is not eating or drinking."* In the Law of Moses, we see that being right before God deals with many things, including which animals we eat and what we are allowed to eat. But now that the Law has been fulfilled in Christ Jesus, we have freedom because the kingdom of God does not lie in the Law but in the grace of God. Simply stated, the Father came making a way through the Law, Jesus came making a way through the cross, and the Holy Spirit came teaching us to walk in the freedom of the kingdom of God.

In verse seventeen, Paul tells us three things that the kingdom of God is: righteousness, peace, and joy in the Holy Spirit. Over the next three days, we will look at what it means to walk in these, but today we want to look at the source of this freedom, the Holy Spirit. The Spirit's presence is near and active, and that should be life-changing to us. He is God just as much as the Father and the Son because they are one. The Spirit has always been and can even be seen moving over the surface of the water during creation (Genesis 1:2). It was during Pentecost that the Spirit was given to those who believe in Jesus as Savior (Acts 2:1–13). Now we are never alone, and the power of the Spirit resides in us. The Spirit comforts us, helps us, teaches us, and bears witness to our spirit that we are saved. The kingdom of God is not eating and drinking, but it is in the Holy Spirit. The kingdom of God dwells in us, and that is what allows us to walk in the spirit. This should change our lives if indeed the Spirit is in us.

———————

RIGHTEOUSNESS IN THE HOLY SPIRIT

For the kingdom of God is not eating and drinking,
but righteousness and peace and joy in the Holy Spirit.

Romans 14:17

The kingdom of God is righteousness in the Holy Spirit. Today, let's break this thought into three parts. First, *"the kingdom of God."* What is the kingdom of God? It is all that God is over. Now God is over all things because He is the Creator, but God's kingdom is the domain that is subject to Him, Heaven. This is why Jesus prayed in the Lord's Prayer, *"Your kingdom come, Your will be done, On earth as it is in heaven"* (Matthew 6:10). It is the place the will of God is done, and His kingdom is coming to earth from Heaven. Oh how we should long to live in His kingdom! Every morning the sun rises, we should long to see the Son standing in the eastern sky, to see His Lordship lived out above our selfishness.

Second, let's look at *"righteousness."* Righteousness is the state of being acceptable or approved by God. Our righteousness is as filthy rags (Isaiah 64:6). So we cannot be righteous in and of ourselves; our best efforts are deserving of Hell. This is why we need a Savior. But through Jesus' death on the cross, we can be counted as right before God. The kingdom of God and His righteousness are to be sought after every day of our lives (Matthew 6:33).

Finally, let's look at *"the Holy Spirit."* Like we said yesterday, the Holy Spirit is God. And of the Father, Son and Spirit, He is the third of the Trinity that is dwelling with us on earth today. It is through the Holy Spirit that we can have a righteousness that is acceptable to God. So we cannot have Heaven on earth in such a way as there is no pain or death, but we can reside in the kingdom of God while on earth because of the righteousness in the Holy Spirit. Through Him, we can walk in the paths of God.

HEAVEN'S HARMONY

For the kingdom of God is not eating and drinking,
but righteousness and peace and joy in the Holy Spirit.

Romans 14:17

There is peace in the kingdom of God. Isn't that what everyone is seeking after? We desire to live our lives in such a way that we are not disturbed. But can we have such peace here on earth? No, if Jesus was oppressed, then we know we will be also. But we can have peace in the Holy Spirit. And what a beautiful peace it is! The Greek word for peace is *eirēnē* which means "harmony." Often we think of living in harmony as a group of people holding hands and singing "*Kumbaya.*" Truth be told, that may not be so far off. When a congregation stands to sing a hymn, and they take their hymnals, those who know how to read the music understand the difference between melody and harmony. The melody is the tune of the song, the main flow of the music, but the harmonies are the other parts that move differently yet complementary to the melody. Some people would say, "How can we live in harmony when everyone is doing something different?" But harmony is just that, people moving and singing differently than the melody but with the same goal. In fact, if everyone sang the melody, the song would be rather dry and boring, but when many voices lift up the same song in full harmony, then the depth and richness of the song can even be felt. So yes, living in harmony can be viewed as a group of people holding hands and singing "*Kumbaya,*" as long as everyone is singing in a complementary way to the melody.

What is the melody of the kingdom of God? It is the glorious song of the Son of God, bringing salvation to an undeserving world! What is the harmony? It is the wondrous song of the Holy Spirit! When the Church, in one accord, sings of the love of the Christ, then we will know the peace of the kingdom of God because then we will know the depth and richness of His harmony!

———————

A SONG OF JOY

For the kingdom of God is not eating and drinking,
but righteousness and peace and joy in the Holy Spirit.

Romans 14:17

What joy is there in the Holy Spirit? Romans 15:13 says, *"Now may the God of hope fill you with all joy and peace in believing, so that you will abound in hope by the power of the Holy Spirit."* The joy that is in the Holy Spirit comes from believing. Whether you are Jew or Gentile, the door of believing has been opened to you, and in believing, there is joy, peace, love, healing, hope, righteousness, power, rest, and so much more. To those who believe in the Son, the sacrifice He made on the cross, and the power He displayed by overcoming death and conquering the grave, there is righteousness so that you may stand approved before the Father as a child of God. For those who believe in the Father and the great love He has for His creation, there is peace. Knowing that the wrath of God is not aimed at you, but rather His grace is aimed at you so that you may enter into His rest. And for those who believe in the awesome and amazing presence of the Holy Spirit Who has transformed your mortal body from a shell of death into a temple of worship and appointed you a priest of worship, there is joy! Walking in the righteousness of Christ, the peace of the Father, and the joy of the Spirit, that is what it is to live in the kingdom of God. May we experience the joy of knowing that though we are fallen and filthy, we have been changed, renewed, and made whole. The kingdom of God is for all people! There is room for everyone, no matter how different they are! The song of praise sung in Heaven was written to be sung by all nations, tribes, and tongues! The kingdom of God is not about what you can or cannot eat or drink; it is about lifting up the magnificent glory of God by walking in the righteousness of the Son, the peace of the Father, and the joy found in the presence of the Spirit. Walk in His joy and be made complete!

LIVING BY THE SPIRIT

If we live by the Spirit, let us also walk by the Spirit.

Galatians 5:25

What is the Christian life other than to be in Christ, to serve Christ, and to be changed by Christ? To know Him and be known by Him, that is what eternal life is all about! When the Spirit of God comes on us, and we are filled with power through Him, the way we live should change. Galatians 5 is full of insights and teaching about living with the Holy Spirit inside of us. We will look at these as the month goes on, but today we look at what it means to live and walk by the Spirit. Let's start at the beginning.

Galatians 5:1 says, "*It was for freedom that Christ set us free; therefore keep standing firm and do not be subject again to a yoke of slavery.*" Through Jesus' death on the cross, we have been set free, and we now live by the Spirit. He dwells in us, and we abide with Him, which bears the fruit of the Spirit. So if we live by the Spirit, we can then walk by the Spirit. Day by day, moment by moment, even step by step, we walk by Him. What this means is we follow the Spirit. To follow Him means that we do not run ahead or wander off, but we stay in such close proximity and give such constant attention to Him that we never leave His side. Verse sixteen says, "*But I say, walk by the Spirit, and you will not carry out the desire of the flesh.*" As we walk by the Spirit or as we said, 'follow the Spirit,' we are being transformed. When we walk by the Spirit we are not walking by our own desires. This comes in a couple of different ways: (1) We deny our desires and choose not to fulfill them (Matthew 16:24). (2) The Spirit of God is at work in us as we follow Him, transforming our desires to be more like His (Romans 12:2). So as we live by the Spirit, we should also walk by the Spirit, and as we walk by the Spirit, we are not carrying out the desires of the flesh. We are being changed moment by moment as the Spirit's presence is near and active.

THE SPIRIT'S FRUIT

But the fruit of the Spirit is love, joy, peace, patience, kindness, goodness, faithfulness, gentleness, self-control; against such things there is no law.

Galatians 5:22–23

Jesus teaches us in John 15:4, *"Abide in Me, and I in you. As the branch cannot bear fruit of itself unless it abides in the vine, so neither can you unless you abide in Me."* Therefore, we as the branch and Christ as the vine are to work in tandem so fruit is grown. The only way this works is for the vine to bring the nutrients to the branch, and then the Spirit of God produces the fruit (Galatians 5:22–23). Our responsibility in this is to simply abide. So, we are to abide in Christ as He is the vine, we are to abide in the Spirit as He is the One Who produces the fruit, and we are to abide in the Father as He is the One Who prunes us and cleanses us so we bear more fruit (John 15:1–3). To know if you are abiding with the Father, Son, and Holy Spirit, just look to see what fruit you are growing. Galatians 5:22–23 gives a list of nine fruits which we call "The Fruits of the Spirit." These nine fruits are actually lifestyles you will exhibit if you are walking in the Spirit each day. In contrast, Galatians 5:19–21 points to fifteen "Fruits of the Flesh." To know who or what you are abiding in, look to see what fruit you are bearing. If you are claiming to follow God, but you are growing fruit of the flesh, then do not stand in denial any longer; go to the Father in confession and allow Him to clean you (1 John 1:9). But if you see you are growing in your love, joy, peace, etc., then worship the Lord Who surrounds you—Jesus on one side, the Spirit on the other, and the Father holding you in His hands. They are working in you as you abide in Them. Over the next nine days, we will look at these fruits which the Spirit's presence is growing in you. Each will have a counterfeit but pray that the Father will reveal those frauds and remove them. The vine of Christ is alive and growing; may you grow in the Fruit of the Spirit.

———————

GROWING IN GOD'S GARDEN

But the fruit of the Spirit is love, joy, peace, patience, kindness, goodness, faithfulness, gentleness, self-control; against such things there is no law.

Galatians 5:22–23

We can never be more Christlike than when we love others. This is because God is love (1 John 4:8). Love is also the fulfillment of the two greatest commandments—to love God and love others (Matthew 22:36–40). Ephesians 5:1–2 tells us, *"Therefore be imitators of God, as beloved children; and walk in love, just as Christ also loved you and gave Himself up for us, an offering and a sacrifice to God as a fragrant aroma."* Love is the key to walking as Jesus walked. Paul even goes so far as to say that if we live the Christian life and do great and powerful things for God yet do not have love, then it is all worthless (1 Corinthians 13:1–3). So where does this love come from? *"We love, because He first loved us"* (1 John 4:19). Love is a fruit of the Spirit; it is what the Spirit grows out of us when we are connected to Jesus and in the hands of the Father. This is why Paul was saying it is worthless to live for Christ yet have no love. God is love, and love is birthed out of His Spirit; therefore anything that we do that does not stem from His love is a fruit of Satan. In God's garden, there are only the plants He planted or the weeds Satan threw in. So you could say you are either a fruit-bearing branch on the vine of Christ, or you are a self-serving weed planted by the deceiver, but love is the indicator. Not the emotional infatuation but a Christlike love. And we know the love of God is very different from the love of self. *"Love is patient, love is kind. It does not envy, it does not boast, it is not proud. It does not dishonor others, it is not self-seeking, it is not easily angered, it keeps no record of wrongs. Love does not delight in evil but rejoices with the truth. It always protects, always trusts, always hopes, always perseveres"* (1 Corinthians 13:4–7). Is the Spirit seen in you by the way you love?

JOYFUL WORSHIP

But the fruit of the Spirit is love, joy, peace, patience, kindness, goodness, faithfulness, gentleness, self-control; against such things there is no law.

Galatians 5:22–23

The Spirit's presence is near and active, and as we will see today, His presence bears the fruit of joy! Something to meditate on is *chara*, the Greek word for joy in Galatians 5:22 which means "gladness." The root word of *chara* is *chairō*, which means "to rejoice." *Chara* is a noun, person (The Holy Spirit), place (The Spirit's presence), and Thing (The fruit of abiding in the Spirit). But the root word *chairō* is an action verb. Note that a root word comes before its counterpart meaning, rejoicing precedes joy. We desire to live with joy, but this comes when we rejoice in Who the Spirit is and what He has done. Therefore when we follow Him, dwell with Him, and live in His love, we can't help but rejoice. When we rejoice, the fruit the Spirit which grows in us is "*joy!*" Nehemiah tells us that the joy of the Lord is our strength (Nehemiah 8:10). To better understand this, let's look at Psalm 126. This is "A Song of Ascent," which means it was probably a Psalm sung by families as they ascended the hill going to Jerusalem for the annual feasts. Psalm 126 remembers how God set the exiled captives free and brought them back to the Promise Land. God set them free, and they were filled with joy, so they rejoiced.

> *A Song of Ascents. When the Lord brought back the captive ones of Zion, We were like those who dream. Then our mouth was filled with laughter And our tongue with joyful shouting; Then they said among the nations, "The Lord has done great things for them." The Lord has done great things for us; We are glad. Restore our captivity, O Lord, As the streams in the South. Those who sow in tears shall reap with joyful shouting. He who goes to and fro weeping, carrying his bag of seed, Shall indeed come again with a shout of joy, bringing his sheaves with him (Psalm 126:1–6).*

If you do not abide in the Spirit, how will you rejoice in Him? His fruit of joy is born out of the time you spend with Him, and without joy, how will you worship Him?

NO GREATER PEACE

But the fruit of the Spirit is love, joy, peace, patience, kindness, goodness, faithfulness, gentleness, self-control; against such things there is no law.

Galatians 5:22–23

Paul tells us in Philippians 4:7, *"And the peace of God, which surpasses all comprehension, will guard your hearts and your minds in Christ Jesus."* The peace of God comes when we spend time with the Holy Spirit. This all-encompassing peace is what allowed Jesus to sleep during the storm (Matthew 8:24). It was this peace of the Spirit that washed over Stephen when he was being stoned to death (Acts 7:55–56). Peace is what allows you to wait on the Lord even when the world stands against you. Jesus tells His disciples in Matthew 10:16–20, *"I am sending you out like sheep among wolves. Therefore be as shrewd as snakes and as innocent as doves. Be on your guard; you will be handed over to the local councils and be flogged in the synagogues. On my account you will be brought before governors and kings as witnesses to them and to the Gentiles. But when they arrest you, do not worry about what to say or how to say it. At that time you will be given what to say, for it will not be you speaking, but the Spirit of your Father speaking through you."* What a blessing peace is; how else could we keep our mouth shut in the midst of accusations? How can we sleep when danger surrounds us? How can we worship Christ when we are being persecuted for His name? The peace that passes comprehension, which comes from the presence of the Spirit, is our lifeline; but beware, everything in this world strives to keep us distracted from the Spirit's presence, disillusioned to God's power, and demoralized by the fear of death. A fruit of the Spirit is a peace that calms all of this, but we will not know it unless we know the Spirit. Do not miss the joy of walking in the love of God, which produces a peace greater than death itself. What do we have to fear when the Spirit is near? We can know that the God Who is in us is greater than the evil in this world! (1 John 4:4).

———

WE WAIT BECAUSE WE TRUST HIM

But the fruit of the Spirit is love, joy, peace, patience, kindness, goodness, faithfulness, gentleness, self-control; against such things there is no law.

Galatians 5:22–23

Patience is a fruit of the Spirit, and it is also the first attribute of love mentioned in 1 Corinthians 13:4-7. Our God is a patient God, and He has been patiently waiting for over six thousand years for the redemption of His creation. Patiently He is still teaching us to be patient, but we are such slow learners. As we abide with the Spirit, He shows us that there is no need to rush, He is over all things, and nothing takes place that will overthrow His plan. When we wait on the Lord, we are able to not only run and walk in the strength of the Spirit, but we are also able to mount up on wings like eagles (Isaiah 40:31). But whether we are walking, running, or flying, it can only be done if we are waiting patiently on the Lord. Patience is a skill learned over time because it involves trusting God to uphold what we cannot do ourselves. This leads us to a greatly misunderstood verse of Scripture. *"And He said to them, "Because of the littleness of your faith; for truly I say to you, if you have faith the size of a mustard seed, you will say to this mountain, 'Move from here to there,' and it will move; and nothing will be impossible to you"* (Matthew 17:20). How many times have I prayed for a mountain in my life to move, only to find the mountain is still firmly rooted in the morning. It is so easy to look at the mountains of life and lose heart, to doubt the very goodness of God or even His existence because He isn't fulfilling this seemingly simple promise. But nowhere in this Scripture does it say that the mountain will immediately jump up and run across the road. Sometimes God moves mountains instantly, but more times than not, mountains are moved one inch at a time. If we lose patience, then we lose the miracle of God. Mountains move as we patiently wait for God to do what we cannot do. We wait because we trust Him. The Spirit is enough!

———————

THE FLAVOR OF KINDNESS

But the fruit of the Spirit is love, joy, peace, patience, kindness, goodness, faithfulness, gentleness, self-control; against such things there is no law.

Galatians 5:22–23

Paul uses the metaphor of fruit on a tree to illustrate a life that is lived in connection to the Spirit. The uniqueness of this metaphor is that fruit is not merely experienced by the way it looks but in the way it tastes. Today meditate on the flavor of kindness. Colossians 3:12–13 tells us a bit of what kindness tastes like, *"So, as those who have been chosen of God, holy and beloved, put on a heart of compassion, kindness, humility, gentleness and patience; bearing with one another, and forgiving each other, whoever has a complaint against anyone; just as the Lord forgave you, so also should you."* Kindness has the sweet flavor of compassion and the boldness of humility, yet at the same time the savoriness of gentleness and patience. Kindness should so enhance our lives that others will hunger to eat at the table of our life. They should have a better understanding of Christ just by being around us.

On the flip side, Paul tells us of the putrid flavor of a life absent of kindness. *"But now you also, put them all aside: anger, wrath, malice, slander, and abusive speech from your mouth"* (Colossians 3:8). A life of wrath and abuse is a life that tears down and leads to death. Those who come to your table, and eat the bitter fruit of death, will become sick to their stomach. Yet those who come to your table and eat the fruit of the Spirit's kindness will find refreshment and be restored. We are able to be filled with the flavor of kindness only when we have been infused with the kindness of Jesus. Christ showed us compassion, humility, gentleness, and patience because that is Who He is; this is the Gospel of the cross. Now we are to imitate that Gospel in the compassion, humility, gentleness, and patience we have for others (Ephesians 5:1).

———————

WHO IS GOOD BUT GOD

But the fruit of the Spirit is love, joy, peace, patience, kindness, goodness,
faithfulness, gentleness, self-control; against such things there is no law.

Galatians 5:22–23

When Jesus was approached by a man, who called Him *"good,"* Jesus replied, *"Why do you call Me good? No one is good except God alone"* (Luke 18:19). You nor I are good, yet Paul tells us in Ephesians 5:8–9 *"for you were formerly darkness, but now you are Light in the Lord; walk as children of Light (for the fruit of the Light consists in all goodness and righteousness and truth)."* Therefore, I am not good but the Spirit, Who bears fruit in me, grows *"goodness"* in me. Goodness means "uprightness of heart and life." God produces in me an uprightness of heart and life that I do not have myself. My heart is my soul, the place of thought and emotion, and often I may look at a temptation and reluctantly walk away from it, but in my heart, I desired it. Maybe I thought the consequences were too costly to act on the temptation, but no one knows the secret thoughts of the heart. Within our hearts, we desire and lust after the forbidden. It seems we get away with this guilty pleasure, but God knows our hearts; this is why He must grow in us goodness of heart. God also grows in us the fruit of goodness or uprightness of life. This would be our actions. What good is it to give God the praise of our lips, but our life still reflects the sins we indulged before we were saved? This is why we need a redeeming Savior Who can remove the seeds of sin and sow in us the seeds of the fruit of the Spirit. The fruit that the Spirit nurtures in us is called the fruit of the Light, and it consists in all goodness and righteousness and truth. We live in a world that preaches the gospel of self-fulfillment, self-reliance, and self-love but know this; our self is not good. It can't do what God must do in us!

O Lord, may I not rely on my own goodness but rather stand in awe of Your goodness growing inside of me.

———————

AN UNDESERVED GIFT

But the fruit of the Spirit is love, joy, peace, patience, kindness, goodness, faithfulness, gentleness, self-control; against such things there is no law.

Galatians 5:22–23

Today we look at the fruit of faithfulness which comes from abiding with the Spirit. It is important to remember the fruit of the Spirit is not nurtured by us. If we have faithfulness, then it is only because God's faithfulness is present in us. Psalm 36:5 says, *"Your lovingkindness, O LORD, extends to the heavens, Your faithfulness reaches to the skies."* God's faithfulness is so expansive, nothing on earth can outdistance it. His faithfulness is the Gospel! *"For by grace you have been saved through faith; and that not of yourselves, it is the gift of God"* (Ephesians 2:8). How would we even know Who the Spirit is apart from faith? His faith in us! Our faith and the Spirit's faithfulness are inseparable. It is impossible to please God apart from faith (Hebrews 11:6) therefore we must walk in faith, serve in faith, love in faith, hope in faith, and lay down our lives in faith. James 2:26 tells us, *"For just as the body without the spirit is dead, so also faith without works is dead."* We are dead apart from the faithfulness of God. But do not think God's faith in us is a neat and tidy thing. On the contrary, God's faithfulness growing in us borders on insanity. James 1:2–4 commands us to consider it a joy when we encounter different trials because they are a testing of our faith, and that testing is what perfects and completes us. We are to rejoice when we go through trials because God is testing our faith. He is testing to see if we hold to His faith in the same manner He holds to His faithfulness. If we do not cling to faith during trials then our faith is dead, and thereby we are, too. Jesus does not turn away from us because we sin; he came to us while we were filled with sin, so His faithfulness is an undeserved gift. God faithfully loves us, and that is everything!

———

THE TEST OF GENTLENESS

But the fruit of the Spirit is love, joy, peace, patience, kindness, goodness, faithfulness, gentleness, self-control; against such things there is no law.

Galatians 5:22–23

The fruit of gentleness is expressed in a disposition that is mild and a spirit that is meek. The story that most displayed Jesus' gentleness would be Mark 10:13–15:

And they were bringing children to Him so that He might touch them; but the disciples rebuked them. But when Jesus saw this, He was indignant and said to them, "Permit the children to come to Me; do not hinder them; for the kingdom of God belongs to such as these. Truly I say to you, whoever does not receive the kingdom of God like a child will not enter it at all.

Think about it, why would kids want to be around some rabbi? And why did the disciples try to get rid of the kids? If Jesus was a sour-faced, cranky crab of a man, then the kids would not have been staying around Him long enough to cause trouble. If the kids were perfect little angels, then the disciples would not have cared if they were around. Either there were loads of ankle-biters, or they were causing a ruckus. But either way, we can deduce the kids were throwing the disciples off their usual ministry routine. To think of Jesus, the Savior of the World, the King of Heaven and earth, and the Creator of the universe, allowing kids to climb on Him, getting muddy footprints on His robe. Kids are loud and know no social cues as to what to say or when to say it. Some of the babies may have been drooling on Jesus' shoulder, and their diapers may have smelled bad. But Jesus was more concerned about the souls of children than He was the cleanliness of His robe. The smell of their praises was more potent than the smell of their diapers. His gentleness was all the kids cared about. When the disciples tried to free their teacher, He gently showed love for the children and bold disapproval for what the disciples were doing. Gentleness is tested by children. Do kids run *to* you or *away* from you?

———

MERCY AND GRACE FOR ALL

But the fruit of the Spirit is love, joy, peace, patience, kindness, goodness,
faithfulness, gentleness, self-control; against such things there is no law."

Galatians 5:22–23

What do you do when everything inside you screams to do something that isn't right, even if it's justified? If someone has treated you unfairly, then our human nature tells us to respond in like kind, and wouldn't the world view our response as warranted? By the standards of this "eye for an eye" world, revenge is not only justified but necessary to keep the bullies and warlords at bay. But Jesus preaches a different message in Matthew 5:43–44, *"You have heard that it was said, 'You shall love your neighbor and hate your enemy.' But I say to you, love your enemies and pray for those who persecute you."* Jesus did not teach us to live a life of revenge but to walk in mercy and grace. This is most evident on the cross when the people were yelling at Jesus to save Himself if He truly was the Son of God, but Jesus simply prayed that God would forgive them because they didn't know what they were doing (Luke 23:34). Jesus modeled for us what true love looked like, and it came in the form of mercy and grace. Mercy holds back what we deserve, and grace gives us what we don't deserve. Often we struggle to give mercy and grace to others because they deserve the wrath, but this is where the fruit of 'self-control' comes into play. We must control the rising emotions of what we want and what they deserve, but we cannot do that on our own. The world cries for us to do whatever we want, even if it's sinful, but our life is not about us. This mindset is to be taken captive and brought into obedience to Christ (2 Corinthians 10:5). Jesus controlled Himself on the cross and gave you and me mercy and grace; now we, through the Spirit, are able to give the same mercy and grace to others. It may not seem right to love those who wrong us, but that is how Jesus loved us. Mercy and grace are for all people, whether we like it or not.

———

BUT THE SAME SPIRIT

Now there are varieties of gifts, but the same Spirit.

1 Corinthians 12:4

The gifts given by the Holy Spirit are incredible yet also mysterious. Are they talents? Are they strengths? Are they the Spirit's way of making our weaknesses strengths? How quick we are to focus on the many gifts instead of the One Spirit Who gives the gift. There is no complete list of gifts in Scripture, so for us to focus on the gifts before we adoringly look at the Spirit would be an injustice. The Spirit's presence is near and active; therefore the fruit of the Spirit is grown in our lives when we spend time with Him, but the gifts of the Spirit are given as they are needed to complete the work of the Lord. These gifts may be given for a season or for a lifetime as is desired by the Spirit. A gift of the Spirit, when used in conjunction with the fruit of the Spirit and used in the Potter's hands, is truly a holy thing.

These gifts could be words of wisdom, faith, healings, speaking in different tongues, interpreting tongues, teaching, service, exhortation, mercy, and many others (1 Corinthians 12:8–10; Romans 12:7–8). So we must ask the question, why does the Spirit give these gifts so randomly? First, the Spirit is God, and His ways are sovereign and absolute. Second, the Spirit knows the plan the Father has for us and what we need to accomplish it. Finally, there are varieties of gifts, but the same Spirit. It is hard to lead when you have multiple leaders. Each leader leads where they think best. So if we were in charge of what gifts we get, then we would abuse the generosity of God, but there is One Spirit, and He gives all the gifts as is best for God's glory. There are so many pieces at work in this world, God, humans, fruits, gifts, ministries, effects, miracles, fillings, etc. All of these work together in such a way our finite minds cannot understand. How can we doubt the Spirit's purpose, presence, and power, when it is Him Who holds all things.

———

THE MINISTRY OF TRUST

And there are varieties of ministries, and the same Lord.

1 Corinthians 12:5

The Holy Spirit gives us gifts as He sees fit so we can use those gifts to fulfill a ministry. A ministry is what we often define as a "calling," and it can be anything that deals with Christ-centered service to others. It is what God calls us to do to make the Gospel known to the lost. For someone who has been called to the ministry of teaching and training disciples, the Spirit might give to them the gift of teaching, wisdom, and shepherding. The gifts would be the tools used to fulfill the called ministry.

But we do need to note a great danger here. Just as we can desire the gift more than we desire the Spirit, we can also do a ministry based on our own desires more than our desire to serve the Lord. A perfect example of this is Martha when she was working so hard to prepare things for Jesus while Mary was just happy to be with Jesus (Luke 10:38–42). The same Greek word used for ministries in 1 Corinthians 12:5 is used in Luke 10:40 when it says, *"But Martha was distracted with all her preparations."* Churches are full of people who are doing ministry, but they forget that the tools used to accomplish that ministry come from abiding with Christ, which is what Mary was doing well. It all starts at the Vine (John 15:5). God calls us to more ministries than we can even imagine, but the same Lord is the foundation. What are you doing "to honor the Lord" that in reality, you can do on your own? If all you do are tasks you can accomplish, then you can rest assured that the Father has called you to more. God's hands are in the impossible and our weaknesses. What glory does He receive if we do not depend on Him? While we know this in our head, do we really trust God enough to walk away from our comfortable self-made, do-good ministry and embark on the journey of depending on God with a ministry that only He could accomplish?

THE EFFECTS OF THE SPIRIT

There are varieties of effects, but the same God who works all things in all persons.

1 Corinthians 12:6

It is the Holy Spirit that makes the world go round. Philippians 2:13 says, *"for it is God who is at work in you, both to will and to work for His good pleasure."* God is the One Who does this work in us. This is why Paul teaches that there are a variety of gifts that are to be used in a variety of ministries, and there are even a variety of effects or outcomes, but it is God Who works all those effects in them. How wonderful it is to know that God not only loves a sinner like me, but He desires to use me to fulfill His plan. His Spirit gives me gifts so that I can do things that are beyond my ability. Those gifts are the tools used in the ministry of serving others which He has called you to. Those people whom you minister to are being shaped and molded by God as you serve them. This is the glorious wonder of God's plan for you (Jeremiah 29:11).

But let us not lose sight of a very valuable truth, there are a variety of effects which God works, but these effects are in *"all persons."* This means no one is beyond hope. God never turns a cold shoulder to anyone. Satan will get in our ears and tell us that the people around us are too far gone or that God doesn't want the likes of them. But truth be told, God affects all people whom we minister to with the gifts of the Spirit. Do not turn away from any soul; God never will. God loves sinners, no matter if they are liars, murderers, Muslims, adulterers, Hindu, molesters, abusive, Buddhists, prideful, cheaters, atheists, worriers, racist, homosexuals, Protestants, gossips, rich, poor, young, old, male, female, or any other fallen human being. The Spirit works in them to bring them to salvation. We are fellow workers with God! (1 Corinthians 3:5–9). Praise God, He does what we cannot do!

COMMON GOOD

But to each one is given the manifestation of the Spirit for the common good.

1 Corinthians 12:7

To each one of us who has answered the call of the Holy Spirit to follow Christ, we have received a manifestation of the Spirit. To manifest something is to make it known or visible. A manifestation is to shine a light on something so it can be seen. So if each one of us has been given a manifestation of the Spirit, then that means we have had a Heavenly light shine on our lives so that the Holy Spirit can be seen in us. Basically, we have been gifted to do what we cannot do ourselves so that we can be a part of a ministry that is greater than us, so that the effect would be not a triumphing of self but a making the Spirit seen so others could know Him. Again we are the tools of the Spirit to make much of the Father. But let's not miss one last great truth in this passage. How often is it that people pray for help in a time of need? These prayers are not just uttered by Christians but by non-believers, too. They may throw out a prayer saying, "Nothing else has helped, maybe there is a God and if so, maybe He will help me." But note that this verse tells us that the manifestation of the Spirit was given to us for the *"common good."* This means for the good of others, saved and lost. We are the tools the Spirit uses to help the common good but only when we allow Him to work His effects through us. Could you imagine a world where there was no need for government assistance, no welfare, no food stamps, and no shelters? Though there will always be needs, there does not always have to be needs going unmet that could be met. God created us to make His great name known by helping others through the gifting of the Spirit. When we do not allow Him access into our lives, then others go in need, and the Church is seen as a selfish country club. Hope for this world is seen when the light of God shines on the Spirit Who is inside us working for the common good.

THE JOURNEY

Peter said to them, "Repent, and each of you be baptized in the name of Jesus Christ for the forgiveness of your sins; and you will receive the gift of the Holy Spirit."

Acts 2:38

In this verse, the path to justification, sanctification, and glorification has been laid out so neatly. Peter is preaching to the people at Pentecost, and he is telling them how they can know that Jesus was the Messiah promised from the Old Testament (Genesis 3:15). Peter is also showing them how they can know this Christ, based on His miracles and signs. The people were *"pierced to the heart"* (Acts 2:37) and wanted to know how to be saved. Peter responds by telling them to *"repent."* Christ's death on the cross is what paid our debt to sin, and the grace of God is what extends salvation to us. Repentance is our role in accepting this forgiveness. This is justification or justice being paid for our sin. Next, Peter tells the people to *"be baptized in the name of Jesus."* Baptism is not a requirement for salvation but a step of obedience. Baptism should be our first opportunity to be a missionary, to tell others what Jesus did for us. This obedience is called sanctification: the process of being sanctified or set apart to become more like Christ. Finally, Peter tells the people to receive the gift of the Holy Spirit. While the receiving of the Holy Spirit is still a part of the process of sanctification, it is also a reflection of what life was supposed to be and a prelude to what life will be in Heaven. This is glorification, the act of being glorified or reinstated to the glorious presence of God. That is what life is all about, being with Christ, bowing before the Father, and being filled with the presence of the Spirit. Peter was walking the people through the Gospel narrative, salvation, growing, and reunion! All of us must walk this journey if we are to know the Father and be known by Him!

O Lord, thank You for the gift of the Spirit! May we not lose sight of His guiding hand from this day until we reach Heaven's throne!

THE LORD OF THE TEMPLE

Or do you think that the Scripture speaks to no purpose:
"He jealously desires the Spirit which He has made to dwell in us?"

James 4:5

How easy it is to take God's grace and view it as a free pass to sin. We would never say that, but it is how we live a life of habitual sin. Paul asks the question in Romans 6:15, *"What then? Shall we sin because we are not under law but under grace? May it never be!"* Our sin separates us from God; therefore, grace is what God gives to us so that we are able to be restored to Him. When we continue to sin, it does not trump the grace originally given, but it does quench the Spirit of God (1 Thessalonians 5:19). Paul also goes on to say in 1 Corinthians 6:19–20, *"Or do you not know that your body is a temple of the Holy Spirit who is in you, whom you have from God, and that you are not your own? For you have been bought with a price: therefore glorify God in your body."* God gives us His Spirit to live in us; this is what the Bible calls reconciliation. *"Now all these things are from God, who reconciled us to Himself through Christ and gave us the ministry of reconciliation, namely, that God was in Christ reconciling the world to Himself, not counting their trespasses against them, and He has committed to us the word of reconciliation"* (2 Corinthians 5:18–19). So through all of this, we can learn that God gave us grace leading to salvation. He also gave us His Spirit to live inside our body, reconciling us as His temple. But we no longer belong to ourselves but rather, God owns us, and He jealously desires the Spirit inside us because it is His Spirit. Therefore, should we go on sinning because grace covers it? No! We must surrender ourselves to the Spirit within us because He is the Lord of the temple.

––––––––

INSEPARABLE

By this we know that we abide in Him and He in us,
because He has given us of His Spirit.

1 John 4:13

"The name of the LORD is a strong tower; The righteous run into it and is safe" (Proverbs 18:10). There is great security in Christ! Though we don't always understand what He is doing, we know He is Emanuel. That is also the beauty of 1 John 4:13, *"We abide in Him and He in us."* The Greek word for abide is *menō*, which means "to remain or to continue to be present." When the Spirit abides in us, He remains and continues to be present. Nothing draws Him away or severs Him from us. There is security in that! But also when the Spirit abides in us, we also abide in Him. This means that we remain in Him and continue to be present with Him. One word that describes this is inseparable. In order for the Spirit of God to be Emanuel, Who dwells in us as a temple, there must be a union between us that is inseparable. No wonder Jesus describes His relationship to us as a Bride and Bridegroom. God's design for marriage was patterned after His desire to be inseparable from us. God hates divorce because it is an attempt to divide what God made inseparable. What security would there be in a marriage if God made it okay to get a divorce? You would live in constant fear that your spouse would get tired of you or mad at you, then leave. Likewise, what security would there be if God chose to leave us any time we disobeyed Him or turned our back on Him. God knew who He was saving long before He ever sent His Son to die on the cross. *"But God demonstrates His own love toward us, in that while we were yet sinners, Christ died for us"* (Romans 5:8). Our security in Christ lies not in our ability to keep Him happy but in His inseparable love for us. The Spirit's presence is near and active because He abides in us and we in Him.

WATER, BLOOD, AND THE SPIRIT

This is the One who came by water and blood, Jesus Christ; not with the water only,
but with the water and with the blood. It is the Spirit who testifies, because the
Spirit is the truth. For there are three that testify: the Spirit and the water and the
blood; and the three are in agreement.

1 John 5:6–8

What *"water and blood"* means has been heavily debated. Some theologians believe this to mean that the water is the natural birth of Jesus and the blood is the death of Jesus on the cross. Other theologians believe the water to be the baptism of Jesus and the blood to be the communion He gave the disciples before the cross. Finally, others believe the water and blood to be symbolic of the water and blood that came out of Jesus' side when the soldier ran the spear through Him on the cross. Because of the Gnostic mindset, which was so prevalent in John's day, that all matter was evil, it would seem natural for John to point to Jesus being fully human and fully divine. But in either of these theories, what we need to see is that the water and the blood testify with the Spirit as to Whom Jesus is. This is something that John had already written about years before, *"When the Helper comes, whom I will send to you from the Father, that is the Spirit of truth who proceeds from the Father, He will testify about Me"* (John 15:26). Jesus came to bring salvation to all who had disobeyed the Father, how we know we are in need of His saving is through the Holy Spirit. He is the truth—the truth about our sinfulness and the truth about Who Jesus is. If we see an apple tree that has no apples on it, what good is it? We need to understand where the apples have gone. If we learn that deer have been eating all the apples, then we may know the cause, but we still have no apples. It is only when we learn how to keep the deer away that we have apples to eat. It's the same with the Spirit. He teaches us that it is our sin that keeps us from God, and it is Jesus Who opens that path back up.

MYSTERY OF MYSTERIES

For you have not received a spirit of slavery leading to fear again, but you have received a spirit of adoption as sons by which we cry out, "ABBA! Father!"

Romans 8:15

Truly, there is no greater mystery than that a God would love His fallen creation to the point, He would sacrifice His own Son so that He could adopt the fallen, making them family. We killed God's only Son, yet He loves us and cherishes us. Every name of God is so powerful, Emmanuel, Provider, Rock, Lamb, and Almighty, but arguably the name that is most awesome is *"ABBA! Father!"* We can almost understand a God Who would want to be with His creation, or Who would desire to provide for them, but how could a God love His backstabbing creation to the point He would adopt them, becoming their Father? The Father's love is deeper and more mysterious than all the dark water of the ocean. Not only does the Father love us with a mind-bending love, but He also unites us with Himself through prayer. This is our direct line of communication to Him, anytime, anywhere, about anything. The Father hears our cries and our requests and responds with compassion and power. Then in those times, we don't even know what to pray our ABBA Father intercedes for us. *"In the same way the Spirit also helps our weakness; for we do not know how to pray as we should, but the Spirit Himself intercedes for us with groaning too deep for words"* (Roman 8:26). Also in Romans 8:34, Scripture says, *"who is the one who condemns? Christ Jesus is He who died, yes, rather who was raised, who is at the right hand of God, who also intercedes for us."* How great is the mystery of God's love? We can run to Him as a child, with outstretched arms, and He desires to lift us up and to wrap us in an embrace as only a Father can. It is a love that protects, that blesses, and that is moved in response to the cries of His child. Great is the love of our Father!

WOULD YOU WALK WITH GOD?

He saved us, not on the basis of deeds which we have done in righteousness, but according to His mercy, by the washing of regeneration and renewing by the Holy Spirit, whom He poured out upon us richly through Jesus Christ our Savior.

Titus 3:5–6

When Adam and Eve were in the garden, everything was *"good."* There was no death, no pain, no sorrow, nor loss. God walked in the midst of the garden, and they had communion with Him (Genesis 3:8). But when they allowed the lust of the eyes to gain mastery of their lives, that communion was severed (1 John 2:16). That walk with God in the garden became a running from Him (Jonah 1:3). Despair replaced joy (Exodus 32:1), striving replaced peace (Galatians 1:10), and murder replaced love (Genesis 4:8). Hearts and minds became filled with evil all the time (Genesis 6:5), and man desired to be god instead of being with Him (Genesis 11:4). But it was God Who loved us even in our refuse-covered bodies (Malachi 2:2–3), our malignant-infected souls (Jeremiah 17:9), and sin-sick spirits (Roman 5:8). The Father sent His Son to save us, and He sent His Spirit to dwell in us. The Holy Spirit of God brought about regeneration and renewing in our lives. Regeneration means rebirth or reproduction. Renewing means renovating or a complete change for the better. What started as whole was broken and lost, but then through the work of Jesus on the cross, it was reborn, and through the Spirit, it was reconciled to new life. We can't understand all we have lost, nor can we fathom all that was given so that we may be made new. The questions we are to answer now are, how is life different because of that regeneration and renewing? If only we could go back to the garden where we could walk with God! Yet through the renewing of the Spirit, we can! Do you walk by the Spirit (Galatians 5:16)? Is there a difference between your sin-laced life and your Spirit-infused Life? Life has been made new; stop walking in the old and take a walk with God.

IN THAT VERY HOUR

When they bring you before the synagogues and the rulers and the authorities, do not worry about how or what you are to speak in your defense, or what you are to say; for the Holy Spirit will teach you in that very hour what you ought to say.

Luke 12:11–12

Trusting God can be very difficult because, at its very basic level, trusting Him is letting go of your life. We have been taught from birth to be safe so as to protect our life. But to trust God is to relinquish your precious life into His hands. If you had a priceless vase, you wouldn't let just anyone hold it. You certainly wouldn't take it to a place where people wanted to throw rocks at your vase. Yet this is precisely what it is to trust God; there are no guarantees of another day. Trusting the Spirit is to put your life into His hands and to accept the outcome, whatever it may be. Jesus, in Luke 12, was talking to a large group of people. He told them that persecution was coming but when people come and arrest you, and put you on trial, and charge you with all kinds of things, not to worry about your defense. He was saying, don't try to formulate the best course of action to protect your life but rather trust the Spirit to give you words. The Spirit's words do not come in advance so you can rehearse them, but rather they come in that very hour. In essence, your very precious life is being threatened because of Jesus; therefore you should put that life into the hands of the Spirit Who will wait until the last minute to tell you what to say. This is a great mystery! How can we trust the Spirit to preserve our life? This mystery requires us to understand His love for us. He gave us life, and He will protect it, but our life on this earth is not His goal, as it is ours. He will guide us day by day all the way to His glorious presence if we will trust Him. This will defy logic, and the world around us will not understand, but truly, the words of the Spirit, in that very hour, are our only Salvation. Total trust, total surrender, total obedience!

———

SEALED BY THE SPIRIT

Do not grieve the Holy Spirit of God,
by whom you were sealed for the day of redemption.

Ephesians 4:30

A letter of vast importance was written by the king. He signed his name on it and put it in an envelope. Tipping his candle, he allowed the hot wax to spill out onto the envelope's flap, and then with the pressing of his ring, the letter is marked. The wax hardened in the undeniable shape of the king's signet. The letter is then handed to the king's trusted servant to be delivered. This servant carries the seal of the king, and the king's joy or disgrace is bound up in this servant's completing his task.

You and I are servants of the King of kings, not only servants but also heirs through Christ. The King has a message for us to deliver, which states that *"all have sinned and fall short of the glory of God"* (Romans 3:23) and *"for whoever will call on the name of the Lord will be saved"* (Romans 10:13). This message is called the Gospel, and it is good news for all humanity! (John 3:16). This message was not sealed with wax but with the blood of our Brother, Jesus Christ, and the signet used to mark it is the Holy Spirit. As children of the King, we have been sealed for the day of redemption! There is nothing more glorious than to bear the seal of the Spirit! But how sad it is to know that by our actions and thoughts, we can grieve that very same Spirit of God. Ephesians 4:25–31 contains a list of things we do that grieve Him. The things listed in these verses are things we may do on a daily basis. They are the things we do when we should be out delivering the message of the Gospel. We are servants of the King, not free agents that pick and choose what we want to do. The Father loved us enough to sacrifice His only Son, and how often do we squander Jesus' blood for a fleeting moment of entertainment or vindication.

O Lord, please grieve our hearts for what breaks Yours! May we be faithful, as servants who bear the seal of the Spirit, to deliver Your Gospel message. Amen.

ONE

Being diligent to preserve the unity of the Spirit in the bond of peace.

Ephesians 4:3

Unity bound by peace, that is the blessedness of the Spirit's presence. Unity can be summed up in a single word, *"One."* The body of Christ is made up of many parts, but there is only one body, and for it to function, the many parts must be united. Paul goes onto say, *"There is one body and one Spirit, just as also you were called in one hope of your calling; one Lord, one faith, one baptism, one God and Father of all who is over all and through all and in all"* (Ephesians 4:4–6). Unity comes when all the parts join together in peace. But what is this peace? Psalm 133:1–3 explains the power of unity and peace, *"Behold, how good and how pleasant it is For brothers to dwell together in unity! It is like the precious oil upon the head, Coming down upon the beard, Even Aaron's beard, Coming down upon the edge of his robes. It is like the dew of Hermon Coming down upon the mountains of Zion; For there the LORD commanded the blessing—life forever."* When brothers and sisters live together in unity, it is pleasant and good; in fact, God even compares this to the sacred oil which anointed Aaron's head when he was before the Lord. Also, God compares it to the dew that falls on mount Hermon which is where He gave the commandment leading to eternal life through Jesus. The unity of believers is compared to the act of worship and the path of salvation; therefore, we should not be trivial about it. It is as serious to God as the death of His Son. We are so quick to bicker with others about things of earthly interests, not eternity, and when we do that, the body of Christ suffers injury. The Spirit's presence is near and active, and when we are united in His presence, then we are bound by peace. This makes the heart of God soar like worship and salvation. So let us be diligent to preserve this unity of the Spirit in the bond of peace!

JULY

The Creator's Words Are Power and Authority

LIGHT WITHOUT A SOURCE

Then God said, "Let there be light;" and there was light.

Genesis 1:3

"Then God said," not 'then God went to work' nor 'then God raised His hand' nor 'then God sent workers.' No, simply, *"then God said."* That is power beyond anything we can imagine. In fact, that is power beyond anything our minds can comprehend. We are a creation that is incapable of creating anything from nothing; therefore, our brains short circuit at the thought of the creation of the universe. Even science, with all its brilliant minds, cannot come up with an answer to how the universe was created from nothing. The Creator's words are power, the power to do the impossible, the power to do the necessary, and the power to love a creation in a way it cannot love its Creator back.

His words are also authority. The word of God has authority over death and life and over light and dark. Notice during the creation account in Genesis 1 that on day one, God spoke, which created light, but it was not until day four that God created the sun, moon, and stars. The word of God has the authority to create a substance without a source. Light without a light source is beyond our understanding and will either cause us to be in awe of His authority, or because of ignorance, to doubt His reality. The difference lies in whom we see as the center of creation. If we as humans are the center, then our logic and understanding is the standard of God's existence, but if God is the center of creation, then it doesn't matter if we comprehend all the nuances of God's existence. We must come to a point where we are okay with not holding all the answers. Science will never be able to explain everything apart from God, and we will never be able to explain everything pertaining to God. So either way, we will be without total understanding. The Creator's words are power and authority because they are, not because we understand them. Good thing He is a loving God!

ASCRIBE TO THE LORD

Psalm 29:3–11

"The voice of the LORD is upon the waters." **Rain**

"The God of glory thunders." **Thunder**

"The LORD is over many waters." **Tsunami**

"The voice of the LORD is powerful." **Volcano**

"The voice of the LORD is majestic." **Snow**

"The voice of the LORD breaks the cedars." **Hurricane**

"Yes, the LORD breaks in pieces the cedars of Lebanon." **Tornado**

"He makes Lebanon skip like a calf, And Sirion like a young wild ox." **Drought**

"The voice of the LORD hews out flames of fire." **Lightning**

"The voice of the LORD shakes the wilderness; The LORD shakes the wilderness of Kadesh." **Earthquake**

"The voice of the LORD makes the deer to calve." **Famine**

"And strips the forests bare." **Forest Fire**

"And in His temple everything says, 'Glory!' The LORD sat as King at the flood." **Flood**

"Yes, the LORD sits as King forever. The LORD will give strength to His people; The LORD will bless His people with peace." **Peace**

OASIS IN A DRY SOUL

Let the word of Christ richly dwell within you, with all wisdom teaching and admonishing one another with psalms and hymns and spiritual songs, singing with thankfulness in your hearts to God.

Colossians 3:16

Have you ever been at a place in your life where you were spiritually dry? Those times when it seems your prayers are not making it past the ceiling, and you simply have nothing to give because your soul is a barren wasteland. These trying seasons of testing can be overcome only one way. Just like a drought in the desert can be relieved only by a steady rain, a dry soul can be revived only by the Creator's word. And just as a desert will come alive with flowers as the rains fall, so will your soul burst forth with new life as the word of God pours into it. His words are rich, giving the poor in spirit the kingdom. His words are healing, restoring what has been broken. His words are penetrating, exposing the cancerous sin in our hearts.

Paul tells us in Colossians 3:16 that when the word of Christ richly dwells in us, then we overflow! We become an oasis not just for our dry and thirsty souls but also for all those around us. All of a sudden, we become a sprinkler of life-giving water to the other parched souls. The Creator's words spring forth with all wisdom to help those who are confused. His word admonishes, or spurs on, those who are tired and ready to give up. Yes, His word bursts forth in songs, making our hearts sing with a song that cannot be contained. It is a song of thankfulness because it is a song of the Creator's love! You cannot hold back the flood of gratitude that erupts from a heart filled with God's Word.

But be sure of this, a cup that is full of "*stuff*" cannot be filled with anything else. A dry soul that is filled with everything the world has to offer cannot be filled with the Creator's Word. It is possible to yearn to sing the songs of gratitude but to be so full of self that the high praises of God turn to dust in your mouth and blow away.

JULY 4

A DIFFICULT STATEMENT

So Jesus said to the twelve, "You do not want to go away also, do you?"
Simon Peter answered Him, "Lord, to whom shall we go? You have words of eternal life."

John 6:67–68

Jesus said that He was the living bread and that anyone who ate His flesh and drank His blood would live forever. *"This is a difficult statement; who can listen to it?"* (John 6:60). The words of Jesus are not always easy to hear. You cannot choose the words of love, compassion, and healing yet ignore the words of death, discipline, and mystery. In essence, we want the words of resurrection but not the words of crucifixion, but there can be no resurrection without a crucifixion. We are creatures of control, and we want to use that control to get what we want. But Jesus is all about breaking the vice of control in our lives. He does this by teaching us dependence on Him, not accumulating fortunes so we can be self-sufficient. This is why many of the people who followed Jesus had trouble when He said that He was the living bread that came down from Heaven and that they must eat His flesh and drink His blood to abide in Him. We all want to abide with Jesus, but we do not want to eat Him. *"This is a difficult statement."* Jesus looked at the twelve and asked if they were going to walk away, too, but Peter responded, "to whom would we go? You have words of eternal life." The words of Jesus are alive! Where else can you go? No temple, no retreat center, no place on earth holds the presence of a living god! Who else can you go to? No guru, no teacher, no best-selling author exclusively holds the words that give life. There is only One way, One truth, and One life, and that One is Jesus! But you must embrace His words. The Creator's words are power and authority, but they cannot be changed or avoided. The path to Life lies in eating and drinking Christ!

———————

CORE BELIEFS

The grass withers, the flower fades, But the word of our God stands forever.

Isaiah 40:8

Can truth change? Is it possible for something to be true today but not true tomorrow? For instance, if you own an old rusty green car but you paint the car bright red, then did you just change the truth? The car was green, this is true, but the car is no longer green; it is red. Does this mean the truth has changed? No, circumstances change, and characteristics change but the truth that this is a car remains. Just like the prophet Isaiah said, *"grass withers and flowers fade,"* these are both progressions of life that bring about change, but the truth that withered grass is still grass and faded flowers are truly flowers remains true. Truth continues even when appearances change. Allow this to permeate your mind: the world around us changes, but God Who is true does not change, although we live in a world that is trying to change our core beliefs:

"God is dead."

"What defines a male or female?"

"When does life begin?"

"Sins are not wrong for everyone."

"You can determine your own truth."

The truth of these thoughts was established by God at creation; therefore, they are truths that remain today. We may try to paint the car a different color, but no matter what you do, it is still a car. Isaiah tells us that the circumstances of life will change, but *"the word of our God stands forever."* Ever since Adam and Eve were kicked out of the garden, humans have been at war, trying to overthrow the word of God. They have tried to prove that their way is better than God's, but no one has ever been able to do this. Sure the wicked may have prospered while on this earth, but not a single person has ever outsmarted or overpowered death. We have painted circumstances and glossed over attributes until many believe they have changed truth, but the word of God still remains!

———

HE IS THE WORD

In the beginning was the Word, and the Word was with God, and the Word was God.

John 1:1

"In the beginning was the Word." That *"Word"* is Jesus Christ, the Son of God. The Creator's Word is power and authority because the Creator's Word is His Son. John 1:2 goes on to say, *"He was in the beginning with God."* Jesus was not created; He was in the beginning. Not only was He in the beginning, He was the Creator. *"All things came into being through Him, and apart from Him nothing came into being that has come into being"* (John 1:3). Jesus is the Word of God; .when Jesus speaks, things happen. When Jesus told the servant to fill up the water pitchers, the water was empowered to become wine (John 2:7-10). When Jesus spoke and called Lazarus to come out of the grave, Lazarus' corpse was given the authority to stand up (John 11:43). When Jesus was woken up by the disciples crying out in the boat because of the raging storm, Jesus simply spoke the words *"Hush, be still,"* and the storm was obliged to become calm (Mark 4:39). When Jesus speaks, there is an outpouring of power because He is the Word! Therefore, the promises that Jesus spoke are likewise powerful. When Jesus said, *"I am with you always, even to the end of the age"* (Matthew 28:20), this is a promise of great power. It is a restating of His name Immanuel (Isaiah 7:14). Life should be very different for us if the Word of God says He is going to be with us always. Likewise, His commands are just as authoritative. When Jesus tells us to love Him with all our heart, mind, soul, and strength, He expects this to be done (Mark 12:30). The power of the Creator's Word should not frighten us, but it should create in us a fear of the Lord. *"The fear of the LORD is the beginning of wisdom, And the knowledge of the Holy One is understanding"* (Proverbs 9:10). Wisdom and understanding come from the Word, they come from Jesus, and that affects our lives!

———

BECAME, FLESH, DWELT, US

And the Word became flesh, and dwelt among us, and we saw His glory,
glory as of the only begotten from the Father, full of grace and truth.

John 1:14

There are such powerful words in this verse! Let's look at a few of them.

- **Became**: The Greek word for became is *ginomai,* and it means "to become or begin to be." Jesus, the Word, was not flesh before, but He became flesh at that point.

- **Flesh**: This Greek word is *sarx,* and it means "the soft substance which covers the bones and is permeated with blood." Flesh also carries with it the idea of frailty and mortality.

- **Dwelt**: The Greek word for dwelt is *skēnoō,* which means "to tabernacle or abide."

- **Us**: The Greek word for us is *egō,* and it literally means "I, me, or my."

When we put this all together became, flesh, dwelt, and us, we see what is meant when the end of the verse says, *"and we saw His glory."* Jesus is the Word (John 1:1–5), and the Word began to be, He was changed from His heavenly being into an earthly body. This frail mortal flesh that Jesus put on was the covering He would be known by as He walked this earth and hung on the cross. His Heavenly body would not have been able to submit to the destruction of the nails; therefore, Jesus began to be mortal. He took on this flesh, and He sojourned or lived here among us. He abided here not just with the people of this earth but with 'me'! The Creator's Word began to be frail so that He could live here with me. This is the Word of God, the *"glory as of the only begotten from the Father"*! Praise God! We worship not a weak and frail God but a God Who became weak and still overcame so that we could partake in His overflowing *"grace"* and *"truth"*!

REJOICE TODAY

This is the day which the LORD has made; Let us rejoice and be glad in it.

Psalm 118:24

When creation started, God spoke, and things began to happen that are way beyond our understanding. Things that science is just now starting to understand in its most basic ways. The Creator's Word, Jesus, spoke, and things that were not became things that are. And the things that were made began to produce what had never been. Time became a reality when *"God called the light day and the darkness He called night. And there was evening and there was morning, one day"* (Genesis 1:5). This differentiation of evening and morning is what became known as one day. Time began that first day, and with it a clock to measure the length of days and seasons but also a timer which would count down the days before Christ would set all things back in order. The fall had not even happened yet, but God in His foreknowledge was laying the groundwork for Salvation. Not only would the Word of God set time in motion, but it would also give us a reference for today. The psalmist would write of today when he said, *"This is the day which the LORD has made."* Today is the day that Jesus created when He made evening and morning that first day. The very moment you sit reading this is the exact moment God created when He set Salvation in motion, when He created a place to come and dwell with us, when He said His first recorded words, *"Let there be light"* (Genesis 1:3). Today is the day that the Lord has made, now *"let us rejoice and be glad in it."* Let us praise the Maker of today because He is also the Creator of yesterday when Jesus hung on a cross in our place. He is the Creator of tomorrow when Jesus will step out of Heaven and call us home. Today, we rejoice because of yesterday and tomorrow; what an honor to serve an All-Powerful Creator!

———————

WORDS OF REBUKE

"A son honors his father, and a servant his master. Then if I am a father, where is My honor? And if I am a master, where is My respect?" Says the LORD of hosts to you, O priests who despise My name. But you say, "How have we despised Your name?"

Malachi 1:6

I cannot imagine hearing any greater words coming from the mouth of our Heavenly Father than "I love you." But in terms of impact, words of discipline are equally important. Discipline is a sign of love because a parent disciplines their child so that they are kept safe (Revelation 3:19). While discipline is not fun, it is for our betterment. The book of Malachi is a book of rebuke and discipline. The priests whom God had appointed to come before the Father in the temple were not following His commands. In fact, they were making a mockery of worship. In Malachi 1:6, the Creator tells the priests that they honor their fathers and a servant respects their master, but He is both Father and Master, yet He is receiving neither honor nor respect from them. He goes as far as to say that the priests despise His name, to which the priests ask, *"How have we despised Your name?"* The very ones who were to uphold the name of Jehovah had become so complacent in their duties that they did not even understand how far off the mark they were. They didn't remember that God has many names and they are all attributes or characteristics of Him: Provider, Sustainer, Helper, Healer, Wonderful Counselor, Mighty God, Everlasting Father, Prince of Peace, etc. What would we have to do to become disrespectful of the Creator's name? Just like the priests, you wouldn't have to do anything. Complacency is the murderer of respect and honor. Do absolutely nothing in the wonderful, sweet name of Jesus, and you will automatically despise Him. The Creator's words are an inconvenience to anyone who is not respecting or honoring His name. But those who disrespect His name do not know the love of His heart.

———————

UNDESIRABLE GIFTS

"But when you present the blind for sacrifice, is it not evil? And when you present the lame and sick, is it not evil? Why not offer it to your governor? Would he be pleased with you? Or would he receive you kindly?" says the LORD of hosts. "But now will you not entreat God's favor, that He may be gracious to us? With such an offering on your part, will He receive any of you kindly?" says the LORD of hosts.

Malachi 1:8–9

Why is it that the Creator's Words are power and authority? It is because when He speaks, He does the impossible. In this life there are things which are either eternal or finite, omnipotent or limited, spiritual or worldly. God is the former; we are the latter. So then who should receive first dibs at honor, God or a governor? Of course, God and most people would agree, but this is not how we live our lives. If you had enough money only to pay your tithe or your taxes, which would it be? All too often we bow to the prestigious while God falls into the shadows of their limelight. We do everything in our power to make people of power comfortable so that we can stay in their good graces, but God we treat as a second-rate asset. We turn to God when we feel there is something to gain. This is exactly what the priests in Malachi's day were doing. They had grown complacent in their worship, so instead of giving God their best, they were offering Him their lame, sick, or undesirable gifts. Sin is defined as "missing the mark," but who determines what the mark should be? If God, then every time we miss that mark, it is because we are choosing something we want over God's desire. The worship the priests gave to God was a mere token of half-hearted ritual because the real worship, the best gifts, they saved for people of this earth. God asks the priests, would you give your governor a gift like that? Would you? Of course not, but yet we give it to God with hopes He will bless us. How wicked we are to think we can give our Creator our leftovers and He will give us His best.

SHUT THE DOOR

"Oh that there were one among you who would shut the gates, that you might not uselessly kindle fire on My altar! I am not pleased with you," says the LORD of hosts, "nor will I accept an offering from you."

Malachi 1:10

Is God pleased with our worship today? Churches can overflow with people, they can passionately sing, and the preacher can deliver a message with great urgency but is God pleased? The priests in Malachi's day were going through the motions of worship, but God was not pleased because He was not the focus of that worship. In your church, is God the focus?

Three words that would do us well to learn are ordinance, sin, and preference. Ordinance is something we are commanded to do. Sin is something we are not to do. Preference is something we would rather do. In our worship, all three of these words play a part. The Creator gave us ordinances which we are to carry out because they are pleasing to Him. He also told us things we are to abstain from because sin hinders worship. But preferences are the ways we carry out those ordinances or how we abstain from sin. The Bible does not explicitly tell us how to carry this out, so we have some liberty to choose. For example, worship is an ordinance but worship style is a preference. We are told to not forsake the gathering together but whether that takes place in a cathedral, sanctuary, restaurant, or a house is a preference. Churches have split or closed their doors because of fights over preferences. Is God in Heaven saying, "I wish there were one among you who would shut the doors of the church so that you would not uselessly hold worship services. I am not pleased with you nor will I accept your worship?" Be very careful to follow the ordinances, abstain from sin, and show grace in preferences. Even if you do not care for it, it's not about you!

———

THE PROFANED NAME OF GOD

*"For from the rising of the sun even to its setting, My name will be great among
the nations, and in every place incense is going to be offered to My name,
and a grain offering that is pure; for My name will be great among the nations,"
says the LORD of hosts.*

Malachi 1:11

The Creator was speaking to His priests who had become lazy in performing their duties in worship. God was rebuking them and calling them back to worship that was honoring to Him. But in verse eleven, God tells them that from the beginning of the day to the end of the day, His name will be great all over the earth. The holy, awesome, powerful, worthy, exalted, and righteous name of God is not made great based on our worship of Him; it is great because He is great! The Creator simply invites us into worship by making that name known. The Father does not need our worship nor our ministry. He opens the door to His presence, not so He is fulfilled but so that we may know Him.

The priests in Malachi's day did not know it, but God knew that soon He would be fulfilling Genesis 3:15, *"And I will put enmity Between you and the woman, And between your seed and her seed; He shall bruise you on the head, And you shall bruise him on the heel."* The time for the coming of the Messiah was drawing near. God had set things up so that those who served Him would point to this Christ, but now because of their selfishness, the very priests who were supposed to be honoring the Lord would not recognize His coming. In fact, Malachi 1:12 tells us that those priests were profaning the name of God. The Messiah would come not as a king but as a baby, and the priests in the temple missed it, but it was the widows, the orphans, the lame, and the outcast shepherds and fishermen who would take up the mantle of making the name of the Creator known among the nations. His name is great whether you lift it up or not, but He desires to hear your voice calling out His praise.

A NEW COMMAND

*And now this commandment is for you, O priest. "If you do not listen, and if you
do not take it to heart to give honor to My name" says the LORD of hosts, "then I
will send the curse upon you and I will curse your blessings; and indeed,
I have cursed them already, because you are not taking it to heart."*

Malachi 2:1–2

If we want to understand the Creator's words to us through the book of Malachi, then we must understand we are a royal priesthood (1 Peter 2:9). This bears weight in how we serve the Lord. In Malachi 2:1–2, the Creator gives a new command and with it a strong punishment for breaking it. The command has two parts:

1. The priests are to *"listen."* When was the last time you stopped everything so that you could just listen to God? We live in a day where productivity is held side by side with success and often godliness. We have quickly lost the lesson Jesus taught Martha. He told her that Mary had chosen well by sitting at His feet, listening to Him, whereas Martha was concerned about doing too many things. What we do in service to the Lord is precious, but what we do will prove hollow if we have not taken the time to listen to His voice.

2. The second part of this new command is that the priest must take it to heart to give honor to His name. Serving the Lord doesn't just happen. There is a decision that must be made. We give honor to His name by the words of our mouth, the thoughts in our mind, and our actions. Simply put, if we are to take it to heart to give honor to God, then we must have the mindset of a servant twenty-four hours a day. We must lay ourselves aside so that God is continually lifted up.

The penalty for not obeying this new command is a curse. Consider this curse and whether or not you are willing to test the Lord. Lucifer stopped listening to God and took it to heart to give honor to himself. God cursed him most severely. The Creator is not to be tested in this—*"listen"* and give honor to His name.

SEASONS OF LIFE

*He sends forth His command to the earth; His word runs very swiftly. He gives
snow like wool; He scatters the frost like ashes. He casts forth His ice as fragments;
Who can stand before His cold? He sends forth His word and melts them;
He causes His wind to blow and the waters to flow.*

Psalm 147:15–18

Winter is a season of picturesque snowy landscapes, children laughing as they sled, and warming yourself by the fire. But winter is also a time of dormant trees, bitter cold, gray skies, and long nights. Depression can run rampant during the long winter months. It doesn't take long to begin desiring the new life of spring. The psalmist writes in Psalm 147:15–18 about the Creator's words which bring winter's cold. It could be that at the word of God, you go through seasons of winter, but do not lose heart; His word also brings spring. Let's dig deeper into these verses. Verse fifteen says that God sends His command to the earth. Sometimes it seems as though God is very distant—as if He is in the comfort of Heaven and we are struggling on earth. Instead of being Emmanuel, He seems to be silent, absent, or very far away. Verses sixteen and seventeen remind us that these winter seasons are full of snow, frost, ice, and cold. They cover our lives like a wool blanket and weigh us down, seemingly stifling life and crushing hope. *"Who can stand before His cold?"* We look at these winter seasons of life and wonder where God is? Why isn't He intervening? The Father's silence seems cold, crushing, and overwhelming. Finally, verse eighteen rings out; God speaks again and changes the season. Spring comes at the word of the Creator. He melts the snow and causes the life-giving streams to flow. Seasons of winter come at the command of God, but spring likewise will come at the exact moment the Creator desires. He knows we cannot stand before His cold, but the worship that comes in the seasons of spring can be sung only by those who have shivered in the winter.

EQUALITY WITH GOD?

Calling a bird of prey from the east, The man of My purpose from a far country. Truly I have spoken; truly I will bring it to pass. I have planned it, surely I will do it.

Isaiah 46:11

Our finite minds cannot understand all God has done, is doing, or will do. Isaiah 46:11 serves to show the Creator's unmatched power and authority. Throughout this chapter, God is speaking of the inabilities of idols. They are man-made and have no power to help or save. God goes on to say, *"To whom would you liken Me And make Me equal and compare Me, That we would be alike?"* (Isaiah 46:5). God throws the gauntlet down saying, compare them to Me; you decide who has power. He goes on to show His authority in verse eleven, where He makes a prophecy about the unborn Cyrus king of Persia, who would over one hundred years later, allow the Israelites to return from captivity. Jeremiah the prophet would also prophecy about their return, *"For thus says the LORD, 'When seventy years have been completed for Babylon, I will visit you and fulfill My good word to you, to bring you back to this place"* (Jeremiah 29:10). Finally, we see the fulfillment of this in Ezra 1, where God stirred the spirit of Cyrus so that he made a proclamation that the Jews could return to Israel.

The Father showed His power and authority over man-made idols to overcome, direct hearts, and foresee the future. The Lord said, *"Truly I have spoken; truly I will bring it to pass. I have planned it, surely I will do it."* Nothing is too great for God! The Creator set things in motion over six thousand years ago that are being brought about today. It is His good plan which is being accomplished. He does what no idol can do, He does what we cannot do, He does what only He can do, and yet He calls us to walk with Him and to join Him in this life. Will you trust Him over the gold and silver of this world? Will you trust Him more than yourself? Who is equal to God?

FINDING JESUS

"For the mountains may be removed and the hills may shake,
But My lovingkindness will not be removed from you, And My covenant of peace
will not be shaken," says the LORD who has compassion on you.

Isaiah 54:10

In a world where nothing seems to last and philosophies try to teach that there is no truth, God says, *"My lovingkindness will not be removed from you."* The mindset of our society is that the idea of an interacting god is now taboo because it doesn't work for all people. Even as a church, we can fall into this mindset, where we view Sundays as our spiritual day and the other six days are our normal days. We miss God because the Creator does not infuse our daily lives. But God is not dead, and He is still present in all the days; we simply do not see Him. Where is He? Closer than we may think, but we must learn to look for the God Who is not the god we desire. Learn to see His moving, His effects, and His fingerprints.

Sometimes I play a game when I am in public. It's called "Who is Jesus?" I look at all the people around me, and I try to figure out which one would be Jesus if He was walking around in bodily form. Would He be the person who is most visible or the person who fades into the background? Is He the person with the most money or the homeless man on the street corner? I enjoy playing this game for a couple reasons: One, it reminds me to be mindful of the Creator's presence, and two, it teaches me that Jesus is all around. He never leaves me, but He can easily be missed. The religious leaders in Jesus' day missed the Son of God because they were searching for someone to fix an earthly problem, not an eternal restoration. We can fall into the same trap. His love, kindness, peace, and compassion are not shaken even if everything around us is changing and challenging. Can you look past the temporal uncertainty and find the Creator's love today?

WISDOM FROM ABOVE

But the wisdom from above is first pure, then peaceable, gentle, reasonable,
full of mercy and good fruits, unwavering, without hypocrisy.

James 3:17

James writes of wisdom that is from above, which is from God. Wisdom is understanding, but it is not just knowledge; it is the knowledge of the Creator. Wisdom comes from God (Ephesians 1:17), and it is rooted in Him (Proverbs 9:10). The wisdom from God is very different from the wisdom of man, though they can be confused. The wisdom of man is self-preserving, self-sustaining, and self-centered. But the wisdom of God is God-focused. To illustrate this, think of the phrase, "pot no saw dog tub keep a was I." In worldly wisdom, this is foolish babbling, but because the wisdom from God looks at things backward, He reveals to us that when you read this right to left it says, "I saw a peek, but God was on top." In this world things don't always make sense, and often it appears that God is moving backward or not fulfilling His promises, but when we look at it backward through His wisdom, we catch a peek, a simple glimpse, and we see that God is still on top; He is still victorious and sovereign.

Wisdom is also something that grows, like fruit on a tree, but likewise, we must stay connected to the tree for this fruit to grow (Luke 2:52). Wisdom from above changes things if we walk in it. In James 3:17 there are eight attributes of wisdom that are vital to walk in. Over the next eight days, we will explore them. But today, we want to take note of two words in this verse, "first" and "then." These are very important because they tell us that these eight attributes are listed in order. *"Wisdom from above is first pure, then peaceable..."* We cannot walk in the wisdom that is *"reasonable"* until we walk in the wisdom that is *"first pure."* So over the next eight days, we will not randomly look at wisdom, but we will follow its path. This will require us to look at life backward because then we get a peek of God, where wisdom from above comes from.

———————

MUDDY WATER

But the wisdom from above is first pure, then peaceable, gentle, reasonable, full of mercy and good fruits, unwavering, without hypocrisy.

James 3:17

The word pure is defined as "to have no fault, immaculate, clean." Wisdom from above is, first of all, pure. Nowhere in wisdom is there anything that compromises its purity. Think of it as opening a new bottle of water. The water in the bottle is drinkable because it is pure. Now, if you took that water and poured it in the dirt then scraped the mud into a cup, that would not be drinkable water because it is no longer clean. No one would desire to drink that water! Wisdom from above is first pure, meaning without fault. Carnal wisdom is the mindset that says, "What's in it for me?" This self-centered thinking is totally contrary to the wisdom of God. So who is to say what purity is or is not? Why can't we say that water which has been poured into the dirt is still pure? Why can't we say that purity is in the eye of the beholder? Someone in this world might like the taste of muddy water. Who is to say that pure water and pure muddy water must be viewed differently? Truth be told, anyone can define purity as they wish and many people today do, but in the judgment to come, you will not be judged based on your definition but on God's standard of purity. This is why God gives a spirit of wisdom. He teaches us what is pure. Isaiah 11:2 says this of Jesus, *"The Spirit of the LORD will rest on Him, The spirit of wisdom and understanding, The spirit of counsel and strength, The spirit of knowledge and the fear of the LORD."* This passage goes on to say that Jesus will delight in the fear of the Lord, which is the beginning of wisdom, that He will judge with righteousness, fairness, and faithfulness. Wisdom from above is first pure as defined by Jesus and taught by His Spirit. It will not be self-centered but will center around the fear of the Lord, righteousness, fairness, and faithfulness.

RESURRECTED LIFE OF PEACE

But the wisdom from above is first pure, then peaceable, gentle, reasonable, full of mercy and good fruits, unwavering, without hypocrisy.

James 3:17

Earthly wisdom is self-focused. It teaches us how to get what we want or how to become self-reliant. So many ideals that teach us how to help others are still anchored in self. We are happy to serve others as long as it does not cost us too much. We love it even more if we can serve others and be served ourselves. We call this a "win-win situation," but we walk away from serving when it becomes a "win-lose situation." It is hard to serve others when there is a cost. Our pride is too overwhelming. Lucifer's first sin was pride, and that pride still acts as the catalyst to all other sins (Proverbs 11:2). The wisdom of this world is founded on an arrogance that looks to a philosophy or even man-made religion to make it seem noble, but it is still rooted in self. The wisdom from above is quite the opposite. Jesus teaches that we must die to self (Matthew 16:24). This is so vital to wisdom because pride will breed war. Pride looks out for only one, whereas wisdom from above brings peace because it is a laying down of self and a serving of others. While people can strive for peace in the world around them, peace without purity first will only end in a war of pride. The Creator's words are first of all pure, then they are peaceable. True wisdom is built by a peace that passes all understanding, the mouth of Christ. But just like all things pertaining to Christ, the peace He brings is not like the peace the world gives (John 14:27). The wisdom from above is not peaceable with the wisdom of the world; in fact it rejects the self-focused wisdom which wars against it. The peace of God is not with this world but is between Him and His children. So the wisdom we are to walk in does not promote self-reliance but rather Savior-reliance, but this will not save us; it will kill us. Then and only then will the Savior resurrect us to a new life of peace.

SMOOTH AS SANDPAPER

But the wisdom from above is first pure, then peaceable, gentle, reasonable,
full of mercy and good fruits, unwavering, without hypocrisy.

James 3:17

Wisdom does not live in a hole. What this means is, wisdom is not meant to be kept to yourself but to be taught and given to others. Wisdom that is hoarded is never applied and therefore not wisdom at all. Proverbs 27:17 says, *"Iron sharpens iron, So one man sharpens another."* Wisdom is meant to be applied to those around us so that we can sharpen and strengthen each other. But understand that the handling of iron at various stages is different. When a forger is shaping iron, they will heat it to very hot temperatures and hit it hard with a hammer. But when someone is sharpening iron, their technique is much more gentle. They will use a metal file to remove the burs, then finally, they might use a leather strop to hone the edge so that it is razor-sharp. When we sharpen one another, we cannot beat each other into submission, but rather we are to gently file away the burs that keep us from being Christlike. There is a saying I like to use when describing certain people within the Church. These people are what many would say are gruff. They mean well; they just come across as harsher than others. I like to say of them, "They are as smooth as sandpaper." They simply have a rougher personality. Often people who are as smooth as sandpaper are kept at arm's length because no one wants to be rubbing elbows with someone so coarse, but if we never encountered people who rubbed against us, then we would never become smooth. There is a massive difference between a rough cut board and a fine piece of furniture. The difference is all the sanding that took place to smooth it out. We are to gently smooth each other out by our interactions; this requires wisdom. If we try to change people, we end up beating them like a forger-shaping metal. Gently, with the Creator's words, we are to love each other, and that will sharpen them not change them.

———————

REASONABLE WISDOM: FAITH LIFE

But the wisdom from above is first pure, then peaceable, gentle, reasonable,
full of mercy and good fruits, unwavering, without hypocrisy.

James 3:17

When I was younger, I worked at a business where my supervisor literally would say to me, "Go over there and get me that." When I hesitated, not knowing where "there" was nor what "that" was, he would get angry at me and begin cursing at me. This may sound silly, but I assure you, he was very serious. There is no wisdom in operating this way. James tells us that wisdom from above is *"reasonable."* The Greek word for reasonable is *eupeithēs* which means "easily obeying or compliant." My supervisor was not wise in his direction to me because I couldn't know what he wanted; therefore, there was no way I could obey him. The Creator's words to us are wise in that we can obey them. Not that our selfish hearts always want to. When asked which command was the greatest, Jesus' response was simple: Love God with everything and love your neighbor as yourself. The wisdom from above is not complicated, "Love God and love others." Moses told the people of Israel, *"I call heaven and earth to witness against you today, that I have set before you life and death, the blessing and the curse. So choose life in order that you may live, you and your descendants, by loving the LORD your God, by obeying His voice, and by holding fast to Him; for this is your life and the length of your days, that you may live in the land which the LORD swore to your fathers, to Abraham, Isaac, and Jacob, to give them"* (Deuteronomy 30:19–20). Moses was calling the people to choose life, by loving the Lord and by obeying His voice. There is life in the wisdom of God if we will *"hold fast to Him."* But there is death for those who choose to walk in the logic of this world. Following this reasonable wisdom of God over logic can be difficult because it requires faith over sight, but for those who choose to walk in it they are filled with life.

———————

DEATH OF THE GIVER

But the wisdom from above is first pure, then peaceable, gentle, reasonable, full of mercy and good fruits, unwavering, without hypocrisy.

James 3:17

Each morning when I fix breakfast for my family, one of my tasks is to fix coffee for my wife. I grind the beans and boil the water, then using a French Press, I brew her coffee. Finally, I pour the coffee into a cup where I'm supposed to leave room for lots of cream, but it seems I always forget and fill the cup to the top. Then as I carry the coffee to the table, I end up sloshing it everywhere, dripping it on the floor and on the table. By the time I sit it down in front of my wife, I've spilled enough so that there is room for cream. Spilling the coffee is not my intention; I just can't help it because of how full the cup is.

James teaches us that this is the same as wisdom from above. When the Creator speaks, His words are overflowing with mercy. This is the essence of Romans 5:8 *"But God demonstrates His own love toward us, in that while we were yet sinners, Christ died for us."* God's mercy overflowed to us even when we were sinning and living contrary to His plan. Now we are to operate in like manner. We are to walk in wisdom that spills over with mercy. How does our life reflect the Father's when someone cuts us off or says harsh things to us or takes from us. Our nature is to fire back at them, seeking balance. They hurt you, so you hurt them back in balance, but the wisdom of God does not hold to balance but to forgiveness. Forgiveness is never balanced because it requires mercy instead of vengeance. Mercy is giving someone what they do not deserve, just as Jesus did not open the floodgates of wrath that we deserved. How can we possibly live such an unbalanced life? The truth is, we cannot. In order to live a life of overflowing mercy, we must lay down our life. Death of self is the only way to walk in the Creator's words. This is the example Jesus displayed on the cross. Mercy equals the death of the giver.

———

GROWING THE FRUIT

But the wisdom from above is first pure, then peaceable, gentle, reasonable,
full of mercy and good fruits, unwavering, without hypocrisy.

James 3:17

If the Creator's words are power and authority, then they must evoke change. His words must be a catalyst that brings the potential and makes it actual. The wisdom from above comes from the mouth of the Creator, and therefore we are changed if we will listen and obey it. This change is not like going from dry to wet but like going from ice to fire. The change that comes from following His wisdom is an altering change. Your very substance is changed. But change reveals itself differently in each of us. James teaches us that the wisdom from above is full of good fruits. What this means is as we walk in the wisdom of God, we are being altered, changed, refined, fitted, and molded into a vessel of honor to the Master. Life no longer looks the same, nor do we interact with others in the same way. But remember, fruit is grown while it is on the tree; it doesn't just appear one morning. Likewise, the good fruit of God grows in our lives while we walk in God's wisdom. As we have already stated, these attributes of wisdom are in a hierarchy. Wisdom from above is first pure, then peaceable, then gentle, then reasonable, then full of mercy, and then full of good fruits. These good fruits are growing in us as we walk in purity, peace, and gentleness. Sometimes years will pass before the fruit on the tree is ready to be harvested. Do not give up, do not lose heart; the Creator's words are power and authority, so they will affect our lives. He will change us from the inside out, and He will develop this change as we grow. Daily we will be challenged to walk in the wisdom of the world, but if we will seek Jesus first, then we will learn that we have no need to see over the waves of life's storms. The Creator is greater than the storm, and that is all we need. Trust God to do what only the Creator can do, grow the fruit.

NO ROOM FOR ERROR

But the wisdom from above is first pure, then peaceable, gentle, reasonable,
full of mercy and good fruits, unwavering, without hypocrisy.

James 3:17

Wisdom from above is *"unwavering."* What does this mean? First off, you need to ask yourself, what is the purpose of wisdom? Wisdom is not the end, but a means to an end. The Creator did not call us to walk in wisdom but to walk in righteousness. Wisdom is the Creator's teachings on how to walk in righteousness (Matthew 5:48). Imagine for a second you are the pilot on a space shuttle, and you are about to dock with the space station. Your survival and the survival of your crew rest in your ability to line up the shuttle with the space station's door. If you sway to the right or the left, even a little, it could be catastrophic. Wisdom is not the act of docking your shuttle with the space station but rather the knowledge of *how* to do it. God has given us very specific guidelines, laws, and commandments we are to follow if we are to walk in righteousness. He then gives us the wisdom to obey those guidelines, laws, and commandments. For example, we are called to worship the Father in spirit and in truth (John 4:23–24). So the aim is the worship of God, just as the aim of the space mission was to dock with the space station. Wisdom from above shows you how to do this unwaveringly. If we get off even a little with something like pride, arrogance, or selfishness, then we will miss righteous worship. This would be the same as wavering on the docking with the space station and destroying both the station and the shuttle. Now don't lose sight of the truth; we do not have the ability to live that righteous life. This is why God sent Jesus to pay our debt, and He sent the Holy Spirit to teach us to walk in wisdom. We cannot earn salvation, but we do have a responsibility to walk in the wisdom of the Spirit so we can complete God's mission for our lives. Wisdom from above is a fine line; there is no room for wavering toward self.

HYPOCRISY AT ITS FINEST

But the wisdom from above is first pure, then peaceable, gentle, reasonable,
full of mercy and good fruits, unwavering, without hypocrisy.

James 3:17

Jesus, in Matthew chapter 23, gives eight woes to the Pharisees and scribes. The seventh woe is found in verses twenty-seven and twenty-eight, which say, "*Woe to you, scribes and Pharisees, hypocrites! For you are like whitewashed tombs which on the outside appear beautiful, but inside they are full of dead men's bones and all uncleanness. So you, too, outwardly appear righteous to men, but inwardly you are full of hypocrisy and lawlessness.*" This is a very serious indictment Jesus is giving to the scribes and Pharisees. Meditate on some of the words Jesus used: "*whitewashed tombs,*" "*full of dead men's bones,*" "*uncleanness,*" "*appear righteous,*" "*hypocrisy,*" and "*lawlessness.*" If you were to boil all this down to one word it would be "*hypocrite.*" The Greek word for hypocrite is *hypokritēs* which means "an actor or pretender." This word gives the image of someone wearing a mask. They appear one way because they are masquerading as something they are not. So when James says that the wisdom from above is without hypocrisy, he is saying there is wisdom in being who you profess to be. The Pharisees received honor because they appeared so righteous on the outside, but inwardly their true motives were festering, decaying their heart. Jesus, Who can see the heart, called them out. They were full of death because the wages of sin is death (Romans 6:23). So we end today with a question: Are you a whitewashed tomb? A good performer can convince an audience that they are who they portray. But a confused actor will convince even his- or herself. In the end, it's not what you say but what is on the inside that reveals the truth. Are you a hypocrite?

WISDOM'S PATH

But the wisdom from above is first pure, then peaceable, gentle, reasonable,
full of mercy and good fruits, unwavering, without hypocrisy.

James 3:17

Wisdom from above begins with the fear of the Lord, and the fear of the Lord begins with His presence. We revere Him because of Who He is, and we know Who He is because, through Christ, the veil was ripped giving us access into His presence. This wisdom is first of all *"pure,"* not containing any sin. Because He is pure, this brings peace. The peace of God does not always bring peace with others because there is enmity between the world and God, but His wisdom does bring peace between Him and His children. Next, because there is peace, not strife, there is gentleness. When there is no war between parties, there is no need to stand on guard, but rather they can be vulnerable or gentle. Next, because motives are pure and the attitude is peaceable and gentle, wisdom teaches that we can be reasonable. Choices can be made with an open mind because we are not looking for the other person to betray us. There is a trust which allows us to not expect the bad but rather love. Next, wisdom, because it trusts, will be *"full of mercy and good fruits."* We are at peace, therefore vulnerable, which allows us to forgive the trespasses of others, showing mercy. This is what Jesus did to us on the cross, which births good fruits in our lives. Through God's wisdom, we then can walk a line of righteousness without wavering. We find God's grace to be sufficient, and we do not need to turn elsewhere for fulfillment. Finally, the wisdom from above is *"without hypocrisy"* because there is no need to appear one way but act another.

Through the knowledge of Who God is, there is purity, peace, vulnerability, trust, death of self, fruits of the Spirit, no need to turn to the right or the left, nor need to hide because He is enough. Therefore through the Creator's words, we can walk in the light of the Truth.

NEEDED THORNS

And He has said to me, "My grace is sufficient for you, for power is perfected in weakness." Most gladly, therefore, I will rather boast about my weaknesses, so that the power of Christ may dwell in me.

2 Corinthians 12:9

The Apostle Paul was in a unique position because of the calling God had for his life. God's plan for our lives will shape the circumstances that happen to us. This was very evident for Paul. God told Ananias to go lay hands on a blind, humble Saul, but when Ananias showed reluctance, God told him, *"Go, for he is a chosen instrument of Mine, to bear My name before the Gentiles and kings and the sons of Israel; for I will show him how much he must suffer for My name's sake"* (Acts 9:15–16). God chose Paul to receive revelations and understandings so he would be able to spread the gospel to the Gentiles, to kings, and to Jews. But because of these revelations, it would have been easy for Paul to boast about all he was doing, so God allowed him to have a thorn in his flesh. This thorn was something that kept Paul humble and dependent on Him. Three times Paul prayed that God would remove this thorn, but three times God told him the same thing, *"My grace is sufficient for you."* Did God have the power to remove this thorn? Of course He did, just as He has the power to grant us any request we make of Him, but God's plan supersedes our desires. The Creator knows exactly what we need even when we do not. So when Paul asked for the thorn in his flesh to be removed and God said *"No"* it wasn't because God couldn't but because Paul needed this thorn to accomplish God's plan.

The Creator's words are power and authority, and that is exactly what He was saying to Paul, "I have the authority and the power to remove this thorn, but My grace is what you need even more. This thorn makes you weak, but that is where my power is perfected. I know you don't want to feel weak, but in your weakness, you are actually strong. Trust Me to take care of you! Relish in My love!"

TESTED WORDS

Every word of God is tested; He is a shield to those who take refuge in Him.
Do not add to His words Or He will reprove you, and you will be proved a liar.

Proverbs 30:5–6

What is the weight of a word? A single word has the power to destroy and drive a wedge between the closest of family members. Many marriages have ended because of the power of a destroying word. A word has the power to brighten a day. When someone is down in the dumps, a word of encouragement can lift them to the summit of a mountain. Truly our words have the ability to tear down and to build up. But our words are finite and only have the ability to operate within this finite realm. Yet the words of the Creator are living words. His words create life and destroy life for eternity. Nothing, not even Satan himself, has the power to overthrow a single word of God. Satan's fate is sealed because God spoke it. *"Every word of God is tested."* They are as sure as salvation (John 10:28), as high as Heaven (Isaiah 55:9), and as true as Jesus (John 1:1). There is unfathomable power in the words of God! Satan knows the words that come from his mouth do not hold a candle to the words of God. Satan may have power, but even he cannot speak things into existence. The Devil is a created spirit just like all the other angelic beings. Therefore Satan does not use his words to create a force greater than God; no, he uses his words to deceive and to mimic. He cannot overpower God's words, so he intermingles lies in with God's words so he can then sell them to us as truth. If he can deceive us into believing these lies, then we walk not in the ways of God but in the ways of the father of lies (John 8:44).

The Creator's words are tested and shown to be true. There is refuge in Him for all who run to Him. But for those who, like Satan, would dare try to add to His word, they will be proved a liar, and the outcome would be that of a liar (Revelation 21:8).

———————

ACCURATELY HANDLING THE WORD

*Be diligent to present yourself approved to God as a workman who does not need
to be ashamed, accurately handling the word of truth.*

2 Timothy 2:15

There are two men mentioned in the Bible that probably most people know nothing about. Their names are Hymenaeus and Philetus. We know very little about them but what we do know is very weighty. Their words spread like gangrene (2 Timothy 2:17). They used to follow the truth, but now they teach wrong doctrines (2 Timothy 2:18). Paul handed Hymenaeus over to Satan because he was blaspheming (1 Timothy 1:20). So, even though we do not know much about these two, we do know that they have gotten tied up in their words and are now in a bad place. The verse we are looking at today is 2 Timothy 2:15 but first, let's look at the verses that sandwich it. *"Remind them of these things, and solemnly charge them in the presence of God not to wrangle about words, which is useless and leads to the ruin of the hearers"* (verse 14). *"But avoid worldly and empty chatter, for it will lead to further ungodliness"* (verse 16). In both of these verses, Paul is warning people not to get caught up in worldly words, which are *"useless,"* *"leads to the ruin of the hearers,"* and *"lead to further ungodliness."* Words can quickly lead to destruction. But in verse fifteen, we see words that lead to life. Paul tells us that we do not need to be ashamed but to be like a workman or a servant who can rightly divide the word of truth. These words are not of the world, not words of logic or poetry; these are words of truth, coming from the Truth (John 14:6). Hymenaeus and Philetus were two people who were more concerned about their words than the words of the Creator, and because of that, they were immortalized in Scripture as blasphemous, gangrene spreading, tools of Satan. God's words are right; take the time, rightly needed to show yourself an unashamed workman of the King. Know His words. Speak His words. Live His words. Be changed by His words.

A CALL TO SERVE

And we know that God causes all things to work together for good to those who love God, to those who are called according to His purpose.

Romans 8:28

Do you remember those movies about the pioneers where 'Paw' was out working in the fields, and 'Maw' was cooking in the kitchen? She would walk out on the front porch and ring the dinner bell and yell, "Come and get it!" Then 'Paw' would come to the house, ready to eat his vittles. This is a prime example of a "calling." The signal goes out to get someone's attention, letting them know their presence is desired for a purpose. This is the same method used by God to call us to Him. The Creator's words are power and authority; therefore, when He calls you to His purpose, it is no small thing. When the God of Heaven calls you by name, you are changed for eternity. This is why we can walk through the challenges of this life; we have a hope that we have been called by our Maker to do His work. When the King sends out His servant, He makes sure the servant has everything he needs because if they cannot accomplish the task, then it is the King Who has need. When God sends us out, He sends us as a servant but also as His sons and daughters. We are His pride and joy, so He will make sure we have what we need because He loves us. Does this mean that we will never know need? Yes and no. We *will never know need* because whatever we need to accomplish His command will be given to us. We *will know need* in that we will not have everything we desire. Remember, God calls us to His plan, not ours. So, when we follow the King, we are equipped to finish the job, but we may know hunger, pain, loneliness, and even death. Does this make the King a selfish dictator? No, if anyone knows the pain of following the King, it is His Son. No pain we will ever know can compare to the pain Jesus experienced, being separated from the Father on the cross. And praise God, through Jesus' death, we will never know that separation!

I AM COMING QUICKLY

He who testifies to these things says, "Yes, I am coming quickly."
Amen. Come, Lord Jesus.

Revelation 22:20

Emmanuel has interacted with His creation since the beginning. Why? Because He desires to be with them. When sin separated us from Him, He became a man to close that gap.

- God created the heavens and the earth. (Genesis 1:1)

- The Father walked in the garden in the cool of the evening. (Genesis 3:8)

- Jehovah came down to meet His children on Mount Sinai. (Exodus 19:11)

- The Lord marched before David's armies to strike the Philistines. (2 Samuel 5:24)

- Jesus was born as a little baby in a manger. (Luke 2:7)

- Christ was sacrificed on the cross then rose from the dead. (1 Corinthians 15:3–4)

- The Holy Spirit filled the believers at Pentecost. (Acts 2:4)

- The Prince of Peace will step out of Heaven, and all the Christians will be taken to meet Him in the air. (1 Thessalonians 4:16–17)

- *The King of Kings* will one day return to reign forever! (Revelation 22:1–5)

Jesus said, *"I am coming quickly"* therefore, it is sure! God's desire is for His people; that is why He created mankind, walked with them, was born, died, rose again, and will come back!

AUGUST

The Father's Love Is Still and Consuming

A FORESHADOWING OF SALVATION

So the LORD scattered them abroad from there over the face of the whole earth; and they stopped building the city.

Genesis 11:8

The Father's love is deeper than the ocean. There is no way we can fathom the all-encompassing depth of God's love. His love is experienced in the first heartbeat of a newly conceived baby; it is felt in the last faint heartbeat of an elderly saint as they cross into eternity. The Father's love is a dark hole, without limits, not understandable nor measurable. But His love is grasped by a mere child as they talk to Jesus. Hallowed is the love of God!

What then does the Tower of Babel, the account of God confusing the languages of a wayward people, have to do with His incredible love? EVERYTHING! The Tower of Babel is found in Genesis 11, which is preceded by the account of Noah and the flood in Genesis 6–10. Both of these stories seem to chronicle the sinfulness of the world and God's punishing them. But to see the Tower of Babel as God's judgment is to miss the point altogether. Not just the point of the story but of God's story, the whole of Scripture. With Noah, God poured out judgment on the entire world except for Noah and his family. The world died because the wages of sin is death. But the gift of God is eternal life through Jesus Christ our Lord (Romans 6:23), which is the heartbeat of God confusing the languages of Babel. Did God have the right to kill them because of their waywardness, just like He did in the days of Noah? Yes, but instead of condemning them, the Father showed mercy. That same mercy is extended to us at the cross. Now God did not leave them to their vices, nor does He leave us. He moved them forward into a better understanding of Who He is and a fuller understanding of how vial their sin was. The Tower of Babel is actually a foreshadowing of salvation, as is all of Scripture. It is a picture of the Father's still and consuming love.

GUARDED LOVE

Call to Me and I will answer you, and I will tell you great and mighty things, which you do not know.

Jeremiah 33:3

This is an incredible verse, reminding us that when we call on God, He hears and responds and teaches us things we do not know. We do not serve an idol that does not have the power to respond, but we serve a living God Who knows what we need before we ask. The Son, Who is Life, did not stay in Heaven but came to earth as a human, so we could have forgiveness and restoration. The Spirit of God is our teacher, Who teaches us and guides us through this life if we will listen. We serve a Father Who loves us deeply! But please note that this verse, like a teabag that steeps in water, steeps in the verses surrounding it. This prophecy, when taken in its context, becomes all the more rich. If you go back to the first verse of this chapter, you learn more details, *"Then the word of the LORD came to Jeremiah the second time, while he was still continued in the court of the guard, saying."* So, this is the second time God has spoken to Jeremiah while he is imprisoned. To understand even more, you have to go to Jeremiah 32:1-5. Jeremiah was imprisoned because he spoke the word of the Lord to the king, but the king did not like the unfavorable message, so he confined him. Now in chapter 33, Jeremiah hears from God again saying, *"Call to Me and I will answer you . . ."* The Father's love reaches down to us when we are imprisoned for being obedient. Jeremiah, while under guard, received the Father's love by hearing His word, that *great and mighty* word *which* he *did not know.* God unfolded to Jeremiah in chapter 33 that Israel and Judah will indeed fall because of their waywardness but would also rise again through the Branch of David, which will never leave the throne but will reign as King and Priest forever. Even in prison, God hears and answers our cries with words of restoration and glory through Him!

GLOBAL CHANGING LOVE

Those that entered, male and female of all flesh,
entered as God had commanded him; and the LORD closed it behind him.

Genesis 7:16

If there was ever a historical event that utterly changed the course of human history yet is so incredibly misunderstood, it would be the flood. Never before in history, nor after, has the earth known the widespread destructive power of the flood. A global event that shifted the continents, created oceans, raised mountains, and ripped canyons, cannot be measured by modern-day methods. We cannot even fathom life before the flood because of the drastic change in the earth's topography which in turn altered environments, wind patterns, and weather. The animal kingdom was changed beyond comprehension as the new environment may not have been suitable for some animals which couldn't adapt; therefore, they died out, which changed the food chain for animals that could adapt. Now they have to adapt again to a diet with the extinction of their once plentiful prey. No, we have no idea what effect the flood had or is still having today.

Now with the same magnitude of force that the flood came on the earth, allow this truth to alter your life: once the provisions, the animals, Noah's family, and Noah were on the ark, *"The LORD closed it behind him."* God closed what? God closed the one door of the ark! The Father, Who was the architect Who designed the ark in Genesis 6, made plans for only one door (Genesis 6:16). Why is this paramount? Because if you were to be saved from the most catastrophic event in history, you had to go through the one door of the ark that God controlled. Likewise, if you are to be saved for an eternity in Hell, you have to go through the one door that is Jesus Christ! (John 14:6). The Love the Father has for mankind is greater than the flood of His wrath. He loves You to death, the death of His Son that is.

OPEN YOUR MOUTH

Open your mouth for the mute, For the rights of all the unfortunate. Open your mouth, judge righteously, And defend the rights of the afflicted and needy.

Proverbs 31:8–9

"Open your mouth." Are you willing to open your mouth on behalf of others who are not able to speak for themselves? In the world we live in, we have slaves *of* society and slaves *to* society.

A slave *of* society is someone who has been put in a certain place because of the society around them. This is someone who lost their job because of cutbacks. They are forced to take a job making less money which makes making ends meet very difficult, so they pick up another job and work more hours just to have their basic needs met. They didn't ask for it; it happened to them.

A slave *to* society is someone who is used by society to move forward. This is when a politician uses the homeless, immigrants, elderly, unborn babies, or any other voiceless minority as a platform to get elected but then never does anything to help them once in office. They seem to be more profitable for society if they are kept as stepping stones to power.

There are many slaves all around us every day. You, in fact, might be a slave *of* society or *to* society. The question is, will you open your mouth for them? There is a price to pay for anyone who opens their mouth for the mute, the unfortunate, and the needy. The price by God's standard is called *"holiness."* It must be given, not taken. It must be continual, not convenient. It must be true, not forged. This is what Jesus paid when He opened His mouth for us, who had no voice against Satan's accusations. We were slaves to sin, but Jesus interceded on our behalf so we could know true freedom. His holiness He gave freely, continually, and truly. What He offered us, He asks us to offer to others. It will cost us something; in fact, it will cost us everything. Holiness, when given, is known by another name—love!

DO YOU NEED AN IDOL

To whom then will you liken God? Or what likeness will you compare with Him?

Isaiah 40:18

What simile could you use to describe God? Finish this sentence, "God is like _____." It is impossible to accurately compare God to anything in this finite world. Even though God in perfect wisdom created humans, it is impossible to compare the Creator to His creation. It's not like comparing apples and oranges; it is more like trying to compare apples and apple trees. But here lies the problem, when we struggle to see God around us, or we do not understand His ways, we look to compare Him to something so that we can make sense of Him. This does not work, so we start to search for alternatives for God that we can understand. The Biblical word for this is an idol.

"As for the idol, a craftsman casts it, A goldsmith plates it with gold, And a silversmith fashions chains of silver. He who is too impoverished for such an offering Selects a tree that does not rot; He seeks out for himself a skillful craftsman To prepare an idol that will not totter" (Isaiah 40:19–20). An idol is something fashioned by man to simulate God; it does not rot or totter and is understandable to our finite mind. It tries to answer the question, "God is like _____?"

But we cannot answer this question fully; God is much too grand and holy to be put in a box such as our brain. So what are we supposed to do? If we cannot comprehend God, then how can we trust Him? The answer in a word is *"Faith."*

"Now faith is the assurance of things hoped for, the conviction of things not seen" (Hebrews 11:1) .

It takes faith to trust the Father when you cannot see or understand Him. Faith is what keeps you locked in when the world is laughing at churches and distorting the Church. "God is like _____?" We cannot accurately answer this, but through faith, we can be okay with that. Through faith, we can worship Who we don't understand.

LAWS AND BROKEN LAWS

Come and see the works of God, Who is awesome in His deeds toward the sons of men. He turned the sea into dry land; They passed through the river on foot; There let us rejoice in Him!

Psalm 66:5–6

The Father's love for His children is amazing! In fact, it is beyond this world! When God created the world, He put certain laws of physics in place. These laws were to bring order to the physical world; without them, the world would break down in disorder. These laws have nothing to do with mankind other than humans have to respect them. Laws such as gravity, buoyancy, length of day marked by the sun, seasons determined by the moon, and thermal dynamics, govern our lives, but we did not create them; we simply discovered what God set in place millennium ago. Without these laws, we would cease to exist.

Now with that in mind, hear the praise of the psalmist, *"He turned the sea into dry land; They passed through the river on foot."* According to the governing laws of physics, water does not stand up. Gravity pulls it back down, but in both of these instances, God broke His own laws of physics and created a miracle. Miracles are not made for all the time because if gravity didn't apply to water, then what would we drink? Rain would be impossible, and oceans would float into space. We need these laws, but God knows when it is best to break them for His awesome glory. The Father broke this law the first time to free His children; He broke it the second time to give them His promised land. His wisdom provided physics, and His compassion provides us with miracles. He knows which we need and when but either way, *His deeds toward the sons of men* are awesome! Through God, Peter walked on water, Joshua saw the sun stand still for a day, Lazarus came back to life, food was multiplied, and water stood up! Awesome are the works of God! *"Let us rejoice in Him!"*

———————

A WEEKEND OF HEALING

Therefore be imitators of God, as beloved children.

Ephesians 5:1

If you could memorize only one verse of Scripture, which would be the best one? Ephesians 5:1 would be the verse I would desire to know. God revealed this verse to me years ago while I was going through a very difficult season of life. I was in college and was struggling with depression and anxiety. One day my mom, who is usually a very compassionate shoulder to cry on, gave me some tough love by telling me to stop focusing on myself and go serve someone. With that in my mind, I pulled my Bible out and stumbled across Ephesians 5:1, which is now my life verse. I asked myself: "How can I imitate God? What did He do?" The answer, I learned, was to imitate Jesus.

A couple days later, while horse playing at a lake with a friend, I was kicked in the chest, cracking a rib, making it very painful to breathe. So now, with a hurt rib and mentally struggling, I signed up to go with another college's Bible club to their fall retreat. I knew maybe three or four students going, but then to top things off, the only space for me to ride was on a van from another college where I knew no one. I was demoralized and lost.

As we rode down the road, I quickly learned that this group of unknown students were oddballs. I was really regretting my decision to go on that trip when God spoke to my heart and reminded me to imitate Jesus. Quickly, I began to see not a group of unique individuals but rather something beautiful. This group consisted of people who were socially awkward and outcasts, but they had come together and become a family. They embraced me into their family, and that weekend I began to heal. I couldn't run and play ultimate frisbee because of my rib, and my anxiety kept me from hanging out in the crowds, so I spent three days being loved and loving some of the greatest people I've ever known. They imitated Jesus to me! Do you know Jesus enough to imitate the Father's love?

———

PERSEVERANCE AND ENCOURAGEMENT

For whatever was written in earlier times was written for our instruction, so that through perseverance and the encouragement of the Scriptures we might have hope. Now may the God who gives perseverance and encouragement grant you to be of the same mind with one another according to Christ Jesus, so that with one accord you may with one voice glorify the God and Father of our Lord Jesus Christ.

Romans 15:4–6

Paul was writing this letter to the church in Rome to spur them on so they wouldn't fall prey to Satan's traps. Satan fights so hard against the Church, seeking to devour anyone he can (1 Peter 5:8). He is a thief who steals, kills, and destroys through a variety of different deceptions (John 10:10). Think of it as the Church is resting on a tripod; the Devil seeks to knock a leg out from under it so that everything collapses. Do not think this is child's play; Satan will kill children, rape women, and consume good men with addictions to reach his goal. He will convince brother to betray brother, and husband to hand his wife over to his schemes. He blinds parents, so they work long hours to afford the technologies that bring Satan into their homes. As a master of disguise, Satan can even lead a church from the pulpit so that the church grows stagnant and ineffective, or even worse, falls into moral failure, defacing the glorious name of Jesus.

This is not a new foe we face; Satan has been attacking God's children since the Garden of Eden. Neither is the method for fighting back new. Paul reminded the Christians in Rome to turn to Scripture because God is the giver of perseverance and encouragement. When Satan is hitting the hardest, it is only through perseverance and encouragement that the Church can stay on track. These gifts from God bind us together, allowing us to lift a unified voice that glorifies the Father. Satan will not stop fighting the Church, but God will never stop giving perseverance and encouragement through His Word.

———

A BEACON OF LIGHT

Come near to Me, listen to this: From the first I have not spoken in secret, From the time it took place, I was there. And now the Lord God has sent Me, and His Spirit.

Isaiah 48:16

For four thousand years, the world waited. Generation after generation passed Genesis 3:15 down to the next one, *"And I will put enmity Between you and the woman, And between your seed and her seed; He shall bruise you on the head, And you shall bruise him on the heel."* Those who sought after Jehovah knew that the day was coming when the seed of the woman would bruise the head of the servant. They craved it, they longed for it, they celebrated it in advance, but mostly they waited. Even Isaiah, the prophet, wrote about that blessed day when the Father would set things right, but notice the words he used. He prophesied from the Deliverer Himself Who said to *"Come near Him."*

What is it that we learn if we come near to Him? We learn something beautiful! In this verse, Jesus uses the Hebrew word `attah which means "And now." *"And now the Lord God has sent Me . . . "* The Deliverer said, 'and now' I have been sent! It is time! Today is the day! The wait is over! But the wait was not over; it would be centuries before the Deliverer would be placed in the manger and even a little longer before the sending of *'His Spirit.'* But this prophecy shot out like a beam of hopeful light from a lighthouse. To all mankind, drowning in a sea of hopelessness, Jesus said, 'it is time!' The Father loved His children enough to send His only Son and His Spirit. But what's incredible is that this prophecy may have been like a lighthouse saying, *"Come near to Me,"* but when all was said and done, Jesus came to us like a rescue boat. He came into the churning sea to save a wretched sinner like me. He said, *"Come near to Me,"* but not until He came to us first!

Lord Jesus, what a wonderful Savior You are! Thank You for coming to us, so we could come to You!

HOPE AND LOVE TO THE NATIONS

Opening his mouth, Peter said: "I most certainly understand now that God is not one to show partiality, but in every nation the man who fears Him and does what is right is welcome to Him."

Acts 10:34–35

What is the greatest news you have ever received? Was it when you and your spouse found out you were pregnant? Was it when you found out the person you loved so much wanted to marry you? Was it when you heard that your cancer was gone? Was it when you heard your child say *"I love you"* for the first time? In all of these, your heart soared, and you were overcome with the emotions of awe and wonder. The message of these announcements was love and hope. This is because love and hope are two gifts that transcend this mortal life. Paul says in Romans 5:5, *"and hope does not disappoint, because the love of God has been poured out within our hearts through the Holy Spirit who was given to us."* Hope and love move us from today into eternity, and they place us in the palm of the Father. He loves us, and it is in Him that our hope is rooted. So in hope and love are the ingredients of the greatest news ever; salvation to the world (John 3:16). Understand that for centuries the vast majority of the human race was on the outside looking in, as God had chosen the Jews to pour out His hope and love. It would seem that the Gentiles were merely the servants and handmaidens of God's bride. But now! Through the love of the Heavenly Father, salvation is extended not just to the Jew but also to the Gentile. Peter announces that *"in every nation the man who fears Him and does what is right is welcome to Him."* The greatest news ever received is that you are welcome to God. Salvation is made available to everyone on earth, no matter your race and no matter your past. Anyone who calls on the name of the Lord will be saved! (Romans 10:13). Salvation belongs to our Lord, and He has given it to all mankind. Hope and love to the nations!

CONSUMING FLOOD

You will seek Me and find Me when you search for Me with all your heart.

Jeremiah 29:13

The Father's love is still and consuming. What does that mean? It means the love the Father has for us is not some illusive carrot that is being dangled in front of us. It is still, and it can be found. Therefore we can know the love of God while we are in the land of the living. We can know His patience as we fall over and over, learning to walk with spiritual legs. We can know His kindness as He blesses us with His favor even though we do not deserve it. We can know His humility as we remember Him in communion. The Father's great love for us is very real, and it can be known because it is still, never changing, and not hiding. If the love of God changed, then today He might love us unconditionally, but tomorrow there might be a condition to His love that would cause us to forfeit our hope in Him. No, the Father's love does not keep a record of our wrongs but rather washes them away. The Father's love is also consuming because if we are to know His love, then we are to search for Him with all our heart. We can not go after God with a half heart. A half heart of service to God is, in reality, a whole heart serving of self. Think of it this way, if you searched for God with only half your heart, then what decides whether you serve God or serve yourself? Your selfishness is what becomes the standard. If serving God is comfortable and convenient, then that's what you do, but if God's plan is painful or interrupts your plans, you would choose to serve yourself. Either way, selfish motives are the gauge; therefore, a half-hearted search for God is actually a whole-hearted serving of self. The Father's love consumes everything (Hebrews 12:29). We find the Father when we search for Him with all of our heart. The Father's love for us is never changing, and it consumes us completely. Let go of your selfish desires and allow His consuming flood of love to wash over you!

PROMISED ETERNAL LIFE

This is the promise which He Himself made to us: eternal life.

1 John 2:25

God promised eternal life:

"In the hope of eternal life, which God, who cannot lie, promised long ages ago" (Titus 1:2).

Eternal life is knowing God:

"This is eternal life, that they may know You, the only true God, and Jesus Christ whom You have sent" (John 17:3).

Jesus came so we could know God:

"And we know that the Son of God has come, and has given us understanding so that we may know Him who is true; and we are in Him who is true, in His Son Jesus Christ. This is the true God and eternal life" (1 John 5:20).

God gave eternal life:

"And the testimony is this, that God has given us eternal life, and this life is in His Son" (1 John 5:11).

We have abundant life now:

"The thief comes only to steal and kill and destroy; I came that they may have life, and have it abundantly" (John 10:10).

Rejecting God is eternal death:

"These will go away into eternal punishment, but the righteous into eternal life" (Matthew 25:46).

Eternity has been set in our hearts:

"He has made everything appropriate in its time. He has also set eternity in their heart, yet so that man will not find out the work which God has done from the beginning even to the end" (Ecclesiastes 3:11).

Choose wisely:

"If it is disagreeable in your sight to serve the LORD, choose for yourselves today whom you will serve: whether the gods which your fathers served which were beyond the River, or the gods of the Amorites in whose land you are living; but as for me and my house, we will serve the LORD" (Joshua 24:15).

THE FRUIT OF TRUST

Blessed is the man who trusts in the LORD And whose trust is the LORD. For he will be like a tree planted by the water, That extends its roots by a stream And will not fear when the heat comes; But its leaves will be green, And it will not be anxious in a year of drought Nor cease to yield fruit.

Jeremiah 17:7-8

Do you trust the Father? Are you willing to surrender everything to Him? This means that you would take your greatest desire, marriage, kids, health, security, or long life and hand it to God and let Him decide if you should get it. It is easier to say you surrender to God than it is to leave your deepest longing in His hands. So again, the question is, do you trust the Father? Are you willing to obey Him no matter what He asks? Maybe you would be willing to be a missionary on the other side of the globe, but are you willing to obey Him when He asks you to pray with someone in the grocery store? Surrender and obedience are the fruit of your trust in the Father. Jeremiah tells us that the person who trusts the Lord is like a tree planted by the water. They do not need to worry because the water replenishes life. And why would we worry when our leaves are green, and we are yielding fruit? But don't miss the fact that this tree planted by the water is living in a year of drought. We are quick to trust God when we are in a season of harvest but when we are surrounded by drought and everyone is pointing to how dry and dead everything is, we stop trusting God, and we rely on ourselves. We start looking for sustainable water in a person, a hobby, or a career. What I mean by *"sustainable water"* is something that promises us security and control. These seasons of drought will unequivocally tell us whether we trust the Father. There is no way to surrender your life or walk in obedience to God unless you trust in Him as the root you draw your sustaining water through. The root takes no heed to how dry the river gets because it is sustained by water much deeper than a river bed.

COME TO ME

Jesus said to them, "I am the bread of life; he who comes to Me will not hunger, and he who believes in Me will never thirst."

John 6:35

"*He who comes to Me.*" In Mark 11:28, Jesus said, "*Come to Me, all who are weary and heavy-laden, and I will give you rest.*" Also, in Luke 18:16, "*But Jesus called for them, saying, 'Permit the children to come to Me, and do not hinder them, for the kingdom of God belongs to such as these.'*" How joyous it is to come to Jesus—to see Him kneel down to embrace a little child or to see Him holding the gate open so you can walk through. What could be better than to walk—no, run—into His presence! Unworthy as we are, broken and dirty, yet Jesus happily welcomes us into His courts. All the more, the Father's love is still and consuming! Hear Jesus' teaching, "*No one can come to Me unless the Father who sent Me draws him; and I will raise him up on the last day*" (John 6:44). The love of the Father moves Him to utter a calling to us! The same voice which spoke the furthest reaches of the universe into existence has also called us by name! He has called us to come, eat and drink, saying, "*I am the bread of life; he who comes to Me will not hunger, and he who believes in Me will never thirst.*" Life is in Jesus; satisfaction, love, family, hope, joy, and forgiveness is in Him! The cry of the Father echoes through time, saying, "*From the dirtiest pigsty to the marble floors of a palace, come to My Son and be filled.*" But not everyone will come to Him. Sadly, many will hear the call and will search for the meaning of it, but in the end, Jesus will be too hard for them to stomach. They will refuse to follow a mere baby in a manger, a dead man on a cross. They will die with their ears ringing with the fading call of the Father saying, "Come to My Son." "*You search the Scriptures because you think that in them you have eternal life; it is these that testify about Me; and you are unwilling to come to Me so that you may have life*" (John 5:39–40).

THE FATHER'S JOY

For they disciplined us for a short time as seemed best to them, but He disciplines us for our good, so that we may share His holiness. All discipline for the moment seems not to be joyful, but sorrowful; yet to those who have been trained by it, afterwards it yields the peaceful fruit of righteousness.

Hebrews 12:10–11

When Samuel went to Jesse's house to anoint the next king of Israel, Samuel saw the tall son, the strong son and the smart son. *"But the LORD said to Samuel, 'Do not look at his appearance or at the height of his stature, because I have rejected him; for God sees not as man sees, for man looks at the outward appearance, but the LORD looks at the heart'"* (1 Samuel 16:7). God is able to see what we are not, straight to the heart. So when God disciplines us, it is not just for what we have done but for what is in our hearts. Unrighteousness is more than just the evil things we do; it's also the evil that we are—our motives, thoughts, and desires. Think of it like a beautiful flower garden that has become overrun with weeds. If the gardener took a knife and started cutting the weeds down, the garden would look brand new, but in no time, the weeds would grow back and once again overtake the garden. If the gardener wants to save the garden, they would have to dig up the roots of the weeds so they would not grow back. God, in His infinite love and wisdom, is not cutting out the weeds in our hearts but also digging up the roots. This is not fun, but His desire is for righteousness, and He knows that as long as our hearts harbor the root of sin, righteousness will be choked out. We must be trained to walk in righteousness because that is where joy and peace grow. This is pleasing to the Father! But when we are more concerned with our pleasure, we begin to sprout unrighteousness in our hearts. God disciplines us so that we can share in His holiness. There is joy when the Father dances through His flower garden singing over us.

———————

INSEPARABLE

For I am convinced that neither death, nor life, nor angels, nor principalities, nor things present, nor things to come, nor powers, nor height, nor depth, nor any other created thing, will be able to separate us from the love of God, which is in Christ Jesus our Lord.

Romans 8:38–39

Paul says that he has become convinced of something. Convinced to the point that he is willing to hang his life on it. He is convinced of the Father's inseparable love. The Christians in Rome are the recipients of this letter, and Paul is spurring them on, exhorting them to trust God and to walk not in their own strength but the security of the Father. It is easy for us to think of God's love for mankind as dependent on our right actions, but Paul is teaching that God's love for us could never be supported by our perfection because we all fall every day. *"For I know that nothing good dwells in me, that is, in my flesh; for the willing is present in me, but the doing of the good is not"* (Romans 7:18). If His love for us depended on our love for Him, then we would be separated from Him again because of our disobedience, just as Adam and Eve were separated from Him by their original sin. But Paul is saying, the Father's love and salvation are held in the hands of His Son, and nothing can separate it from us. He even goes as far as to list ten things that may seem powerful enough to divide us from God but in fact, none of them can. Nothing can separate us from His love, not death or life, the very foundation of our existence. Neither angels nor principalities, no powers beyond this world can touch His love. Neither things present nor things to come, time itself isn't enough. There are no powers strong enough to break God's bond with us. Height nor depth nor any other created thing could possibly separate us from the Father's love! There are forces on earth and powers below that can end our life, but nothing can take our lives out of God's grasp. We can boldly rest in Him because God is enough for eternity!

LIFE AND DEATH

For I am convinced that neither death, nor life, nor angels, nor principalities,
nor things present, nor things to come, nor powers, nor height, nor depth,
nor any other created thing, will be able to separate us from the love of God,
which is in Christ Jesus our Lord.

Romans 8:38–39

Possibly one of the most relatable people in the Bible is Jonah. The first chapter of the book of Jonah was about him trying to run from the Father's presence. Jonah's first attempt was to run away and hide. He got on a ship sailing the opposite direction and went below deck and fell asleep (Jonah 1:5). His second attempt to run beyond the grasp of God's hand was to commit suicide. He told the sailors to throw him into the sea. He knew that the storm was raging because He was running from God. He could have asked the captain to turn the boat around so he could go to Nineveh, but instead, he was willing to end his life (Jonah 1:12). The men finally threw Jonah overboard, and sure enough, the storm did calm down on the surface of the sea (Jonah 1:15), but in chapter two, we learn that the storm under the water continued to rage (Jonah 2:1–6). Jonah found out that neither in death or life could he escape God's presence. The love of the Father actually unites these two ends of the spectrum, making them one point. To know the love of the Father is to die to self, and to die is to know life like never before! Jonah, like many of us, tried to do things his own way, but instead of finding solitude in life or death, he found torment. See, the Father's love is expressed through His presence. What on earth could compare to the life-giving, self-denying presence of God? Anything you want more than His presence is your idol. God gives His presence to those He loves, and neither life nor death can separate you from it. Jonah learned this the hard way. But in the belly of the fish, he found God's presence and remembered His love and turned back to Him. Don't run from the Father's presence; relish in His love!

———————

FIGHTING DEMONS

For I am convinced that neither death, nor life, nor angels, nor principalities, nor things present, nor things to come, nor powers, nor height, nor depth, nor any other created thing, will be able to separate us from the love of God, which is in Christ Jesus our Lord.

Romans 8:38–39

"Are they not all ministering spirits, sent out to render service for the sake of those who will inherit salvation?" (Hebrews 1:14). Angels and principalities are those beings that hold a bearing on our lives, yet we cannot see them. Angels and fallen angels, or demons, interact with us every day, helping or hindering our walk with God. When Lucifer was cast from Heaven, he took with him a third of the angels, which became his minions of deceit (Revelation 12:4). Satan's angels build strongholds in our lives, and they attack our spirits trying to rob us of joy, steer us toward evil, and kill us. Paul tells us in Ephesians 6:12, "*For our struggle is not against flesh and blood, but against the rulers, against the powers, against the world forces of this darkness, against the spiritual forces of wickedness in the heavenly places.*" Satan is trying to set up dominion in our lives so that we cower to him instead of bowing to the Sovereign King. To do this, he must separate us from the grace-filled love of God or at least make us think we have been separated. God already has power over the angels and principalities because He created them. "*And in Him you have been made complete, and He is the head over all rule and authority*" (Colossians 2:10). Therefore, think about His love over their power. First Corinthians 13 gives us several attributes of the Father's love—patient, kind, hope, etc. If we cannot be separated from the Father's love, and if Jesus is the head over the rule of Satan, then what does it mean when we struggle with our patience, kindness, and hope? It means Satan has distracted us from God's power. In these times we need to remember, nothing can separate us from the Father's love, which is flowing through us.

IS GOD SOVEREIGN

For I am convinced that neither death, nor life, nor angels, nor principalities,
nor things present, nor things to come, nor powers, nor height, nor depth,
nor any other created thing, will be able to separate us from the love of God,
which is in Christ Jesus our Lord.

Romans 8:38–39

Either God is sovereign, or He is not. He cannot be sovereign in some areas and not in others. And if God is sovereign, then why are we trying to take control from Him? So if God is sovereign, then salvation must be complete and completed. How could a God Who is in control of everything give salvation to His children that still has to be finished? Likewise, how could He give salvation that isn't sealed? Wouldn't He know that we weren't going to live up to the standards of righteousness? This is the heart of what Paul is saying in these verses, nothing can separate you from the Father's great love for you. Your former sins were forgiven at salvation, but if your current or future sins weren't also covered, then what good was the gift of salvation? The sovereignty of God is over your past, present, and future. Your present life is in the hands of God and is under what Paul said earlier in this chapter, *"And we know that God causes all things to work together for good to those who love God, to those who are called according to His purpose"* (Romans 8:28). Everything in your current life is working for your good, not just your good moments but also your failures. If God isn't bigger than your failures, then He would not be much of a Savior. Also, God's sovereignty is over the things yet to come. The Father has already revealed the outcome of His war on evil; Satan, the demons, and death will all be thrown into the lake of fire. It is finished; the war has already been won. So the question remains, is God sovereign or is He not? Because if He is, then neither things present nor things to come can separate us from the love of the Father, but if He is not sovereign, then the outcome is still up in the air.

A MORE GLORIOUS POWER

For I am convinced that neither death, nor life, nor angels, nor principalities,
nor things present, nor things to come, nor powers, nor height, nor depth,
nor any other created thing, will be able to separate us from the love of God,
which is in Christ Jesus our Lord.

Romans 8:38–39

Paul tells us that there are no powers that can separate us from the Father's love. Powers or forces around us come in many different forms. The Greek word for *"powers"* is *dynamis* which is where we get the word dynamite. We can think of it like a land mine that the enemy has buried in our path. When we step on these mines, it is like a stick of dynamite blowing up right under our feet. The impact of the blast rocks our world and sends shrapnel whirling through our family. We are left dazed and confused as we assess the damage. Our enemy is no respecter of persons. He will attack children, women, and men alike. Everyone is affected by the power of his dynamite. Many church-going, Bible-believing Christians will be knocked off course by these *"powers."* While this explosive *"power"* has the ability to damage families, destroy ministries, and cripple our spirits, they do not have the power to separate us from the Father's love. And while it may seem like Satan's powers are more powerful than God's or at least more apparent, just remember, the God Who is in you is greater than the prince of darkness, who is in the world (1 John 4:4). Satan uses his powers to create chaos and confusion; God is wise, not random. We may wonder why God allows all these explosions to go off around us, but His ways are perfect. He is also with us, and His glorious power is majestic (Acts 1:8). The Spirit of God, Who is a greater power, has come on us, and He is leading the charge against the enemy. When we walk the path of the Holy Spirit, we do not carry out the desires of the flesh (Galatians 5:16). God's love is greater than Satan's dynamite, so do not lose heart. Stand courageous!

GRIPPED BY GRACE

For I am convinced that neither death, nor life, nor angels, nor principalities,
nor things present, nor things to come, nor powers, nor height, nor depth,
nor any other created thing, will be able to separate us from the love of God,
which is in Christ Jesus our Lord.

Romans 8:38–39

In Greek mythology, the stories that have been handed down were in some ways an attempt to explain the events around us. When bad things happen, people look for a cause. For the Greeks, they looked to see what the rambunctious and mischievous gods were doing. Often they would memorialize the story by giving a physical object one of the names of their gods. For example, the planets in our solar system have Greek names that coincide with Greek gods. Also, things they did not understand were given stories to try to explain them, such as the "nether world" being inside the earth. Every world religion is in some way an attempt to answer the questions—why do things happen the way they do, and how do we explain what we do not know? For the Greeks, they looked to the heights, the gods they named the planets after. Or they looked to the depths, the evil lurking in the nether world. They wanted to understand the forces around them. For Christians, we likewise look to God or Satan to answer these questions. Maybe God is teaching or testing us; maybe Satan is oppressing or tempting us. We want to understand good and evil. The apostle Paul likewise dealt with people who were looking to the heights of the heavens and depths of the earth to understand their power, but he reminded them that neither of these has the power to separate them from the Father's love. God is greater than the understanding we so desperately desire. In fact, there is nothing created by the hands of God nor the minds of man that can separate us from His love. Nothing is stronger than the grasp of God's grace-filled love! When nothing makes sense, trust the Father, His love is still and consuming!

———————

TODAY IS THE DAY

The Lord is not slow about His promise, as some count slowness, but is patient toward you, not wishing for any to perish but for all to come to repentance.

2 Peter 3:9

When you look at the panoramic of Scripture, the Father's love is undeniable. God set a covenant before the people of Israel, and they agreed to keep His law. But there has never been even a single person, other than Jesus, who has kept that law. *"For all have sinned and fall short of the glory of God"* (Romans 3:23). Paul tells us, *"For the wages of sin is death, but the free gift of God is eternal life in Christ Jesus our Lord"* (Romans 6:23). Therefore every person who has ever walked this earth has disobeyed God and deserves death. This may seem like a harsh penalty, but on one hand, the people agreed to the covenant, knowing death was the penalty, and on the other hand, God can make the penalty as harsh as He wants because He already knew He was going to send His Son to die in our place (Romans 5:8). Salvation through Jesus' death and resurrection has been made available to everyone. No one is exempt from the grace and mercy of the Father, but that same grace and mercy are not forced on them. Paul tells us the path to salvation: *"that if you confess with your mouth Jesus as Lord, and believe in your heart that God raised Him from the dead, you will be saved; for with the heart a person believes, resulting in righteousness, and with the mouth he confesses, resulting in salvation"* (Romans 10:9–10). Salvation has been made available, but we must confess and believe. The penalty for anyone who refuses to confess Jesus as Lord and believe in His resurrection is death, eternal separation from the Father. God could easily wipe out all the sinners who refuse to accept His Son's great offer of Salvation but instead, He is patient. One day He will fulfill his promise, but today He holds back His wrath so we may turn and be forgiven. Today is the day of salvation.

GUILT NO MORE

Then the LORD commanded the fish, and it vomited Jonah up onto the dry land.

Jonah 2:10

Jonah chapter two is a great example of a prayer from an honest heart. Jonah had received a call of God that demanded obedience, but Jonah was looking either at his own inabilities or his own disdain for God's task. God's yoke and burden are light, only when you look at them through the Spirit's ability to carry them in you. But Jonah, like most of us, looked at God's call and was overwhelmed because he focused on himself. The fear, dread, and hatred of this calling crushed Jonah's willingness to worship God, and so he ran in the opposite direction, even to the point of trying to end his life. So it is here at the end of Jonah's life that the Father's love reached down and collided with Jonah's fear, dread, and hatred. It was as Jonah's life was fading to dark, like the last few seconds of a candle before it burns out, that he remembered the Father's love. He cried out to God and repented of his self-centered, self-serving, and self-saving heart. The Father, in a beautiful display of mercy and grace, then did something that should resonate in all of our ears; He had the fish vomit Jonah up onto the dry land (Jonah 2:10). This is vitally important because the Father could have had the fish vomit Jonah on the ocean floor so he would have to struggle to the top of the waves. Or the fish could have vomited him in the middle of the ocean so he would have to swim for days on end. Or even vomit him into the mire and mud. But in the Father's love, the fish vomited Jonah onto dry land, so he would be ready to complete God's task. The Father's love is not vindictive against us for our sins. He calls our sins what they are, an abomination, but He also gives grace completely. His grace covers our disobedience and places us fully back where we need to be to accomplish His plan. We still have the consequences of our actions, but we do not have the guilt.

SONS AND DAUGHTERS

"And I will be a father to you, And you shall be sons and daughters to Me,"
says the Lord Almighty.

2 Corinthians 6:18

"What partnership have righteousness and lawlessness?" (2 Corinthians 6:14). Truly there can be no partnership between these two things. In the same verse, Paul uses the image of two oxen being yoked together. Together they can pull so much stronger than one ox alone, but when a wild ox is yoked together with a trained ox, then they do not pull in tandem. In this case, the two oxen pull contrary to each other, and the result is they may pull less together than one ox alone. But when Paul focuses on the partnership between righteousness and lawlessness, these two powerhouses are opposites; therefore, they do not just struggle to pull together, but it would be like yoking two oxen but putting one facing forward and the other facing backward. They constantly pull against the other so nothing can be accomplished. This is why Paul teaches that righteousness and lawlessness have no partnership together. Of course, we can see how the teachings of the Bible and the teaching of pop culture have no partnership but what if you follow that line of thinking to its logical end? What could possibly be more righteous than God? Nothing. What could possibly be more lawless than our sinful heart? Nothing. What partnership does God have with us? We may pull against Him, but through the narrative of Scripture, we see the beauty of *'Love,' 'Forgiveness,' 'Repentance,' 'Grace,' and 'Adoption'*. Don't miss the incredible love in what God has done for you. Verse eighteen says God speaks to the lawless and tells them, *"And I will be a father to you, And you shall be sons and daughters to Me."* We now have a partnership together, not because we overcame our lawlessness but because righteous Jesus stepped into our lawlessness and turned us around. The Father's love took the lawless and made them sons and daughters!

LOVED FIRST

In this is love, not that we loved God,
but that He loved us and sent His Son to be the propitiation for our sins.

1 John 4:10

If the book of 1 John had a keyword, it would have to be *"love."* John speaks of love for God, love for others, and the love God has for us. He even goes so far as to let us know that He, Himself is love. But why is love so important? Let's see what John tells us about this love:

Beloved, let us love one another, for love is from God; and everyone who loves is born of God and knows God. The one who does not love does not know God, for God is love. By this the love of God was manifested in us, that God has sent His only begotten Son into the world so that we might live through Him. In this is love, not that we loved God, but that He loved us and sent His Son to be the propitiation for our sins. Beloved, if God so loved us, we also ought to love one another (1 John 4:7–11).

The Father's love for us is so deep, and we are to be rooted in it. We know what love is only because the Father first loved us (1 John 4:19). The love of God was shown by sending His Son to be the propitiation for our sins. What does that mean? It means Jesus' death appeased God's wrath. So God loved us so much that He poured out the wrath He had for our sins on Jesus. Now that we have the love of the Father, we can know Him. We can know love because He is love. Having experienced God's love, we know what love is and with that we can then love God back by loving others. The Father's love is never stagnant; it never stands still. It is active and responsive, which is how God is toward us. He moves in our lives, shaping us so we can be active and responsive toward others. We are to walk in love as Christ loved us (Ephesians 5:2).

Father, thank You for loving us! May we love You deeply as we love others today. Please help us to walk in Your love as we know You more!

———

WAITING ON GOD'S GRACE

Therefore the LORD longs to be gracious to you, And therefore He waits on high to have compassion on you. For the LORD is a God of justice; How blessed are all those who long for Him.

Isaiah 30:18

The Father's love for you and for me is more vast than the ocean and deeper than the ocean floor. Actually, His love is so great it goes from Heaven all the way to earth. It spans life and death. The Father reigns in Heaven but He looks on us with passion; He looks on us with love! Isaiah even tells us that *"the LORD longs to be gracious to you."* Let's explore this further. The Hebrew word for longs is *chakah*, which means "to wait." The word *chakah* is used three times in this verse. Twice in reference to the Lord and once in reference to mankind. *"Therefore the LORD longs (chakah) to be gracious to you, And therefore He waits (chakah) on high to have compassion on you. For the LORD is a God of justice; How blessed are all those who long (chakah) for Him."*

Chakah is a word that is much easier said than lived out. Throughout Scripture, Israel said they would wait for the Lord, but when push came to shove, they moved on without God. But the Father truly lives out *chakah*. He is a God of justice, and justice demands the death of all those who sin against Him. But He *chakah* (longs) to be gracious to us and therefore *chakah* (waits) on high to have compassion on those of us who will *chakah* (long) for Him. Do we desire our Savior as He desires us? This is easy to sing on Sunday mornings but will we continue to *chakah* (wait) for Him on Monday morning? Do we still *chakah* (long) for Him on Friday evening? The Father waits patiently for us to learn to *chakah* so His grace can wash over us. Do not take His patience nor compassion for granted. His blessings are only for those who learn to *chakah* in action, not just word.

Father, may I chakah (long) for You as You chakah (wait) on me!

OUR BELOVED'S HANDS AND FEET

Indeed, He loves the people; All Your holy ones are in Your hand,
And they followed in Your steps; Everyone receives of Your words.

Deuteronomy 33:3

In Deuteronomy chapter 33, Moses is at the end of his life. He has led the Israelite people all the way to the border of the promised land, and he gathers everyone and blesses them. One by one, he goes through the tribes of Israel and speaks blessings of them. For forty years, Moses has led them. They celebrated the victory over Egypt, and they mourned the wrath of God for their stubbornness. In verse three, Moses goes on to speak of God's love for His people! Moses says that all of the holy ones of God are in His hand. He holds them and sustains them (Isaiah 41:10).

What better place could we be than in the hand of God? The Potter's hand, the nail-pierced hand, the righteous right hand, the uniting hand, the mighty hand, the hand that lifts us up! Not only were they in His hand, but the beloved people of God *"followed in Your steps."* This literally means to lie down at Your feet. To lie down at the feet of God is to take our rightful place of worship. Just as the hand of God is a secure place, His feet are the site of worship. His wounded feet, the feet that crushed the head of the serpent, the feet that stand on the enemies of God, and the feet that rest on the earth as a footstool. The hands and feet of God are our blessings!

Finally, in verse twenty-six, Moses says, *"There is none like the God of Jeshurun, Who rides the heavens to your help, And through the skies in His majesty." Jeshurun* in Hebrew means "upright one" and is another name for Israel. The Father, in His majesty, races to our side in order to help us. The King, in His majesty, runs to the side of His servants so that we may have the blessing of His hands and feet! No other religious figure has the majesty nor the humility of our Father. Praise God for His hands and feet!

REDEMPTION'S SONG

*But God, being rich in mercy, because of His great love with which He loved us,
even when we were dead in our transgressions, made us alive together with Christ
(by grace you have been saved).*

Ephesians 2:4–5

The Father's love is still and consuming! Just like a calm pool of water can be seen through, water that has been stirred up is cloudy. God's love is like still, calm water, revealing to us His great masterpiece! Once we see His hand at work and experience His love in action, we become consumed in it! It washes over us as a redemptive tidal wave and prepares us for eternity with Christ! But let's not miss the grandeur of it by simply looking at a couple verses; let's look at the context of our verse today:

And you were dead in your trespasses and sins, in which you formerly walked according to the course of this world, according to the prince of the power of the air, of the spirit that is now working in the sons of disobedience. Among them we too all formerly lived in the lusts of our flesh, indulging the desires of the flesh and of the mind, and were by nature children of wrath, even as the rest. But God, being rich in mercy, because of His great love with which He loved us, even when we were dead in our transgressions, made us alive together with Christ (by grace you have been saved), and raised us up with Him, and seated us with Him in the heavenly places in Christ Jesus, so that in the ages to come He might show the surpassing riches of His grace in kindness toward us in Christ Jesus. For by grace you have been saved through faith; and that not of yourselves, it is the gift of God; not as a result of works, so that no one may boast. For we are His workmanship, created in Christ Jesus for good works, which God prepared beforehand so that we would walk in them (Ephesians 2:1–10).

The love of God at work in our sinful lives is the essence of His masterpiece! Perfection collided with iniquity, and the result was redemption's song!

IN THE END, THERE'S HOPE

So then you are no longer strangers and aliens,
but you are fellow citizens with the saints, and are of God's household.

Ephesians 2:19

Hope has got to be one of the most precious gifts God has given us! When everything around you is falling apart, and you are standing alone in a barren wasteland, hope that the Father will rescue you is the only thing you have to hold on to. *"God is our refuge and strength, A very present help in trouble. Therefore we will not fear, though the earth should change And though the mountains slip into the heart of the sea; Though its waters roar and foam, Though the mountains quake at its swelling pride. Selah"* (Psalm 46:1–3). In this we have hope! When you stand before the Father on judgment day, you cannot alter the outcome, so you hope Jesus will step up and say, *"Daddy this one is with Us!"* When nothing else is left, that is when hope is the brightest or the darkest. The difference is where you place your faith. If your faith lies in your ability and the empire you have created on this earth, then the hope you have about the life to come is very bleak and dark because it is out of your control. But for someone who puts their faith in the blood of Jesus and the love of the Father, the hope they have of eternity is as bright as the noonday sun. What an incredible honor it will be to hear the LORD say, *"Well done, good and faithful slave . . . enter into the joy of your Master"* (Matthew 25:21). But even more thrilling it will be to hear the Father say, *"Welcome My CHILD!"* No one is excluded from being adopted into the family of Christ! What a great day it will be when our King, with tears of joy brimming in His eyes, lifts His hands and declares that we are indeed home! We will sing, and we will dance, at least for the first ten-thousand years, then we will do it all over again! It pleases the Father so deeply to love us so richly and to open His arms and welcome us into His charge. He will dance for eternity because of the joy of calling you His own!

LOVE NEVER FAILS

Love never fails; but if there are gifts of prophecy, they will be done away;
if there are tongues, they will cease; if there is knowledge, it will be done away.

1 Corinthians 13:8

Three little words that change everything: *apapē oudepote piptō.* In Greek this means, "Love never fails." Can you imagine what it would mean if you changed any of these three words? "People never fail." "Cars never fail." Or "Love sometimes fails." "Love shouldn't fail." Or "Love never dies." "Love never sleeps." If you change any of these words, everything falls apart. What hope is there if the love of the Father has the possibility of failing? Nothing would be solid. No foundation would stand without love being the bedrock it's built on. *"Love never fails."*

The same idea of *"never"* is used in Genesis 8:21 when God receives Noah's offering, *"The LORD smelled the soothing aroma; and the LORD said to Himself, "I will never again curse the ground on account of man, for the intent of man's heart is evil from his youth; and I will never again destroy every living thing, as I have done."* Twice in this verse, God declares something He will never do. What would it have meant for Noah and his family to step off the ark only to hear God say, "I probably won't ever destroy the earth again"? If that had been what God had said, Noah and his family would have stayed in the ark and kept a stockpile of food on board just in case. Never must mean never, or there can never be trust, and without trust, there can never be love. Without love, we can never have hope, and without hope, we are dead already. The rainbow is a symbol, not just of God's wrath turned away from mankind but also as a reminder that His *"love never fails"*!

"For God so loved the world, that He gave His only begotten Son, that whoever believes in Him shall not perish, but have eternal life" (John 3:16).

———

THE FATHER'S SHOUT

The LORD your God is in your midst, A victorious warrior. He will exult over you with joy, He will be quiet in His love, He will rejoice over you with shouts of joy.

Zephaniah 3:17

For years Jerusalem will be in ruin and its people exiled. This was the prophecy of Zephaniah, but in the last chapter of his book, he prophesied about a new day! A day when the Father's love would reach out to His children. His anger would be spent, His lesson would be taught, and then He would set the stage for the arrival of His Son. It would be time for the outcast to come home. There will be joy, there will be singing, and there will be dancing! *"When the Lord brought back the captive ones of Zion, We were like those who dream. Then our mouth was filled with laughter And our tongue with joyful shouting; Then they said among the nations, 'The Lord has done great things for them.' The Lord has done great things for us; We are glad. Restore our captivity, O Lord, As the streams in the South. Those who sow in tears shall reap with joyful shouting. He who goes to and fro weeping, carrying his bag of seed, Shall indeed come again with a shout of joy, bringing his sheaves with him"* (Psalm 126). When the outcast are welcomed in and the prisoners are set free, the Father overflows with joy because His great plan is unfolding. Zephaniah tells us that on that day, the Father will be there with His children, and He will rejoice over them. What causes God to break out in song? According to Zephaniah, it is His great love for us. He disciplines us when we walk away because He loves us too much to leave us separated from Him. When we turn back, He shouts for joy! To Israel He would come as a victorious warrior, with shouts of joy! Later, Jesus would likewise declare His love for us with the shout, *"It is finished!"* (John 19:30). And there is coming a day when the Lord will again shout for joy and sound the trumpet, as He calls His children home! (1 Thessalonians 4:16–17).

SEPTEMBER

The Rabbi's Teachings Are Life and Truth

GOOD RABBI

And Jesus said to him, "Why do you call Me good? No one is good except God alone."

Mark 10:18

One day, as Jesus was about to go on a journey, a man, whom we know as the *"rich, young ruler,"* came running up to Him and knelt down before Him addressing Him with honor. *"Good Teacher, what shall I do to inherit eternal life?"* (Mark 10:17). Jesus responded, *"Why do you call Me good? No one is good except God alone"* (Mark 10:18). This short exchange tells us some important information:

1. Jesus was considered a Teacher or a Rabbi.
2. He was a Rabbi Who knew the path to eternal life.
3. No One is good except God.

Therefore, if God is the only One Who is *"good,"* yet Jesus is *"good,"* then He must be God. If Jesus is a good teacher, it would be in our best interest to listen to Him and to obey what He says. If we listen and obey, we find eternal life, but as the rich, young ruler finds out, if we don't listen and obey, we find sadness and grief (Mark 10:22). So what are the teachings of the good Rabbi? He teaches the only way to true Life. The world tells us unlimited ways to find eternal happiness, security, and overflowing joy, but none of their teachings deliver what they promise. The evidence of the shortcomings of the "self-help" industry is in their very existence. Why would you need two books on discovering the meaning of life? If the first one delivered what it said, why would you need another one? The very fact that we have thousands of books promising to teach us the way to happiness shows us that they cannot give you what you want. If the world could explain eternal life, then there would never need to be another book on the subject. Yet bookstores are overrun with books on how to extend your life. Jesus, the good Rabbi, knows the path of eternal life. Not only does He know it, but He also paved the way, and He will walk it with you if you will listen and obey. Will you learn from the good Rabbi?

NEVER TO SEVER

I am the vine, you are the branches; he who abides in Me and I in him,
he bears much fruit, for apart from Me you can do nothing.

John 15:5

Every moment we are alive, we have the opportunity to commune with the God of all creation. But if we desire to abide with Him, how do we go about it? Conventional thought is to have a daily quiet time. There are books on the subject of how to have a quiet time, and there are workbooks that you can work through during your quiet time. We teach the importance of a daily quiet time in churches, seminaries, and Bible studies. I have even heard a quiet time equated to the need for a car to stop and get gas. If the car doesn't take the time to get filled up, then it won't run very long. If we do not take the time to daily fill up with God, then we likewise won't run long. But this analogy, though it sounds good, is not as wise as one may think. The Rabbi chose not to equate communion with the Father to a car filling up with gas but rather a branch to a tree. How silly it would be to say, "If you (*a branch*) want to abide with Christ (*the Tree*) then you must daily have your quiet time; this way the branch can connect to the Tree for thirty minutes!" No branch can survive connecting and disconnecting from its life source. While a car can drive for hours on a single five-minute stop at a gas pump, we do not have that ability. What the Rabbi was teaching in this verse is that we cannot ever disconnect from Jesus. Our abiding time with Jesus should go from sunrise to sunset and all through the night. The moment we disconnect from the Vine is the moment we dry up and die. Listen to what the Rabbi said: *"For apart from Me you can do nothing."* It could be that the Church is so hindered today because we are trying to connect to Jesus for a few minutes in the morning or a couple hours on Sunday; then we disconnect to do our thing. With that amount of abiding in Christ, we are dead, and the Life-giving sap of the Vine is not in us.

MISCONCEPTIONS AND COUNTERFEITS

Pilate said to Him, "What is truth?" And when he had said this,
he went out again to the Jews and said to them, "I find no guilt in Him."

John 18:38

What is truth? Truth is a funny thing because there can be only one truth. There can be counterfeits, there can be misconceptions, and there can be flat-out lies, but in the end, there can only be one truth. Jesus stood before Pilate and heard him ask, *"What is truth?"* Jesus knew full well what truth was; He had already told the disciples that He is the Truth (John 14:6). The Son of God knew the Truth, but the people were blinded by their misconceptions and counterfeits. Pilate would eventually give in to the demands of the people to crucify Jesus, but in an attempt to cleanse himself from any injustice, he called for a basin of water to wash his hands, saying, *"I am innocent of this Man's blood"* (Matthew 27:24). What he thought was liberation was actually eternal condemnation on himself. The *"truth"* he thought he was holding to was actually a counterfeit. When the people saw Pilate wash his hands and claim innocence of Jesus' blood, they arrogantly cried out, *"His blood shall be on us and on our children!"* Likewise, the truth they believed was simply a misconception. Their greatest hope should have been that the blood of Jesus would have been on them and their children, but what they cried out for was condemnation. Counterfeits and misconceptions claim to be the truth, but they always end up being a lie. There can be only one truth; that is what the Rabbi teaches. There are many misconceptions about Jesus, and there are loads of counterfeits, but none of them lead to the Father. Our hope is Christ alone!

Rabbi, teach us to know the difference between Your truth and the world's counterfeit. Right any misconception we hold to and may we walk in the Truth of Jesus!

———————

FOLLOWING THE STEPS OF CHRIST

A pupil is not above his teacher; but everyone, after he has been fully trained, will be like his teacher.

Luke 6:40

Could you imagine what it would be like to follow Jesus, hearing Him teach, watching Him interact with others, forgiving, loving, and worshiping? Oh, the things you would learn from walking in the footsteps of the Rabbi. His words would ring out in your ears and sink deep into your heart. When you tried to serve others but things didn't go the way you were hoping, He would be there to encourage and instruct. How wonderful to have received the call to be one of the disciples! We would never rise above our Teacher, though that would be the temptation, but we would be able to learn to walk like Him. We must be careful not to become prideful of the opportunities or understandings we glean from our time with Jesus. This is what caused Lucifer's tragic fall. He forgot where his rightful place was. The creation will never rise above the Creator, nor will the pupil outsmart the Teacher. Why do we insist on becoming more than God? Why can't we simply relish in the shadow of the Almighty (Psalm 17:8)? Isn't His rest enough (Hebrews 4:1)? Do we need more than His grace (2 Corinthians 12:9)? What more could we desire beyond being adopted into His holy family (Romans 8:15)? Jesus desires to fully train us, just as He did the disciples. To fellowship with us and to journey with us. To utilize us in His ministry and to give us baskets of leftover food to carry. The Rabbi is ready to teach if we will listen and obey. But be ready because Jesus' methods are unorthodox and always lead to the death of the pupil. This is one of the Rabbi's first lessons—life can come to us only if we have died to self. He will teach us to count trials as joy, desire weakness over strength, love our enemies, forgive those who hurt us, and walk by the Spirit instead of the patterns and traditions of our culture. We cannot rise above Him, but if we follow Him, we can learn to walk as He did.

MAGIC TRICKS AND MISDIRECTION

The good man out of the good treasure of his heart brings forth what is good; and the evil man out of the evil treasure brings forth what is evil; for his mouth speaks from that which fills his heart.

Luke 6:45

Magicians for centuries have tried to give the illusion that they could take one substance and change it into another. For several years, throughout college, I was an amateur magician, doing birthday parties and church get-togethers. The gist of every magic trick I did was the same—to change something into something else. I would put a silk scarf into a hat and then pull out a dove. It is impossible for silk to become a dove, but that is what gives magic its allure. It gives the appearance of doing the impossible. But to pull it off, magicians have to use some form of misdirection. They get you to focus on one thing while they are making the switch out of sight.

This same principle of misdirection is utilized by Satan. He promises you the ability to have your fleshly desires and your righteousness, too. More or less, Satan is saying you can put in a silk scarf and pull out a dove. The Rabbi, on the other hand, tells us in Luke 6:45 that what goes into the heart is what comes out of the heart by way of the mouth. If you put lustful images into your heart by looking at porn, then evil is what will come out of your mouth. If you put gossip in your heart when you talk with your friends, then evil will come out of your mouth. If you put a silk scarf in a hat, a silk scarf is what will come out unless a trick is being played.

On the flip side, if you worship God and that fills your heart, then worship is what will come out of your mouth. If you put unity in your heart by forgiving others, then love is what will come out of your mouth. No matter what Satan tries to sell you, what goes into your heart is what comes out of your mouth; any promise of something different is a misdirection. The Rabbi's teachings are life and truth, not flash and smoke.

———

LORD, LORD

Why do you call Me, "Lord, Lord," and do not do what I say?

Luke 6:46

The Rabbi is teaching a lesson, which we call the Sermon on the Mount. He has reached a very pivotal part in this teaching where He, in essence, asks the people around Him the question, *"Who am I?"* He is saying, "I hear the title you are calling Me, but it is not lining up with how you live your life." In Matthew's version of the Sermon on the Mount, Jesus adds, *"Not everyone who says to Me, 'Lord, Lord,' will enter the kingdom of heaven, but he who does the will of My Father who is in heaven will enter. Many will say to Me on that day, 'Lord, Lord, did we not prophesy in Your name, and in Your name cast out demons, and in Your name perform many miracles?' And then I will declare to them, 'I never knew you; depart from Me, you who practice lawlessness'"* (Matthew 7:21–23). So in actuality, Jesus is asking the people to consider Who He is, but not to answer with words or even with their actions but with their heart. What does that mean? The concept of *heart* has become very fluid in today's world. Certainly, I am not saying our emotions are what we should stake our eternity on because emotions are so fleeting. The Bible even says that "the heart is deceitful . . . and sick" (Jeremiah 17:9). It could be that the Rabbi is trying to teach us that words can lie and actions can be deceiving, but in our heart, meaning our spirit, that is where we swear our allegiance. God is a spirit, and in our spirit is where the Holy Spirit interacts with us. In Proverbs 20:27, the Bible says, *"The spirit of a man is the lamp of the LORD, Searching all the inner depths of his heart."* Don't be fooled because God certainly isn't. He desires our heart/spirit to bow to Him, not the words of our mouth, which can lie, nor our actions, which can operate out of convenience. God is worthy of true worship, which is in spirit and truth, not actions and words (John 4:23–24).

THE HEART OF PRAYER

Pray, then, in this way: "Our Father who is in heaven, Hallowed be Your name."

Matthew 6:9

"Pray . . ." We could do a whole devotional of just this one word. God speaks, and God listens. What does He say? What should we say? Jesus the Rabbi is going to teach us some of the inter-workings of prayer. In this verse, there are three things that we need to understand if we are to pray with the heart of Jesus.

Our Father: I believe the first thing we need to learn from the Rabbi is the focus of prayer. How much of our daily prayers are consumed with our wants and desires? But Jesus teaches us that we are to start with the Father. Not just my Father or your Father but *our* Father. This means your prayer is to be united with the prayers of others. Together we call out to our Father. We address Him for Who He is, not as a cosmic Santa Claus or magic genie but as our Father, the One Who adopted us into His family through the blood of His only Son. To pray, we must first know the *Who*.

Who is in Heaven: The second thing we need to learn about prayer is what the Father's position to us is. He is in Heaven; we are not. We would not even have access to Heaven if it were not for the Father's grace. He is great, and we are nothing. He is perfect, and we are sinners. So when we pray, we need to know the *where* of the *Who*.

Hallowed be Your name: Finally, the Rabbi points us to why we pray to our Father in Heaven; it is because He is Hallowed. The Father has a name that is greater than any other. At the mere mention of His name, mountains bow to the ground, and the seas lift up their waves in worship. We would not even know *holy* if it were not for the Father. The Rabbi teaches the heart of prayer comes when we know the *Who*, the *where*, and the *why* of the Father.

TRUE CONTENTMENT

Your kingdom come. Your will be done, On earth as it is in heaven.

Matthew 6:10

Total surrender is the act of laying everything down and leaving nothing in your reserves. In essence, it is putting all your eggs into one basket and then letting them float over Niagara Falls. Total surrender to God brings no certainty of your desired outcome. In fact, biblical history shows us that surrendering to God brings you Pharaoh's army, angry giants, fiery furnaces, lion's dens, raging storms, crosses, and jail cells. But those who surrendered to God also found parted waters, guided stones, fireproof robes, sleepy lions, calm waters, forgiveness, and unlocked cell doors. The Rabbi teaches that we should pray that God's will may be done here on this earth just as it is in Heaven. This is not easy when the subject of your prayer is the healing of a loved one or the restoration of something lost. Placing it in God's hands means Heaven and earth could be moved to bring it about, or God may say it's time to let it go. This possibility is why we hold resources back when we surrender to God. This might be why Ananias and Sapphira held back some money in Acts 5. Luke tells us in Acts 2 that the people in the Church sold their possessions so that they could give to others as there was need. No one needed to store up stuff for themselves because everyone's needs were being met. Ananias and Sapphira joined in this movement, but they held some money back in reserve and because of that, their lives were taken from them. When we pray, *"Your kingdom come. Your will be done, On earth as it is in heaven,"* we surrender to God's Lordship, we lay down our desires, and we open ourselves up to pain, loss, and death as we hope for eternity. Those who trust the Rabbi will know His presence, but those who hold in reserve will never know true contentment.

HEAVEN'S BEST

Give us this day our daily bread.

Matthew 6:11

"Then the LORD said to Moses, "Behold, I will rain bread from heaven for you; and the people shall go out and gather a day's portion every day, that I may test them, whether or not they will walk in My instruction" (Exodus 16:4). When the Rabbi taught us to pray for our daily bread, one would have to think that He was remembering Moses and the children of Israel as they received their daily manna in the dew. During the night, God would rain down manna from Heaven, the bread of angels (Psalm 78:25), and they would go out each day and get what they needed. Never were they to gather more than a day's worth, nor were they to store a surplus. Each day, God would give them what was needed for that day.

How wonderful it would be to have God bring home your groceries every day! To have Him ring your doorbell and say, "Good morning! Here is your breakfast, lunch, and dinner, as well as snacks." To know only plenty and never need. Why would you need surplus unless there were days God did not deliver? One of the Rabbi's lessons of prayer was to pray that the Father—Who is in Heaven, Who is holy, and to Whom we are to submit—would once again put us on His grocery route. But do we trust Him to provide our daily bread? Would we keep a surplus hiding in the cabinets just in case? Would we be content eating manna every day? After we have known the convenience of aisle after aisle of food at the grocery story, from which we pick and choose what we eat, would we want God's provision each day? Daily bread brings security, but it requires surrender. Yet if we are not willing to surrender, then there is no security. The Father simply asks us to trust Him to bring manna in the dew. Daily He pours out Heaven's finest, yet we complain because we want more of what the world has put together. Daily security, Heaven's best, no surplus, total surrender—the Rabbi teaches, if this is what you want, then pray for it.

———————

SEPTEMBER 10

OUR DEBT FORGIVEN

And forgive us our debts, as we also have forgiven our debtors.

Matthew 6:12

Matthew 18:23–35 contains the parable of a king who settled debts with his slaves. One slave owed him more money than he could ever pay back, so when the king ordered for him, his wife, and his children to be sold off to repay the debt, the slave fell to the ground and pleaded for more time. Can you imagine how earnestly this slave begged for merciful patience? His family was hanging in the balance. There was nothing this slave could do to save them or himself because it truly was impossible to repay what he owed. In the mind of the slave, the best-case scenario would be that the king gives him more time to repay, and then for the slave to do enough good things for the king that the king would continue to extend his patience. He was hoping to go to his deathbed still having the debt but having played a game of "Do enough good to stay safe" and "Outsmarted the king." But the king felt compassion for the slave (Matthew 18:27). The king, who had every right to sell off this man and his family to recoup what he had lost, decided not to grant him more time to do the impossible but rather to simply forgive the debt entirely. These words would have rung out in the ears of the slave like a thousand bells tolling at once. Forgiveness was never an option in his mind. Forgiveness meant no more trying to do enough good to stay in the king's good graces or trying to outsmart the king. He was free, no longer a slave to the debt he was crushed by. Forgiveness— what incomprehensible compassion. The Rabbi used this parable as a way of teaching the forgiveness of the Father. At best, you and I could hope to pacify or appease God with our attempt to be good, but this would be an impossible task. The King of kings had every right to open the gates of Hell and throw us in, but God in His immeasurable compassion forgave our debt, setting us free from the prison of sin. Hallelujah, what a Savior!

———

FORGIVE

And forgive us our debts, as we also have forgiven our debtors.

Matthew 6:12

The Rabbi continued in the parable of Matthew 18:23–35 that we looked at yesterday, but where yesterday we ended with praise, today we end with repentance. The slave who had his debt forgiven walked away from the benevolent king with a song of thanksgiving in his heart. But on his way home, he saw another slave who owed him a sum of money. This slave begged and pleaded with the first for more time to repay the debt, but the forgiven slave was unwilling to extend the same grace he had received, so he had the slave thrown in prison until he could pay back the debt. When some of the other slaves heard about the forgiveness of the king and the lack of forgiveness shown by the first slave; they told the king about it, and the king called the forgiven slave back in. *"You wicked slave,"* the king said, *"should you not also have had mercy on your fellow slave, in the same way that I had mercy on you?"* And with that the king threw the slave into prison until he could pay back his impossible debt.

This teaching of the Rabbi is challenging, not to understand but to practice. It is with great joy that we receive the forgiveness of the Father, but it is with great difficulty that we let an offender go free. It is one thing to forgive an accidental infraction, but one that costs us dearly is not easily forgiven. Yet, the Rabbi is not nearly as concerned about what was taken from us as He is concerned about what we do with what is given to us. He restores what has been taken, but He takes what we withhold. *"For if you forgive others for their transgressions, your heavenly Father will also forgive you. But if you do not forgive others, then your Father will not forgive your transgressions"* (Matthew 6:14–15). So great is the forgiveness of the King! So horrifying is the justice poured out on us instead of His Son! Today celebrate with those who sinned against you as you both walk away forgiven.

FOLLOWING TEMPTATION OR GOD

And do not lead us into temptation, but deliver us from evil.
For Yours is the kingdom and the power and the glory forever. Amen.

Matthew 6:13

When following the Spirit of God, there can be nothing but blind trust. Looking upon the invisible and listening for a voice that speaks to our spirit is not easy to follow. Emotions and fleshly desires often speak louder than the still, quiet whisper of our Lord. We must be careful with every step we take, to know that it is the Lord Who leads us; otherwise, we may fall into great sin in the name of Jesus. Understand that Jesus never tempts us, but when we follow our mind's version of Christ, then we can end up bound by the cords of sin. The Rabbi is teaching here that we are to pray and ask the Father to lead us as a Good Shepherd leads His flock to green pastures and still water (Psalm 23).

Temptation is everywhere, and its pull on our lives is strong. It does not matter the time of day or night, nor whether you are male or female, rich or poor, young or old, Methodist, Lutheran, Baptist, Charismatic or Episcopalian, temptation calls to all people and desires to do the bidding of Satan. Satan will masquerade as an angel of light, bidding his victim come and follow him much to the same tune as Jesus calling the disciples. Many who follow him believe they are living right, but they have been deceived. He promises us the world if we will only bow down to him (Matthew 4:9). We must be alert, ever vigilant, because the devil desires to overthrow God's plan through us. Therefore we are to pray, "Lord, do not lead us into temptation." The Good Shepherd leads us on level paths if we will only follow Him with trust. The Rabbi knew blind trust was not easy, so that is why He taught that all who have seen the Rabbi have seen the Father. *"So faith comes from hearing, and hearing by the word of Christ"* (Romans 10:17).

DRAWN TO HIS SIDE

And do not lead us into temptation, but deliver us from evil.
For Yours is the kingdom and the power and the glory forever. Amen.

Matthew 6:13

The Rabbi knew the cords of sin could not be broken by our own abilities. These cords bind us and hold us captive, pulling us down deeper into death. Scripture tells us, *"His own iniquities will capture the wicked, And he will be held with the cords of his sin. He will die for lack of instruction, And in the greatness of his folly he will go astray"* (Proverbs 5:22–23). We need a Deliverer Who will cut the cords that bind us. Addictions have a way of boomeranging back around, blindsiding us and growing even more toxic in our souls. The Rabbi teaches us to pray and ask God to deliver us from evil, but how does this deliverance come? In a remarkably beautiful way.

The Greek word for deliver is *rhyomai,* which means "to draw to one's self." God delivers us by drawing us to His side. But God cannot be in the presence of evil; He is holy and righteous. So how can we come to His side? He throws us a lifeline, a rope that we can grab onto and allow Him to pull us to Himself. That Lifeline is Jesus. The Rabbi Who is telling us to pray and ask the Father to deliver us from evil is the very Lifeline the Father sent to be the Deliverer. Just as a lifeline dangles between a ship and a man overboard, Jesus spanned the gap between Heaven and earth with His arms outstretched on the cross. Now He fights for us; He goes before us, and He teaches us to walk in His ways. Have you ever known God to alleviate the strain of temptation? Have you ever seen Him shut the door on a sin you were trying to commit? Sometimes God, through Jesus, draws us to Himself, and other times He calls us to come to Him through Jesus. Either way, the deliverance is found in His presence. In His presence is all the kingdom, power, and glory forever! When we pray for deliverance, the Rabbi draws us to Himself, where evil cannot exist.

NO LOOKING BACK

But Jesus said to him, "No one, after putting his hand to the plow and looking back, is fit for the kingdom of God."

Luke 9:62

The call to follow Jesus is an all-consuming call. It affects every facet of our lives, from where we are living to the thoughts we think about. When Jesus was walking down the road, He encountered three different people who were interested in following Him, so He taught them about the cost of the calling. Jesus told the first person, *"The foxes have holes and the birds of the air have nests, but the Son of Man has nowhere to lay His head"* (Matthew 8:20). The second person wanted to first bury his father, but Jesus said, *"Allow the dead to bury their own dead; but as for you, go and proclaim everywhere the kingdom of God"* (Matthew 8:22). And to the third person who wanted to first say good-bye to their family, Jesus said, *"No one, after putting his hand to the plow and looking back, is fit for the kingdom of God."* The Rabbi was teaching those who wanted the fame of being a part of the healings, the feedings, and the growing crowds that following Him does not lead to fame but to a letting go of home, family, and dreams. Anything that we hold onto must be let go so that our hands are free to cling to God. Lifted hands in worship must first be empty. Hands of mercy cannot serve while holding the things of this world. So the Rabbi taught these three people the importance of letting go. We are to keep our eyes focused on the One Who has called us. It is so easy to hear the call and to jump in with both feet, with visions of notoriety, but once we see that the fame of following Jesus is often just persecution in the making, we want to run away. Jesus said anyone who puts his hand to the plow but then looks back is not fit for the kingdom of God. Never mistake the call to follow Christ as a guarantee of fame and bliss. His call is a guarantee to service, hard work, love, and peace for those who keep their eyes focused on Him.

———

WHAT THE LAWYER LACKED

And he answered, "You shall love the Lord your God with all your heart,
and with all your soul, and with all your strength, and with all your mind;
and your neighbor as your self.

Luke 10:27

A lawyer once asked Jesus a very perplexing question, *"Teacher, what shall I do to inherit eternal life?"* What could be better than to have someone wanting to know how to spend eternity with the Father? But the Rabbi knew that this was a test. Jesus knew there was nothing the lawyer could do to inherit eternal life. Jesus' response of loving God with everything was correct, yet impossible. If we could love God with all our heart, soul, strength, and mind and love our neighbor as ourselves, then we would have kept the Law perfectly, thereby gaining access into Heaven. But no one can fulfill the Law completely except Jesus. Jesus answered his question, but the lawyer knew he was also being tested. He couldn't deny that he had fallen short of perfection and therefore needed something or Someone to save him.

So if we cannot fulfill this command, then what is the purpose of trying to live by it? The Rabbi understood where this command originated. This command was known as the *shema,* and it was found in Deuteronomy 6:1–2:

> *Now this is the commandment, the statutes and the judgments which the LORD your God has commanded me to teach you, that you might do them in the land where you are going over to possess it, so that you and your son and your grandson might fear the LORD your God, to keep all His statutes and His commandments which I command you, all the days of your life, and that your days may be prolonged.*

In these verses we see why God would command us to obey a Law that we cannot fulfill. God wanted people to know, the obeying of these commands was so the generations to come would *"fear the LORD your God."* To fear Him, to trust Him, to obey Him, and to love Him. The Rabbi knew the lawyer still lacked this.

ALL IS EVERYTHING

And he answered, "You shall love the Lord your God with all your heart, and with all your soul, and with all your strength, and with all your mind; and your neighbor as your self.

Luke 10:27

Anytime the Rabbi tells us to do something with our *"all,"* we need to pay special attention. When He tells us that what we are supposed to do with our *"all"* is the foundation for the whole Law and the prophets (Matthew 22:40), we need to dedicate our lives to it. The absolute most important thing we could do is to love God with our *"all."* Jesus teaches that our *"all"* includes our heart, mind, soul, and strength. Basically, this means everything that is our inside and our outside. When you break this down, God craves our love for Him to flow from our desires, emotions, physical ability, and our intellect. What does this look like? The Father understands what it means to love with *"all"* His desires. He desires none to perish but all to come to repentance (2 Peter 3:9). His desire was for the world to be reconciled to Him, so He stopped at nothing until the way was made, even giving His Son as the ultimate sacrifice. Jesus also understands loving with *"all"* His emotions. He would experience agony to the point of sweating blood before going to the cross, but His prayer was for the Father's will to be done (Luke 22:44). Christ's love for mankind was also with *"all"* His physical ability. He would absorb the beatings and carry the cross until He had no strength left, and Simon of Cyrene would have to help (Luke 23:26). Finally, the Father knew what it was to love us with *"all"* His intellect. He planned out our existence, even down to how many hairs would be on our head and how many days we would live (Jeremiah 29:11; Matthew 10:30). God Almighty understands what He is asking of us when He demands our *"all."* He understands it because He has already given us His *"all"* so we can give it back to Him. It costs us nothing because it all belongs to God, but it requires everything we have!

SEPTEMBER 17

A LIFE OF SELFLESSNESS

And he answered, "You shall love the Lord your God with all your heart, and with all your soul, and with all your strength, and with all your mind; and your neighbor as your self.

Luke 10:27

Do nothing from selfishness or empty conceit, but with humility of mind regard one another as more important than yourselves; do not merely look out for your own personal interests, but also for the interests of others.

Philippians 2:3–4

Have this attitude in yourselves which was also in Christ Jesus, who, although He existed in the form of God, did not regard equality with God a thing to be grasped, but emptied Himself, taking the form of a bond-servant, and being made in the likeness of men. Being found in appearance as a man, He humbled Himself by becoming obedient to the point of death, even death on a cross.

Philippians 2:5–8

For this reason also, God highly exalted Him, and bestowed on Him the name which is above every name, so that at the name of Jesus every knee will bow, of those who are in heaven and on earth and under the earth, and that every tongue will confess that Jesus Christ is Lord, to the glory of God the Father.

Philippians 2:9–11

Learning to love your neighbor as yourself is truly a mark of theology. *Theo* means "God," and *ology* means "the study of." If we desire to live a life of loving others as Christ loved the Church (Ephesians 5:2), then we must study God, namely Jesus, the God-man to Whom we can humanly relate. What were His actions and motives? Jesus, as King, emptied Himself and took on the form of a bond-slave, and even laid down His life for us. To walk with love for our neighbors as Jesus did, we must walk the paths Jesus walked. This cannot be done as long as we look at our status or our merit; these come not from ourselves but are given by the Father.

———

BESEECH THE LORD

And He was saying to them, "The harvest is plentiful, but the laborers are few; therefore beseech the Lord of the harvest to send out laborers into His harvest."

Luke 10:2

Luke chapter ten is a passage of Scripture where the Rabbi is commissioning His followers to go out and prepare all the places He is going to go. His instructions to them were not a coach's speech about, "Go, fight, win!" Nor did He lay out some grand program on "How to Reach Your World in Twelve Easy Steps." Actually, His instructions were very simple: First, pray. He did not teach them to pray anything about themselves being bold, wise, or effective; He taught them to pray that God would do the work. Their role was to *"beseech the Lord of the harvest."* They were to cry out to God for the souls of humanity:

O Lord God of Heaven and earth, we beg You, for Your great Name, please raise up laborers who will go into the harvest! Maker of all creation, we beg You to not let one single fruit of this harvest fall to the ground and perish! May cities be brought to their knees; may they repent; may they know the love of the Lord of the harvest! You, O Lord, are too wonderful for words, too great for comprehension, but You alone can raise up an army of laborers who will go before You, preparing the way! We are Your vessels; use us as You see fit!

Their next set of instructions was to trust the Lord of the harvest to provide for their needs. Don't worry about where you will sleep or what you will eat or what you will wear. You are not to try to provide security for yourself but rather allow God to meet your needs in a way that lifts His great Name among a lost people.

Finally, the Rabbi told them to *"go."* "You have prayed, and you are trusting; now go." Jesus' method for reaching the world today has not changed; we have just stepped in and tried to establish ourselves. The Rabbi's lesson still rings true: "Pray, trust, go!" God will do the work.

SEPTEMBER 19

THE UNKNOWN STRANGER

*Listen to this! Behold, the sower went out to sow; as he was sowing,
some seed fell beside the road, and the birds came and ate it up.*

Mark 4:3–4

Who are the people you pass on the road every day? What are their names? What is going on in their lives? Most of the people we encounter but never engage will move on in obscurity. Their name is never known to us; their existence is quickly forgotten; and their story is lost before it was ever read by us. But that is not so with God. He wrote His story on their heart, and He knows them most intimately. He overflows with passion and compassion for every person who walks down the road. They are special to Him, and because of that, He has placed you on the same road at the same time. He has given you His Word and commissioned you to go and make them disciples (Matthew 28:19–20). The living Word of God is to flow out of your mouth and your actions so that those around you will hear His voice beckoning them to know Him. But that is the convicting truth the Rabbi teaches in this verse. Those who walk down the street may hear the Word of God, but that seed, though sown, was never planted. That seed was no more planted than the seeds cast before the pigeons at a park. Satan swoops in and snatches the Word of God out of their ears well before it engages their brains and especially before it roots itself in their hearts. But sadly, we have no clue because we are not looking at the people we pass on the road. Most often, our actions say, "If someone's story is to be written, let it be mine." But the story that stands first to be written is that of the Rabbi. What is our story, if it were not for the Rabbi speaking Life into our souls? So can we engage every person we pass on the road? No, our focus should not be on the people we pass but on the One Who knows all hearts. When we look through the lens of Christ, we will see the people we daily pass clearer than we ever have.

———

THE ROCKS AND THE SUN

Other seed fell on the rocky ground where it did not have much soil;
and immediately it sprang up because it had no depth of soil. And after the sun
had risen, it was scorched, and because it had no root, it withered away.

Mark 4:5–6

"Listen to this! Behold, the sower went out to sow" (Mark 4:3). The sower went out and began to broadcast the seed over a field. They knew that if the seeds were scattered now, soon with water and sunlight they would be ready to harvest. He tossed the seeds here and there with the hope of a great reaping to come. But not all of the seeds the sower sowed would be harvested. Some of them would die before they bore fruit.

One such seed would land in the rocks. Any farmer can tell you that if you have rocks in your field, you will not have as good a harvest. So maybe the sower would prepare the soil each year, and when he came to a rock, he would toss it over at the edge of the field. Now when the sower cast out seed, some of the seeds would land in those rocks. The plant would quickly grow, but the rocks would stop any roots from taking hold. Then when the sun, which is needed for growth, hit the plant, it had no way to get adequate water, and it would shrivel up and die.

The Rabbi teaches that this seed in the rocks is like the person who hears the Word of God and quickly grows with joy, but because of persecution, they quickly die not having sufficient roots. When persecution or trials come, we will waste away if we are not being nourished by the Living Water of the Spirit. So a question to ponder is: are you a seed in the good soil or a seed among the rocks? Both grow, but one is only temporary (Mark 4:17). The sun is both needed and deadly to plants. Likewise, trials are both needed and deadly to us. Persecution, along with *"water from on high,"* can grow us (James 1:2–4), but trials alone will scorch us and we will wither away.

Father, please supply us with water to grow through trials, not dry up and die. Amen.

FINITE MASQUERADES

Other seed fell among the thorns, and the thorns came up and choked it,
and it yielded no crop.

Mark 4:7

God knew mankind would suffer hardships while in this world. This is why the Father led His children throughout the Old Testament, the Son became a man and walked with us during the Gospels, and the Holy Spirit was sent to dwell in the hearts of the Church to this very day. They even gave us Their Word, so we could have Their love letter, guiding statutes, and teaching. But still, we struggle to walk in Their ways. Jesus knew of the power of Scripture. *"For the word of God is living and active and sharper than any two-edged sword, and piercing as far as the division of soul and spirit, of both joints and marrow, and able to judge the thoughts and intentions of the heart"* (Hebrews 4:12). But even with the power of Scripture, the Rabbi warned that many things can derail His Word from taking root in our hearts. Satan can steal it; persecution and trials can block the roots; and the worries of the world, the deceitfulness of riches, and the desires for other things can choke it out like weeds in a garden. Is the Word of God weak? Not at all, but the human heart is easily distracted. The world seems to tower over us with anger, hatred, and acts of violence. We wonder when will that violence be turned on us? Death looms in the shadows, and we fear sickness and pain. Likewise, the world is full of greed, coveting, and fraud; who can we trust? Even our own thoughts tell us to take from the weak. The world dangles shiny trinkets and supposed shortcuts in front of us; how are we to navigate this life of landmines? These worries, deceptions, and desires will choke us out if we do not find our solace in the healing Word of God. The Rabbi's teaching is just as pertinent today as it was then; nothing of this world will satisfy the longings of our soul. Our eyes desire the finite masquerades, but our soul yearns for eternity, that which only the Authenticity of Heaven can produce.

———

A MULTIPLYING HARVEST

Other seeds fell into the good soil, and as they grew up and increased,
they yielded a crop and produced thirty, sixty, and a hundredfold.

Mark 4:8

Finally, we see some good news about some of the seeds this sower threw out. After the birds ate some, the sun baked some, and the weeds choked some, now some seeds have landed on good soil, and they received water, which enabled their roots to grow deep and which sustained them when the sun was hot. Once harvest time came around, they were loaded with fruit.

Let's take a second to examine the arithmetic of this parable. For the sake of ease, let's say that the sower had four seeds. One fell on the road, and the birds ate it. One fell in the rocks and sprouted but withered with the heat of the sun. One fell among the weeds, which choked it out when it grew up. Finally, one seed fell on good soil and grew to harvest. It would appear that the Lord of the harvest is not very good at what He does. Three out of four seeds perished. But where the world deals in subtraction, the Lord of the harvest deals in multiplication. That one seed would produce thirty, sixty, or even a hundred times more seeds. Again if the sower then threw out those sixty seeds and three-quarters of them perished, the remaining fifteen seeds would produce nine hundred more. The world cannot stop the Lord of the harvest! One simple seed in His hands is enough to cover the world with the Gospel!

So what is the Rabbi's lesson? We may sow the seeds, water the seeds, and even chase away birds, remove the rocks, and pull the weeds, but it is God Who makes them grow (1 Corinthians 3:6). Satan will stop at nothing in his attempts to overthrow the grace of God; but he cannot steal, wither or choke out the Word of God from enough people to stop the harvest. The worries and desires of this world are very real, but the love of the Rabbi is far surpassing that of the hatred of the birds along the road.

THE LIGHT OF THE WORLD

Then Jesus again spoke to them, saying, "I am the Light of the world;
he who follows Me will not walk in the darkness, but will have the Light of life."

John 8:12

"Light and dark." The light comes from Jesus, and the darkness is from the world. We wander around in darkness unless we follow the Light, walking where He walks and waiting when He stops. Jesus is a great Light, shining brightly, illuminating the shadows. We cannot fathom all the depths of what it means for Jesus to say, *"I am the Light of the world."*

Jesus would later say something similar but completely different. *"You are the light of the world. A city set on a hill cannot be hidden"* (Matthew 5:14). So first we learn that Jesus is the *"Light of the world"* and then He says that His disciples are the *"light of the world."* Who is the light of the world—Jesus or those who follow Him? The answer is found in a most unique place.

Genesis 1:16 says, *"God made the two great lights, the greater light to govern the day, and the lesser light to govern the night; He made the stars also."* In the Creation account, God created two lights, a greater light for the day, which is the sun, and a lesser light for the night, which is the moon. Now science teaches us the moon is not actually light but simply a rock. Yet if you have ever walked outside in the darkness of night, when there is a full moon, then you could possibly even have seen shadows cast by the light of the moon. Where does this light come from? It comes from the sun, the greater light, reflecting off the surface of the moon. The same is true for us being the *"light of the world."* We are not lights but rather reflections of a greater Light, Christ Jesus. The Rabbi taught that while He was on the earth, He was the *"Light of the world,"* but when He left, we would be the *"light of the world"* by being reflections of Him. *"The people who walk in darkness Will see a great light; Those who live in a dark land, The light will shine on them"* (Isaiah 9:2).

FORGIVING LOVE

But I say to you, do not resist an evil person;
but whoever slaps you on your right cheek, turn the other to him also.

Matthew 5:39

Sometimes when the Rabbi taught, He would teach the masses something new, and other times He would teach an individual how to right a misconception they had been living by. Living with a misunderstanding can be the difference between Heaven and Hell. One of the major reasons for the opposition to Christianity, aside from Jesus' claim to being the only way to Heaven (John 14:6), is that sometimes believers will act out of a misunderstanding of Scripture. The Bible calls this holding to a form of godliness but denying its power (2 Timothy 3:5). When we believe a misconception, we are denying the power of God, which hinders others from seeing the Body of Christ rightly. We can see the Rabbi righting a misconception at the Sermon on the Mount, when He reminded the people that they had heard it said, *"An eye for an eye, and a tooth for a tooth"* (Matthew 5:38). But the people used this as a means to seek revenge on others when they were wronged. Jesus righted this misunderstanding by saying, *"But I say to you, do not resist an evil person; but whoever slaps you on your right cheek, turn the other to him also."* This was unthinkable! Why would we allow the person who harms us to then harm us again? Was the Rabbi calling them to be a doormat so others could walk on them? No, but God is calling us to become more like Him. All of us are guilty of betraying the Father. In fact, we are guilty of crucifying His only Son. Therefore with the understanding of *"An eye for an eye,"* God should betray us to death, but instead, He loved us (Romans 5:8). No revenge fell on us but rather on Jesus. Likewise, we are to allow God to dish out revenge on our enemies. God is big enough to handle those who lash out at us, and He is big enough to put the same forgiving love in us that is in Him.

———————

GIVING IT ALL

If anyone wants to sue you and take your shirt, let him have your coat also.

Matthew 5:40

The Rabbi's teachings were much more than just words. Words are much more intellectual, a conveying of information, but the teachings of the Rabbi are applicational. Information for the sake of information does not bring about growth, yet information that is practiced brings maturity. Jesus taught those listening to the Sermon on the Mount a lesson that in its informational form sounded foolish but in its application, was unfathomable. He told the people that if someone sued you and took your shirt, then you were to give them your coat also. From this one verse, we can infer a couple things. First, if someone is suing you, then they have a grievance against you. And if the court sides with them, then justice has sided against you saying that you were deficient in your dealing with this person. You were in the wrong. Next, if this person is taking the very shirt off your back, then we can assume that you do not have an ox or a goat or any money. You are down to the clothes you are wearing. At this low point in your life, when you have nothing but your clothes, you are found in the wrong, and now someone is trying to even take your shirt. Jesus tells you to go even further and to give them your coat as well. To a Jew, this was unimaginable because the Law made provisions for your coat. *"If your ever take your neighbor's cloak as a pledge, you are to return it to him before the sun sets, for that is his only covering; it is his cloak for his body. What else shall he sleep in? And it shall come about that when he cries out to Me, I will hear him, for I am gracious"* (Exodus 22:26–27). The Rabbi was saying to give that which no one was to take. Why? Because love, God's love, covers our needs, even down to what we will lay down with at night. Following the Rabbi takes total trust. We do not need to make provision for ourselves. Nothing with God is infinitely more than everything without Him!

WALK TWO MILES

Whoever forces you to go one mile, go with him two.

Matthew 5:41

Have you ever heard the saying, "Walk a mile in someone else's shoes"? The heart of this saying is, in order for you to understand another person, you must walk with them, experiencing their life, wade through their trials, and celebrate their victories. You have to get into their world and draw near to them. This is exactly what Jesus did to us. He came to earth to walk in our shoes, experience our life, wade through our trials, and celebrate our victories. He is Emanuel, which draws Him near to us. This is how Salvation came to mankind. But the Rabbi's teaching does not end here. No, He walked a mile in our shoes so that we could then walk a mile in His shoes. When Jesus spoke of someone forcing you to go one mile with them, everyone immediately thought of the Romans. A Roman soldier had the ability to force anyone to carry their stuff for one mile. This was one of Rome's ways of putting the Jewish people in their place. But the Rabbi was teaching them to not just fulfill their servitude but to also freely go a second mile with them. In essence, "walk a mile in their shoes." Not only would you be freeing yourself from the oppression of Rome, but you would also have the opportunity to get to know the person. Just like Jesus, you would have to chance to step into their world and shine the light of Christ in the shadows.

This teaching is still valid today as well as still difficult. How do we love those who oppress us? Maybe instead of trying to overthrow them, we should do what Jesus did: "go with the FLOW"—**F**-forgive, **L**-love, **O**-opportunities to serve, **W**-worship. Usually, when we think of *"going with the flow,"* we think of taking the path of least resistance, but in this case, it is walking a second mile with someone who wants to rise above us. Instead of fighting them, we serve them, just as the Rabbi served us.

GIVE FREELY; LIVE FREE

Give to him who asks of you, and do not turn away from him who wants to borrow from you.

Matthew 5:42

Over the past several days, we have looked at some of the Rabbi's difficult lessons. They have been hard because they go against the fundamental lie Satan has fed us, that we deserve something more. Since the dawn of time, mankind has sought to rise above its position before God. Our position is one of humility. We own nothing, and we can do nothing; our very being can be attributed to only the Creator. Therefore when we hold on to something as if it were ours, we are ignorantly stealing from God. Another way of looking at this is to understand that we are slaves to God. Yes, slaves! Because we have been bought with a price (1 Corinthians 6:20). A slave has no rights, no property, no house, no food, nor possessions. Everything they have is because their master gave it to them. Likewise, God is our Master, and He must be our Master if we are to bear His name (Romans 10:13); therefore, we own nothing. So when the Rabbi taught the crowds to give their other cheek to the person who just slapped them or to give their coat to the person who took their shirt or to walk another mile with the person who forced them to walk the first, it was to bring them freedom from the slavery of man and the imprisonment of this world. We are bound by no one except the Father. No one rules us, but He and no one else takes from us that He does not repay. For the person who has nothing, what can be taken from them? If we serve God, then we must hold the things of this world with loose hands. It isn't ours—it is God's—and He has told us to give it to him who wants to borrow it. If they don't give it back, then you have lost nothing; it was never ours. When we take possession of what belongs to God, then we fall prey to Satan's lie that we deserve something more. But when we humbly steward what the Master entrusts to us, we can serve others. Give freely; live free!

———————

THE RABBI'S LIFE

This is eternal life, that they may know You, the only true God,
and Jesus Christ whom You have sent.

John 17:3

On the night before He was crucified, the Rabbi had the opportunity to eat a meal with His disciples and to pray for them. He knew the time had come, and He used His last few hours with them in prayer. He prayed in the upper room, and then He prayed on the Mount of Olives. Jesus spoke in His prayer of what eternal life really is. The true nature of life was a continuous theme throughout the Rabbi's ministry. In John 10:10, He said, *"The thief comes only to steal and kill and destroy; I came that they may have life, and have it abundantly."* The life Jesus came to give was not normal life but abundant life. Again the Rabbi would teach about life: *"Jesus said to him, "I am the way, and the truth, and the life; no one comes to the Father but through Me"* (John 14:6). Finally, in the High Priestly Prayer Jesus said, *"This is eternal life, that they may know You, the only true God, and Jesus Christ whom You have sent"* (John 17:3). Life—true life, abundant life, eternal life—can only be found in the Rabbi. These words are very churchy and very spiritual when said plainly, but what do they mean? Remember, they were spoken, not by a mere man but by the Rabbi; there is an eternal lesson in them. All of us will pass away, and the life we live here on earth will end (Hebrews 9:27). But our life does not stop at death. Death is simply the threshold through which we transition from a fallen world of restraints and curses into the glorious presence of the Rabbi, where death can no longer parade its pain. But death is not the beginning of life. Life abundant began when we took the first step into grace. It is at the cross of Calvary that Life submitted to death on our behalf; yet three days later, death was diagnosed terminal. Death is rendered powerless in the knowledge of Who the Rabbi is!

———————

FULLY LOVED

For this reason I say to you, her sins, which are many, have been forgiven,
for she loved much; but he who is forgiven little, loves little.

Luke 7:47

The Rabbi entered into the home of a Pharisee named Simon, and a sinful woman came up behind Him and began to wet His feet with her tears, then wipe them off with her hair. She poured perfume on His feet, which angered Simon. Jesus, knowing his heart, then told a parable about two debtors—one owing a large sum of money and one owing a smaller amount of money. Neither of them could pay their debts, so the lender forgave them both. The Rabbi then asked Simon, *"So which of them will love him more?"* Simon answered the one who was forgiven more would love him more. Jesus then turned to the sinful woman and forgave her.

The love this lady had for the Rabbi was great, while the love Simon had for Him was self-love. Simon saw very little need to be forgiven. What had he done to need a Savior? At least he was not like the sinful woman. But Jesus knew how sick and wicked Simon's heart was. Yet this woman, whose sins were great, loved so deeply.

It is easy to see the Rabbi's lesson on the correlation of love and forgiveness, but let's take a moment to meditate on the Rabbi. Who did He love more? The religious Simon or the repentant sinner? How beautiful is the thought that God's love for us is not based on our love for Him? If the Father is Love, then there is no way He could love more or love less. His love is complete. The heart of the Father beat with love for Simon, even in his arrogance and self-righteousness, because the love of the Father can break and mend his deceived soul. Likewise, the Father overflowed with love for the bruised flower who anointed the feet of His Son. Her list of sins was long, but forgiveness made that list blank. The Rabbi knew both sinners fully, and He longed to be fully known.

GREATER IS HE

And He said to them, "Why are you afraid? Do you still have no faith?"

Mark 4:40

Twice the Rabbi told the disciples to get in the boat and go to the other side. Both times the disciples would encounter life-threatening storms in the middle of the lake. Both times, the disciples would struggle with the sea. Both times, one or more of the disciples would cry out for the help of the Rabbi. Both times the Rabbi would calm the storm. And both times the Rabbi would question the faith of the disciples (Mark 4:35–41; Matthew 14:22–33).

What is it about the other side of the lake that Jesus desired? Could it be that Jesus wanted to show His Lordship over storms? Was He trying to show the need for faith? Maybe He simply wanted to minister on the other side of the lake. In any or all of these, the Rabbi taught the disciples that God is greater than any created thing. The first time they *"crossed over to the other side,"* the disciples were worried about the boat filling up with water (Mark 4:37), but Jesus was asleep in the stern of the boat. The second time they *"crossed over to the other side,"* the disciples were rowing hard against the wind and waves (Mark 6:48), but Jesus was taking a walk . . . on the water. The Rabbi was not concerned about any created thing because He was the Creator. What could weather do to Him that He could not calm? What could demons do to Him that He could not banish? What human could touch Him without His allowing them? What disease could hurt Him where He could not heal it? Jesus simply rose above all these things. For the disciples, they could be harmed by weather, demons, humans, and sickness, but that might be why He called them to the other side. He was teaching them that, "greater is He who is in you than he that is in the world" (1 John 4:4). Could you imagine sleeping or taking a walk during the storms of life? Jesus could! Could you imagine simply abiding with Jesus while the waves crash over? There is no better place!

———

OCTOBER

The Redeemer's Song Is Pure and Restoring

HE SEES ME BEAUTIFUL

Like a lily among the thorns, So is my darling among the maidens.

Song of Songs 2:2

The Redeemer's song is pure and restoring; it also rings out in our spirit. Take some time to still your mind and listen for His voice. God is singing a song over us, and it is a song of love and rejoicing! This song is sung from the book of Genesis to the letter of Revelation; it's redemption's song. In the middle of it all, we find a small book that usually goes unnoticed. Song of Songs, which means "the best of the songs," is perched in the middle of Scripture and separates the books of Poetry from the Major Prophets. The meaning behind Song of Songs is debated and could be a poem about Solomon's love for his first wife. It could be simply a fictitious, romantic poem. Others debate that it is an allegory about the Father's love for Israel, and others think it parallels Jesus' love for the Church. I believe that all of these are true. The Redeemer is wise enough to write His song on the hearts of His children for all generations. Can You hear the voice of the Bridegroom echoing off the walls of eternity: *"Like a lily among the thorns, So is my darling among the maidens"* (Song of Songs 2:2). In the eyes of Christ, the world pales in comparison to how He sees us. If you can, let your mind get a handle on the fact that He doesn't see our sins, our pride, our lusts, or our ugly, but rather sees us as a lily among the thorns. The Redeemer sees us as beautiful! This is so difficult for us because we struggle to see past our mess, but Jesus sees the Bride He longs for. What holy love it must be to have such blinding grace for an adulterous lover of this world.

I laid down and I did dine,

On flesh and forbidden fruit.

But of this mess You did protest,

And make my heart brand new.

CALL AND RESPONSE

Like an apple tree among the trees of the forest,
So is my beloved among the young men.
In his shade I took great delight and sat down,
And his fruit was sweet to my taste.

Song of Songs 2:3

Yesterday we talked about the song that the Redeemer is singing over us in the Song of Songs. Today we look at the song we sing back to Him. In music this is called "Call and Response." In the Christian walk, it is called "Worship." The Redeemer's song is pure and restoring, so the lyrics that flow out of our soul should be righteous and whole. The Bridegroom compared us to a lily among thorns; we, in turn, make a comparison, too, *"Like an apple tree among the trees of the forest."* Could you imagine walking in the forest and seeing all the pine trees with their needles, all the broad leaf trees with their acorns and nuts, but there in the middle of them is a lone apple tree? Smaller in stature but loaded with large, round, juicy, sweet, and beautiful apples. Apples can be used for so many things, applesauce, apple pie, apple butter, apple cider, cooked apples, and apple cider vinegar. And what a delight it is on a summer's day just to sink your teeth into an apple and let the juice run down your chin. Compared to all other trees ("things of this world"), He is greatly to be savored! *"In His shade I took great delight and sat down."* There is no greater place to be than in the shade of the Lord. It is there that we find "great delight." That does not mean all of life is fun when we walk with Christ, but when we are listening to His song, there is nowhere else we would rather be. Take time today just to sit and abide in the shadow of the Almighty. Reach up and take some of the fruit of His tree and taste how sweet He is. And when you sit and eat His fruit, it will begin to grow in you as well. The sweetness of the fruit of the Spirit will grow in you and through you (Galatians 5:22–23).

"O taste and see that the LORD is good; How blessed is the man who takes refuge in Him" (Psalm 34:8).

THE NARRATIVE OF LOVE

He has brought me into his banquet hall, And his banner over me is love.

Song of Songs 2:4

The narrative that is intertwined in the Song of Songs is a beautiful story of love, but it is also overlaid with the most beautiful song of redemption. Solomon goes and visits a vineyard He owns and leases out. While there, he meets a girl and falls in love. He then has to leave for a time. The young lady waits and longs for her lover to return. She watches the mountains, longing to see him bounding over the top of them. Finally, the day comes that she lifts up her eyes, and there he is in all his glory, coming to get his bride and take her home to be with him. Together they go to the palace where they celebrate with a wedding! Truly the book of Song of Songs is a "poetic love mystery." But how could we overlook the similarity to Christ's love story with His Church? He left His throne to come into our world; He displayed His love for all to see on a cross, then had to leave for a time. For those who long and watch for His return, they will one day see Him bounding through the clouds, coming to take His Bride to her new home. Together they will celebrate their love with a wedding. All of Heaven will rejoice and cry out, *"Holy, Holy, Holy is the Lord God Almighty!"*

"He has brought me into his banquet hall, And his banner over me is love" (Song of Songs 2:4). Oh, the joy that will be on that day when we can gaze into the eyes of Love! But that joy is not reserved for that day but is now available to everyone who longs for it! Jesus said, *"In My Father's house are many dwelling places; if it were not so, I would have told you; for I go to prepare a place for you. If I go and prepare a place for you, I will come again and receive you to Myself, that where I am, there you may be also"* (John 14:2–3).

Jesus retells the narrative of the Song of Songs: "I came; I'm leaving; I'll return; I'll take you to be with Me!"

THE LORD'S GLORY

But the angel said to them, "Do not be afraid; for behold, I bring you good news of great joy which will be for all the people; for today in the city of David there has been born for you a Savior, who is Christ the Lord."

Luke 2:10–11

The night Jesus was born, shepherds were watching their sheep when an angel appeared to them. The Bible says that the glory of the Lord shone around them. In Exodus 34:29, we get a better understanding of what this means: *"It came about when Moses was coming down from Mount Sinai (and the two tablets of the testimony were in Moses' hand as he was coming down from the mountain), that Moses did not know that the skin of his face shone because of his speaking with Him."* People could tell that he had been with God because of the appearance of his face. It is the same way with the angel in Luke 2; the glory of the Lord shown all around not just him but also the shepherds. When we have been in the presence of God, His glory shines on everyone near us. Jesus explains this truth in another way, *"You are the light of the world. A city set on a hill cannot be hidden; nor does anyone light a lamp and put it under a basket, but on the lamp stand, and it gives light to all who are in the house"* (Matthew 5:14–15). The light that emanates from us is not our light but the glory of God. It comes from us being in His presence, and it shines on all who are in the house. The angel had been in the presence of the Lord, and the glory of the Lord shown on the shepherds. The Bible then tells us that a great multitude of the heavenly host joined the angel, and they were saying, *"Glory to God in the highest, And on earth peace among men with whom He is pleased"* (Luke 2:13–14). If one angel who had been in the presence of the Lord caused the glory of the Lord to shine forth around those shepherds, can you imagine what it must have been like when the host of Heaven joined in? The Redeemer's song of peace rang out that night, and the sky was illuminated with the glory of the Lord!

GOD'S HEART SONG

The LORD your God is in your midst, A victorious warrior. He will exult over you with joy, He will be quiet in His love, He will rejoice over you with shouts of joy.

Zephaniah 3:17

We all have a mental image of God. It may have been influenced by cartoon representations or Hollywood portrayals, but we all have an image that pops into our minds. Maybe you see the Father as a holy version of your earthly father. Maybe you have conjured up an image based on your experiences in life. In all of these, we fall miserably short of imagining the appearance of God because we are trying to portray Him in human terms. In essence, we are trying to put an image together based on a description. It would be like trying to put a jigsaw puzzle together without knowing what the picture was. Someone may say that the image in the puzzle is very strong or that the image is vivid and glorious. The description does not help you put the puzzle together; it just describes an aspect of the finished product. Likewise, we have been given lots of attributes of God—*loving* (1 John 4:16), *truthful* (John 14:6), *compassionate, gracious, slow to anger and abounding in lovingkindness* (Exodus 34:6), *a strong fortress* (2 Samuel 22:33), and so many other things. But do these attributes help you know what God looks like? No, they help you know His heart. The heart of our Redeemer is beautiful! His heart is so full of joy that He sings, shouts, and dances as He walks through our midst. The Redeemer's song flows through our streets and can be heard in our backyards. The crickets join in, and the birds chirp in harmony; the thunder echoes in time with His heartbeat. We may not know what He looks like, but we can know His heartsong. But beware—sins have a way of dulling our ears. It drowns out the melody of the Father and clouds our minds so that all we hear is noise. When we lose our way, simply look overhead; that is where the Redeemer will be, exulting with joy!

"Please help me to quiet my soul and listen to Your song as You sing in my midst!"

UNITING HEAVEN AND EARTH

And one called out to another and said, "Holy, Holy, Holy, is the LORD of hosts,
The whole earth is full of His glory."

Isaiah 6:3

Isaiah was a man called by God to be a prophet, to receive His message, and to deliver it to the desired recipient. In the year of King Uzziah's death, Isaiah would receive a vision from God that would be beyond anything he had ever experienced because, in this vision, he saw the Lord. Now Scripture tells us this: *"But He said, You cannot see My face, for no man can see Me and live!"* (Exodus 33:20). Therefore on the day that Isaiah saw the Lord sitting on a throne, he died. Not physically but fleshly. Isaiah worded it this way: *"Woe is me, for I am ruined! Because I am a man of unclean lips, And I live among a people of unclean lips; For my eyes have seen the King, the LORD of hosts"* (Isaiah 6:5). That very day, Isaiah received a calling to be a prophet; this calling, like all callings from God, can only be accomplished if we are dead to self and alive in Him. Isaiah was enlisted into the service of the Redeemer to prophesy about the coming Suffering Servant (Isaiah 53). This would be a daunting task, but Isaiah had been blessed with a couple very special gifts. First, he had seen the Lord sitting on His throne! This alone would change his life forever. Second, he had heard the seraphim singing the Redeemer's song: *"Holy, Holy, Holy, is the LORD of hosts, The whole earth is full of His glory."* What a beautiful sound and what an awesome opportunity it was for Isaiah to hear and see what true worship was like. This would fuel him for the task ahead. Finally, Isaiah was touched by a coal from the altar of God, which took away his iniquity and forgave his sins (Isaiah 6:6–7). Now he had something to sing about. Isaiah was changed that day. He saw the Lord; he heard angelic worship; he experienced cleansing and forgiveness; and he was called to join in singing the Redeemer's song, which unites Heaven and earth.

———————

ANSWERING THE CALL

Ah Lord GOD! Behold, You have made the heavens and the earth by Your great power and by Your outstretched arm! Nothing is too difficult for You.

Jeremiah 32:17

Now the word of the LORD came to me saying, "Before I formed you in the womb I knew you, And before you were born I consecrated you; I have appointed you a prophet to the nations." Then I said, "Alas, Lord God! Behold, I do not know how to speak, Because I am a youth." But the Lord said to me, "Do not say, 'I am a youth,' Because everywhere I send you, you shall go, And all that I command you, you shall speak. "Do not be afraid of them, For I am with you to deliver you," declares the Lord (Jeremiah 1:4–8).

Jeremiah received the all-powerful, all-authoritative, and all-scary call of God, which said, I've called you to be a prophet to the nations. Jeremiah's response is greatly worth noting. He said, *"Alas, Lord God!"* The word a*las* in Hebrew is *"ahahh,"* which is an exclamation of emotion. In essence, Jeremiah was freaking out. He began listing the excuses of age and ability, but God would not let that deter him. In the end, Jeremiah would be obedient to what the Redeemer had planned for him, and he would watch the Father do great things. Many chapters later, Jeremiah would once again use the exclamation *ahahh.* *"Ah Lord God! Behold, You have made the heavens and the earth by Your great power and by Your outstretched arm! Nothing is too difficult for You"* (Jeremiah 32:17). Jeremiah would exclaim "ahahh," but this time, instead of listing excuses, he sang the Redeemer's song, saying, "Nothing is too difficult for You." God's call is bigger than our ability, but His call was never for us to accomplish alone. We proceed in the strength and ability of the God of the universe (Ephesians 6:10). Only a Redeemer as great and marvelous as Christ Jesus can take our *ahahh* of fear and turn it into an *ahahh* of worship! *"Ahahh,"* the Redeemer's song is pure and restoring!

AN ELEVENTH HOUR PRAYER

While I was fainting away, I remembered the LORD,
And my prayer came to You, Into Your holy temple.

Jonah 2:7

The Redeemer's song is pure and restoring, but what is His song? What are the words? What is its tune? Jonah was a man who found the Redeemer's song in the eleventh hour. Living life in the eleventh hour is a life of zero certainties. Jonah said, *"While I was fainting away ... "* Jonah felt like he was *"fainting away,"* but he hadn't yet learned that God would not allow him to *"faint away"*—not until He was ready for him to—and God was not ready for Jonah to come home. Also, it's important to note, God does not ask us to serve Him; He calls us. Another way of saying this is, God tells you where to go, what to say, and when to show up. For Jonah, he didn't want to go where God said or to say what God wanted, nor did he then or ever want to go anywhere near Nineveh; but God didn't ask Jonah to go to Nineveh—He told him. Jonah thought he could outsmart God by running from Him. When that didn't work, Jonah thought he could outsmart God by simply dying. But you will never be able to best God, especially in death because He is Life. So when Jonah tried to die, God simply made him live. For three days, Jonah would survive in the belly of the fish, but while he thought he was *"fainting away,"* God was simply waiting for the opportune moment. It was during this time in the fish that Jonah learned what the Redeemer's song was. It is the song of a broken and contrite heart. The words are honest and true. They stem from repentance and lead toward obedience. Praise is the refrain, and worship is the chorus. Humans cannot sing the Redeemer's song until they have become undone. God's anthem is too great to be sung with half a heart. It is never too late to sing a song of prayer to God; the eleventh hour is exactly when the Redeemer's song most clearly resonates. That is when we lay aside ourselves and humbly turn from our disobedience to the light of God!

WORSHIPPING SELF

Those who regard vain idols Forsake their faithfulness.

Jonah 2:8

Jonah found the Redeemer's song while *"fainting away"* in the belly of the fish. It was there that he confessed his sin. Jonah said, *"Those who regard vain idols Forsake their faithfulness."* What is an idol? An idol is a physical representation of *a god.* What is the purpose of an idol? When it comes to religion, the bottom line is *faith.* It takes faith to believe in the God of the universe because we cannot see Him, or touch Him, and Satan tries to create doubt in those times we see God's hand at work, saying there are scientific or psychological reasons for it. Likewise, it takes faith to believe in some other god. You cannot see Allah, or Buddha, or Krishna, nor could the people in Bible days see Baal, Ashtaroth, or Dianna. Finally, it even takes faith to be an atheist. If there is no God, then where did we come from? Religion always goes back to what our origin is. There are no guarantees in religion, and that is why we must have faith. As humans, we desire proof of the unknown, and often if we cannot find proof, then we will create our own. This is where idols come in. We believe in a god that we cannot see, so when doubts rise up, we create something physical to represent the unseen. We believe god embodies this idol, and that way we can take him with us and cling to him. As Christians, we do this, too. It might be the cross necklace we clutch or a Christian fish on our vehicle that we hope will ward off speeding tickets. It is what we hold to when we want more than just faith. For Jonah, he had bowed down to the most common idol of all—*self.* Jonah's own vanity was what he worshipped. Like many of us, his gauge of obedience was what he wanted or what he felt comfortable with. He would forsake his faithfulness because he regarded himself over God. But while in the fish, Jonah would confess this sin and turn back to the Redeemer.

IT IS FINISHED

But I will sacrifice to You With the voice of thanksgiving.
That which I have vowed I will pay. Salvation is from the LORD.

Jonah 2:9

Finally, Jonah is ready! From the very first moment he received God's call to go to Nineveh, he has been running. How incredibly scary it is to run toward death. Jonah struck out on his own, determined to evade the call of God. This never works; God simply wears you down until you have nothing left. Just like a fisherman wears out a fish so that once it's exhausted, he can easily reel it in. Jonah had run hard and was now exhausted. With nothing left, He declared to God, *"That which I have vowed I will pay. Salvation is from the LORD."* In essence, "I'm utterly empty, Lord; I surrender." Have you ever stood before God, having been stripped of everything? Literally, having nothing left in you? Vulnerable, exhausted, even fearful of His response. But even if His response was harsh, you're so empty, you could no longer make a defense. Utterly and totally, your life, your hopes, your failures, your eternity lies in the hands of Someone other than you. You lay your head on the ground and close your eyes; there is nothing else you can do. Your mind echoes the words of Jesus, *"It is finished"* (John 19:30). But as you lie there exhausted, you begin to hear something so unexpected that you can't quite figure out what it is. Then in disbelief, you realize the Redeemer is singing a song over you! As you lay in the belly of the fish, the sound of His voice fills the space around you with a melody that strikes deep into your heart! Your exhaustion is replaced with joy, and your fears melt to peace. In the darkness of your prison, you listen to the Redeemer's song. Renewed, refreshed, and revived, you surrender to God's plan. *"That which I have vowed I will pay. Salvation is from the LORD."* "I will go to Nineveh!" Why? Because the Redeemer sang His song *"while I was fainting away"* (Jonah 2:7).

DAVID WAITED

He put a new song in my mouth, a song of praise to our God;
Many will see and fear And will trust in the LORD.

Psalm 40:3

Psalm 40 was written by David, and in it, you can hear the wisdom of a shepherd, the fear of a fugitive, and the confidence of a king. David knew what it was to find the presence of God in each of these walks of life. That's how he could write, *"I wait patiently for the LORD; And He inclined to me and heard my cry"* (Psalm 40:1). Where did this patience come from? Scripture tells us, *"Love is patient"* (1 Corinthians 13:4); also *"patience"* is a fruit of the Spirit (Galatians 5:22). Patience comes from abiding with God. David would not have known how to wait patiently on the Lord unless he had walked with Him. He knew the Father cared about him, but he also knew the Father was preparing him for what was ahead. David continued his psalm by saying, *"He brought me up out of the pit of destruction, out of the miry clay, And He set my feet upon a rock making my footsteps firm"* (Psalm 40:2). Do not miss the details; David was patiently waiting while he was in the miry pit of destruction! Yes, he was crying out to God, but still, he waited until God inclined His ear and brought him out of the pit. The Redeemer's response is amazing toward those who cry out to Him yet wait patiently for Him to move. David was pulled out of the mire and placed on a rock. For anyone who has sunk low in despair, you know *'waiting'* and *'patience'* are not what fills your thoughts. But David waited. Finally, God reached down and brought him out. David went from sinking to standing and from crying out to singing a new song of praise! How glorious is our Redeemer! He can take someone crying out in the pit of destruction and raise them up to a firm foundation. He puts a new song of praise in their mouth, and many will see what God has done and will trust in Him! That is redemption at its finest. The world will know how great He is when we sing the song of one who waited.

———————

WHO THE REDEEMER IS

Let all who seek You rejoice and be glad in You;
Let those who love Your salvation say continually, "The LORD be magnified!"

Psalm 40:16

David continues Psalm 40 with an exhortation to make the Redeemer known. He says, *"Let all who seek You rejoice and be glad in You."* Those who feel that God is boring do not know Who God is. For those who seek Him, they will rejoice; they will be glad. This is not prosperity but reality. Why? Why is there joy for those who seek God? It is because of the Redeemer's song! David said, *"Let those who love Your salvation say continually, 'The LORD be magnified!'"* When our eyes are fixed on Him and Who He is, when we magnify and make much of His attributes, then we no longer see the storms of life, the sins that prevail, the pains that torment, or the needs that are still lacking. When we look at Him, we sing about His *"righteousness," "faithfulness," "salvation," "lovingkindness,"* and His *"truth"* (Psalm 40:10). We sing the Redeemer's song because this is Who He is:

Righteousness—*"He made Him who knew no sin to be sin on our behalf, so that we might become the righteousness of God in Him"* (2 Corinthians 5:21).

Faithfulness—*"If we are faithless, He remains faithful, for He cannot deny Himself"* (2 Timothy 2:13).

Salvation—*"And all flesh will see the salvation of God"* (Luke 3:6).

Lovingkindness—*"How precious is Your lovingkindness, O God! And the children of men take refuge in the shadow of Your wings"* (Psalm 36:7).

Truth—*"And you will know the truth, and the truth will make you free"* (John 8:32.)

David made known the righteousness, faithfulness, salvation, lovingkindness, and truth of God to the *"great congregation"* (Psalm 40:10) because when you seek the Redeemer, He is magnified!

THE SONG OF THE CROSS

Into Your hand I commit my spirit; You have ransomed me,
O LORD, God of truth.

Psalm 31:5

What a glorious Psalm! For Jesus to utter these words of David with His dying breath makes them hold such richness (Luke 23:46). To be sure, what words could we possibly say that could hold more weight? They are the essence of salvation. How else can we be saved other than to commit our spirit into the hand of the Redeemer? We are not saved of our own ability; therefore, we cannot assure our salvation through any means other than to hope the Father is a God of His word.

Many people would wager there is no better place to be than in the hand of God? But according to the writer of Hebrews, *"It is a terrifying thing to fall into the hands of the living God"* (Hebrews 10:31). What is salvation for some is judgment for others. The hands of the Redeemer are perfectly capable of forming the intricacies of the human heart, as well as forge the mountains of the Himalayas. But His nail-pierced hands are also capable of differentiating who is to be ushered into Heaven's gates and who is to be put out. *"Into Your hand I commit my spirit"*—how sobering a thought to think of the cut-and-dry decision His hand will make for each one of us. There is no "in between" or "almost." Simply "salvation" or "judgment." But let us not forget the rest of the verse: *"You have ransomed me, O LORD, God of truth."* The Redeemer's song rang out from the cross and drove a wedge in eternity, splitting from Heaven to Hell, because either the God of truth ransomed you or He didn't. Life and death are surprisingly separated, not by fathoms but merely by the handbreadth of Christ. Hold your life, and you will lose it (Matthew 16:25); commit your life into the hand of God, and you will be saved. The Redeemer's song was never clearer than when He sang it from the cross.

Oh, God, into Your hands, I commit my spirit! Deliver me to Your side because without You, I am lost.

———————

BROKEN HEART

A Psalm of David. A Maskil. How blessed is he whose transgression is forgiven,
Whose sin is covered!

Psalm 32:1

Do you need a restored soul? Sin robs us of our vitality because it separates us from God, Who is our Source of life. Most of us really are not bothered by our sin. We do not like to get caught, nor do we like doing things we know we shouldn't, but to truly mourn our sin, we do not. This lack of brokenness leads us to dry seasons of life. David said, *"When I kept silent about my sin, my body wasted away Through my groaning all day long. For day and night, Your hand was heavy upon me; My vitality was drained away as with the fever heat of summer. Selah"* (Psalm 32:3–4). David knew the dry days and sleepless nights of hiding his sin. There are times when God allows us to flounder and drift away, feeling the very depths of hopelessness, because as long as we continue to sin yet feel no remorse, then why would we desire a Redeemer? Finally, David could stand it no longer; he humbled himself before God saying, *"I acknowledged my sin to You, And my iniquity I did not hide; I said, "I will confess my transgressions to the Lord"; And You forgave the guilt of my sin. Selah. Therefore, let everyone who is godly pray to You in a time when You may be found; Surely in a flood of great waters they will not reach him. You are my hiding place; You preserve me from trouble; You surround me with songs of deliverance. Selah"* (Psalm 32:5–7). Did you catch David's words? After having withered in his sin, David exposed them with confession. Confessing your sins makes you vulnerable to loss, but when you hate your sin more than the risk of losing everything, then you are mourning your sins. You crave the presence of God more than your fleshly desires. At this point, David said, *"You surround me with songs of deliverance."* That is the Redeemer's song! It is pure and restoring, exactly what a broken heart needs.

———

DARK WORSHIP

And in your lovingkindness, cut off my enemies And destroy all those who afflict my soul, For I am Your servant.

Psalm 143:12

When David wrote Psalm 143, he was brutally honest about what was going on in his mind. He was not acting as if the struggles of this life were wonderful and every temptation from Satan was mere playtime. On the contrary, David came before God with honor and raw emotion. David spoke of his struggles in three divisions: *life, spirit,* and *soul.* Listen to his words: *"For the enemy has persecuted my soul"* (Psalm 143:3). *"He has crushed my life to the ground"* (Psalm 143:3). *"My spirit is overwhelmed within me"* (Psalm 143:4). *"My souls longs for You, as a parched land* (Psalm 143:6). *"My spirit fails"* (Psalm 143:7). *"In Your righteousness bring my soul out of trouble"* (Psalm 143:11). *"And destroy all those who afflict my soul"* (Psalm 143:12). David was in a dark place. He had not forgotten God; in fact, he looked to the Redeemer alone for his salvation, but David was tired of the struggle. So this psalm is what you might call *"Dark Worship,"* meaning the worship that comes when our heart is in a dark place. David was trying to sing the Redeemer's song, but he felt closer to the grave than to God's presence. He knew the answers of praise, thanksgiving, and abiding in the presence of God, but the struggle was intense. This psalm holds so many real-life truths and honest woes, but the best part comes in the very last line. In the midst of all the struggles, David said, *"For I am Your servant"* (Psalm 143:12). The Redeemer's song, when sung in *"Dark Worship,"* produces *"sweet surrender!"* David was willing to stay in the throes of war if that was what God desired. The resolution of this psalm was not deliverance but surrender; that is what the Redeemer's song is all about. A redeemer is one who does for someone else what they couldn't do alone. If the Redeemer doesn't deliver as you desire, will you still surrender to Him? Powerful words, powerful surrender, powerful worship!

———

HIS MAJESTY

On the glorious splendor of Your majesty And on Your wonderful works, I will meditate.

Psalm 145:5

When was the last time you allowed your body, soul, and spirit to come together in focused meditation on Who the Redeemer is? The Hebrew word for meditate is *siyach,* and it means to "muse, study, ponder or to put forth thoughts." Think of it this way, you could spend your entire life looking at nature, the flowers, the birds, and the clouds; never would you be able to behold all of their beauty. For every nuance, you discover there would be hundreds more that go unnoticed. Then when you add in the dimensions of sound, smell, and touch, you would be even more dumbfounded by the myriad shades of beauty. But to know you are this mesmerized by creation, just imagine the infinite wonders of the Creator! That is what David was singing about when he wrote Psalm 145:5. He meditated on two different aspects of God: *the glorious splendor of Your majesty, and on Your wonderful works.* Let's take a moment to meditate on the first one.

What *is* the glorious splendor of God's majesty? Take a moment to prayerfully meditate on each of the following attributes of the Redeemer's splendor: holy, mighty, wise, perfect, all-knowing, all-powerful, present, healing, hopeful, righteous, King of kings, Lord of lords, forgiving, Divine, sinless, suffering Servant, merciful, enduring, lovingly-kind, gracious, rich in blessing, Creator, Sustainer, Deliverer, Lion of Judah, Provider, the only One Who can open the seven seals, Friend, Brother, Everlasting Father, Counselor, Prince of Peace, Mighty God, majestic, beautiful, true, a rock, a refuge, sheltering wings, strong righteous right hand, our banner, victorious, Sunrise from on high, Living Water, Bread of Life, Beginning and the End, First born of the dead, Father of lights, Light of the world, Lamb of God Who takes away the sins of the world, and so much more!

OCTOBER 17
THE WORKS OF THE REDEEMER

On the glorious splendor of Your majesty And on Your wonderful works, I will meditate.

Psalm 145:5

How glorious are the works of the Redeemer! Let us meditate on them as we praise His holy Name!

At creation, we saw His **powerful word**.
In the Garden of Eden, we saw His **provision**.
With the curse, we saw His **justice**.
At the flood, we saw His **wrath**.
At the Tower of Babel, we saw His **mercy**.
With Abraham, we saw His **covenant of love**.
In the plagues, we saw His **power over all gods**.
At the Red Sea, we saw His mighty **protection**.
With the Law, we saw His **righteousness**.
During the time of Judges, we saw His **patience**.
With the kings of Israel, we saw His **jealous rule**.
With the words of the prophets, we saw His **severity**.
During the exile, we saw His **compassion for the remnant**.
As the Israelites returned, we saw His **promise fulfilled**.
At the Nativity, we saw His **humility**.
In His earthly life, we saw His **testimony**.
With the disciples, we saw His **wisdom**.
With the religious leaders, we saw His **righteous anger**.
During His trial, we saw His **silence**.
On the Mount of Olives, we saw His **agony**.
In His death, we saw His **salvation**.
In His resurrection, we saw His **validation**.
At His ascension, we saw His **calling**.
At Pentecost, we saw His **closeness**.
Through the apostles, we saw His **plan unfurl**.
At salvation, we saw His **amazing love**.
In Revelation, we see His **Kingdom come**!

O Lord God, King of Heaven and earth, great are the works of Your hands! May I meditate on them day and night!

———

ENTHRONED UPON PRAISES

Praise the LORD! For it is good to sing praises to our God;
For it is pleasant and praise is becoming.

Psalm 147:1

In this psalm, the Psalmist makes a most emphatic demand of the reader to *"praise the LORD!"* Praise, the ascribing to the Lord what is due to Him. The psalmist says that praising God is good, pleasant, and becoming. Why? How can it be that proclaiming Who God is can be so good for the proclaimer? Are we promised riches or health or long life if we praise God? Did Jesus promise that we would be kept safe from evil people, destructive beasts, or the elements if we praise the Father? Does Scripture teach that if we praise the Spirit of the living God, we will live in the sweet spot of life, and nothing will be trying or difficult? In all of these, the answer is no. We are not promised healing, protection, or provision if we praise God, but we are told to praise the Lord because it is good, pleasant, and becoming. What might this mean?

Psalm 22:3 says, *"Yet You are holy, O You who are enthroned upon the praises of Israel."* This is the litmus test of self-denial and worship. This verse explains the difference in the attitude of our hearts and the words of our mouths. We may say that the Redeemer is the Lord of our life, but when push comes to shove, we want what we want, when we want, and how we want. And if that isn't what we get, then we kick and scream. That is not good, pleasant, or becoming because there is no praise in it. Yet for those who do not get what they want but are still able to praise God, they are the ones who truly desire God to be lifted higher than they. God is enthroned upon praises; that is why it is good, pleasant, and becoming. It is the fulfillment of our role as worshippers of the Almighty. Does your heart truly want the Redeemer to be on His throne, or do you want to be on that throne? Our complaints and our praises tell the truth of our hearts. We may not receive the healing, protection, or provision we desire; but when God is seen on His throne, everything is as it should be.

HUMBLE STATE

For He has had regard for the humble state of His bondslave; For behold, from this time on all generations will count me blessed. "For the Mighty One has done great things for me; And holy is His name."

Luke 1:48–49

Can you fathom a world without arrogance? Arrogance is an archenemy to the children of God. Through Christ, we can do anything (Philippians 4:13; Matthew 19:26), but apart from God, we can do nothing (John 15:5). So for us to speak of who we are and what we can do is arrogance. For us to surrender to our inability and to cling to God's strength is humility. Humility is one of the heart attitudes that most aligns itself with Christlikeness—total dependence on the Father (John 5:30; 8:28). All throughout Scripture, we find God calling the weak, the untrained, the timid, and the sinner. Time after time, people would try to run from God's call because they were overwhelmed with His instructions, but when it came to Mary, her response was starkly different. Mary, a female in a male-dominated society, who being unmarried had no real resources of her own, who had no husband to get pregnant by, whose very life would be at stake if she got pregnant out of wedlock, and who didn't even have the money to bring a lamb to offer to the Lord but rather offered two turtle doves (Luke 2:24; Leviticus 12:7–8). Who was Mary that the Redeemer should take notice of her? She was a humble bondslave of the very Baby she would carry. Mary was humble enough to know that her inability plus God's ability was all she needed. She did not run from God's call or give excuses. Actually, she praised God for His blessings. When most people would be running away or objecting to God's call, Mary sang the Redeemer's song. *"For the Mighty One has done great things for me; And holy is His name."* The Redeemer came into this world through the willingness of a humble woman's devoted heart. May we be humble enough to bow below the arrogance of this world; there we will find a worthy song to sing to our King.

NIGHT COMES BEFORE MORNING

I will extol You, O Lord, for You have lifted me up, And have not let my enemies rejoice over me. O Lord my God, I cried to You for help, and You healed me. O Lord, You have brought up my soul from Sheol; You have kept me alive, that I would not go down to the pit. Sing praise to the Lord, you His godly ones, And give thanks to His holy name. For His anger is but for a moment, His favor is for a lifetime; Weeping may last for the night, But a shout of joy comes in the morning.

Psalm 30:1–5

The Redeemer's song rings out in our lives like a life preserver in the middle of a stormy ocean. The life preserver makes us sing and dance, but we do not like the thought of being tossed in the waves. Usually, we do not appreciate the victory unless we first experience the war. That is why it is called the Redeemer's song. We sing it once we have been redeemed. David noted this juxtaposition; to be lifted up is to first be laid low. David was healed, but not until he had cried out. God kept David alive but not until he had gone down to Sheol. Time after time, we see God's redemption and salvation and mercy but not before the fall, the pain, and the accusation. David even framed it this way: *"Weeping may last for the night, But a shout of joy comes in the morning."* You cannot have a morning without a night. Nights are tough; they are dark, full of shadows and unknown noises. But morning comes with new light, understanding, and relief. No one wants to endure through the night, but how sweet the shout of joy is that follows. The Redeemer's song is pure and restoring! It resounds most true at the first glimmer of Light after a night of fighting. But to rest as He sings over you is to know the healing and restoration which makes you whole.

O Lord, the pain is so great, the fear is so intense, the struggle is so hard, and the hopelessness is so deep. Please hold me during this night. I cannot see You, but You say You are near. Please come with Your mercy at the first light of dawn.

ASAPH'S WORSHIP (PART I)

Whom have I in heaven but You? And besides You, I desire nothing on earth.

Psalm 73:25

The ark of the covenant was highly important to the children of Israel. The lid of the ark was where the presence of Jehovah rested. After the children of God had been separated from the ark for a while, King David brought it back to Jerusalem. He had a tent built for it to be housed in, and he appointed priests to worship before the Lord. *"He appointed some of the Levites as ministers before the ark of the Lord, even to celebrate and to thank and praise the Lord God of Israel: Asaph the chief, and second to him Zechariah, then Jeiel, Shemiramoth, Jehiel, Mattithiah, Eliab, Benaiah, Obed-edom and Jeiel, with musical instruments, harps, lyres; also Asaph played loud-sounding cymbals"* (1 Chronicles 16:4–5). Could you imagine being Asaph, chosen by King David to play the cymbals before the Redeemer? But Asaph's job was more than just cymbals: *"Then on that day David first assigned Asaph and his relatives to give thanks to the Lord"* (1 Chronicles 16:7). *"So he left Asaph and his relatives there before the ark of the covenant of the Lord to minister before the ark continually, as every day's work required"* (1 Chronicles 16:37). Asaph and his family ministered before the Lord continually, giving thanks and making music. He was chosen for this high honor not just because he was of the priestly line of Levi but because he knew the Redeemer's song. He would write in Psalm 73:25, *"Whom have I in heaven but You? And besides You, I desire nothing on earth."* Asaph was consumed with the Redeemer's presence. Tomorrow we will look at a psalm of thanksgiving Asaph sang as he ministered before the Lord, but today, ask yourself if you desire the presence of God more than the things of this earth? The answer will lie in whether your words, attitudes, and actions are praising to God or complaining, arrogant, and self-serving.

"O Lord, may we be consumed in Your presence."

––––––––

ASAPH'S WORSHIP (PART II)

Then on that day David first assigned Asaph and his relatives to give thanks to the Lord.

1 Chronicles 16:7

Today, worship alongside Asaph as he sings the Redeemer's song:

Oh give thanks to the Lord, call upon His name; Make known His deeds among the peoples. Sing to Him, sing praises to Him; Speak of all His wonders. Glory in His holy name; Let the heart of those who seek the Lord be glad. Seek the Lord and His strength; Seek His face continually. Remember His wonderful deeds which He has done, His marvels and the judgments from His mouth, O seed of Israel His servant, Sons of Jacob, His chosen ones! He is the Lord our God; His judgments are in all the earth . . . Sing to the Lord, all the earth; Proclaim good tidings of His salvation from day to day. Tell of His glory among the nations, His wonderful deeds among all the peoples. For great is the Lord, and greatly to be praised; He also is to be feared above all gods. For all the gods of the peoples are idols, But the Lord made the heavens. Splendor and majesty are before Him, Strength and joy are in His place. Ascribe to the Lord, O families of the peoples, Ascribe to the Lord glory and strength. Ascribe to the Lord the glory due His name; Bring an offering, and come before Him; Worship the Lord in holy array. Tremble before Him, all the earth; Indeed, the world is firmly established, it will not be moved. Let the heavens be glad, and let the earth rejoice; And let them say among the nations, "The Lord reigns." Let the sea roar, and all it contains; Let the field exult, and all that is in it. Then the trees of the forest will sing for joy before the Lord; For He is coming to judge the earth. O give thanks to the Lord, for He is good; For His lovingkindness is everlasting. Then say, "Save us, O God of our salvation, And gather us and deliver us from the nations, To give thanks to Your holy name, And glory in Your praise." Blessed be the Lord, the God of Israel, From everlasting even to everlasting. Then all the people said, "Amen," and praised the Lord (1 Chronicles 16:8–36).

CONTRASTED LOVE

I will bear the indignation of the LORD Because I have sinned against Him,
Until He pleads my case and executes justice for me.
He will bring me out to the light, And I will see His righteousness.

Micah 7:9

Jesus was eating a meal at Simon the Pharisee's house; while there, a known sinful woman came and began to wash His feet with her tears and dry them with her hair. Then taking perfume, she began to anoint His feet. Her presence alone was in contrast to the piousness of a Pharisee. Likewise, her crying must have stood out amongst the laughter of a dinner party. Finally, imagine the stark difference between the scent of dinner and the smell of perfume. This woman was an overload to the senses and a distraction to what was going on. But the Redeemer loved it! Knowing Simon's heart, Jesus told a parable about two debtors being forgiven sums of money. One was a large sum and the other smaller, but neither could repay it. Jesus then asked Simon, which debtor loved the forgiver more? Simon correctly replied, *"the one who was forgiven more"* (Luke 7:36–50). The Redeemer had painted a radiant picture of love in colors just as stark as the presence of an immoral woman in the house of a Pharisee. This woman loved Jesus much because she had been forgiven much. She sang the Redeemer's song because it was in direct contrast to the condemning song of society.

As the prophet Micah said, *"I will bear the indignation of the LORD Because I have sinned against Him, Until He pleads my case and executes justice for me. He will bring me out to the light, And I will see His righteousness."* Like the sinful woman, we sing the Redeemer's song because we have been forgiven much. We love deeply because we have been brought into the light, and we now see the righteousness of God, and it is in stark contrast to our filth. In spite of this, He loved us deeply, forgiving our sins and raising us up to new life!

WAITING ALL THE DAY

To You, O LORD, I lift up my soul.

Psalm 25:1

Who would desire God's heart more than a man after God's own heart? (1 Samuel 13:14). David lifted up his soul to the King of kings and the Lord of lords. He longed to live in the house of the Lord all the days of his life (Psalm 27:4). Why would David long so hard to be in God's presence, yet we fall short of that all too often? It could be that David had sung the Redeemer's song, and in it, he made a humble request: *"Make me know Your ways, O LORD; Teach me Your paths. Lead me in Your truth and teach me, For You are the God of my salvation; For You I wait all the day"* (Psalm 25:4–5). David was humble enough to know that no matter what height he rose to, he would never understand all there was to know about the Almighty. So he prayed, "Lord, make me know Your ways, teach me Your paths, lead me in Your truth, and teach me." Those four requests can be prayed only if the last line of this verse is true: *"For You are the God of my salvation; For You I wait all the day."* David knew the redemption that came through the Father's love, and because of that, he was willing to wait on the Redeemer. How can you wait on the Lord if you do not know His ways, His paths, His truths, and His wisdom? The ways of God are higher than our own (Isaiah 55:9). When we see cancer, God sees beautiful surrender. When we see hopelessness, God sees His way up. God's ways are complete. The Shepherd's paths are full of green grass and still water, but they are also in the shadow of death and within view of the enemy (Psalm 23). The truth of the Savior is unbending. Never will the truth of God compromise with the world to make life easier. So if we desire to know His ways, to walk His paths, and to live in His truth, then we need the Redeemer to teach us. It is in His teaching that we stop trying to conform to this world because it makes life easier (Romans 12:2). His teachings teach us to wait on Him in His holiness. David had learned how he could say, *"To You, O LORD, I lift up my soul."*

THE SONG OF LIFE

For You are my hope; O Lord GOD, You are my confidence from my youth.
By You I have been sustained from my birth; You are He who took me
from my mother's womb; My praise is continually of You.

Psalm 71:5–6

If you could draw out your life like a line, that line would sometimes go up, and sometimes it would go down. Our timeline tells the story of God as we journey with Him and when we turn our back on Him. But if you will look closely at your timeline, then you will see the Great Shepherd's guiding hand at work. From the time you were born until the day you die, God directs your steps. In Psalm 71, the psalmist is reflecting on the Redeemer's guidance through life. All throughout Scripture, we see how the Father loved His children. He knew them from the womb (Psalm 139:13); He taught them in their youth (Psalm 71:17); and He even holds them in their old age (Isaiah 46:4). If an artist were to draw your timeline from beginning to end, it would not be a straight line, but rather it would curve and contour as life shifts and changes. When the artist had finished, I do believe you would see the image of a fingerprint, God's fingerprint. It would bear witness to a lifetime of memories. Times you fell, times you took steps of faith, times He rescued you, times of celebration. Our life is nothing but a picture of His redemption, His love, and His grace. It is no wonder that Jesus said, *"Permit the children to come to Me; do not hinder them; for the kingdom of God belongs to such as these"* (Mark 10:14). The children are His children, and He holds them and loves them. He can already see their timeline drawn out. The Redeemer's song is lived out in children, in youth, and in old age. It is the song of life! Take time to listen to children sing the Redeemer's song; they sing it from an honest heart of childlike faith. Listen to a youth sing as they seek to understand life in the uncertainty of it. Listen to the elderly sing His praise as they remember His guiding hand throughout their timeline. Listen and sing along.

SOURCE OF PRAISE

I will rejoice greatly in the LORD, My soul will exult in my God; For He has clothed me with garments of salvation, He has wrapped me with a robe of righteousness, As a bridegroom decks himself with a garland, And as a bride adorns herself with her jewels. For as the earth brings forth its sprouts, And as a garden causes the things sown in it to spring up, So the Lord GOD will cause righteousness and praise To spring up before all the nations.

Isaiah 61:10–11

Where does the Redeemer's song come from? Is it simply the sum of the words we put together in our brain then speak with our mouth? Physically, yes, our brain sends the message to our mouth; then our mouth moves in conjunction with our lungs pushing air past our vocal cords, which form sounds recognizable by our brain as words. So physically, we can speak the words of the Redeemer's song, but spiritually, it is sung from a much richer source. The song of the Redeemer is a response to what God has done in us. *"He has clothed me with garments of salvation, He has wrapped me with a robe of righteousness."* The Father does what we cannot do, and that is like a seed planted in His own garden. That seed germinates and sprouts, eventually bearing the fruit of praise. *"My soul will exult in my God."* The Redeemer's song can be faked to the human ear because the human ear is a physical body part that receives physical sounds, but God is a Spirit, and nothing but spirit worship will bring joy to His heart (John 4:23–24). But note that the Redeemer's song is not just sung in praise but also lived out in righteousness before the nations (Isaiah 61:11). This righteousness is not my own, but that of Christ placed on me like a robe. Christ's robe on me!

The Father is not interested in a verbal chorus of hollow praises, but what pleases His ears is a heart that has been touched by the hallowed righteousness of God. That is where the Redeemer's song flows from.

———

ACCEPTABLE FASTING

Behold, you fast for contention and strife and to strike with a wicked fist.
You do not fast like you do today to make your voice heard on high.

Isaiah 58:4

What is an acceptable fast before God? Plainly stated, it is one that lifts up His glory, not our desires. Is your humility masking your selfishness? Listen to what God tells His children through the prophet Isaiah:

Is it a fast like this which I choose, a day for a man to humble himself? Is it for bowing one's head like a reed And for spreading out sackcloth and ashes as a bed? Will you call this a fast, even an acceptable day to the Lord? "Is this not the fast which I choose, To loosen the bonds of wickedness, To undo the bands of the yoke, And to let the oppressed go free And break every yoke? "Is it not to divide your bread with the hungry And bring the homeless poor into the house; When you see the naked, to cover him; And not to hide yourself from your own flesh? "Then your light will break out like the dawn, And your recovery will speedily spring forth; And your righteousness will go before you; The glory of the Lord will be your rear guard. "Then you will call, and the Lord will answer; You will cry, and He will say, 'Here I am.' If you remove the yoke from your midst, The pointing of the finger and speaking wickedness, And if you give yourself to the hungry And satisfy the desire of the afflicted, Then your light will rise in darkness And your gloom will become like midday. "And the Lord will continually guide you, And satisfy your desire in scorched places, And give strength to your bones;

And you will be like a watered garden, And like a spring of water whose waters do not fail. "Those from among you will rebuild the ancient ruins; You will raise up the age-old foundations; And you will be called the repairer of the breach, The restorer of the streets in which to dwell"(Isaiah 58:5–12).

When you fast, may your heart sing of God's great love, not your deepest desire!

———————————

CREATION SINGS

For the Lord takes pleasure in His people;
He will beautify the afflicted ones with salvation.

Psalm 149:4

Have you ever listened to the symphony of creation? The singing of the crickets in the evening, the chirps of the birds at dawn, the laughing of a child in the park, and the rustle of leaves in the fall. Creation is singing the Redeemer's song all around us if we will take the time to listen. Have you noticed the flowers turning to face the sun, the limbs of trees reaching up to the heavens, and the clouds carrying water to their proper place? Creation is a masterpiece of worship. Have you ever experienced the scent of a morning glory blooming in a garden or the smell of a crisp, cool, fall morning? The beauty of creation is missed if not experienced with gratitude. Have you ever felt the roughness of the bark, the smoothness of an eggshell, or the softness of a baby's hair? Creation, when felt, draws us to worship as we have never known before. Have you ever tasted the sweetness of a wild blueberry, the tartness of a green apple, or the delight of a carrot? Creation begs you to taste and see the goodness of the Lord (Psalm 34:8). Creation gives honor to its Creator, and we would do good to take note of its obedience. Take time today to simply stop what you are doing and just listen to the renewing symphony, admire His gorgeous masterpiece, smell the scent of gloriousness, feel life with the faith of a child, and savor the taste of God's delight! Start by meditating on the words of Psalm 149:1–4.

Praise the Lord! Sing to the Lord a new song, And His praise in the congregation of the godly ones.

Let Israel be glad in his Maker; Let the sons of Zion rejoice in their King.

Let them praise His name with dancing; Let them sing praises to Him with timbrel and lyre.

For the Lord takes pleasure in His people; He will beautify the afflicted ones with salvation.

———————

NOT ONCE BUT TWICE

In that day this song will be sung in the land of Judah:
"We have a strong city; He sets up walls and ramparts for security."

Isaiah 26:1

"In that day." "This song will be sung." This verse raises two questions that I want us to look at over the next couple of days. First, in what day will this song be sung? And second, who will be singing this song?

To understand what day Isaiah is talking about, we must go backwards to chapter twenty-five. Let's focus on verses seven through nine:

And on this mountain He will swallow up the covering which is over all peoples, Even the veil which is stretched over all nations. He will swallow up death for all time, And the Lord God will wipe tears away from all faces, And He will remove the reproach of His people from all the earth; For the Lord has spoken. And it will be said in that day, "Behold, this is our God for whom we have waited that He might save us. This is the Lord for whom we have waited; Let us rejoice and be glad in His salvation.

That day is referring to the coming of Christ. The long-awaited day when the King of kings will come and forgive our sins and right the curse, fulfilling Genesis 3:15. But in looking at these verses, we find an issue. Jesus came to this earth over two thousand years ago as a baby; the veil of the temple was ripped in two at the cross; and the veil over the nations that blinded the Gentiles was removed. This we now see. But death has not been swallowed up for all time, and God has not yet wiped the tears from all faces. This dilemma exists because, like many of the people in first-century Israel, they were looking for the Messiah to come and set up His kingdom. Actually, what took place was the Redeemer came to reveal His love for mankind; He then left with a promise to return for His bride. The veil was removed the first time; He will banish evil and death the second time. So *in that day* has already come, but it is also yet to come. The Redeemer's coming is not once but twice.

———

FILLED WITH HIS SONG

In that day this song will be sung in the land of Judah:
"We have a strong city; He sets up walls and ramparts for security."

Isaiah 26:1

Yesterday we looked at which day Isaiah was talking about when he said, *"In that day."* Today we want to examine who will be singing on that day? Isaiah 26:9 tells us when the earth experiences God's judgments, the people of the earth learn righteousness. We see this when there is a natural disaster or war breaks out. People turn to the Redeemer for protection. But Isaiah goes on in the next verse to say, *"Though the wicked is shown favor, He does not learn righteousness; He deals unjustly in the land of uprightness, And does not perceive the majesty of the LORD"* (26:10). The fallen world we live in is full of evil, and it is set up to favor those who are evil. They may appear to be living on easy street, but they lack some very vital elements of life.

- **Love**: While they may love others and things, they cannot grasp what true love is.
- **Peace**: Peace can be experienced only in the presence of the Spirit of God.
- **Contentment**: You can never know *enough* until you have surrendered to God's grace being enough.
- **Joy**: Joy follows the path of rejoicing. While money can buy you temporary happiness, eternal joy can only come through rejoicing in Who the Redeemer is.

"In that day," the wicked may appear to be favored, but they will not perceive the majesty of the Lord, and without that, they will never know the Redeemer's song. Who will sing the Redeemer's song on that day? The righteous will sing it with love, peace, contentment, and joy! Today we sing His song because He came to us and bought us with the blood of His Son, but when He returns, we will sing it because never again will we taste death, never again will a tear make it to our cheek, never again will the nations stand as a reproach before God. We will sing because the Redeemer has filled us with His song.

A JOURNEY OF PRAISE

For the choir director; on Muth-labben. A Psalm of David. I will give thanks to the Lord with all my heart; I will tell of all Your wonders. I will be glad and exult in You; I will sing praise to Your name, O Most High.

Psalm 9:1–2

Every word of Scripture is included for a purpose. So while many of us breeze over the instructions written before a psalm, there is purpose in them. David wrote Psalm 9 to be sung by the choir. He instructed the choir director on how this psalm was to be sung. Try to imagine being present at the tabernacle back during the reign of King David. Journey with me as we listen to them sing. You stand outside the tabernacle in the light of the sun as everyone is milling about. The choir stands ready, and the choir director steps into place. On his signal, every voice in the choir begins to quietly sing, *"I will give thanks to the Lord with all my heart; I will tell of all Your wonders."* The sounds of the instruments linger as the voices fade out. Now the singers get slightly louder as they sing, *"I will be glad and exult in You."* Hear the melody, the harmonies, the crescendos, and the rests. Their voices, now louder, sing, *"I will sing praise to Your name."* At this point, the choir director is standing on his tiptoes, hands raised, trying to summon every man, woman, and child in the choir to unleash every decibel to the glory of God. And with one last resounding voice, they sing, *"O MOST HIGH!"* The sound is so deafening yet so beautiful. Even after the choir stops singing, you can still hear the sound echoing off the mountains, continuing into eternity. No one speaks because what else could be said? The Redeemer's song has been sung! From eternity to eternity, the name of the Lord is praised!

O Father, I am not worthy to sing Your song. It is pure and restoring, and my heart longs to sing it. May I join in with all creation and the voices of worshippers past, present, and future, as Heaven and earth sing Your song of redemption.

———————

NOVEMBER

The Healer's Touch Is Certain and Complete

WHY NOT HEALED

The Lord is near to the brokenhearted And saves those who are crushed in spirit.

Psalm 34:18

What would you do if you heard there was a man who was healing people in your town? What in you is broken, sick, or hurting that you want to be healed? To what length would you go to be touched by this healer? Healing is a tricky thing because sickness and pain are products of the fall. God cursed humanity because of the sin of Adam and Eve, and at that point, their bodies began to decay; their minds began to dull; and their heath began to fail. Therefore when we go to the Healer and ask Him to heal our hurts and sickness, we are actually asking Him to take back the curse brought on by our disobedience. It is so easy to look at God with anger wondering how He could be so calloused not to heal the pain of this world, but it was because of our callousness that the pain came to be. God would be righteous if He never healed anyone of anything; that is why He is so benevolent when He does pull back the effects of the curse for someone and brings healing. So the question that is front and center is why would God choose to sometimes heal and other times not? To answer this question, we must start by acknowledging God's ways are higher than ours; therefore, we may never understand His reasonings. Next, we must understand that God does not heal everyone all the time for the same reason He kicked Adam and Eve out of the garden and away from the Tree of Life. His desire is not for His children to live eternally in a fallen world but to be with Him in His perfection. Lastly, the Healer doesn't always heal because when we are hurt, we will either turn to Him or walk away from Him. For those who will walk in faith, they will experience love like they have never known. The Healer is, *"near to the broken-hearted and saves those who are crushed in spirit."* This life will end, and for those who are known by Him, they will experience healing greater than this world has ever known.

HEALING TO YOUR BODY

Do not be wise in your own eyes; Fear the Lord and turn away from evil.
It will be healing to your body And refreshment to your bones.

Proverbs 3:7–8

What does fearing the Lord and healing have to do with each other? Very simply, the Lord is the Healer, and He knows better than we do. Also, the Lord is the Creator, knowing our inner workings. Finally, the Lord is also our Sustainer and knows what we need, even more than we do. To better understand this, we should turn to the Law. Of the more than six hundred laws God gave to Moses, a good chunk of them are laws dealing with the health of Israel. What to eat and what not to eat. Even down to where to go to the bathroom. Why would the divine God of the universe care about all these nitpicky things? Aside from Him desiring our obedience, it has to do with our health. We now know through science that the foods deemed unclean are potentially harmful. It could be that they contained harmful parasites or could aid in the growth of cancers or heart disease. Where we live in proximity to the disposal of our bodily waste is keenly important to our health. There are numerous diseases linked to contact with feces. Today we do not think about it because of septic tanks and public waste systems, but when the Israelites left Egypt, they were starting over in the wilderness, an outbreak of cholera could have wiped out their whole nation. Years later, Solomon told this proverb to the people, *"Do not be wise in your own eyes."* They might not have thought God's health commands still applied because they lived in an established land, but pride goes before a fall (Proverbs 16:18). You do not know better than the One Who knows all things. We are to fear Him and give immediate obedience. The Healer knows what is best, and it is not for us to question His instructions. We are just to obey them. Will God grant healing every time we obey? That is not for us to know, but healing and refreshment come to those who fear the Lord.

———

TOUCHING FAMILIES

When Jesus came into Peter's home, He saw his mother-in-law lying sick in bed with a fever. He touched her hand, and the fever left her; and she got up and waited on Him.

Matthew 8:14–15

Typically we envision the disciples as these twelve bearded, burly men who were rough around the edges, but culturally there is the possibility that they were much younger, maybe even teenagers. For Jewish kids who had memorized the Torah and the Prophets, there was a chance a rabbi would come and ask them to follow him. If no rabbi extended the invitation, then they would join the family business. For some of the disciples, we know that they were in their family's business. James, John, Peter, and Andrew were fishermen, and they left their families to follow Jesus (Matthew 4:18; Luke 5:10). But other than this, we do not know much about the disciple's personal lives or ages. We know Jesus called them, and they left everything to follow Him. One of the only other tidbits we know about a disciple's personal life is that Simon Peter was married. His wife was never mentioned, but his mother-in-law was. Matthew 8:14–15 tells us that she was sick with a fever. We do not know the extent of this illness, except she had a fever and was in bed. The Healer walked into His disciple's house, saw the woman sick in bed, and He reached out and touched her hand. No words were exchanged, no rebuke of the fever—simply a touch, a Healer's touch. The fever left her, and she got up and started serving Him. That's how it is when we have been touched by the Healer—we wait on Him and we cling to Him because without Him, we would still be sick, physically and spiritually. We may not know much about the disciples, but we do know this—Peter answered Jesus' call to follow Him, and because of that, healing came to his family. The Healer's touch can still heal our families today!

O Lord, please touch our families, raise them up, and bring healing to them! Amen.

THE TOUCH OF FREEDOM

*So Jesus was saying to those Jews who had believed Him, "If you continue in My word,
then you are truly disciples of Mine; and you will know the truth,
and the truth will make you free."*

John 8:31–32

The Healer's touch is certain and complete, but His healing is not always physical. Sometimes His healing touch is mental; sometimes it is emotional; and sometimes it is spiritual. The healing that comes from Christ is complete on all sides. Therefore, we must look at the whole of a man. We are more than just a body; we are also soul and spirit. Jesus heals all of us.

The sin in our lives brings bondage and death, but healing brings freedom and, therefore, life. Our life prior to the cross is nothing but chains. We were shackled to sin and bound by our love of self. No matter what we did, we were incapable of breaking free. But then Jesus did the incomprehensible by purchasing us out of the hands of death and then set us free. *"So if the Son makes you free, you will be free indeed"* (John 8:36). This is the truth of the Gospel! Jesus—the Way, the Truth, and the Life (John 14:6)—came to set us free. This very truth is what John says, *"will make you free."* The touch of Christ does not mean you will be healed of all diseases, nor does it mean you will be healed from all emotional hurts, but no longer will you be bound by the chains of sin. The voice of the accuser will cease to hold power over you. *"You are from God, little children, and have overcome them; because greater is He who is in you than he who is in the world"* (1 John 4:4). The Healer is greater than the hurter, and on that day, the Healer set us free to live and love as we have never known before. The door of our cell is knocked off its hinges, and the gate of the prison is standing open. Jesus stands at the gate and calls us out, much like He called Lazarus to walk out of death (John 11:43). The healing touch He gives is an eternal freeing from the grip of sin. Are you free indeed (John 8:36)?

SETTING CAPTIVES FREE

Rejoice with those who rejoice, and weep with those who weep.

Romans 12:15

It's been said, *"Laughter is good medicine,"* but there is also something to be said for tears. Often we look to a doctor to heal us physically, a pastor to heal us spiritually, and a psychologist to heal us emotionally, but we serve a God Who wants to be our defense against the trials of life. A pill may relieve a headache, but it will come back; finite healings bring temporal relief, but a touch of the hand of Christ can bring restoration forever. It is true that God's healing comes in His way and His time, which often is different from our own, but while we wait, we are not alone. If we weep, the Church is to weep with us. When someone rejoices, we are to rejoice with them. Our sicknesses on this earth, whether physical, spiritual, or emotional, are nothing more than captivity, a time spent under the painful rule of a tyrant. But as we see in the Old Testament, captivity is temporary for those who cling to God. And when you are set free, you leave with so much more than you ever imagined. Do not think I am saying this is easy, but do hear me say, healing is very real! That is why we weep with those who weep and rejoice with those who rejoice. We live this life together, and together with Christ as the Great Physician, we will worship Him when sick and when healed!

> *When the Lord brought back the captive ones of Zion, We were like those who dream. Then our mouth was filled with laughter And our tongue with joyful shouting; Then they said among the nations, "The Lord has done great things for them." The Lord has done great things for us; We are glad. Restore our captivity, O Lord, As the streams in the South. Those who sow in tears shall reap with joyful shouting. He who goes to and fro weeping, carrying his bag of seed, Shall indeed come again with a shout of joy, bringing his sheaves with him (Psalm 126:1–6).*

TRUSTING FOR TODAY

Heal me, O Lord, and I will be healed; Save me and I will be saved, For You are my praise.

Jeremiah 17:14

Total trust in God is way more than trusting Him with your afterlife. Believing God exists and that He has paid the debt you could not pay and will call you righteous on the day of judgment are the foundational blocks of our faith, but they are in no way the sum total of our trusting faith. James tells us that, *"Even so faith, if it has no works, is dead, being by itself"* (James 2:17). Therefore faith cannot rest solely on what Jesus did or what will happen when we die but also on what happens while we live. Total trust means we surrender to whatever God deems necessary in our lives. If the Healer allows sickness into your life, will you embrace it because you trust Him in life? If He allows persecution to come to you, will you receive it because God is Sovereign? If pain comes to your family, will you praise God in the midst of the seeming unfairness? To trust God with your afterlife is tough, but that is trusting God with something you have no control over. Yet trusting God in the midst of circumstances you can control or at least take part in, that is a surrendered faith. When you look to the Healer for His touch yet it seems He is not listening to your cries, it is hard to not try to take over. I'm sure the disciples failed at this many times. Why does God wait when it would be so easy for Him to bring healing? If we truly believe it would be that easy for God to bring healing, then why do we struggle to surrender when He doesn't? If He is Sovereign over one, then He must be Sovereign over the second. Jeremiah said, *"Heal me, O Lord and I will be healed; Save me and I will be saved, For You are my praise."* The reverse of this verse is just as true. "Don't heal me, O Lord, and I will not be healed; Don't save me, and I will not be saved, For You are my praise." Total trust and surrender says, whether God heals or not, He is still my praise.

A CONTINUAL FEAST

All the days of the afflicted are bad, But a cheerful heart has a continual feast.

Proverbs 15:15

In the twenty-third Psalm, David wrote, "You prepare a table before me in the presence of my enemies." Can you fathom what it would be to sit down at the table of the Lord? Tables are often a central fixture within a home. It is a place where families come together to be renewed. They are renewed physically by the food they eat. They are renewed as a family as they sit around the table and talk about their day. They may even be renewed spiritually as the family lifts up prayers of thanksgiving for God's provision. Renewal prepares us for what is still to come; the day is not yet over. A table may represent renewal, but it can also represent unity. The members of a family go in different directions throughout the day, but a table gives a single location to come back to. When the day draws to a close, they can sit together, united as a family. Finally, a table can also be the site of healing. Christ prepares a table before us in the presence of our enemies. Night and day, our enemy, the devil, seeks to devour us (1 Peter 5:8). It seems we are never out of the reach of his claws which tear into our spirit. But when we are being renewed and united at the table of the Lord, then we are being healed. "All the days of the afflicted are bad." The days of the afflicted are full of dread, pain, misery, fear, and torment. "But a cheerful heart has a continual feast." Yes, there is hope for the afflicted! It comes when the Healer pulls out a seat at His table and offers you to come and sit down. As you sit down, He wraps a towel around His waist and kneels before you with a basin of water, and washes your feet. As He washes the dirt of the day away, the scars and wounds of affliction also begin to disappear. You then sit at the table of the Lord, renewed in Him, united to Him, healed by Him, and now cheerful because of what He has done for you. A continual feast at the table of Christ!

DYING NO MORE

But when this perishable will have put on the imperishable, and this mortal will have put on immortality, then will come about the saying that is written, "DEATH IS SWALLOWED UP in victory. O DEATH, WHERE IS YOUR VICTORY? O DEATH, WHERE IS YOUR STING?"

1 Corinthians 15:54–55

What greater healing could there be than to be healed from all maladies for all time? That is exactly the future for all those who are known by Christ (Matthew 7:23). The apostle Paul, in his first letter to the Church in Corinth, taught that there was a day coming when the very agent of sickness would be done away with. That agent is death itself. Death is the penalty for sin (Romans 6:23), and seeing as we all have sinned, we all are in the process of dying. Death comes to us in many ways, sickness, violence, old age, accidents, etc. But this death is simply the first death; the second death is far worse. The second death is separation from God for all eternity in the lake of fire (Revelation 21:8). Jesus' death on the cross rendered this death dead, for all those who have the life of resurrection. Jesus' resurrection, much like a garment, is to be put on, thereby making the perishable, imperishable, and the mortal, immortal. Through the resurrection, we can sing, "Death is swallowed up in victory. O death, where is your victory? O death, where is your sting?" In Heaven, there is no death, no sickness, nor hurt or pain. Death will be thrown into the lake of fire and its sting taken away. This is the true healing the Healer longs to bring, the removal of the curse of sin. But understand that this curse is not just whitewashed away. No, it was extended in all its fury onto the Son of God. The blows that were meant for me were given in full strength to Jesus. The nails that should have pierced me pierced Jesus' hands and feet. God did not go easy on His Son because of His love for Him, but rather laid on Him the full torrent of wrath because of His love for us!

THE BLIND SHALL SEE

The LORD opens the eyes of the blind; The LORD raises up those who are bowed down;
The LORD loves the righteous.

Psalm 146:8

The psalmist of Psalm 146 sang a beautiful song of praise to God! It was a psalm of surrender and a psalm of admiration. When praising the Healer, it is easy to allow the pride of life to slip in and disorient our focus. We may think we are praising God, but all the time we are talking about ourselves. When we say, *"I praise God because of me, me, me,"* we are not really praising God; we are only acknowledging ourselves at God's expense. But the Psalmist of 146 showed no interest in elevating self in his praising the Father. He was contrite, surrendered, honoring, and hopeful. Our heart song must be all of these if we are to truly praise His name. To lift up the Healer is the highest honor we, as His creations, can have. To love Him, praise Him, sing of Him, meditate on Him, and to tell of Him, nothing could be more fulfilling. So think about it when the psalmist said, *"The LORD opens the eyes of the blind."* Blindness comes in three different veins. The first two are either you are born blind, or you were born with sight, but you lost it. The third type of blindness has nothing to do with your physical sight but everything to do with how you see the Messiah. To go from the darkness into Light would be life-altering, but to receive your spiritual sight, that would be Life itself. The healing of sight is linked to the healing of the heart. The healing of the heart is what allows us to praise the Healer; the healing of sight is what we sing about. Praise God for what you have seen (Luke 2:20). But just like the psalmist, to sing about what you now see is to be surrendered, contrite, and honoring of the Healer, not self. This is much easier said than done. We can sing a pretty song that is full of hollow words, but to sing a hallowed song, we must disappear in the glory of His greatness.

BOWED LOW ENOUGH

The LORD opens the eyes of the blind; The LORD raises up those who are bowed down; The LORD loves the righteous.

Psalm 146:8

Bowed down is the symbol and position of a slave. Not just a slave but a broken slave, one who knows their place before their Master. How low is a slave supposed to bow? There is a correlation between how low a slave bows and the status of the master. If the master is mean, vial, and worthless, then the slave may bow his body, but his heart stands in resistance to the master. If the master is kind, protective, and gentle, then the slave will bow his body and heart. But if the Master is the King of kings, then the slave will not bow out of duty but because the Master is worthy of the bow. *"For it is written, "As I live, says the LORD, every knee shall bow to Me, and every tongue shall give praise to God"* (Romans 14:11). There is no choice; you will bow because every knee is going to bow before the Master. But for everyone who bows before the Healer as a slave, He will raise them up. They will be raised up as brothers and sisters of the Prince of Peace for their contrite heart before the Master. Who are we to even look on the face of Him Who created everything? Are we worthy enough to look into the eyes of the Savior Who hung naked and broken from the cross? Is there anything righteous in us that could earn even a moment in the presence of the Sustainer of all? No! Resoundingly no! Nothing could possibly be good enough in us to earn us anything before the Christ. Our righteousness is filthy rags (Isaiah 64:6). We bow before God with our faces pressed into the dirt not because we are humble but because He is worthy. We would have to bow down six feet below ground before we reached a depth we deserved. Death and burial—that is our rightful position before God, but *"The LORD raises up those who are bowed down."* I'm worthy of death, but the Healer raises me up to Life!

A HEART MADE RIGHT

The LORD opens the eyes of the blind; The LORD raises up those who are bowed down;
The LORD loves the righteous.

Psalm 146:8

Healings come in all shapes and sizes. Some are as dramatic as the dead being raised to life, and others may be as unseen as the healing of an emotional scar. Sometimes the healing takes place in the public eye, and sometimes they take place in the silence of our hearts. Every healing is a touch of the Healer's finger and never to be undermined. The earthly healings of the Healer also last for a varied amount of time. For Jairus' daughter, she was only twelve when she died. So when Jesus raised her from the dead, she still had her whole life in front of her (Mark 5:42). But when Lazarus was raised from the dead, he was already an adult (John 11:44). Both this little girl and Lazarus would die again, yet their life span after their healing was varied. God's healings come in all different shapes and sizes and for different lengths of time, but they are all erased when our mortal lives end. When we enter Heaven's gates, we will all be totally healed of all things for all time. So what is the Healer's greatest healing? Raising the dead? Setting the demon-possessed free? Protecting the orphan or widow? The greatest healing may seem small compared to the raising of the dead, but it is far more earth-shattering and much longer lasting. It is being touched with the love of the Father. If this doesn't seem like much of a healing, I would dare say you have never experienced His love. Odds are, if you do not value the love of God, then you are probably so consumed with your own love that you do not see just how vile you really are and how the love of a perfect God heals you from sin (John 3:16). *"The LORD loves the righteous."* He does not love you because you are righteous, but you are righteous because He loves you! His touch can make a dead heart beat again, but His love can take a sinful heart and make it righteous.

———————————

GREATER LOVE

I will heal their apostasy, I will love them freely,
For My anger has turned away from them.

Hosea 14:4

Healing can come in different areas of our lives, physically, mentally, emotionally, socially, and spiritually. It is easy to overlook the need for spiritual healing because it isn't so clearly seen. But the wedge driven between God and us because of our sin is very real; therefore, the healing needed to reconcile that wound is also very real. Hosea uses the word *apostasy,* which means "waywardness or faithlessness." A beautiful picture of God healing the waywardness of Israel is found in Ezekiel 16. The story goes, God finds a little baby laying in a field, still with the blood of birth on it. No one cared for this baby, and it had been left to die. But God came along and took the child in, cleaning it and clothing it. In time the child would grow up into a beautiful young lady, and God would make a covenant of marriage to her, and He would heap riches and blessing on her. But her fame would go to her head, and she began to look for love in other places. She began to play the harlot with every man that passed by and even used the gifts God had given her to prostitute herself to others. Finally, God received her back, remembering His covenant with her, but He would make a new covenant with her, an everlasting covenant (Ezekiel 16:60). This story is a prophecy about God's love for Israel and how Israel turned from Him and ran after idols and sought love in every other avenue. But God would remember His covenant with Israel and would not only take her back but He would also heal her *apostasy.* The wedge of sin has the power to destroy. If it is not healed and restored, then it has the power to condemn us to Hell for eternity, but as God said through Hosea, *"I will love them freely."* And He loves and heals us also, even when we turn our back on Him. Our apostasy is great, but His healing and love are greater!

ARISE (PART 1)

A father of the fatherless and a judge for the widows, Is God in His holy habitation. God makes a home for the lonely; He leads out the prisoners into prosperity, Only the rebellious dwell in a parched land.

Psalm 68:5–6

"Arise, O Father; Your children cry out.

The enemy kills; the thief comes to steal;

Despising Your Name, their hatred they spill.

Now Your children wait; before You they kneel."*

The words of this poem are the heart's cry of the children of God as they long for Christ's return. As David said in Psalm 68, *"A father of the fatherless . . . is God in His holy habitation."* God, in His infinite wisdom, chose to reveal Himself to His creation as their Father. Why? Because in the Jewish culture, who needed help more than the orphan and widow? Neither had a defender or provider. They were cast aside and forsaken, but the Healer came to His people not as a king, though He is a King; not as a conqueror, though He is a Conqueror; and not as a scholar, though His wisdom is unmatched by any above the earth or below. No, the Healer came as a Father to the fatherless. Who claims the fatherless? Who comes to their defense? Who protects them from harm? Who provides for them when there is nothing left? Who teaches them the ways of life? Who brings them security in the night? Who goes before them when the path is unclear? Who sings them to sleep when the darkness closes in? Who calls them by name, calming their heart? Who ushers them into Heaven when this life is done? It is the Father! In this poem, you can hear His heartbeat. It was the Father's love that sent Jesus the first time, and it will be the Healer's touch that sends Him the second time!

"In peace I will both lie down and sleep, For You alone, O LORD, make me to dwell in safety" (Psalm. 4:8).

*See Appendix

NOVEMBER 14

ARISE (PART 2)

A father of the fatherless and a judge for the widows, Is God in His holy habitation.
God makes a home for the lonely; He leads out the prisoners into prosperity,
Only the rebellious dwell in a parched land.

Psalm 68:5–6

"Arise, O Warrior; it's time to go home.

The battle is over, the victory won.

The slain have fallen; the enemy's thrown.

We look to the sky, return where You've gone."*

The psalmist continues in Psalm 68:5 by saying that the Healer is *"a judge for the widow in His holy habitation."* What could be more moving than the broken heart of a widow? According to Paul, a widow is not just a woman who has lost their husband but a woman who has lost her husband and has been left alone (2 Timothy 5:5). Either she has also lost her children, or she never had them. Who is there to plead her case or to provide for her need? Who will sit with her and listen to her words? It is the Healer, that's Who! He is the Warrior Who rises to the defense of the needy. Jesus modeled this compassion for us when He interacted with a widow from the town of Nain. He was entering the town just as this widow was going out to bury her only son. She had already buried her husband and now her son. She was alone; she was broken; and she was scared. As Jesus looked at her, He felt compassion (Luke 7:13). It was not the compassion of pity but the compassion of empathy. He chose not to just feel sad but also to get involved. That is what the Healer does; He steps into a world of need and gets involved. He brought His habitation down to us and stood as Judge for the widow. The proud He makes low, but the humble He raises up in the light of His presence (James 4:6). He defends His children, striking the enemy with the words of His mouth. He binds their wounds and mends what has been broken.

*See Appendix

ARISE (PART 3)

A father of the fatherless and a judge for the widows, Is God in His holy habitation.
God makes a home for the lonely; He leads out the prisoners into prosperity,
Only the rebellious dwell in a parched land.

Psalm 68:5–6

"Arise, O Shepherd; the lions are near,

Your flock has scattered; they tremble in fear.

Who will defend them? It was You Who died,

Now Your grave stands empty; they need not hide."*

Continuing with Psalm 68, the psalmist writes, *"God makes a home for the lonely."* How gracious it is that the Healer makes a home for the lonely, but what good is a home to someone who is alone? Loneliness is not a matter of where you are but who is around you. When you feel alone, it is easy to feel unwanted and neglected. Probably the worst emotion we can be inflicted with is a sense of being alone and therefore unloved. It goes against the very name and nature of God, *Emmanuel.* Jesus is *"God with us";* that is why He came to the earth. We are to take comfort in the truth that the Healer will never leave us nor forsake us. There will undoubtedly be times when others walk away from us. Family will neglect us; friends will betray us; and it will appear that we stand alone; but we are most assuredly not alone! For the lonely, there is healing simply in the knowledge that the Spirit desires to always be with us, not figuratively but literally! But let's not stop there; let's dig deeper. In Psalm 68:6, the Hebrew word for *home* is *bayith* which literally means "household or family." God not only makes a home for us, but He also takes us into His family. He is Emmanuel, and because of that, we are connected to every Christian, past, present, and future. It is Satan's lies that tell us that we are alone, and it is a lamb that is isolated that is the prey of the lion. You are not alone! Do not cower in the shadows. Through Christ we already have victory. Victoriously we stand, together!

*See Appendix

ARISE (PART 4)

A father of the fatherless and a judge for the widows, Is God in His holy habitation.
God makes a home for the lonely; He leads out the prisoners into prosperity,
Only the rebellious dwell in a parched land.

Psalm 68:5–6

"Arise, O Musician, and take a bow,

All Heaven and earth are singing Your praise!

For years You have waited, but we see now.

You are King over all; Your song we raise!"*

What are we supposed to do with this abundant life that God has given us (John 10:10)? It is easy to get mixed up and lost in the chaos. What is right? What is wrong? Where should I go? When is the right time? It is easy to become paralyzed with options or to become ridged in rules. If we are not careful, this abundant life can become a prison cell in which we serve a life sentence. But the psalmist reminds us that *"He [God] leads out the prisoners into prosperity"* (Psalm 68:6). Who praises louder than a prisoner set free? Listen to the song of God's children as they return from captivity: *"When the Lord brought back the captive ones of Zion, We were like those who dream. Then our mouth was filled with laughter And our tongue with joyful shouting; Then they said among the nations, 'The Lord has done great things for them.' The Lord has done great things for us; We are glad. Restore our captivity, O Lord, As the streams in the South. Those who sow in tears shall reap with joyful shouting. He who goes to and fro weeping, carrying his bag of seed, Shall indeed come again with a shout of joy, bringing his sheaves with him"* (Psalm 126:1–6). This life does not have to be a prison cell. The Healer knows the way we should go and the time we should act. Fix your eyes on Christ (Hebrews 12:2). Trust Him (Proverbs 3:5–6). Follow His Word (Psalm 119:105). Wait on Him (Philippians 3:20). And sing the healing song of freedom (Psalm 40:3).

*See Appendix

ARISE (PART 5)

A father of the fatherless and a judge for the widows, Is God in His holy habitation. God makes a home for the lonely; He leads out the prisoners into prosperity, Only the rebellious dwell in a parched land.

Psalm 68:5–6

"Arise, O Potter; Your vessel is good,

A beauty to see and ready to use.

Now held in Your hand, the work has begun,

How perfect its cracks, its Maker we muse."*

The psalmist goes on to say, *"Only the rebellious dwell in a parched land."* The inverse of this statement must mean, *"those who are not rebellious dwell in watered lands."* Now in order to not preach a Gospel built on exaggerations and misconceptions, we must acknowledge and just because you follow God does not mean that everything is going to be easy and everyone who rebels against Him will live in utter ruin. To understand what the psalmist is saying, you need to understand that God sees water differently than we do. This water is life, and it flows out of the throne of the Lamb (Revelation 22:1). He gives it without cost (Revelation 21:6), and those who drink of it will never thirst again (John 4:14). There will still be difficult times for those who follow Christ, but they will have something the world does not. Jeremiah says it this way: *"Blessed is the man who trusts in the LORD And whose trust is the LORD. "For he will be like a tree planted by the water, That extends its roots by a stream And will not fear when the heat comes; But its leaves will be green, And it will not be anxious in a year of drought Nor cease to yield fruit"* (Jeremiah 17:7–8). There will still be heat and drought, but our source of life comes not from the sun but the Son. Nor does our hope come from earthly rivers but from the water of life flowing from the Lamb. He touches the fatherless, the widows, the lonely, the prisoner, and the thirsty, making them whole.

*See Appendix

BEARING OUR BURDEN

Blessed be the Lord, who daily bears our burden, The God who is our salvation. Selah.

Psalm 68:19

The psalmist starts this verse with a directive to *"bless the Lord."* What a wonderful, merciful, loving, and powerful Healer we serve! Don't miss this opportunity to do just that! Tell Him how great He is and how much you long to abide with Him! He is our salvation! He is the very thing we couldn't do, and because of that, we have life today! We do not exactly know what the word *Selah* means, but one possibility is "to stop and ponder or meditate." If we are more concerned with the schedule of our day or meeting our own desires than we are abiding in Christ, then it is very doubtful we have ever been touched by the grace of the Healer. Turning a blind eye to Christ's goodness is a heart that has not been restored. Someone who can't take the time to worship the Almighty because of their labor is someone who has never entered the rest of Christ (Hebrews 4:1). But for those who have been cleansed by the blood of the Lamb, this psalm says He daily bears your burden. Note a couple things about this. First, what incredible grace the Healer shows to His creation. He, being King, is willing to lift the burden of those beneath Him. But God not only lifts our burden, He also bears or carries that burden. Secondly, He *daily* carries our burden. This could mean while He has the power to totally eliminate our burden, He chooses to daily take it and carry it as we walk with Him. Finally, our burdens are placed in Jesus' hands *only* if we place them there; He does not take them from us. The Bible says in 1 Peter 5:6–7, *"Therefore humble yourselves under the mighty hand of God, that He may exalt you at the proper time, casting all your anxiety on Him, because He cares for you."* Part of the healing the Healer gives us is the opportunity to hand Him our anxieties, to let go of the thing we so desperately want to keep within our control. Because of His love, He daily bears our burden.

———————

NAME OF HEALING

She will bear a Son; and you shall call His name Jesus,
for He will save His people from their sins.

Matthew 1:21

Today let's look at the healing of Joseph, Jesus' earthly father—a man who is talked about every year but rarely considered. Joseph received a message from an angel, telling him that his soon-to-be wife was going to give birth to a baby that was not his. This baby was actually put there by the Spirit of God and was going to be the Savior of the world. Any Jew would have been thrilled to have a front-row seat to the Messiah's coming, but almost any man in Joseph's position would have been asking, why does He have to come through my wife? I'm sure Joseph had dreams for his family, but now he would be constantly defending his wife and Son against anyone who didn't believe their story. Maybe he instantly started thinking of names—names that would get him off the hook. If Joseph was to raise the Son of God, then he could name Him Joseph Jr. so others would praise him. Or he could name Him Loammi, which comes from the book of Hosea and means *not my people,* so he'd be able to say, "Don't look at me; He's not my child." But Joseph didn't have a say; the angel told him to name the baby Jesus, which means *Jehovah is salvation.* Joseph believed the angel and did what God desired, but this could not have been easy for this soon-to-be husband. He would experience wounds from skeptics such as family and friends for the remainder of his life. Yet for Joseph, there was healing. Every time he called Jesus' name, there was ointment applied to his wounded heart. Joseph could not claim his DNA brought salvation, leading him to pride, nor could he run from this child, leading to lostness. No, Joseph would find healing not in fathering salvation but in speaking His name. Joseph was blessed to love Him and to watch Him grow (Luke 2:52). Today, the name of Jesus is still healing those who call on it (Romans 10:13).

MOVED TO INVOLVEMENT

When the Lord saw her, He felt compassion for her, and said to her, "Do not weep."

Luke 7:13

There is something about Jesus raising the widow's son that intrigues me, making it one of my favorite miracles (Luke 7:11–17). Of these seven verses, verse thirteen is the one that shoots fireworks in my spirit, and that is because of one small phrase: *"When the Lord saw her."* I believe that this sighting was more than just seeing with His eyes. Jesus saw her, but He was moved in His core. Another way of saying it is, there was a physical response to an emotional stirring. His response was one of compassion, the Bible says. Why? Was it because He was thinking of His own mother? It is believed that Joseph had already passed away, and Mary was now a widow. Perhaps, Jesus was remembering that day in Nazareth when Mary walked out of the city, following as Joseph's body was carried to its resting place. Or maybe Jesus was thinking about the day to come when Mary would look on her Son's lifeless body being taken down from the cross and carried to a tomb. We do not know the reason Jesus was touched by looking at this mother, but we know that He was so moved that He physically responded. It is easy to be emotionally stirred, but to allow that to move us to a physical response is not so easy. It will cost us something to stop a funeral procession. But the Healer was willing to pay the cost; He stopped the coffin and told the grieving mother, *"Do not weep."* The healing of Christ is truly bringing life where there is death. He looks at us and sees the death in our hearts, and is so moved with compassion that He physically intervenes. He touches our lifeless heart, and though it has pumped blood since we were in the womb, now it pumps life! The Healer was emotionally stirred to the point He physically intervened; He was willing to pay the cost of getting involved; and because of that, life was given, and a family rejoiced.

———————

THE WELLS WITHIN

She said, "No one, Lord." And Jesus said, "I do not condemn you, either. Go. From now on sin no more."

John 8:11

I find then the principle that evil is present in me, the one who wants to do good. For I joyfully concur with the law of God in the inner man, but I see a different law in the members of my body, waging war against the law of my mind and making me a prisoner of the law of sin which is in my members. Wretched man that I am! Who will set me free from the body of this death? Thanks be to God through Jesus Christ our Lord! So then, on the one hand I myself with my mind am serving the law of God, but on the other, with my flesh the law of sin (Romans 7:21–25).

Paul is speaking of the war that is raging inside of us. The law of God versus the law of sin. The Bible teaches that you cannot have both sweet and bitter water coming from the same well (James 3:11); therefore, how do we produce actions flowing from the law of God and the law of sin? Inside our heart there is not simply one well but two. From one flows life through the law of God (Proverbs 4:23) and from the other, death through the law of sin (Romans 6:23). So what can we do? Life and death mingle together inside of us. Paul looked at this dilemma and exclaimed, *"Wretched man that I am! Who will set me free from the body of this death"* (Romans 7:24). The answer followed, *"Thanks be to God through Jesus Christ our Lord"* (Romans 7:25). Jesus is the answer, but how? Does He plug up the well of sin in our heart? Not until we get to Heaven. So what are we to do with this war inside of us? For this we look to Romans 8:1: *"Therefore there is now no condemnation for those who are in Christ Jesus."* Just like the woman who was caught in adultery, the sin was present in her life, but Jesus did not condemn her. Is this license to sin? No, it is a license to be healed from the ravages of this war. This adulterous woman should have died, and death was served but not to her; it was placed on the bleeding back of a crucified Christ.

SOUNDNESS OF MIND

The people went out to see what had happened; and they came to Jesus,
and found the man from whom the demons had gone out, sitting down at the feet of Jesus,
clothed and in his right mind; and they became frightened.

Luke 8:35

Fear is a prison. Fear is a thief. Fear is a fierce task master. Fear is a tool of Satan. Fear says, *"I cannot."* Fear stands in direct opposition to God, and therefore it is already a defeated foe!

The secret to fear is that it can have control over you only as long as it reigns as most powerful. When the waves of the storm seem bigger than God, fear grips your heart. When death looms more powerful than the One Who gives life, fear will steal your joy every moment of every day. When fear weaves itself into your mind, you become anxious, and God becomes the weaker Warrior, blindly waving His sword, wounding Himself and those who fight alongside Him. Fear will distort your mind, and if it is allowed to live there, it will taint your spirit as well. *"For God has not given us a spirit of fear but of power, and love, and discipline"* (2 Timothy 1:7). The Greek word for discipline is *sōphronismos* which means "an admonishing or calling to soundness of mind." The Spirit of God that abides in us is not a weak demigod who cannot control the elements of His world. No, the Healer is far superior to the waves, to sickness, to your enemies, and even to evil spirits because He is the Creator of all of these. Each of these bow to Him and respond to His command. Just as the man in Luke 8, who had a legion of demons terrorizing him, when Jesus gave the command for them to exit, they who utilized fear became scared themselves. Then the man who had lost his mind was sitting there in his right mind because his mind had been called to soundness. This man was no longer scared of his demons because he now knew the One Who was greater. He had soundness of mind because the Healer's touch is certain and complete.

THUS THE HEALER'S PRESCRIPTION

*And My people who are called by My name humble themselves and pray and seek
My face and turn from their wicked ways, then I will hear from heaven,
will forgive their sin and will heal their land.*

2 Chronicles 7:14

"And My people who are called by My name"

"This is His commandment, that we believe in the name of His Son Jesus Christ, and love
one another, just as He commanded us" (1 John 3:23).

"Humble themselves"

"He must increase, but I must decrease" (John 3:30).

"And pray"

"The end of all things is near; therefore, be of sound judgment and sober spirit for the
purpose of prayer" (1 Peter 4:7).

"And seek My face"

"You will seek Me and find Me when you search for Me with all your heart" (Jeremiah 29:13).

"And turn from their wicked ways"

"Therefore repent and return, so that your sins may be wiped away, in order that times
of refreshing may come from the presence of the Lord" (Acts 3:19).

"Then I will hear from heaven"

"We know that God does not hear sinners; but if anyone is God-fearing and does His will,
He hears him" (John 9:31).

"Will forgive their sin"

"For He rescued us from the domain of darkness, and transferred us to the kingdom of His
beloved Son, in whom we have redemption, the forgiveness of sins" (Colossians 1:13–14).

"And will heal their land"

"Heal me, O LORD, and I will be healed; Save me and I will be saved, For You are my
praise" (Jeremiah 17:14).

O Lord, may I know Your healing touch as I long for Your holy presence. You are
Lord of all! Amen.

————————

VALIDATED FORGIVENESS

"But, so that you may know that the Son of Man has authority on earth to forgive sins,"
He said to the paralytic, "I say to you, get up, and pick up your stretcher and go home."

Luke 5:24

The Healer's touch is certain and complete, which is why the healing of a paralytic man was most irritating to those who did not believe Jesus was the Christ. This particular day, Jesus was teaching, and a large crowd had gathered to hear Him. At the same time, a group of men were carrying a paralytic on a stretcher, bringing him to the Healer to be touched. The problem was, so many people had come to hear Jesus that these men could not get their friend in the house. So they went up on the roof, made a hole, and lowered the stretcher down with ropes, right in front of Jesus. Now to the religious leaders, Jesus was not just a nuisance; He was also a mystery. How was this unpredictable Rabbi doing such supernatural things? Everyone in the room waited, excited to see if the Healer would once again do the impossible. And if Jesus would have just touched this man and healed him, He would have been admired as a healing hero. But Jesus looked at the paralytic and the group of men who had brought him, then said, *"Friend, your sins are forgiven you"* (Luke 5:20). Everyone was confused; they were expecting healing, but instead, they heard forgiveness of sins. The religious leaders were trying to figure out what just happened. No one could forgive sins except God. How could an eccentric Rabbi dare to tell someone their sins were forgiven? But then Jesus did the very thing that would put a pebble in the shoe of His listeners for the rest of their lives. He said, *"so that you will know the Son of Man has authority to forgive sins . . . pick up your stretcher and go home."* Boom! Jesus validated His forgiveness of sins by doing what the religious leaders could not do; He healed the man. The Pharisees did not believe Him to be the Messiah, but they could not deny the paralytic had been healed.

———

COMPASSION AND FAITH

When He had said this, He spat on the ground, and made clay of the spittle, and applied the clay to his eyes, and said to him, "Go, wash in the pool of Siloam" (which is translated, Sent). So he went away and washed, and came back seeing.

John 9:6–7

It was rare that Jesus did things normally. It seems that He always went the extra mile to do things backward or in a mind-bending way. Why? Why would Jesus capitalize on putting His listeners in moral turmoil? Even those the Healer healed were often asked to do what no one would dream of doing to be healed. Through the lens of physical healing, this doesn't make a lot of sense, but through the lens of spiritual healing, you can start to understand. We must remember why Jesus came to this earth. *"And hearing this, Jesus said to them, "It is not those who are healthy who need a physician, but those who are sick; I did not come to call the righteous, but sinners"* (Mark 2:17). Jesus did not come so fallen humans could live longer, happier, and healthier lives. No, it was so that we could live eternally with the Father. Sin stood as the obstacle blocking the gates of Heaven, so Jesus came to become a new gate. His love for humanity moved Him to compassion, but His compassion required Him to make a way out of our death. That is what His death on the cross was; yet while His death made salvation available to the entire world, it did not force it on them. No, salvation is for those who have faith that He is the Son of God. We are saved by grace (compassion) through faith (Ephesians 2:8). God's compassion made it possible for us to receive His gifts: the breath of God is life (Genesis 2:7); the blood of Christ is salvation (Romans 5:9); the Spirit of God is love (Romans 5:5); and the saliva of Jesus is healing (John 9:7) to those who have the faith to be obedient. The Healer may ask to smear spit-made mud in our eyes, but if that is the source of sight, then who are we to argue?

RIVER OF HEALING

*So he went down and dipped himself seven times in the Jordan,
according to the word of the man of God; and his flesh was restored
like the flesh of a little child and he was clean.*

2 Kings 5:14

Deep are the roots of sin that grow out of our hearts and draw nutrients from the manure of self-service! The love of self was what claimed the lives of Adam and Eve, and it is still the sin that taints our hearts today. Every day we are tempted to experiment with ways to elevate our wisdom over God's. The Healer desires to give healing to us and to strengthen what has been broken, but we are so hard-hearted that we would rather live with our infirmity than receive His healing through obedience. Just as Naaman left Elisha's house in a rage because the healing that was being extended to him was not done in a way suitable to his status. Naaman would have stayed a leper until he died because it wasn't leprosy that was eating his heart but rather pride. The healing touch of God comes when our hearts are humble enough to bow before Him. Isn't it ludicrous that the one who is sick has the audacity to say the means of healing isn't good enough? We look at Naaman and scoff at his disregard for the Healer, but we are just as guilty, if not more so. At least Naaman did turn back and obey. Many of us will go to our graves turning a blind eye to the healing extended to us. It is so easy to cry out to God over and over about the same thing, yet we do nothing more than give Him lip service. We can be so obstinate toward God that we refuse to lift a single finger to help reach those damned to Hell, yet we will pour out our own accolades before Him as if He owes us for our service. Shame on us! If the King tells us to wash seven times in the Jordan, it does not matter what river we would rather wash in; we should run to the river and dive in head first. Our healing has zero to do with us and everything to do with the Healer.

THE DEPTH OF HEALING

And he fell on his face at His feet, giving thanks to Him. And he was a Samaritan.

Luke 17:16

In the days of Jesus, people who were diagnosed with leprosy were forced to live in seclusion, away from their families. Understandably, those with leprosy would band together and live in colonies. One day as Jesus was traveling between Samaria and Galilee, He encountered one such family. There were ten lepers, raising their voices together, asking for the Healer to give them mercy. Jesus did not give them a touch of healing but rather a hope of healing. He told them to go show themselves to the priest as Moses had commanded. It was while they were on their way that they became clean. Can you imagine that short journey? The ten of them are standing together, demoralized, ostracized, and dying, when all of a sudden, Jesus walks by. They look at each other, and with decaying lips, they smile. Together they run toward Jesus but are careful to keep their distance. They cry out for mercy, and Jesus instructs them to go to the priest. Uncertain of what was to happen, they turn toward the temple and begin to run. As they run down the streets, they notice their bodies are moving in ways that they haven't in a long time. They feel different; they feel energized with power in their muscles. Their joints don't ache, and their senses return. They look down to see that their skin is clean and restored! They shout for joy in the very streets they had just moments before tried to be invisible in. They dance and talk all at the same time. *"What should we do? Go to the priest? Go to our families?"* Yet in the heart of one, gratitude overflowed, and he ran back to Jesus and fell on his face. Oh, the joy of a heart that recognized the gift of the Healer! Not just its source but also its depth. This man's skin was restored; his family was reunited; but even more, his heart was healed. That is why he fell on his face at the feet of Jesus. He understood the depth of his sickness and, therefore, the depth of his healing.

———————

FRIEND VERSUS ENEMY

But Jesus answered and said, "Stop! No more of this."
And He touched his ear and healed him.

Luke 22:51

In the book of Proverbs, Solomon writes, *"Faithful are the wounds of a friend, But deceitful are the kisses of an enemy"* (Proverbs 27:6). Faithful versus deceitful, wounds versus kisses, friend versus enemy—if you broke this down, you could say, *"A faithful friend may wound, but a deceitful enemy may kiss."* With this proverb in mind, overlay it on Jesus' encounter in the Garden of Gethsemane. Judas, a friend of Jesus, signaled the soldiers by kissing Jesus. This gesture of love was actually motivated by deceit. A sign of love was actually the gateway to death.

Still with this proverb in mind, consider Malchus. As the soldiers grabbed Jesus, Peter drew his sword and cut off the right ear of a man named Malchus, a slave of the high priest. Peter meant this wound for his enemy, but Jesus stopped him and then faithfully healed the mangled ear.

Now with both Judas and Malchus in perspective, let's see who is enemy and who is friend. James 4:4 says, *"You adulterers! Don't you realize that friendship with the world makes you an enemy of God? I say it again: If you want to be a friend of the world, you make yourself an enemy of God."* Judas was a friend of Jesus who made himself an enemy by siding with the world. Malchus was an enemy of Jesus who was shown the faithfulness of a friend. But what was Jesus' response? Did He devise a plan of revenge on either? No, He went to the cross and died the death that was meant for both of them. Judas nor Malchus were the enemy; they were the objects of His love (Mark 10:45). Satan is the enemy, and Jesus kept that in view. The wounds of Jesus offer healing to all who make themselves enemies of God.

———————

SIGHT MADE WHOLE

Moved with compassion, Jesus touched their eyes;
and immediately they regained their sight and followed Him.

Matthew 20:34

Can you imagine what life must have been like for a blind person in the days of Jesus? It was probably like it is for us today who try to decipher John's revelation of the end times. In the book of Revelation, John described things he had never seen before, things he had no understanding of. Now we are to take that information and try to put it together in a logical manner, even though we do not have the mental ability to grasp it. The conglomeration of things past, present, and future that we come up with is probably a far cry from what John actually saw. Likewise, a blind person in Jesus' day would have to take descriptions of things they have no concept of and try to put them into a working mental image. Undoubtedly, the two blind men outside Jericho had heard about a man named Jesus of Nazareth, who taught with authority and did miraculous healings and even raised the dead. These two men had no way of knowing Who Jesus was nor if what they had heard was fact or fiction. Strange events have a way of becoming tall tales that become outright lies. These men had heard of the events, the tales, and the lies; then they put it all together as best they could. At the end of the day, they believed Jesus was their only Hope. Not just to regain their sight but for salvation. They unashamedly cried out to the *Son of David,* the title given to the long-awaited Messiah. They put all their eggs into one basket, and at the risk of becoming even more publicly scorned, they continued to cry for the Son of David to have mercy on them. At last, the Healer touched their eyes, and their sight was restored. What was once skewed for them had now become clear. They saw Jesus clearly! That is, they saw His physical body clearly. They already had a right view of Him spiritually, and that is what made all the difference.

HAVE YOU BEEN HEALED

He made Him who knew no sin to be sin on our behalf,
so that we might become the righteousness of God in Him.

2 Corinthians 5:21

The Healer's touch is certain and complete. Is it certain and complete in your life? Have you truly experienced the healing of Christ, or have you just grown accustomed to the ailments of your life? Obviously, I'm not speaking of your physical body but of your spirit. Our disobedience to God has driven an eternal wedge between us and the Father, a wedge that has allowed poison and pollution to drain into our soul. We are sick in body, possessed in soul, and dead in spirit. In short, we need the Healer's touch! Through Christ's death on the cross, salvation has already been bought. Jesus, Who knew no sin, became sin for us. Now, in Him, we can become the righteousness of God. But do not miss the fact that when God saves us, He does not immediately take us home to Heaven. He heals us for a reason. He heals us so we can continue the work of the harvest.

Listen to the words of Paul in 2 Corinthians 5:18–21:

Now all these things are from God, who reconciled us to Himself through Christ and gave us the ministry of reconciliation, namely, that God was in Christ reconciling the world to Himself, not counting their trespasses against them, and He has committed to us the word of reconciliation. Therefore, we are ambassadors for Christ, as though God were making an appeal through us; we beg you on behalf of Christ, be reconciled to God. He made Him who knew no sin to be sin on our behalf, so that we might become the righteousness of God in Him.

The Healer reconciled us for a reason; we are to be His ambassadors. The sick, lame, possessed, and dead that Jesus healed could not keep their mouth shut. They jumped, sang, danced, and shouted; and their anthem was, "I once was sick, but now I'm healed, and it was Jesus Who made me whole!" Have you met the Healer?

———————

DECEMBER

The Shepherd's Staff Is Long and Safe

THE SHEPHERD'S PRESENCE

The LORD is my shepherd, I shall not want.

Psalm 23:1

What image floods your mind when you think of the word *peace*? You might think of a scenic overlook in the mountains or a sandy beach with the sun shining on you and waves crashing nearby. Still others would simply like to be at their own home for a quiet evening with family. Virtually anywhere can be a peaceful place; therefore, I want you to ponder this question: What makes your peaceful place peaceful? A scenic overlook can be beautiful unless you are standing there when an electrical storm is going on. The ocean is glorious unless you are caught in a rip tide. And a quiet evening at home is special, but tragedy can strike at any moment. I am in no way trying to breed fear in your life but rather to get you to grasp the source of peace. How many times have we said something like, *"If I can just make it to the end of this week, things will settle down"; "If I only had more money, I wouldn't struggle so much"; or "If my kids would only do what I say then I could have a moment's peace."* Peace is something that we all search for and even pay great amounts of money to get, but if the truth be told, the peace we manufacture or buy is short-lived. The reason for this is that peace is not a place or a circumstance but rather a Person. It is the Shepherd! Jesus is the Shepherd, and we are His sheep. Sometimes He leads us to scenic overlooks, sometimes to sandy beaches; other times He lets us rest at home, and still other times He leads us into the fires. But we can still be at peace because peace is not made; it is found. If something can manufacture peace, then something else can wreck it. If your peace is based on someone doing something, then it would be impossible for you to have peace if they did not do it. *"The LORD is my Shepherd, I shall not want."* Peace is found in the Shepherd's presence, not the circumstances of life. His presence is greater than any challenge we encounter, but the sheep must fix their focus on the Shepherd.

———————

MADE TO LIE DOWN

He makes me lie down in green pastures; He leads me beside quiet waters.

Psalm 23:2

The twenty-third Psalm must be one of the most tranquil passages in the Bible. To think of the Shepherd's protection, provision, and presence is so reassuring. On nights when you wake up and the stresses of the world come rushing in, you can meditate on this psalm, and it brings rest to a frazzled mind. But the second verse is confusing. The Lord *makes* me lie down in green pastures. The Hebrew word for *makes me lie down* is *rabats,* and it is what is called a *causative verb,* meaning it's an action done to you. So lying down is something the Shepherd causes you to do. Does this mean that the Shepherd physically forces you to the ground? Or is it like a parent who makes their child lie down at nap time? The parent does not pen the child down, but they do not give an option, either. Biblically, we can see the Shepherd both physically and circumstantially making His sheep lie down. Sickness or injury can render you bedridden, and while that may seem harsh, many people have found the love of the Father while lying flat on their back. Also, a loss of a job can put you in a season of inactivity. It may feel like God has pulled the rug out from under you, but the Shepherd knows when you need to lie down in green pastures. The question is, will you fight God, or will you surrender to Him? Sometimes God gives us refreshing green pastures, and at other times God takes away our old brown pasture that we are used to and leads us to new ones. It is easy to celebrate when God gives the new, but it's difficult when He takes away your comfort zone. Job said it this way, *"Naked I came from my mother's womb, and naked I will return there. The LORD gives, and the LORD takes away. May the name of the LORD be blessed"* (Job 1:21). The Shepherd knows what we need, and that is why the peace of the twenty-third Psalm is found in His ability to give and take away as is best to Him.

ETERNITY AWAITS

He makes me lie down in green pastures; He leads me beside quiet waters.

Psalm 23:2

In the eyes of the Shepherd, what exactly are *quiet waters?* Water is mentioned in various forms throughout Scripture. From the Mediterranean Sea to the Jordan River. Are these quiet waters? The Red Sea did not sound so quiet as it parted for the Hebrew children to walk across on dry ground. The Mediterranean Sea did not sound so quiet as Jonah was being picked up and thrown overboard. The Sea of Galilee didn't sound so quiet when Peter took his eyes off Jesus and looked at the wind and the waves. Water when babbling over smooth stones can be relaxing, but when it is crashing over boulders, it can be deafening. The Shepherd leads His sheep beside quiet waters, water that a lamb can safely drink. But the water the Shepherd longs to pasture His sheep beside will not be found until the earth has passed away and a new Heaven and new earth come.

Revelation 22:1–5 says:

Then he showed me a river of the water of life, clear as crystal, coming from the throne of God and of the Lamb, in the middle of its street. On either side of the river was the tree of life, bearing twelve kinds of fruit, yielding its fruit every month; and the leaves of the tree were for the healing of the nations. There will no longer be any curse; and the throne of God and of the Lamb will be in it, and His bond-servants will serve Him; they will see His face, and His name will be on their foreheads. And there will no longer be any night; and they will not have need of the light of a lamp nor the light of the sun, because the Lord God will illumine them; and they will reign forever and ever.

The river of the water of life that flows from the throne of God and of the Lamb, that is the river the Shepherd longs to lead His sheep beside. Oh, how we should long to rest beside this river, knowing the curse is gone, the Shepherd sits on His throne, and eternity awaits! Of this river may we drink!

———

RESTORING SWEET REST

He restores my soul; He guides me in the paths of righteousness For His name's sake.

Psalm 23:3

What does it mean for the Shepherd to restore our soul? The Shepherd provides for our physical needs by providing green pastures for food and quiet waters to drink, but now we see that *"He restores my soul."* Our soul is our heart and mind, our conscience and emotions. In other words, the Shepherd is providing mentally restorative rest for the sheep.

King David wrote in another psalm, *"In peace I will both lie down and sleep, For You alone, O LORD, make me to dwell in safety"* (Psalm 4:8). Sleep, or rest, comes from the safety brought about by the presence of the Shepherd. As a parent, one of the most touching things you do is to sneak into your children's room after they have fallen asleep and simply watch them. You listen to their quiet breathing, and you admire the look of peace on their face. They are innocent because they do not know the possibilities. They do not care about those possibilities because they believe nothing can harm them with you in the next room. Your presence is enough to provide them with rest. It is the same way with the Shepherd. His presence is enough to give His sheep rest. They are full; they are replenished; and they are safe. Their minds think of the Shepherd as their eyes close. Everything is as it should be. As we grow up, it becomes easy to focus not on the Shepherd but on the wolves, and our sleep becomes restless. Romans 12:2 says, *"And do not be conformed to this world, but be transformed by the renewing of your mind, so that you may prove what the will of God is, that which is good and acceptable and perfect."* The restoring of our soul does not come from aligning ourselves with the world and its hollow self-help wisdom, nor fearing the horrors of the world, but rather, restoration is through the Great Shepherd alone. His presence is enough to give us restoring, sweet rest.

———————

FORK IN THE ROAD

He restores my soul; He guides me in the paths of righteousness For His name's sake.

Psalm 23:3

What do you do when you come to a fork in the road? How do you know which way to go? Do you follow your gut, or do you flip a coin? Neither if you want to get where you are going. You know which way to go by looking at the directions. One way might look more friendlier and the other more ominous, but if you want to get to your destination, then you follow the directions. It is the same way in our spiritual walk. The Shepherd is our source of directions. As He leads us to green pastures, quiet waters, and restoration of soul, we are to follow Him. When He turns to the left, we should be right on His heels. When He turns right, we should remain in sync with Him. And if He stays straight, we should not deviate. We are like sheep and easily swayed by wants and feelings (Isaiah 53:6). Our wants and feelings are so easily misconstrued, if we do not keep the Shepherd always before us, then we are in for a lot of trouble. The Bible says that our heart is wicked and deceitful; therefore, we cannot trust what we want (Jeremiah 17:9), but the Bible also says that God gives us the desires of our heart if we seek Him (Psalm 37:4); therefore, when is it okay to follow our desires? Also, what we feel can be misleading because if we want to do something wrong, God convicts us, and if we want to do something right, Satan tries to deceive us. In both ways, we feel a push or pull. When we try to make directional decisions about our lives based on what we want or how we feel, we run the risk of getting lost. The only way to stay on the right path is to follow the leading of the Shepherd, and that comes from following Him every step of the way. The prayer of our heart should be, *"Make me know Your ways, O LORD; Teach me Your paths"* (Psalm 25:4). The Father rejoices in guiding us in the paths of righteousness. It is for His name's sake that He leads us, and that is a holy, righteous name!

FROM DEATH TO LIFE

Even though I walk through the valley of the shadow of death, I fear no evil,
for You are with me; Your rod and Your staff, they comfort me.

Psalm 23:4

The paths the Shepherd leads us on are not always the most scenic nor the safest. But remember, the paths we walk were never meant to be where we stop to dwell. The path is simply the way to the pasture. How often do we look at the path in front of us and shrink back, telling God to find another way? Fear grips our hearts as we look at the world of death all around us. We long to live in Heaven's glory, but we walk in the ravages of evil. As we journey, we slip and fall; we get sidetracked and lose our way. Everything inside us tells us to sit down and cry. We feel stuck like a sheep caught in the thicket. It is easy to see the path as the destination. Somewhere along the way, we have bought into the lie that following the Shepherd is the safest path we can take. Following Christ may be eternally safe, but many lambs have lost their lives walking the paths of the Shepherd. If this leads you to think harshly of the Shepherd, remember it was we who walked away from Him, and it was He Who came to us to lay His life down so we could know Him. We must remember that the pasture we are headed to is not on this earth, and the only way to get there is through death. That is why the Shepherd is worth following; He is the resurrection and the life!

John 11:25 says, *"Jesus said to her, 'I am the resurrection and the life; he who believes in Me will live even if he dies.'"* We all must pass through the path of death, but that is because the pasture of life is on the other side! We may not like this arrangement, but we are mere sheep, and the Father is our Shepherd. We do not have a say in what is right or wrong or even what is fair. The paths of Christ are righteous, and though you walk through death, there is life to any who follow Him.

———————

LIGHT IN THE DARK

*Even though I walk through the valley of the shadow of death, I fear no evil,
for You are with me; Your rod and Your staff, they comfort me.*

Psalm 23:4

This is a beautiful verse and one that is full of theology. One such point is not fearing even though you walk through a dark valley. To start with, I want you to think about light versus darkness. To have a shadow, you must have two things: first, light, and second, something to block the light, creating darkness. In this verse, what is the light and what is blocking it? The second part is easy; *"death"* is what is blocking the light because it is the shadow of death. But the source of the light is not as clear. If this was a literal valley, then we could say it is the sun, but David is writing figuratively about walking through a rough season of life. So when we think of the figurative shadow of death, the light could very well be the opposite, the light of life. John 8:12 says, *"Then Jesus again spoke to them, saying, 'I am the Light of the world; he who follows Me will not walk in the darkness, but will have the Light of life.'"* So in light of the twenty-third Psalm, the Shepherd leads His sheep through some rough times, and during that time, the Light of life gets blocked by death. This could be equated to a lamb turning around and no longer seeing its shepherd. A lamb stands zero chance of survival without the provision and protection of its shepherd. So this raises the question, how is it that death has managed to block the light of the Son? The darkness of death and the light of Jesus are not strangers to each other. When Jesus was on the cross, the sun became dark (Matthew 27:45). When Jesus died on the cross, death overshadowed the world, and the disciples, just like sheep without a shepherd, were afraid because it appeared that death had won. But just like David's declaration, *"I fear no evil because You are with me,"* even when death blocks the Light of life and we no longer can see the Shepherd, evil does not need to be feared. Emmanuel is with us, and that is more powerful than death.

DECEMBER 8

YOUR ROD AND STAFF

*Even though I walk through the valley of the shadow of death, I fear no evil,
for You are with me; Your rod and Your staff, they comfort me.*

Psalm 23:4

It seems like it would get cumbersome for a shepherd to carry both a rod and staff. Perhaps a shepherd did carry both, or maybe David was speaking of different functions of a shepherd's walking stick. The first is the Hebrew word, *shebet,* which means "a shepherd's rod or crook." This rod was long with a crook at the top and was used for a variety of things. The crook was utilized for pulling back a lamb that had separated itself from the shepherd. If it had fallen down a ravine, the shepherd could reach out his rod, hook the lamb, and lift it back up. This rod could easily be used to help direct the herd, pulling back those who wandered off. Next, David talks about the comfort which comes from the Shepherd's staff. The Hebrew word for staff is *mishènah* which means "support or staff." The rod aided in rescuing, but the staff gave the shepherd support as he traversed on rocky terrain. The comfort of the staff was particularly for the lamb that was being carried on the shepherd's shoulders. He would carry lambs that had been injured or were sick. Likewise, a shepherd would sometimes break the leg of a lamb that kept wandering off; he would then carry that lamb on his shoulders until the leg healed, teaching the lamb not to leave the protection and provision of the shepherd. If while the shepherd carried a lamb, he lost his footing and fell, great harm could come to the lamb and the shepherd. So this staff of support helped the shepherd walk with sure footing, keeping himself and the lamb safe. The Good Shepherd's rod and staff bring comfort to His sheep because He reaches out to rescue us, and His steps are sure as He carries us, even when the world seems treacherous. If we are wayward or hurting, the Shepherd's rod and staff are reminders that His presence is a refuge (1 Peter 2:25).

THE SHEPHERD'S TABLE

You prepare a table before me in the presence of my enemies;
You have anointed my head with oil; My cup overflows.

Psalm 23:5

Jesus often talked about feasts and meals shared together because that is where family and friends gather to break bread. They talk about their day; they celebrate their victories; they hold each other accountable for their failures; and they teach each other life lessons. The Shepherd has prepared just such a table for all those in His fold.

Luke 13:22–30 says:

*And He was passing through from one city and village to another, teaching, and proceeding on His way to Jerusalem. And someone said to Him, "Lord, are there just a few who are being saved?" And He said to them, "Strive to enter through the narrow door; for many, I tell you, will seek to enter and will not be able. Once the head of the house gets up and shuts the door, and you begin to stand outside and knock on the door, saying, 'Lord, open up to us!' then He will answer and say to you, 'I do not know where you are from.' Then you will begin to say, 'We ate and drank in Your presence, and You taught in our streets'; and He will say, 'I tell you, I do not know where you are from; depart from Me, all you evildoers.' In that place there will be weeping and gnashing of teeth when you see Abraham and Isaac and Jacob and all the prophets in the kingdom of God, but yourselves being thrown out. **And they will come from east and west and from north and south and will recline at the table in the kingdom of God.** And behold, some are last who will be first and some are first who will be last.*

People will come from the east, west, north, and south to eat at the table of the Lord. What joy will overflow the Shepherd as He gathers His children around a table of worship! He has been preparing this table for a millennium, and what a day of joy it will be!

ANOINTING THE SHEEP

You prepare a table before me in the presence of my enemies;
You have anointed my head with oil; My cup overflows.

Psalm 23:5

So far in the twenty-third Psalm, we have seen how the Shepherd provides for our needs and protects us from our enemies. David continues this Psalm by saying, *"You have anointed my head with oil."* Oil had different purposes in the Bible. There is a healing property to oil, as we can see in Isaiah 1:6: *"From the sole of the foot even to the head There is nothing sound in it, Only bruises, welts and raw wounds, Not pressed out or bandaged, Nor softened with oil."* It was also believed that those who were anointed with the Spirit were filled with Him. *"As for you, the anointing which you received from Him abides in you, and you have no need for anyone to teach you; but as His anointing teaches you about all things, and is true and is not a lie, and just as it has taught you, you abide in Him"* (1 John 2:27). But probably the most common view of being anointed was to be set apart for a task. When David was just a boy watching his father's sheep, Samuel came looking for the next king of Israel. When he saw David, Samuel anointed David's head with oil, symbolizing David was being set apart for the task of leading the nation (1 Samuel 16:13). The priests were anointed for their service in the temple. They were set apart for their worship before the Lord (Exodus 40:15). So which of these is the reason the Shepherd anoints our head with oil? The word anointed literally means "to make fat or to fill with marrow," symbolizing prosperity or strengthening. Whether we are healed, filled, or set apart, our anointing is a symbol of God's prosperity and strengthening being poured out on us. He heals our wounds (Psalm 147:3); He fills us with His own Holy Spirit (Romans 8:9); and He sets us apart as His children (John 1:12). No longer are we His sheep, but we are adopted into the family of God, heirs to the kingdom, and loved by the Father (Romans 8:15).

WHOSE CUP

You prepare a table before me in the presence of my enemies;
You have anointed my head with oil; My cup overflows.

Psalm 23:5

In this psalm, David is using the metaphor that God is like a Shepherd, and we are like sheep. David went to great lengths to keep this metaphor going. Everything he wrote about were things sheep needed or encountered. It is as if David was writing this psalm while tending his father's sheep in the fields *(and maybe he did)*. Sheep need green pastures and water; they are led through rough terrain and are even anointed for different reasons. But the question that I keep pondering is why would a sheep have a cup? Sheep drink from streams, not cups. They have no house to store a cup nor even the ability to carry a cup. So how does a sheep have a cup that is overflowing? The only response to this question that I can come up with is that the cup belongs to the Shepherd, and He has given it to us. Maybe the path He leads his flock on has no water nearby, so the Shepherd has poured His own water into a cup and sat it down so the sheep could drink from it? If this is the case, then the question begging to be asked is what is the Shepherd filling the cup with? Living water? The blood of Calvary? Or the dregs of suffering? Yes, to all! The cup of the Lord overflows with all of these. And just as He has drunk them so are we to whom He gives His cup. The final question we should ask is what happens to the overflow from the cup? Does it spill on the ground and go to waste? May it never be! May we take the overflowing cup of Christ to everyone we come in contact with. Living water for those who thirst for righteousness, the blood of Calvary for the world stained by sin, and the dregs of suffering for a Church that longs to fulfill the commission of Christ. The Shepherd's cup keeps the sheep alive, but only if they drink what He overflows it with. It's not always easy to drink what the Shepherd pours for us, but His presence and compassion accompany His cup.

A SHEPHERD WHO FOLLOWS

Surely goodness and lovingkindness will follow me all the days of my life,
And I will dwell in the house of the LORD forever.

Psalm 23:6

Oh, what a rich verse of Scripture this is! Surely the Shepherd's staff is long and safe, and we can see why in this verse. First, it is important to note that both the words *goodness* and *lovingkindness* are nouns, not verbs. This means that as we live our life, we do not have a wave of good and pleasant things happening to us. This verse does not preach a message of, follow God, and only prosperous things will happen to you. No, it means that as you follow the Shepherd, His attributes of goodness and love are with you. These attributes are not necessarily being done to us but are present in that the Shepherd is present.

Next, we see that not only are goodness and lovingkindness present but they also follow us all the days of our lives. This is vitally important to understand because this could mean the difference in the world revolving around God or us. For God to *follow* can be interpreted a couple different ways: God is being led by us, and God pursues us. In the first, we are the center and God, being secondary, is being led by us. The second, God is the center and we, being secondary, are being pursued or sought after. Do not miss the wonderful, beautiful Good News that God does not follow us but rather pursues us as a shepherd pursues a lost sheep! He left Heaven and pursued us all the way to our cross; then He climbed on it and died in our place! Jesus puts it this way, *"What do you think? If any man has a hundred sheep, and one of them has gone astray, does he not leave the ninety-nine on the mountains and go and search for the one that is straying?"* (Matthew 18:12). Jesus did not follow that lost sheep wherever it wanted to go, but rather, He pursued it and found it and brought it back. That is the goodness and lovingkindness of the Shepherd! (Psalm 119:176).

THE LORD'S HOUSE

Surely goodness and lovingkindness will follow me all the days of my life,
And I will dwell in the house of the LORD forever.

Psalm 23:6

David both started and ended this psalm by calling the Shepherd *"Lord."* There is a difference between a shepherd and a lord. A shepherd is a hired hand, but a lord is an owner. A shepherd lives out in the field, but a lord lives in a great house. David sees God as both a Shepherd Who loves, cares, protects, provides, and watches over the sheep, and Lord, Who is the Sovereign Master, redemptive Owner, and compassionate Possessor of all. Shepherd and Lord seem to be opposite ends of a spectrum: poor versus rich, dirty versus clean, outside versus inside, sent versus sender, and worker versus owner. But Jesus put it this way, *"'I am the Alpha and the Omega,' says the Lord God, 'who is and who was and who is to come, the Almighty'"* (Revelation 1:8). Jesus was saying, "I'm the beginning and the end and everything in between. I am the full spectrum, not just a certain point on it." David understood God to be his everything, and that is why, at the end of this psalm, he points to something ludicrous. In this metaphor, David being the sheep, an animal not known for its cleanliness nor perfumed smell, says that he will dwell in the house of the Lord forever. He did not say he would dwell in the house of the Shepherd but in the house of the Lord, Who is the Owner of the sheep. David is claiming that the owner is going to open up his clean, beautiful, and expensive house and allow dirty, smelly sheep to come in and live. The Lord's house is for His family, not dirty animals! But the Lord knows that through David's line, a Shepherd will come, laying down His life for His sheep, thereby making them children of the Lord, welcoming them into His house, as family, for eternity! The sheep only need to ask for this great honor (Psalm 27:4; Romans 10:13).

THE ROCK OF MY SALVATION

From the end of the earth I call to You when my heart is faint;
Lead me to the rock that is higher than I.

Psalm 61:2

"The LORD is my **rock** and my fortress and my deliverer, My God, my **rock**, in whom I take refuge; My shield and the horn of my salvation, my stronghold" (Psalm 18:2).

"For who is God, but the LORD? And who is a **rock**, except our God" (Psalm 18:31).

"The LORD lives, and blessed be my **rock**; And exalted be the God of my salvation" (Psalm 18:46).

"For in the day of trouble He will conceal me in His tabernacle; In the secret place of His tent He will hide me; He will lift me up on a **rock**" (Psalm 27:5).

"To You, O LORD, I call; My **rock**, do not be deaf to me, For if You are silent to me, I will become like those who go down to the pit" (Psalm 28:1).

"Incline Your ear to me, rescue me quickly; Be to me a **rock** of strength, A stronghold to save me" (Psalm 31:2).

"He brought me up out of the pit of destruction, out of the miry clay, And He set my feet upon a **rock** making my footsteps firm" (Psalm 40:2).

"He only is my **rock** and my salvation, My stronghold; I shall not be greatly shaken" (Psalm 62:2).

"To declare that the LORD is upright; He is my **rock**, and there is no unrighteousness in Him" (Psalm 92:15).

"O come, let us sing for joy to the LORD, Let us shout joyfully to the **rock** of our salvation" (Psalm 95:1).

THE SHEPHERD'S CALL

But he who enters by the door is a shepherd of the sheep.
To him the doorkeeper opens, and the sheep hear his voice,
and he calls his own sheep by name and leads them out.

John 10:2–3

During biblical days, a shepherd could board their sheep in a community sheep pen. This pen was usually built by stacking stones into a rectangle or circle. The stones were stacked high enough that the sheep could not get out and wolves could not get in. There was only one gap in the wall, and that was the gate—one way in and one way out. This is why Jesus said anyone who climbs over the wall to get sheep is a thief. The shepherd did not climb over the wall but rather went to the gate because the gatekeeper knew the shepherd and gave him access. The shepherd would then call his sheep by name, and they would come to him. Did the shepherd call every lamb by its own name? Did a shepherd stand at the gate and roll call the names of a hundred sheep? Or maybe he called his own name, and the sheep, knowing they belonged to him, would hurry to the gate. In this pen, there might be sheep from several different shepherds, each of them knowing their own shepherd's name. When they heard his name, they followed because they knew their shepherd cared for them.

This parable is possibly one of the most teachable parables Jesus gave. There is a reason the angel told Joseph to name Mary's baby *Jesus* (Matthew 1:21). The name *Jesus* means "Jehovah is salvation." The Hebrew root for Jesus is *yasha,* and the Hebrew root for salvation is *yasha.* Salvation comes only through the name Jesus; they are intertwined and inseparable. When the Shepherd comes to call His sheep, He calls them by the only name that brings salvation, *Jesus*! (Acts 4:12). Jesus leads us out of sin by His sweet name; we hear His voice; and we follow because He cares for us.

———

HIS VOICE

When he puts forth all his own, he goes ahead of them, and the sheep follow him because they know his voice. A stranger they simply will not follow, but will flee from him, because they do not know the voice of strangers.

John 10:4–5

What does the voice of the Shepherd sound like? Have you heard it? Imagine being a sheep that follows and depends on its shepherd for everything. You trust your shepherd and stay on his heels every day. One day, the shepherd leads you into a pen and tells you to wait until he returns. Then you watch him turn and leave. What do you do? Do you stand? Do you eat? Do you rest? How can you rest? The shepherd is out of sight. Fear grips your heart, and you cry out, but you do not hear the shepherd's voice. You wonder, was it something you did to deserve this? Could you undo the bad or do enough good to get your shepherd to come back? But each day is silent. Then one day, when you least expect it, you hear a voice that causes your breath to catch; it's your shepherd! He stands at the gate and is calling for you! You run to his side, and he rubs your wool and speaks gently to you. He leads you out of the pen and back onto the trail. You follow him so closely because you do not want to lose sight of him again. You find yourself praying the prayer of David in Psalm 35:22: *"You have seen it, O LORD, do not keep silent; O Lord, do not be far from me."* The silence of God is deafening! Our spirit longs to hear His voice! For thousands of years, we have waited for Him to return like He said He would, but still, we wait. We long to know that even though He said He was going to prepare a place for us, He hasn't forgotten us. But He has not forgotten us. His heart longs for our reunion. The day is coming when the Shepherd will stand at the gate, and with a voice that is loving, excited, powerful, and familiar, He will call us to come to Him, and we will follow Him because He is our Shepherd!

THE GATE

*So Jesus said to them again, "Truly, truly, I say to you,
I am the door of the sheep."*

John 10:7

With an understanding that a shepherd could board their sheep in a community pen, which was walled in on all sides, we will look at the saving relationship of the Shepherd to His sheep. This walled-in pen had only one gate, which was guarded by a gatekeeper. The gatekeeper would not open the gate for anyone except the shepherd who brought the sheep. It was his job to protect the sheep while the shepherd was gone. When a shepherd came to get their sheep, the gatekeeper had to make sure he only got the sheep belonging to him and that no other sheep escaped while the gate was open. The gatekeeper's livelihood rested on his ability to keep out thieves and to keep in sheep. When a shepherd came to the gatekeeper, the door was opened, and the shepherd called out their sheep.

Jesus is the Good Shepherd, and we are His sheep. He has placed us in the pen of this world with a promise to return to get us. What a glorious day it will be when we hear the Shepherd's voice calling us to come to Him. We will run to the gate, and at the bidding of the Shepherd, the gate will be opened. The Good Shepherd will stand there with open arms, lovingly ready to receive His sheep. As we leave the pen, we will walk past a multitude of other sheep who do not respond to the Good Shepherd's voice because they do not know it; they do not belong in His fold. They will continue to sleep or eat grass. When the last of the Shepherd's sheep walk out, the gatekeeper will shut and lock the gate. The sheep will have been separated, those who belong to the Good Shepherd and those who do not. For those who remain in the pen, their destiny has been sealed because the gate has been shut and locked. The Good Shepherd has called out all those who belong to Him (John 14:6), and now He leads them on to green pastures and quiet waters (Psalm 23:2).

———————

I AM THE DOOR

I am the door; if anyone enters through Me, he will be saved,
and will go in and out and find pasture.

John 10:9

In this parable, Jesus was teaching the people about salvation. There is one Door, one Way, one Savior, and one Name by which we must be saved. Anyone who claims there is another way to salvation is not of God but of Satan. It does not matter whether we think this is fair or right; we are clay in the Potter's hands, to be used as He sees fit, period. It is correct to say that the Shepherd is the Doorway to the pasture. Many sheep have refused to go through that door because they want to find pasture their own way. If a sheep could manage to scale the wall and make it to the other side, then that sheep would have found pasture on its own terms. But that is not how God set up this world. How many sheep have been dashed to death, falling from the wall? And what really breaks the Shepherd's heart is that He is standing at the gate calling to these sheep to come to Him. They would find pasture if they would just come to Him. But they are not interested in being saved; they don't want to be sheep; they want one thing, and that is to be their own shepherd. And that will be their demise. But for all those sheep who hear the Shepherd's voice and come to Him, they will find pasture.

It is not that the Shepherd is being unreasonable. He is not saying that He has dismissed all other ways to peace and life just so you have to come through Him. But rather He is saying that all ways lead to death, so in His love, He became the only Way that leads us to life. There are many shepherds, and there are many pastures, but no shepherd can lead you to the green grass and quiet waters of Heaven except the Good Shepherd. The love of the Shepherd is more than the sheep can understand.

O Lord, thank You for shepherding us to Your pastures! You called us and You loved us, now we have hope of new Life! Amen.

———

THE SHEPHERD'S VICTORY

The thief comes only to steal and kill and destroy;
I came that they may have life, and have it abundantly.

John 10:10

Jesus said that anyone who did not come through the door of the sheep pen but rather climbed over the wall was a thief. Jesus went on to say that the thief comes only to steal, kill, and destroy, but what did the sheep do to the thief? Why is the thief so bent on harming and killing sheep? Truth be told, the thief is not interested in the sheep at all; his malice is aimed at the Shepherd. Satan preys on the weak, the hurting, and the isolated because his motto is, *"Hurt the sheep, hurt the Shepherd."* The thief comes to steal, kill and destroy; we are a side note in that, victims in the thief's vendetta against his former Master. Satan came to steal us from the Father, kill the Son, and destroy the Holy Spirit of God. But Jesus refused to stay dead because He is the One Who gives abundant life, Eternal Life! We are the weapon of choice Satan uses to bring pain to the Shepherd. Much like a robber would use an innocent bystander as a human shield to get what he wants, Satan lures us with temptations and sins so that we would be a ticking time bomb ready to go off in churches, in our families, and in a society that already hates the Shepherd. Satan pumps us so full of our own mythology that our pride and arrogance drive us to harm the sheep around us who long for the Shepherd's return. We smear mud on the precious name of Christ every time we speak words of hate and judgment. We misrepresent the Shepherd when we openly preach God's grace but privately sin against Him. How heartbreaking it is that the very sheep whom the Shepherd lovingly died for are doing the bidding of the thief who despises them and hates the Father. Yet praise be to God, the very plan the thief had of killing the Shepherd is the very redemption the Shepherd used to give us Life.

THE GOOD SHEPHERD

I am the good shepherd; the good shepherd lays down His life for the sheep.

John 10:11

To better understand Who the Good Shepherd is, let's look at the inverse of it:

Then the word of the Lord came to me saying, "Son of man, prophesy against the shepherds of Israel. Prophesy and say to those shepherds, 'Thus says the Lord God, "Woe, shepherds of Israel who have been feeding themselves! Should not the shepherds feed the flock? You eat the fat and clothe yourselves with the wool, you slaughter the fat sheep without feeding the flock. Those who are sickly you have not strengthened, the diseased you have not healed, the broken you have not bound up, the scattered you have not brought back, nor have you sought for the lost; but with force and with severity you have dominated them. They were scattered for lack of a shepherd, and they became food for every beast of the field and were scattered (Ezekiel 34:1–5).

Now that we have seen the deeds of bad shepherds, who prey on the sheep, what does the "Good Shepherd" do?

For thus says the Lord God, "Behold, I Myself will search for My sheep and seek them out . . . Then I will set over them one shepherd, My servant David, and he will feed them; he will feed them himself and be their shepherd. And I, the Lord, will be their God, and My servant David will be prince among them; I the Lord have spoken. "I will make a covenant of peace with them and eliminate harmful beasts from the land so that they may live securely in the wilderness and sleep in the woods. I will make them and the places around My hill a blessing. And I will cause showers to come down in their season; they will be showers of blessing (Ezekiel 34:11,23–26).

This covenant of peace will come through the Shepherd laying down His life, on the cross, for His sheep. In this, there are showers of blessing for the Good Shepherd's sheep because His love runs deep and is eternally given.

UNIFYING THE FLOCKS

I have other sheep, which are not of this fold; I must bring them also,
and they will hear My voice; and they will become one flock with one shepherd.

John 10:16

Could you imagine walking down the street and meeting the creation of a mad scientist, who had taken different body parts from dead people and sewed them together much like Frankenstein? But this scientist had put the feet where the ears should have been, and it had three legs for arms. Not to mention its nose was sewn into its knee. Instead of having two eyes, it had two mouths, and where the mouth should be, there was a finger. The creature would be so grotesque that people would fear it, which leads to hate. At best, people might pity it, yet shield their children from the monster.

Sadly, the Church is often seen much like this mad scientist's creation. We have segmented ourselves by denominations and then sects within the denominations. Each church is walking as it sees best, even if it's contrary to its neighboring congregation. Then, so many people within those congregations are not utilizing their spiritual gift; they are picking and choosing what they will do to serve God. So the outcome is a creature far more fearsome than Frankenstein's monster. There is no wonder the world hates, fears, and even pities Christians. So many of us are running around looking like *"sheep without a shepherd"* (Mark 6:34). Jesus taught the people that He was going to take two flocks of sheep, the Jews and the Gentiles, and He was going to bring them together so they would be *"one flock with one shepherd."* But we have allowed Satan's wolves to scatter us into so many different flocks. The world is confused because they cannot see a clear picture of Who the Good Shepherd is. Rather what they see is an un-unified, argumentative, critical, unloving, and clueless conglomeration that calls itself followers of God. This is not what Jesus called His body, but it is what He laid His life down for. He loves His sheep, and He is shepherding them to the Father.

———————

THE SHEPHERD KING

*Like a shepherd He will tend His flock, In His arm He will gather the lambs
And carry them in His bosom; He will gently lead the nursing ewes.*

Isaiah 40:11

"Those who wait on the LORD will soar on wings like eagles" (Isaiah 40:31). They will be renewed and refreshed! The waiting may seem arduous, but there will be rapturous joy that comes with His revealing! But know this, if the waiting is not drawing you closer to the Shepherd, then you are not waiting on Him. To wait does not mean just sitting and watching the grass grow, but rather it is to anticipate, to make ready, and to be consumed in His return.

Isaiah the prophet had the incredible honor of proclaiming the coming of the Shepherd: *"A voice is calling, 'Clear the way for the Lord in the wilderness; Make smooth in the desert a highway for our God. Let every valley be lifted up, And every mountain and hill be made low; And let the rough ground become a plain, And the rugged terrain a broad valley; Then the glory of the Lord will be revealed, And all flesh will see it together; For the mouth of the Lord has spoken'"* (Isaiah 40:3–5). Isaiah was saying, while you are waiting, get things ready. There is a job to do. Isaiah would go on to say, *"Behold, the Lord GOD will come with might, With His arm ruling for Him. Behold, His reward is with Him And His recompense before Him"* (Isaiah 40:10). He is coming to rule, and His arm is strong! He is coming, as the next verse says, *"Like a shepherd He will tend His flock . . ."* (Isaiah 40:11). The Mighty King, the Savior, the Almighty will come not in all His state but as a Shepherd, to lead His flock. The royal robes of the palace will come later, but for now, the King will come as a Shepherd to lead, care for, feed, and love the dirty sheep. It was easy for people to miss Him in first-century Israel, as it is still today; that is why we are to prepare the way. Just like the angels, we are to proclaim His *coming* (Luke 2:13–14). The first time Christ came, it was as the Shepherd; the next time, it will be as the King!

———

THE SHEPHERD'S TASKS

*Like a shepherd He will tend His flock, In His arm He will gather the lambs
And carry them in His bosom; He will gently lead the nursing ewes.*

Isaiah 40:11

God loves us even though we are like sheep who keep wandering off and even become defiant in the face of the Shepherd. Yet the Shepherd never abandons His sheep; He is consumed with love for them. Listen to the job description of the Shepherd in Isaiah 40:11 (emphasis mine): *"Like a shepherd He will **tend** His flock, In His arm He will **gather** the lambs And **carry** them in His bosom; He will gently **lead** the nursing ewes."*

Tend means "to shepherd, rule, and pasture." It is making the hard decisions for what is needed more than fulfilling the wants and desires of the sheep. Basically, this is where we wander away from God because we want to tend ourselves. We want to call the shots.

Gather means "to gather, collect or assemble." The Shepherd calls all of His sheep together. He calls the Church to worship, and one day He will call us to assemble in the sky where we will worship in His presence for eternity.

Carry means "to lift, support, and sustain." The Shepherd lifts us up, higher than the trials of this world. He supports or steadies us with His righteous right hand. And He sustains us as we walk through the dry and dangerous paths of life.

Lead means "to guide or give rest." Jesus guides us to His desired destination—His presence. He knows this life is not easy; that is why He gives us His presence. His presence is where we find rest and nourishment for our bodies and souls.

Any shepherd can tend, gather, carry, and lead; but the Good Shepherd does so with gentleness so that none of His lambs, ewes, or sheep are lost. It is the kindness of the Shepherd that leads us to repentance (Romans 2:4).

———————

FOLLOWING WHICH SHEPHERD

Now when the people saw that Moses delayed to come down from the mountain, the people assembled about Aaron and said to him, "Come, make us a god who will go before us; as for this Moses, the man who brought us up from the land of Egypt, we do not know what has become of him."

Exodus 32:1

Which shepherd are you following? There are so many people and things that pull at us. Advertisements are designed to make you feel like you can't live without their product. Supposed experts declare you need their advice. Everyone has an opinion which they propagate as fact. This is why it is vitally important to keep the Good Shepherd in sight. Even following a good person who is following the Good Shepherd is not enough.

Moses followed God out of Egypt, leading the Jews toward the Promise Land. But when God led him up Mount Sinai, the people fell apart because they had not been following God; they had been following the man who was following God. This is very dangerous, and it is unfortunately something that happens in churches every week. God calls "under shepherds" or pastors to lead their congregations, and we do need to heed their words, but it is so easy for the sheep to sit back and become lazy, not depending on God because it is easier to trust a pastor you can see over a God Whom you cannot.

When Moses was delayed on the mountain, the people turned from what they could no longer see and built an idol they could. This is because they were never supposed to be putting their faith in Moses to begin with. Moses did not free them from Egypt, and his presence did not assure right directions, protection, nor provisions. Moses was following the Good Shepherd just as every person freed from Egypt was to do. This may sound like a recipe for anarchy, with everyone going different directions; but remember, God may call His sheep to walk different paths, but the destination is always the same, making His name great!

A SHEEP'S HOUSE

Know well the condition of your flocks, And pay attention to your herds.

Proverbs 27:23

A house is not built with walls alone, nor is it simply a roof. Houses are made from a variety of plans and have a myriad of parts, but some aspects of a house are needed across the board. A house needs a foundation, walls, roof, windows, and a door. Likewise, our lives are multifaceted, but there are certain areas of our lives that we need if we are to be healthy.

The foundation of a house is critical; likewise, our spiritual foundation must be laid on the Rock (Matthew 7:24). Spiritually, if we are full of doubt and sin, then our lives, like a house without a foundation, will fall.

The walls of a house must be strong, supporting the roof. If you take out a load-bearing wall, the house will collapse. Likewise, physically we must remain strong and healthy.

The roof of a house protects it from the elements of nature, the heat of the sun, and the rain of the clouds. Likewise, our emotional stability protects us from the elements of life. Without stable emotions, we would be tossed around like a ship in a storm.

The windows of a house allow in light and fresh air. Likewise, our mental capacity allows in wisdom and fresh growth. Our mind holds all these aspects of life together.

Finally, a door gives access into the house on the one hand and bars access on the other hand. Likewise, socially we need times of social interaction and times of solitude.

For us to be healthy, we need a house that is well built, complete with a foundation (spiritually), walls (physically), roof (emotionally), windows (mentally), and doors (socially). The Shepherd knows each of us. He pays attention to all aspects of our lives, and He supplies what we need to be whole. Being Creator, He knows what we need better than we do. Being the Good Shepherd, He supplies it.

———

TO SEEK AND SAVE

I have gone astray like a lost sheep; seek Your servant,
For I do not forget Your commandments.

Psalm 119:176

The Good Shepherd knows His sheep, loves His sheep, and has laid down His life for His sheep. It was for this purpose that the Shepherd came to earth—*"For the Son of Man has come to seek and to save that which was lost"* (Luke 19:10). Jesus was solely focused on doing the will of the Father, which was to seek and to save the lost. As sheep, we have the ability to wander, but the Shepherd seeks us out even in the darkest of pits. He then reaches down and pulls us out, saving us from the wages of sin (Romans 6:23). We are set free (John 8:36). We have gone from darkness to light, and now we have a hope that soars through eternity. So if we have been set free, then how is it that we find ourselves right back in the same predicament we were freed from? *"But now that you have come to know God, or rather to be known by God, how is it that you turn back again to the weak and worthless elemental things, to which you desire to be enslaved all over again?"* (Galatians 4:9). How can we settle for things so morbidly evil when life so righteously perfect has been extended to us? It is because even a sheep that has been sought after and saved by the shepherd is still a sheep that is easily led astray. How tiresome it must be for the Shepherd to once again strike out to find a wandering sheep. But He does; the Shepherd continues to seek us, bringing us back into the fold. It is the love of the Shepherd that steadies His course. He is patient and kind, not keeping a record of our wrongs (1 Corinthians 13:5–7). His love is deeper than our ability to sin. Not that His love makes our sin okay. His righteousness makes His justice full! But His grace makes His vengeance fall not on us, but on Himself. We cannot fathom His love, redemption, or sacrifice. The Shepherd's staff is long and safe, able to reach us wherever we wander to, and His righteousness is holy, making His salvation complete!

———————

ETERNAL SHEPHERD

They will hunger no longer, nor thirst anymore; nor will the sun beat down on them,
nor any heat; for the Lamb in the center of the throne will be their shepherd,
and will guide them to springs of the water of life;
and God will wipe every tear from their eyes.

Revelation 7:16–17

We as sheep will encounter wolves who harm us, pits we fall into, thieves who steal from us, and many things that call for our attention, causing us to wander from the Shepherd. Because of all this, it is easy to despair. This world is a scary place, and this life is hard. But in the midst of this despair and fear, there is one thing we can't miss—the Shepherd is with us! Science teaches us that the human eye can only focus on one thing at a time. It is capable of bouncing between things so fast it can put a large picture together, but it can only focus on one thing. So we can not look at this world and the Shepherd at the same time. Either we will focus on despair or focus on peace. What we focus on is what will win the battle for our soul. So know this, we may face wolves, pits, and thieves, but the Shepherd is all we need.

Revelation chapter seven is a passage of Scripture often taken out of context. We read verses nine through twelve and interpret them as if they were about us, in Heaven, worshiping God, along with Christians from Africa, Asia, South America, and Europe. But verse fourteen both asks and answers the question, who are these people? They are the people who came through the great tribulation. They have known the trials of a savage world under the antichrist, and through the Shepherd's leading, they have made it to the throne of God! But do not miss verses fifteen through seventeen, as they worship around the throne, *"the Lamb in the center of the throne will be their shepherd."* Jesus is not just our Shepherd while we toil on this earth; He remains our Shepherd even in Heaven where there are no wolves, pits, or thieves. He will lovingly lead and provide for all of eternity!

THE GUARDIAN OF SOULS

For you were continually straying like sheep,
but now you have returned to the Shepherd and Guardian of your souls.

1 Peter 2:25

We learn from this verse that Jesus is not only our Shepherd but also the Guardian of our souls. The Greek word for "guardian" is *episkopos,* and it means "one charged with the duty of seeing that things to be done by others are done rightly." Even though we are like sheep, we have been given a task to do. This task is called God's plan. Jeremiah 29:11 says, *"For I know the plans that I have for you,' declares the LORD, 'plans for welfare and not for calamity to give you a future and a hope.'"* The Guardian makes sure that we carry out our task correctly, but prior to that, He helps us understand our task and equips us to fulfill it. Learning to discern God's task for us and how He has equipped us for His plan comprises the vast majority of the teaching in churches today, but turning to His reproof is not often talked about. The Shepherd disciplines the sheep He loves because He wants what is best for them (Hebrews 12:6). The Shepherd even left the fold so that the Helper, the Guardian, could come and keep us on the right path. John 16:7–8 tells us, *"But I tell you the truth, it is to your advantage that I go away; for if I do not go away, the Helper will not come to you; but if I go, I will send Him to you. And He, when He comes, will convict the world concerning sin and righteousness and judgment."* Walking in the discipline of the Guardian is not easy because it requires us to once again relinquish our desire to be the shepherd. It is so easy to live like the people in the days of Noah, where everyone was doing whatever they wanted, but that brought on God's wrath. Discipline involves surrender and obedience, apart from our will. Jesus is the very essence of this. Peter tells us, it is by the wounds of Jesus that we are healed (1 Peter 2:24). Our healing comes at the hand of the Shepherd laying aside His will and surrendering to the Father's (Luke 22:42).

———

FOLLOWING THE SHEPHERD'S LEADING

Thus says the LORD, your Redeemer, the Holy One of Israel,
"I am the LORD your God, who teaches you to profit,
Who leads you in the way you should go."

Isaiah 48:17

The Shepherd leads us in the way we should go. What way is He leading you? How does He lead you? Do you know? Do your eyes see Him? Do your ears hear Him? Do you feel His rod and staff directing you as you go about your day? If not, why? Psalm 25:9 says, *"He leads the humble in justice, And He teaches the humble His way."* How does the Shepherd lead His sheep? We know He speaks to us, calling our name (John 10:4) and revealing His plan (Psalm 32:8). He also walks with us so that we can see His hand (Hebrews 12:2). His tender mercies and kindness guide us as we are made new through His blood and set apart for His service (Luke 1:78–79; Romans 2:4). Nature obeys His command, even guiding us (Isaiah 43:2). He uses trials such as sickness to change our direction (John 9:3). He gives us counsel through His Scripture as we read and meditate on it (Psalm 73:24; 2 Timothy 3:16). The Shepherd even puts others in our pathway to encourage and to direct us, but we must be careful who we take counsel from because there are many who would lead us astray (Proverbs 12:26; 22:6). The Shepherd not only leads us in the way we should go, but He also pursues us and rescues us when we get off course (Luke 19:10). It is for His Name that He guides and rescues His children (Psalm 106:8).

But the question still remains, do you know the leading of the Shepherd? As Isaiah 48:17 says, He *"leads [us] in the way [we] should go,"* but as Psalm 25:9 teaches, it is the humble who are led. There is a difference between leading and being led. The Shepherd leads—it's what He does—but those who are humble are the ones who are led. Are you humble enough to be led by the Shepherd?

———

WHAT DOES THIS MEAN

This is the LORD'S doing; It is marvelous in our eyes.
This is the day which the LORD has made; Let us rejoice and be glad in it.

Psalm 118:23–24

Do not miss the greatness of God today! Both verses twenty-three and twenty-four of Psalm 118 begin with the same English word—*this*. But in Hebrew, these are two different words. *This* in verse twenty-four is *zeh,* and it literally means "this." But the word *this* in verse twenty-three is *Iythiy'el* and it literally means, "God is with me." So when you go back and plug that into the verse, you see, "*God is with me, is the LORD's doing; It is marvelous in our eyes.*"

That is exactly the message of the verse right before this one. "*The stone which the builders rejected Has become the chief cornerstone*" (Psalm 118:22). Jesus, the Shepherd, is the Stone that was rejected but has now become our Cornerstone. He is the *This* of verse twenty-three. The Shepherd is with us—not by our doing but through the Father's. That should be marvelous in our eyes! We were sinful, dirty, back-biting sheep, and the Shepherd came to be with us! *This* is where salvation lies, and because today is the day of God-made salvation (2 Corinthians 6:2), let us rejoice and be glad in it!

This truth should make all the difference in the world for us. God is with me because of the Lord's doing. He came as a baby, born into humble means, approachable by all humanity. He lived a life of counter-religious love, yet without sin. He was falsely accused, sentenced to death, and then led away to the agony of the cross. The Shepherd willingly got down on my cross and allowed the nails, which were my damnation, to pierce His hands and feet. The breath which He breathed into our lungs at creation ceased to fill His lungs, and with the Father turning away, the Shepherd laid down His life for His sheep. Yes, the Shepherd came to be with us, not because of us but because of Him! He is the resurrected Good Shepherd, and *This* is marvelous in our eyes!

DO YOU TRUST GOD

Trust in the LORD with all your heart And do not lean on your own understanding.
In all your ways acknowledge Him, And He will make your paths straight.

Proverbs 3:5–6

Throughout this year, we have seen God as the Potter, the Savior, the Counselor, the Servant, the Commander, the Spirit, the Creator, the Father, the Rabbi, the Redeemer, the Healer, and the Shepherd. We have seen His call, His protection, His love, and His teachings. What could possibly be better than to fall in love with the God of the universe Who is already madly in love with you? He loved us so much, He gave His only Son so that we could have undeserved, abundant life! (John 3:16; 10:10). The question that has manifested itself throughout this year has been, do you trust this God? You may believe in Him; you may love what He has done for you; but do you trust Him? Total trust equals total surrender, which equals total obedience. What good is a Savior if you do not trust Him? What good is a Father if you do not trust His love? What good is a Potter if you do not trust how He formed you? Jesus is the Good Shepherd, and His staff is long and safe; we can trust Him. He deserves our whole-hearted trust. We will most assuredly not understand all He is doing, but that is why we must trust Him! We are to acknowledge Him and then take the step of faith needed to be obedient to His leading. Proverbs 4:18 says, *"But the path of the righteous is like the light of dawn, That shines brighter and brighter until the full day."* The Shepherd leads you on the path of righteousness; and if you will trust Him, you will step into the dawn of His light, and He will shine ever brighter in you until His presence is undeniable. I beg you to trust the Potter's hands!

"For this reason I also suffer these things, but I am not ashamed; for I know whom I have believed and I am convinced that He is able to guard what I have entrusted to Him until that day" (2 Timothy 1:12).

APPENDIX

Arise

"Arise, O Potter; Your vessel is good,
A beauty to see and ready to use.
Now held in Your hand, the work has begun,
How perfect its cracks, its Maker we muse."

"Arise, O Father; Your children cry out.
The enemy kills; the thief comes to steal;
Despising Your Name, their hatred they spill.
Now Your children wait; before You they kneel."

"Arise, O Shepherd; the lions are near,
Your flock has scattered; they tremble in fear.
Who will defend them? It was You Who died,
Now Your grave stands empty; they need not hide."

"Arise, O Warrior; it's time to go home.
The battle is over, the victory won.
The slain have fallen; the enemy's thrown.
We look to the sky, return where You've gone."

"Arise, O Musician, and take a bow,
All Heaven and earth are singing Your praise!
For years You have waited, but we see now.
You are King over all; Your song we raise!"

For more information about
Jason Lawson
and

The Potter's Hands
please visit:

www.jasonlawsonbooks.com

Ambassador International's mission is to magnify the Lord Jesus Christ
and promote His Gospel through the written word.

We believe through the publication of Christian literature, Jesus Christ and
His Word will be exalted, believers will be strengthened in their walk with
Him, and the lost will be directed to Jesus Christ as the only way of salvation.

For more information about
AMBASSADOR INTERNATIONAL
please visit:

www.ambassador-international.com

*Thank you for reading this book. Please consider leaving us a
review on your social media, favorite retailer's website,
Goodreads or Bookbub, or our website.*

More from Ambassador International

Through vignettes of fresh water springs and fly fishing analogies, *Theology From the Spring* provides the reader with eyes for seeing how God's creation—the natural world—can provide answers to the oldest divine mystery and make sense of the beauty and chaos we see within the created order.

Join Christine Paxson and Rose Spiller as they explore the answers to these and many other questions about the true Gospel message in *No Half-Truths Allowed: Understanding the Complete Gospel Message.* Learn what Jesus did for you, why He did it, and how you can articulate the Gospel to others.

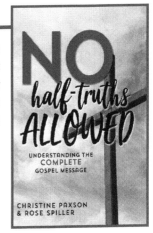

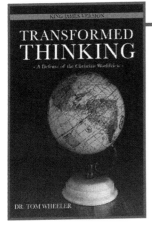

In *Transformed Thinking*, Tom Wheeler clearly lays out the most fundamental beliefs of Christianity and compares them to other worldviews, providing arguments to support his beliefs. Even though this book is purposed for the classroom setting, it would be a beneficial read for any believer who wants to have a firm foundation on which to share their beliefs with unbelievers.